PREDICTING COLLEGE GRADES:

AN ANALYSIS OF INSTITUTIONAL TRENDS OVER TWO DECADES

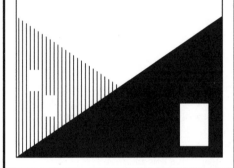

WARREN W. WILLINGHAM
CHARLES LEWIS
RICK MORGAN
LEONARD RAMIST

in collaboration with

WILLIAM H. ANGOFF, NAZLI BAYDAR,
NANCY BURTON, CAROLYN R. CRONE,
GARY L. MARCO, LAURA MCCAMLEY,
FRED MCHALE, JUDITH POLLACK,
MARK POMPLUN, DONALD R. ROCK,
GLORIA WEISS

Sponsored by

THE COLLEGE BOARD
AND
EDUCATIONAL TESTING SERVICE

The College Board is an education association of more than 2,700 secondary and postsecondary institutions, systems, agencies, and associations committed to maintaining academic standards and broadening access to higher education. It offers a wide array of programs and publications to students, parents, schools, and colleges, including the Admissions Testing Program, which encompasses the Scholastic Aptitude Test (SAT), the Test of Standard Written English, and various subject-area Achievement Tests. The Board's headquarters are in New York City.

Educational Testing Service (ETS) is a private, nonprofit corporation devoted to measurement and research, primarily in the field of education. Under contract to the College Board, ETS develops and administers the SAT and other instruments used by colleges and schools. It also develops and conducts testing programs for other sponsors in education, business, and the professions, and carries out extensive research in statistics and measurement, test validity, new forms of assessment, and educational policy and practice. ETS's headquarters are in Princeton.

Compositor: Sandy Callighan
Cover Designer: Robin H. Matlack
Production Coordinator: Mary Ann Halasz

Table of Contents

PART I — Factors Affecting Prediction Trends

Tables

Figures

Preface

The college admissions process in the United States is a complex undertaking. Individual schools and colleges vary a great deal. Students differ widely in their preparation. The principal parties — students, school counselors, and college admissions officers — all have a shared interest in estimating whether freshmen are likely to do well in particular academic programs. Predicting college grades of individual students is by no means exact, but overall, there is a moderately good correlation between a student's college grades and his or her previous school record and SAT scores.

Such correlations vary in size from college to college, but it is more surprising that correlations averaged across colleges vary from year to year. For example, the average correlation of SAT scores with freshman grade average has decreased in recent years, following an earlier increase. Why is that? Have there been changes in the test? In the grade criterion? Only an integrated series of studies could disentangle the host of factors that might be involved in such correlational trends. Believing that a better understanding of trends in validity coefficients would be useful to colleges, the College Board and ETS decided to undertake the studies here reported. We are grateful to both organizations for their support, and particularly to Nancy Cole for her advice and encouragement.

This volume comes in two parts. The results of individual research studies are reported in Part II (Chapters 4-13). Some of those chapters are condensed versions of more detailed accounts available in technical reports.

Chapters 1 though 3 in Part I are less technical and intended for a general professional audience. The purpose of Part I is to furnish useful background information, suggest a framework for thinking about the topic, and summarize what we have found. Chapter 1 may be particularly useful to readers not closely familiar with grade prediction. Note especially the Glossary on page 2. Chapter 2 integrates and summarizes the available evidence on this topic: previously published research reports, the findings of the various studies described in Part II, and results of some additional special analyses that were undertaken in order to answer questions not addressed elsewhere. Chapter 3 attempts to state concisely the main conclusions and comments on some interesting implications of the findings.

A number of ETS staff have contributed to this volume. The senior author organized the work and had overall editorial responsibility.

The other three principal authors, listed alphabetically, made major contributions over an extended period in the effort to produce a coherent analysis of a complex problem. Other contributors assumed responsibility for individual studies as indicated by chapter authorship.

Valuable advice was obtained from several external consultants who were especially generous with their time and expertise: Lloyd Bond, Bert Green, Rex Jackson, Lyle Jones, Robert Linn, Lorrie Shepard, and John Tukey. We are grateful to each of these individuals. Robert Linn reviewed the entire manuscript and early drafts of each of the study reports. His substantial contributions are greatly appreciated.

Special appreciation and thanks are also extended to several colleagues who, in addition to the authors, reviewed all or large parts of this volume and provided much valuable advice: Neil Dorans, Samuel Messick, Lawrence Stricker, Howard Wainer, and members of the Joint Staff Research and Development Committee. Chapter authors have also recognized other reviewers and special contributions in footnotes to individual chapters.

Several staff provided valuable assistance in producing this volume. Linda Johnson had the major responsibility for administrative coordination and helped with many aspects of the work. Joan Stoeckel and Ruth Waks typed most of the final manuscript. Peter Mann edited the volume. We are grateful to all for their very competent work and their willing dedication to task.

Warren W. Willingham

FACTORS AFFECTING PREDICTION TRENDS

Glossary

CGPA	College grade-point average
FGPA	College grade-point average for the freshman year
HSGPA	High school grade-point average
HSR	High school record — refers generally to academic performance in high school; also used whenever correlations for different colleges may be based upon different measures of high school performance (i.e., either rank or grade average, either college- or student-reported)
SAT-M	SAT-Mathematics, the test section or the score
SAT-V	SAT-Verbal, the test section or the score
SAT-V&M	Total SAT score, used only as a college characteristic (i.e., more/less selective), never as a predictor
SAT-V,M	Multiple correlation based upon SAT-V and SAT-M scores; implicit in any reference to the correlation between the SAT and FGPA, course grades, or HSGPA
Corrected correlation	A correlation corrected for multivariate range restriction (SAT-V, SAT-M, HSR) in order to make validity coefficients comparable year-to-year; used in trend analyses unless otherwise indicated (see page 13ff and Note 4-2)
Pairwise trend analysis	A method for estimating the trend in successive yearly averages when data are based upon different colleges in the successive years (see page 12ff and Note 4-1)
College prediction slope	The straight line with slope t that best describes the yearly trend in validity coefficients (HSR, SAT, or both) for a given college (see Figure 1-2)
Low third of class	Students who rank at or below the thirty-third percentile of enrolled freshmen on preadmissions ability measures (HSR and SAT, or SAT alone); similarly, middle or high third
VSS	Validity Study Service — A free service provided by the College Board, enabling colleges to carry out prediction studies tailored to local data and interests

CHAPTER 1

Introduction: Interpreting Predictive Validity

WARREN W. WILLINGHAM

This volume delves into a question that has received surprisingly little attention: Why do systematic changes over time sometimes occur in the correlation between admissions test scores and college freshman grades? There are substantial data on each of the major admissions tests that should be useful in examining this question. For many years, the College Board has encouraged each institution that uses the Scholastic Aptitude Test (SAT) to undertake periodic studies of the relationship of SAT scores to grades on its campus. In 1964, the Board initiated a Validity Study Service, administered by ETS, through which such studies could be carried out at no cost to the college. The results of these validity studies have been compiled and described on several occasions (see Ford & Campos, 1977; Ramist, 1984; Ramist & Weiss, Chapter 5 of this volume; Schrader, 1971).

A chapter (Ramist, 1984) in the latest edition of *The College Board Technical Manual for the Scholastic Aptitude Test and Achievement Tests* summarizes more than 2,000 validity studies. The findings are grouped by type of institution, by academic program, by selectivity of the institution, and so on. Such data provide a useful frame of reference for individual colleges to interpret their own results. This summary also shows, year by year, the average correlation between SAT scores and freshman grade-point average (FGPA) for all validity studies that were carried out from 1964 to 1981. The average correlation coefficient fluctuates to some degree each year, sometimes going up or down for several years in a row. Such a yearly average has not been regarded as a barometer of the SAT's predictive validity, mainly because there is no reason to assume that the changing groups of colleges that participate in the Validity Study Service each year are comparable over time or that they are representative of SAT user-institutions generally.

On the other hand, a downward trend in this average correlation, first noted several years ago, seemed unexpectedly persistent. A study was commissioned to find out whether one would see any such trend in the correlation of SAT scores and FGPA if the correlations were corrected to make the data statistically comparable from year to year. Morgan (1989a) confirmed that statistical artifacts were causing lower correlations, but also found that some decline remained in the average corrected correlation (.51 to .47) from 1976 to 1985. Consequently, the College Board and ETS decided that it was time to examine more carefully the nature of such trends, how they come about, and what they may mean.

We had three objectives in preparing this report. One was to contribute to a better understanding of the various factors that can cause systematic changes in the correlation of SAT scores and FGPA. Toward that end, a framework of such factors is suggested later in this chapter and those factors addressed in more useful detail in Chapter 2.

A second objective was to integrate a number of recent research findings that otherwise would appear only in separate technical reports. Accounts of the individual projects are given in the various chapters of Part II. Chapter 2 provides a synthesis and discussion of all the findings.

A third objective was to consider implications of changes in the observed relationship between admissions test scores and college grades — possible implications for institutions, as well as for the design of admissions tests. These implications are addressed in Chapter 3.

The remainder of this chapter is devoted to several topics that provide useful background. First is a brief but necessary discussion of the role of predictive validity within the larger context of how admissions tests are used and evaluated. Following are some comments on the nature of institutional validity studies, illustrative results of the Validity Study Service studies, and ways in which noncomparable yearly data can cloud interpretation of trends. Finally, we consider a framework for determining why validity coefficients may vary.

PREDICTIVE VALIDITY IN CONTEXT

The correlation between test scores and college grades provides information that is highly relevant to test validity and test use — but not the whole story by any means. In order better to interpret and evaluate evidence concerning predictive validity, it is helpful to consider first how admissions tests are used and on what basis their use is justified.

Test Use in Admissions

Admissions practices are quite diverse among individual institutions and among types of institutions. Although open-door colleges may not use tests for selection at all (except to limit enrollment in oversubscribed programs), the most selective institutions may use both aptitude and achievement tests along with a variety of objective and subjective information. While colleges vary widely in the proportion of applicants they accept, most actively recruit and admit students with different characteristics and accomplishments in order to serve a variety of goals that are deemed important to the institution.

These goals include maintaining an appropriate demographic and ethnic mix of students, attracting competent students with interests in different areas of study, maintaining ties important to the institution, insuring that each class includes students who have the diverse talents that are useful to a college community (e.g., artistic and musical talent, leadership, technical or interpersonal skills — yes, even athletic proficiency). A variety of measures may be useful in achieving these objectives, and different measures have different strengths and play different roles in the admissions process.

In a detailed study of admissions decisions regarding 25,000 applicants to nine private colleges, it was found that personal qualities of applicants carried one-third of the weight in selection overall but played a larger role in the more selective institutions. Among the personal qualities that appeared to make a difference in admissions decisions, the most heavily weighted was minority status (plus), followed by alumni status and having had an outstanding admissions interview (both also plus). Academic qualifications got two-thirds of the weight in admissions decisions. Test scores and high school record (HSR) were equally good predictors of admissions decisions and equally good predictors of freshman grades in these colleges (Willingham & Breland, 1982).

When used in conjunction with HSR, test scores provide an objective alternate admissions credential for students who may not have achieved up to their potential in secondary school or may have modest grade records due to having taken demanding courses. As supplementary information for colleges, the test offers the admissions officer a standard measure on all students regardless of school background and a means of identifying exceptional students whose records may not reflect their abilities.

The academic qualifications of an incoming class are as much determined by the self-sorting decisions of students as by the selection decisions of individual colleges. While many institutions are selective in the sense that their students are more able and better prepared than high school graduates generally, they do not necessarily maintain that selectivity by rejecting a substantial number of applicants. Institutions actively recruit students who can meet their standards, school counselors advise, and students decide among their reasonable options.

In such an admissions process, where recruitment and self-selection are dominant, admissions tests serve somewhat different functions. One is to help each college identify as accurately as possible a small but important group: those applicants the college judges to have little chance to succeed and who are likely to make disproportionate demands on its instructional resources. Another function is to provide a common metric that, with coursework and other requirements, helps the institution signal and maintain consistent academic standards while recruiting students from a wide variety of backgrounds.

Test Validity

The foregoing observations about test use in admissions help to illustrate an obvious point: While different colleges admit students in different ways, any measure that is commonly used for selection has effects throughout the educational system, both direct and indirect. Thus, in considering how one validates or justifies that use, it is necessary to think broadly about likely effects on students and schools. This takes us considerably beyond the perspective of predicting grades.

Both legal precedent and psychometric theory support a broad view of validity. In *Washington vs. Davis* (1975), the Supreme Court ruled that any selection test should be evaluated on the basis of a rational analysis of all the evidence concerning its appropriateness, which may or may not include a prediction study. In some situations, it may be impractical to do prediction studies because the groups are too small. In other instances, the results of a prediction study might have limited credibility because of serious shortcomings in the criterion measure. In any event, contribution to prediction is only one line of evidence. There is a clear consensus in the measurement profession that there is no single basis for deciding whether a test is valid for a particular purpose (American Educational Research Association, American Psychological Association, & National Council on Measurement in Education, 1985; Messick, 1988). The collective evidence should confirm not only that a test measures what it purports to measure, but that its use for a particular purpose is justified by the consequences of such use (e.g., immediate benefit, long-term utility, cost, negative side effects, etc.).

From a practical standpoint, we might pose the following four types of questions in considering the validity of a test like the SAT. These questions are framed in recognition of the fact that the test and the process of admitting students must be evaluated, not on some absolute scale, but against plausible alternatives.

1. Is the content of the test appropriate? Does it measure educationally important knowledge, skills, and developed abilities? Is there alternative content that would serve better?

2. Is the test effective in predicting academic performance? Would other measures work better or prove to be useful supplements? Does the test add useful information to measures already available?

3. Is the test fair to subgroups? Does it fairly represent their educational achievement and their likely success in college? Is the balance of content as fair as possible to diverse groups? Would alternative content or measures be fairer overall?

4. Are the consequences of test use — including all costs, benefits, practical considerations, and side effects — positive overall? If there were no test — or another type of test — would the effects on students, schools, colleges, and the educational system be better or worse?

The purpose in listing these questions is to outline, at least, a broader context of test use and validity that should be considered in evaluating the findings of institutional validity studies. Needless to say, these questions raise a wide range of issues, some narrow and technical, others broadly concerned with the nature of the educational process. Corresponding to these issues, there is a very large literature of research and writing, of which institutional validity studies represent only one piece. It is not our purpose here to review this literature. It may be useful, however, to give a brief indication of its character and to cite a few references that provide an overview of various topics of possible interest.

Over the years there have been several reviews of predictive validity studies of the SAT (Fishman & Pasanella, 1960; Ford & Campos, 1977; Ramist, 1984; Schrader, 1971). Such institutional studies are typically quite limited in scope. They are intended to serve local purposes rather than to explore research issues that might apply generally to such issues as test quality, possible improvements, test interpretation, etc. Such broader issues are more likely addressed in special studies undertaken for that purpose. Special studies carried out at ETS are summarized in the *Program Research Review* (Willingham & Johnson, 1989). It includes annotations of some 60 published research reports over the past five years concerning various aspects of validity and other characteristics of the SAT.

Evidence regarding the appropriateness of test content and the construct validity of the SAT is found in several reviews: Donlon (1984a, especially Chapters 1, 3, and 7), Cruise and Kimmel (1990), and

Marco, Crone, Braswell, Curley, and Wright (1990). Angoff (1971) and Dyer and King (1955) provide further historical perspective on the SAT.

Studies of test fairness to subgroups have been prominent in the research programs of the College Board and ETS for the past two decades. Several reports provide useful overviews of extensive research concerning particular groups of examinees: Hispanic students (Duran, 1983; Pennock-Roman, 1990); Black students (Baratz-Snowden, 1987; Linn, 1982a); disabled students (Willingham, Ragosta, Bennett, Braun, Rock, & Powers, 1988); and women (Clark & Grandy, 1984; Wilder & Powell, 1989). Prior to their use, all SAT items go through sensitivity review to ensure they do not contain material or references that may be objectionable to women, minority groups, disabled examinees, or other groups. In recent years, considerable research also has been directed to statistical methods for identifying items that may have irrelevant difficulty for some groups. Two reports provide a useful introduction to that work: Holland and Thayer (1986) and Schmitt and Dorans (1990).

One might reasonably ask why institutional studies of the SAT seldom include measures other than the test scores and high school record. Some do, but the better answer is that over several decades, intensive looking by researchers across the country has not come up with any other measures that would add information of practical significance in predicting college GPA. Some researchers, notably Nichols and Holland (1963) and Richards, Holland, and Lutz (1967), demonstrated the usefulness of extracurricular accomplishments in forecasting similar behavior in college. Willingham (1985) extended that work by showing that colleges are not likely to select optimally the applicants they characterize four years later as their most successful students overall unless their admissions decisions take account of prior accomplishments outside the classroom. On the other hand, this study confirmed that no additional measure provides much useful information in forecasting FGPA, once high school record and test scores have been considered.

Literature on the broad question of the social and educational usefulness of college admissions tests is quite varied. It embraces empirical analysis and reasoned judgment, as well as diverse points of view. Representative articles and books include those by test critics (Crouse & Trusheim, 1988; Owen, 1985), by ETS staff (Educational Testing Service, 1980; Manning, 1977; Willingham & Breland, 1977), by independent researchers (Elliott & Strenta, 1990; Klitgaard, 1985; Manski & Wise, 1983), and by practitioners in institutions (College Board, 1986b).

PREDICTIVE VALIDITY STUDIES

Studies conducted through the Validity Study Service (vss) constitute the principal source of information concerning the predictive validity of the sat in individual colleges and universities. Trends in the results of these studies are the focus of this report. The following paragraphs briefly describe such studies and provide some illustrative data.

Colleges undertake validity studies in order to obtain a variety of statistical information about the relationship between measures used in admissions and the subsequent success of students in college. The institution provides information to the vss about college grades earned and receives in return a report that provides correlations, prediction equations, and measures of the error in prediction. Colleges can specify use of several predictors but typically use sat scores and a measure of high school performance — either grade average or class rank. Freshman grade-point average (fgpa) is the performance criterion normally predicted. Particular groups of students (e.g., women, engineering majors) may be analyzed as well as, or instead of, the total class. For more detailed information about the service, the reports provided, and the statistical procedures, see *Guide to the College Board Validity Study Service* (College Board, 1988c).

There are several ways that a college can think of the relationship between a predictor and fgpa. One is the slope of the regression line that shows the expected increase in grade average associated with increasing sat scores. Another is the correlation coefficient (r), which is numerically equivalent to the regression slope under certain conditions. Compared to the regression slope, the correlation coefficient has two advantages that likely account for its frequent use. It is expressed on a simple scale where zero indicates no systematic relationship and 1.0 indicates a perfect relationship. Also, a correlation is largely unaffected by the fact that different measures may be expressed on different scales. (See Note 1-1.)

As previously noted, sat scores are always used in conjunction with some measure of high school performance. As Linn (1982b) notes, there are social and educational arguments favoring the use of a common test standard that complements the high school record (hsr), but the extent to which the test adds to prediction is nonetheless important. That is, to what extent does the multiple correlation based on both measures exceed the correlation based on hsr alone? Some improvement in prediction is critical to the argument that the objective test score provides a measure of fairness across diverse secondary schools and gives students a second way of demonstrating their academic capability. Consequently, it is necessary to give close attention to the predictive validity of the school record.

By way of summarizing the previous discussion, we can distinguish three types of measures that are used here to characterize prediction trends. Each answers a somewhat different question.

- *The correlation coefficient* (or sometimes, the regression weight) is used to indicate the predictive power of an individual measure.

- *The multiple correlation* indicates the level of prediction afforded by two or more measures used in concert — normally test scores and high school record (HSR).

- *The increment in prediction that is due to the test* is indicated by the difference between the correlation for HSR alone and the multiple correlation based on HSR and the SAT. The partial correlation of SAT with FGPA holding HSR constant provides similar information.

Validity Study Service Summary Data

Chapter 8 (Ramist, 1984) of the technical manual of the Admissions Testing Program provides a detailed description of the results of institutional studies conducted through the VSS from 1964 to 1981. Other studies reported here provide more recent results. Summary data for selected groups of students and colleges provide a useful overview for purposes of this discussion. Table 1-1 shows average correlations with college grades for SAT, HSR, and a weighted combination of the two. (See Note 1-2.)

The first line of Table 1-1 shows the picture that is by now familiar. College grades can be predicted moderately well, but certainly with no high degree of accuracy. The school record provides a more accurate forecast of FGPA than do the test scores (.48 vs. .42). The two together do better than either alone (i.e., a multiple correlation of .55 or .07 higher than HSR by itself). Used together, the optimal weights for these measures averaged as follows in 685 studies: SAT-Verbal, 26 percent; SAT-Mathematics, 20 percent; and HSR, 54 percent. Among the various groups of students and colleges shown in Table 1-1, there is little deviation from that general pattern.

Table 1-1 also shows group differences in these correlations that are often observed: somewhat higher correlations for women than men, for private than public colleges, and for smaller than larger institutions. The yearly averages also illustrate the trends in SAT correlations noted earlier: an increase in the early 1970s, followed by a decrease. These data constitute a considerable accumulation of valuable information concerning the predictive validity of the SAT and the predictability of college grades. These various comparisons may be misleading, however, because the data are not necessarily comparable across the groups shown. Needless to say, comparability of yearly data is essential to accurate monitoring of trends.

Table 1-1

Correlation of SAT Scores and High School Record (HSR) with Freshman GPA for Selected Groups of Students, Colleges, and Years[*]

		Correlation with Freshman GPA			
	Number of Colleges	SAT[#]	HSR	SAT & HSR[#]	SAT *Increment*
Total	685	.42	.48	.55	.07
Women	574	.46	.49	.57	.08
Men	511	.38	.44	.51	.07
Major:					
Business	100	.37	.43	.52	.09
Liberal Arts	96	.39	.48	.55	.07
Engineering	77	.37	.42	.51	.09
Science	64	.41	.46	.55	.09
Education	61	.42	.49	.57	.08
Nursing	27	.46	.50	.60	.10
Type of College:					
Public 4-year	201	.38	.44	.51	.07
Private 4-year	428	.44	.49	.57	.08
Size of Class:					
Over 1000	108	.39	.44	.51	.07
501 to 1000	151	.41	.46	.54	.08
500 or less	312	.45	.51	.59	.08
Average SAT of Class:					
1200 and higher	22	.35	.33	.44	.11
900-949	117	.44	.50	.57	.07
699 or lower	20	.38	.39	.49	.10
Year					
1970	112	.39	.49	.55	.06
1975	130	.44	.48	.56	.08
1980	181	.42	.46	.54	.08
1985	124	.37	.47	.52	.07

[*] These data are largely from Ramist (1984). See Note 1-2.
[#] Multiple correlations based on SAT-V and SAT-M, and on SAT-V, SAT-M, and HSR as indicated.

COMPARABLE MEASURES

There are three important ways in which yearly correlations may lack comparability. First, the average correlation between SAT and FGPA may vary across years simply because the colleges are different. Validity coefficients vary widely among institutions — from .27 to .57 at the 10th and 90th percentile, respectively (Ramist, 1984, p. 142; see also Boldt, 1986, and Munday, 1970). Variations in the range of talent within institutions are another potential source of variation in all of these correlations. Finally, there is variation among correlations involving the HSR because colleges use different measures of high school performance in validity studies. Each of these sources of noncomparability must be controlled.

Comparable Cohorts of Colleges

Few institutions do validity studies every year. Therefore, the yearly cohort of participating colleges varies even though there are substantial numbers of studies in most years. Knowing that, and knowing there are systematic differences in predictability of grades in different institutions, how can one interpret the yearly averages with any assurance?

In searching for a way to make the yearly averages comparable, one thought is to use data only from those colleges that have done studies each year during the period of interest. The problem with that method is that few colleges do studies every year. With this restriction, only an extremely limited and unrepresentative sample of colleges would remain for analysis, especially if the period of study were long enough to be of much use in charting trends. Another possibility would be to adjust the trend by taking into account yearly differences in key institutional characteristics that tend to be related to the level of validity coefficients. There are several problems with that approach. Morgan (1989a) found, as did Munday (1970), that the institutional characteristics available cannot account for variation in validity coefficients with much accuracy. Furthermore, such adjustments would not necessarily prove useful in achieving comparability for the variety of other statistics one would like to track (means, standard deviations, other correlations, etc.).

Morgan (1989a) dealt with this problem by adapting a repeated-measures technique that had been developed by Goldman and Widawski (1976) for another purpose — to compare grading standards in different college courses where the students overlap only partly. In the process, Morgan extended the power and applicability of the technique by adding slope coefficients and standard errors, making it possible to evaluate trends and their statistical significance. The

Table 1-2

Illustration of the Pairwise Method of Analyzing Trends
Based upon Variable Yearly Samples

	Correlation by Year			
Institution	1979	1981	1983	1985
A	.37	.37		
B	.39		.39	
C	.41			.41
D		.41	.41	
E		.45		.45
F		.	.49	.49
Observed Mean	.39	.41	.43	.45
Pairwise Mean	.42	.42	.42	.42

reason for referring to this technique as a "pairwise" trend analysis is evident from the illustration in Table 1-2.

The pairwise analysis estimates how a group mean is changing over time by averaging differences between pairs of repeated measures within the same institutions. In Table 1-2 it is evident that there is no overall trend within individual institutions since in every case the correlation for a given institution is the same for both years in which it "participated." There is an increasing trend in the observed yearly means only because those institutions with the higher correlations tended to be represented in the later years. The pairwise mean for each year is based upon the average deviation — always zero in this illustration — from the grand mean. (See Note 4-1 for the precise computation.) The pairwise mean correctly shows no yearly change, but indicates .42 each year, which represents the grand mean. Thus, the method takes account of differences in institutional participation each year. Because this technique applies to any type of measure, it has been applied at a number of points in the studies reported here in order to ensure that measures are comparable with respect to yearly representation of different institutions.

Comparable Range of Talent

There are two metrics commonly used for expressing the relationship between a predictor and a criterion: the correlation coefficient and the regression coefficient, the latter being the slope of the regression line as shown in Figure 1-1. The regression line indicates to what

13

extent one can expect, from past experience, that students with higher test scores will make higher FGPAS. The regression line has important advantages as a descriptive measure, because it depicts the real relationship between the test score and the criterion. The regression coefficient (or, more precisely, an equation with several regression coefficients or weights) is what the institution actually uses in estimating how a given student is likely to do. Statisticians tend to favor the regression coefficient (or weight), but this measure is not ordinarily used to characterize test validity, because it varies widely with the scale of the predictor and the criterion and is, therefore, not at all comparable across tests and situations.

The correlation coefficient, on the other hand, always ranges conveniently from zero to 1.0 (plus or minus). For the purposes of this discussion, we can also say that it is insensitive to the particular scale on which the predictor or the criterion might be based. These are important advantages, but the correlation coefficient also has an important shortcoming: Its magnitude is reduced if the range of talent in the group is reduced. For that reason, the measure does not provide comparable estimates of validity in groups that vary in the range of predictor scores, as happens in selection. As Linn, Harnisch, and Dunbar (1981a, p. 662) put it, "The effect of selection on a correlation coefficient is a perennial problem in the conduct and interpretation of criterion-related validity studies. Results for an

Figure 1-1

Effect of College Selection and Self-Selection
on Range Restriction at a Particular College

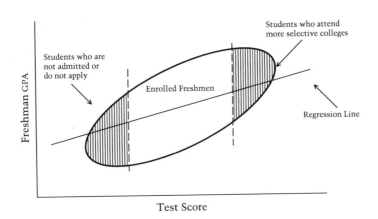

entire unselected population are of primary interest, but criterion data are available only for a selected subpopulation." Figure 1-1 illustrates the effect. The regression line shows that GPA goes up as test scores go up, but the ellipse represents the scatter of scores in an imperfect relationship. At the same test-score level, students vary in their freshman grades, though on average, those with higher scores make higher GPAs. The shape of the ellipse reflects the size of the correlation — a high coefficient looking more like a loaf of French bread, a coefficient near zero looking more like a basketball. As the picture suggests, range restriction, either due to selection by the college or self-selection by the students, will lower the correlation even though the intrinsic relationship between the scores and the FGPA remains the same.

The effect of range restriction can be large. Thorndike (1949) reports an unusual experiment in the Army Air Force during World War II. An entire group of pilot applicants were allowed to enter training irrespective of their scores on the selection test. The test's validity in this group of unselected applicants was .64, whereas the coefficient was .18 within the group that exceeded the normal qualifying score on the selection test. In college admissions, several studies have shown that the range of scores on the predictor is the largest source of variation in validity coefficients (Boldt, 1986; Linn, Harnisch, & Dunbar, 1981a; Munday, 1970). College Board VSS data indicate that the validity coefficient for the SAT averages .36, .45, and .57, respectively, in groups of colleges where the average standard deviation for SAT scores lies in the following ranges: below 80, 90-95, and above 110 (Ramist, 1984, p. 144-147).

There are standard procedures for correcting correlations for range restriction (Gulliksen, 1950). These are often not used because it is difficult to know whether the assumptions are warranted. But after demonstrating that the usual correction likely underestimates predictive validity, Linn et al. advise (1981a, p. 662), "Thus it seems desirable to routinely compute and report corrected correlations along with their uncorrected counterparts. Though still conservative, the corrected values will generally provide a better indication of predictive validity and be less misleading than uncorrected correlations alone."

In order to have a comparable metric for tracking yearly trends in validity coefficients, it is clear that a correction is necessary, because the range of talent within individual institutions can easily vary due to changes in the dynamics of college admissions. We have viewed the range-adjusted coefficients as the appropriate metric for examining trends in validity coefficients, though for other purposes the unadjusted coefficients may also be informative. Accordingly, all trend analyses here are based upon corrected coefficients unless otherwise indicated.

Multivariate range corrections have been used here (see Gulliksen, 1950, pp. 165-166, and Note 4-2), because college admission is multivariate by its nature, and also because Linn et al. (1981b) demonstrated that a univariate correction undercorrects. Finally, the important issue in this analysis is the shape of the trend line for average correlations between SAT and FGPA, not its elevation. Range corrections here use unrestricted standard deviations based upon the population of test takers. *This yields coefficients some 10 percent to 20 percent larger than observed coefficients.* While different range corrections might be argued for different institutions or different test uses, in this instance the critical requirement is to use the same correction across all institutions and years so that the coefficients will be comparable.

Comparable School Records

Depending upon the specifications of individual colleges, the Validity Study Service employs one of four different measures to express the student's academic performance in secondary school: class percentile rank (standardized on a scale of 20 to 80), grade-point average (usually on a 4.0 scale), plus two corresponding measures that are based upon data reported by the student rather than taken from the school transcript. These four measures are similar but not strictly comparable.

Both schools and colleges sometimes have strong philosophical or practical preferences for high school class rank or GPA. Colleges indicate which they prefer to use in their validity studies, and the percentages choosing each are about even. From the standpoint of validity research, the choice is apparently not consequential. The two measures correlate about equally with FGPA. Having two measures is mainly an inconvenience, because with different scales, it is sometimes difficult to pool or summarize data for effective interpretation.

A more serious problem is posed by the choice between high school performance measures based upon student-reported or college-reported (transcript-based) information. Student-reported grade or rank data come from the Student Descriptive Questionnaire, filled out by examinees when they register for the SAT. Such self-reported ranks and GPAS are used mainly for counseling, preliminary admissions screening, and some types of research. In recent years, about one-third of the VSS validity studies have used self-reported school rank or grades. Several special studies have shown self-reported data of this sort to be reasonably accurate when compared with actual transcript data (Freeberg, 1988; Sawyer, Laing, & Houston, 1988; Freeberg, Rock, & Pollack, 1989). Although self-reported measures are known to have somewhat lower validities, it has not been clear to what extent that may be due to the quality of the measure itself rather than to a characteristically lower validity of HSR in institutions that use student-reported information in validity studies.

In any event, the fact that these metrics are not strictly comparable calls for special care in reporting and interpreting student-reported data. In Morgan's (1989a) analysis, for example, it became apparent that a downward trend in the observed correlations between HSR and FGPA may be due partly or largely to increasing representation of self-reported HSRS. As will be noted, this comparability problem has been handled in different ways appropriate to different analyses in the studies reported here. These include analyzing only actual transcript data (Chapter 4), disaggregating data by type of HSR (Chapter 5), and using self-reported data exclusively (Chapter 10).

Institutional Differences in Prediction Trend

These three comparability problems — the cohort of colleges, the school record, and the range of talent — can be handled within the pairwise method of trend analysis as described. But there is an additional problem that must be noted. If there are significant differences from college to college in the *trend* of validity coefficients, then the overall results of a trend analysis will obviously depend upon what colleges one has available for a given study or analysis. As we shall see in the following chapter, there are such systematic institutional differences and, in one sense, this is a mixed blessing. While institutional differences provide important clues in understanding changes in the correlation between predictors and FGPA, these differences can also confuse results, and they are not corrected by the pairwise method or any other statistical adjustment, as far as we know.

An added complication is the fact that, under certain conditions, institutional differences can lead to variations in trend estimates derived from the pairwise method. This is a general technical problem concerning the weighting of institutional data rather than a quirk of the pairwise method itself. Nevertheless, there are practical problems as to what weights are best when some colleges do more validity studies than others, and there are known to be college differences in the trend of results. These matters are discussed in Chapter 6.

Even when care is taken to see that correlations are based upon comparable data from year to year, there are still changes in average validity coefficients over time (see Morgan's study reported in Chapter 4). In attempting to unravel the possible reasons these coefficients change over time, it is helpful to look at a concrete example. Figure 1-2 shows trends in the correlation between SAT scores and FGPA at two institutions over a nine-year period (from Fincher, 1990). The solid lines connect the actual coefficients. The heavy dashed lines show the *prediction slope* for each college, i.e., the straight line that best describes the overall trend in prediction at that college. In 1978, the correlation was about the same for the two institutions. In the ensuing nine years, the correlation of College A fluctuated, but showed essentially no long-term change, while College B experienced a progressive decline — a 13 point drop in the prediction slope from 1978 to 1987. Why the difference? What possible explanations come to mind?

Is the decline in College B merely a chance phenomenon? Not likely. With a small freshman class, validity coefficients may show marked changes up or down over two to three years, but the freshman classes of these two institutions are not small, and the change in College B's correlations is progressive for almost a decade.

Perhaps College B has had a changing clientele, such as an influx of female students in recent years. If so, and if women's grades are less predictable from test scores than men's are, that might account for the change. Again, no: These correlations are based upon male students only, and furthermore, women's grades tend to be more — not less — predictable from test scores.

Could a change in the test account for the decline in correlations for College B? If so, it's not apparent why that didn't affect College A. Perhaps College B is in a hotbed of test coaching, and its SAT scores have been progressively distorted with more coaching activity. That doesn't seem likely. These are two public universities in the same state. Even if there were evidence that coaching affects validity coefficients, it would presumably have similar effects on similarly situated institutions.

These particular hypotheses seem unfruitful in this case, and they only scratch the surface of the problem. There are numerous other possibilities. College B may have become much more selective during this period, or it may have undergone a substantial demographic change on some basis other than gender, e.g., a shift in ethnic representation that is somehow related to predictive validity. Even if the test itself has not changed, the curriculum at College B may have

Figure 1-2

Multiple Correlations of SAT-Verbal and -Mathematical Scores with
Freshman GPA at Two Institutions over a Nine-Year Period

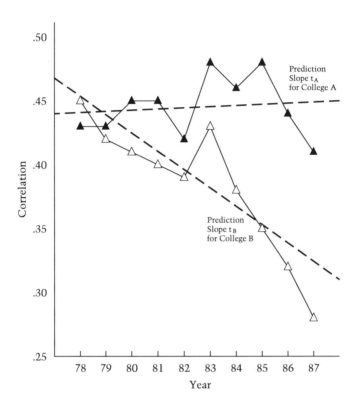

changed in ways that place less emphasis on the academic skills represented in the test. Perhaps remediation and other educational practices have improved the freshman grades of many low-scoring students and effectively "beaten the prediction" of poor performance in college. Or perhaps grading practices have changed more than the actual performance of the students.

This exercise suggests several conclusions. First, the topic is complicated. Any of a number of factors can be involved in lowering or raising the correlation between test scores and FGPA — possibly several factors at once. Consequently, no one study can be sufficient for determining what has and what has not created a change in a particular institution. Furthermore, it seems reasonable to assume that any factor that could change average coefficients at the level of

Table 1-3

Framework for Considering Factors That May Influence the Relationship Between Test Scores and Freshman Grades

Type of Variation or Change	Type of Analysis or Evidence
1. THE SAMPLE	
1.1 Institutional variation in prediction trends	— Stability and reliability of trends; short-term vs. long-term fluctuations
1.2 Type of institutions represented (selectivity, size, control, etc.)	— Comparable validity metrics: single-order, partial, and multiple correlation; regression weights
1.3 Students represented (ethnicity, gender, academic disposition, age, etc.)	— Subgroup analysis: proportional representation, relative performance, comparable validity metrics
1.4 Nature of database (Validity Study Service, national sample, state system)	— Comparison of studies and samples
2. THE PREDICTOR (Test Score)	
2.1 Characteristics of the test (content and statistical)	— Reliability
2.2 Meaning of scores (nature of the construct represented)	— Test specifications, item and test analyses
	— Comparability across forms
2.3 Score variations (due to external factors like coaching, test disclosure, repeat testing)	— Correlation with other measures
	— Internal test structure
3. THE CRITERION (FGPA)	
3.1 Characteristics of grades (courses included, grading practices)	— Reliability
	— Grading practices, distributions, etc.
3.2 Meaning of grades (skills or type of performance valued)	— Comparability across sections, courses, departments
3.3 Grading variations (due to different standards or different performance)	— Correlation with other measures
	— Predictive accuracy in lower/upper class segments
3.4 Educational practices (remediation, placement)	

a single institution could also operate at the national level. Understanding a national trend can be approached with the same sorts of hypotheses in mind, though the problem is more complicated for the obvious reason that there may be differences among institutions.

Finally, rival explanations of changes in validity coefficients fall naturally into three categories that mirror the correlational model: the predictor (the test score), the criterion (the FGPA), and the sample on which the correlation estimate is based. Because a correlation is a measure of association *between* two measures, it can be equally affected by a change in either of the two measures, or by a change in the sample.

These three categories — predictor, criterion, and sample — provide the basis for a framework of possible causes of correlational change. Table 1-3 shows such a framework directed to this topic on a national scale. Several aspects are worth noting. The listed factors vary widely. Some lend themselves to straightforward, if tedious, analysis (e.g., possible changes in the technical characteristics of the predictor over time). Others, like the meaning of grades, are exceedingly difficult to study, especially if one wishes to draw conclusions that may apply to broad segments of education.

This framework is useful only as an heuristic, particularly since the categories tend to overlap. The factors that may affect the predictor and the criterion are parallel to some degree but play out differently. "Predictor" refers here to a test score, but it can apply to high school record as well. Furthermore, it is necessary to take that measure into account because it directly affects two important validity metrics: the multiple correlation based on test scores and HSR, and the increment of that multiple over the correlation of FGPA with HSR alone. Most of the factors listed in Table 1-3 have been examined in studies reported here, though the extent to which they could be evaluated with available data varied, of course. Results of those studies are discussed in the following chapter.

CHAPTER 2

Understanding Yearly Trends: A Synthesis of Research Findings

WARREN W. WILLINGHAM*

As the discussion in Chapter 1 makes clear, there is a wide range of factors that may cause correlations between admissions test scores and FGPA to vary over time. Consequently, the data and other evidence that may be helpful in understanding a trend in such variations come from a variety of sources and special studies. In this chapter, we take up in turn the various issues identified in the three-part framework of Table 1-3: possible changes in the samples upon which correlations are based, possible changes in the predictor, and possible changes in the criterion.

In each of these categories, a number of questions are posed in order to help structure the topic and to examine those issues that seem most important. Prior research and other relevant facts are cited, of course, but the main sources of information are the wealth of data available concerning the SAT and the series of special studies reported in Part II. Findings are cited by chapter and table as appropriate. In the course of preparing this chapter, some additional analyses were undertaken in order to clarify cross-cutting issues or to answer specific questions not addressed in the studies described in Part II. But first, what trend are we talking about?

Estimating Overall Trends

Table 4-1 shows average validity coefficients by year, as compiled by VSS. These include the observed correlations with FGPA for SAT, HSR, and the two predictors combined for each year from 1964 to 1985. (Here and elsewhere, the correlation between the SAT and FGPA or other grade criteria always refers to a multiple correlation based on SAT-V and SAT-M.) The data suggest two general trends. One is a gradual decline in the correlation based on HSR alone, paralleled by a similar decline in the multiple correlation based on SAT scores and HSR. A second and

---

* A number of colleagues have provided valuable assistance in the preparation of this chapter. In particular, I am grateful to coauthors Charles Lewis, Rick Morgan, and Leonard Ramist for numerous dialogues and generous help on several knotty issues, to Rick Morgan for use of a database he developed, to Laura McCamley for data analysis, to Linda Johnson for assistance throughout, and to Neil Dorans, Robert Linn, Samuel Messick, and Larry Stricker for helpful reviews.

somewhat different trend is evident in the relationship of SAT scores with FGPA: a substantial increase in the early 1970s, followed by a similar decrease. As noted in Chapter 1, those trends in observed correlations cannot be trusted, because the year-to-year comparisons are not made on the basis of the same institutions, the same type of high school records, or correlation coefficients with comparable range restriction.

Morgan (1989a) studied validity coefficients from 222 colleges in the period 1976 through 1985, using data that are comparable in those three respects. He did indeed find a decline from .51 to .47 in the average corrected correlation between SAT scores and FGPA, half the change observed in the VSS yearly averages over that period (Table 4-1). On the other hand, he found very little change (.01 or less over that period) in the relationship of HSR to FGPA, in the multiple correlation with FGPA based on SAT scores and HSR, or in the incremental validity of SAT plus HSR over HSR alone.

Morgan's study, reported in Chapter 4, made two important contributions. One was to show that noncomparable measures can substantially distort trends in VSS yearly data — for both the SAT and the HSR. The other was to provide an improved method for studying such trends. Morgan's study was based upon a limited period (1976 to 1985), as well as a limited set of data — only those studies that used college-reported high school records. In a more comprehensive and detailed follow-up study, Ramist and Weiss (Chapter 5) used the same pairwise trend analysis and included all types of high school records (HSR), but based all comparisons on the same type of record. They examined correlational data compiled by VSS from 466 colleges that did validity studies in at least two of five time periods: pre-1973 through 1985-1988. (Both the first and last periods were atypical — the first because it covered eight years, the last because most studies were done in 1985. See Note 2-1.) Figure 2-1 shows their findings regarding the overall trend in corrected validity coefficients through these time periods.

A general finding of the Ramist-Weiss study, confirming the Morgan study, was that changes in validity coefficients over time are considerably reduced when the analysis is based upon data that are comparable from year to year. As Figure 2-1 indicates, an increase of .02 in SAT predictive validity was followed by a gradual decrease of about .04 over the next 10 to 12 years. During this entire time, from the mid-1960s to the late 1980s, pairwise analysis showed little change in the relationship of HSR to FGPA over all colleges combined. On the other hand, the multiple correlation based on both SAT and HSR did decline somewhat from the mid-1970s to the mid-1980s, so there was some change in the incremental predictive validity of the SAT

Figure 2-1

Pairwise Trend Analyses of Corrected Correlations of SAT Scores
and High School Record (HSR) with Freshman GPA by Time Period*

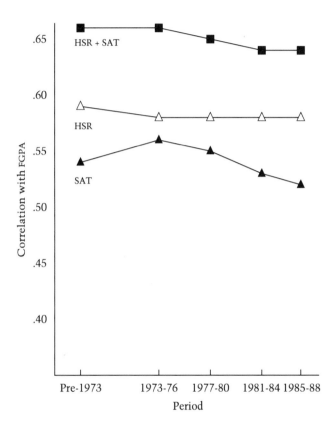

*See Ramist & Weiss, Table 5-6.

over the HSR alone. In the pairwise analysis, that increment increased
.013 in the early 1970s and decreased .020 thereafter.

How dependable are these estimates? Very dependable, from one
standpoint. Using the pairwise method with this sample of colleges,
the overall estimates are statistically very stable — mainly because
they are based upon a great deal of data. But a stable average does not
necessarily characterize the individual colleges accurately. In fact,
for every two colleges where the correlation of SAT scores with FGPA
decreased from the mid-1970s to the mid-1980s, in a third college the
correlation increased. As we shall see, differences from college to
college provide an important clue to understanding trends in validity
coefficients.

Additionally, this sample is not necessarily representative of institutions of higher education generally, or even of sat users. Many institutions routinely do their own validity studies, rather than use the vss, and there are undoubtedly many others that seldom do studies. Also, among those colleges that did participate in the vss during these years, data from 36 percent could not be used in the trend analyses because those institutions either did only one study each or did studies in only one of the five periods. Needless to say, a different group of colleges might give a different answer.

Willingham and Lewis (Chapter 6) used a different method of analyzing trends in order to check on the possibility that trend estimates might vary due to some colleges doing more studies than others. The alternate approach was to determine a *prediction slope* for each college; i.e., the slope of the line that best fits the values (describes the trend) of that institution's validity coefficients in successive years. Thus, the prediction slope provides a numeric index of the degree of change over time and its direction (plus for increasing, minus for decreasing).

Prediction slopes for individual colleges are illustrated in Figure 1-2. This method has the advantage of giving equal weight to studies in estimating the trend for a given college and equal weight to colleges in estimating the overall trend. A disadvantage of the prediction slope in estimating trends is that, being linear, it is not sensitive to a change of direction. But for a period when the general trend does not appear to be changing direction, the average of such slopes for all colleges is a useful alternate method of characterizing the overall prediction trend. (See Note 2-2.)

Figure 2-2 shows an analysis of average prediction slopes using the Ramist-Weiss database, as described by Willingham and Lewis in Chapter 6. (See Note 2-3.) There were two separate analyses: one based on 110 colleges in 1970-74, and another on 387 colleges in 1974-88. For the period 1970-74, the slopes in Figure 2-2 look generally similar to the pairwise trends in Figure 2-1. In this early period both methods of analysis indicate that there was not much change in overall predictability of fgpa (i.e., the corrected multiple correlation based on sat and hsr). The sat correlations were trending up, however, and the hsr correlations were trending down.

Note that there was only a modest increase in corrected sat correlations in 1970-74 even though vss average uncorrected correlations were increasing rapidly in this period. This result reinforces the conclusion of Ramist and Weiss that much of the large increase in observed sat validity coefficients at that time (on the order of .08 to .09) was due to increasing representation of colleges with relatively high coefficients and to decreasing range restriction.

26

Figure 2-2

Average College Prediction Slope for Corrected Correlations of SAT Scores
and HSR with Freshman GPA —Determined Separately
for 110 Colleges in 1970-74 and 387 Colleges in 1974-1988

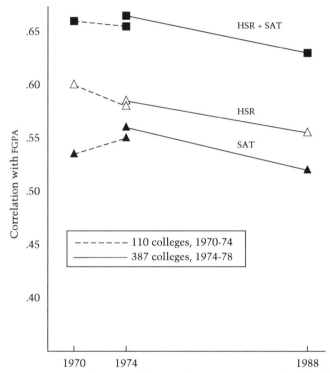

The average HSR slopes in Figure 2-2 suggest a gradual decline in corrected coefficients through the entire period 1970 to 1988. The pairwise trends in Figure 2-1 were flatter. But the main difference apparent in the two analyses is the comparative trend for the different predictors from 1974 to 1988. While the HSR trend was flat in the pairwise analyses, trends estimated on the basis of the average prediction slopes of individual colleges look similar for HSR, SAT, and the two combined. The estimated amount of decline in these coefficients over a decade was .020, .030, and .025, respectively. These results indicate a change in the SAT increment of –.005 (i.e., .025 minus .020).

The differences between Figures 2-1 and 2-2 are not large, but the two methods of analysis do present somewhat different impressions, particularly for the 1974-88 period. Apparently, they give slightly different results partly because the two methods differ in the way they handle variations in the numbers of studies from individual

27

colleges (see Chapter 6), and partly because one method represents an average slope across colleges and the other represents a slope of average yearly points based on college studies. These are not necessarily the same if all colleges do not do a study each year. Is one estimate more correct than the other?

Table 2-1 extends the question. It shows several 10-year trend estimates in the 1974-88 period based on somewhat different samples, measures, and analytical methods dictated by the purpose of each study. The number of colleges and studies in the four analyses varies mainly because number 1 is restricted to studies with transcript-based high school GPAs or ranks, numbers 2 and 3 cover a wider year span, and number 4 focuses on only three years. Also, because it is based on student-reported HSGPAs, number 4 includes a number of studies with HSR mismatches in the VSS database or other characteristics precluding their use in number 2 or number 3. The data in number 2 are almost the same as those in number 3, the main difference being a time span one year longer in the latter.

The results of these various analyses appear to differ for one or more of five reasons: the sample, the statistical method, the use of a period of years vs. a yearly pairwise analysis, the weight applied to

Table 2-1

Estimates of 10-year Change in Corrected Validity Coefficients
During the Period 1974-88*

Study	Studies/ Colleges	Period	10-Year Change in	
			HSR	SAT
1. Morgan (Table 4-3)	778/222	1976-85	−.005	−.040
2. Willingham-Lewis (Table 6-4)	1737/387			
a. Average College Prediction Slope		1974-88	−.021	−.030
b. Slope Weighted By K(K-1)/2			−.005	−.031
3. Ramist-Weiss (Tables 5-5 and 5-6)	1897/399			
a. Pairwise by Period		1973-88	+.005	−.037
b. Pairwise by Year		1974-88	−.001	−.052
4. Morgan (Table 10-1)	443/198	1978-85	−.036	−.056

*See Note 2-11.

28

multiple studies from one college, and the type of HSR. All produce small variations in estimates. Given these variations and the uncertain sample biases that may be present in the particular selection of institutions with usable data that are represented in the VSS database, it is difficult if not impossible to pick a particular number as *the* trend for SAT or HSR validity coefficients.

Table 2-1 does suggest a general conclusion, however. From the mid-1970s to the mid-1980s, there was a gradual decline in the predictability of FGPA (about -.02), reflected somewhat more in SAT scores than in HSR. For a 10-year period during this time, the change in correlations with FGPA was probably in the range of -.03 to -.05 for the SAT and .00 to -.03 for HSR. Did a declining trend continue into the late 1980s? That may not be an unreasonable assumption, but from the very limited data available after 1985, it is impossible to say with any assurance. (See Note 2-4.)

One other trend of interest is the relative contribution of SAT-Verbal and SAT-Mathematics scores in optimum prediction of FGPA. Table 5-7 shows those trends. In the period prior to 1973, there was an increase in the proportion of the prediction weights associated with the test scores (.41 to .46). This change is consistent with the increase in incremental validity of the SAT during that period. It is particularly interesting, however, that practically all of that change was due to an increase in the correlation of the SAT-Mathematics score with freshman grades. From the mid-1970s to the mid-1980s, the corrected validity coefficients for both SAT-V and SAT-M scores declined at the same rate as the total SAT. As a result, the relative weight of the whole test in prediction returned to a level (.39) slightly below that of 15 years earlier, but the increased relative importance of the math score was largely maintained. We move now to an examination of factors that may be related to trends in validity coefficients — first, sample effects.

POSSIBLE CHANGES IN THE SAMPLE

If a change is observed in the average validity coefficient from one year to another, there are two types of potential sample effects to consider: change in the sample of institutions, and change in the sample of students within institutions. One can view institutional sample effects either as different results from college to college or as variation among different samples or classes of institutions. Institutional differences in trends will be examined first, because individual colleges are the basic unit with which we are concerned, and that is where validity studies are conducted and interpreted. Understanding college differences in validity results bears not only on the trend estimates just discussed, but also on several subsequent issues. Sample effects that may be associated with the changing student body in higher education are discussed in a subsequent section on demographic differences.

Institutional Differences in Trends

In their study of law schools, Linn et al. (1981a) suggested that the great majority of variation in validity coefficients among those relatively homogeneous institutions was due simply to variations in the range of talent and to random fluctuations. In undergraduate institutions, on the other hand, Boldt (1986) found considerable variation in SAT validity coefficients from college to college that could not be accounted for by those two factors. This finding suggests that different types of institutions might show different trends in corrected correlations.

Year-to-year differences in validity coefficients for individual colleges are readily observed (Ramist, 1984). While such yearly deviations are often assumed to be mostly sampling fluctuations, institutions are encouraged to do validity studies periodically, partly on the possibility that prediction results may change over time. The first suspicion that there probably were important college differences in prediction trends came from Morgan's finding (Chapter 4) that trends appeared to vary for some types of institutions.

Whether the predictability of FGPA shows different trends from college to college is a significant question for two reasons. If there are consequential institutional differences in trends, then the sample of colleges on which the trend estimate is based can easily affect results. Also, knowing whether prediction trends are similar or different from college to college is helpful in understanding how the trends may have come about. If there are no significant institutional differences in prediction trends, it would appear more likely that some change in a predictor had caused an overall trend to go up or down. On the other hand, significant differences in prediction trends from college to college would point to the FGPA criterion as a more likely source of the change, because the criterion can more easily vary from college to college and year to year.

The prediction trend for a given institution was defined earlier as the slope of a straight line that best fits the validity coefficients from studies the college has done over time (see page 18 and Figure 1-2). Coefficients from individual studies will vary, year to year, but the slope of the line, up or down, shows the trend. The question, then, is whether those slopes look generally similar for different colleges. Figure 2-3 gives a visual answer: enormous variety.

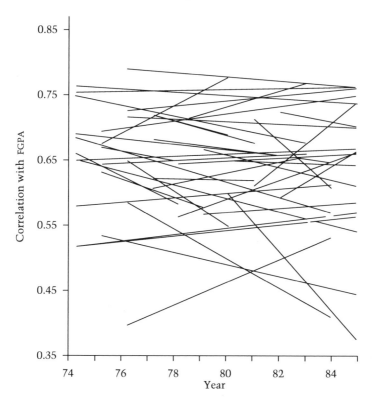

Figure 2-3

College Differences in the Predictability of FGPA —a Representative
Sample of College Prediction Slopes for Validity Coefficients
Based upon SAT Scores and HSR

These college prediction slopes are based on corrected multiple
correlations (SAT and HSR). Using both the school record and an
admissions test means that FGPA is being predicted about as well as it
is likely to be in the individual colleges — assuming that each college
continues to use much the same FGPA criterion. (There is a long research
history and an accumulation of evidence on this point; see Note 2-5.)
Such a prediction slope was computed for all colleges that had done
four or more validity studies since 1974 using the same measure of
high school performance. Thus, the individual slopes may be based
on as few as four or as many as 12 points. A 25 percent sample (every
fourth slope in order of size) is shown in Figure 2-3 simply to
illustrate the differences. There is wide variation in the predictability
of FGPA at these colleges. At individual institutions, the typical
corrected validity coefficient ranges from the .30s to the .70s, even

31

though these corrected correlations do not reflect variations that normally occur due to some colleges being more selective than others. Also, the prediction trends move in all directions. It is not obvious whether there are more going up or down.

The confusing variety of college results illustrated in Figure 2-3 indicates the need for further analysis to separate effects. Through analysis of variance (see Table 6-3), it is possible to identify five components of variation in these correlations. They are listed below, along with the percentage of variation associated with each component when the analysis is based on corrected SAT validity coefficients.

1. College differences in average coefficient — variations in the typical level of validity coefficients from college to college (59 percent of the variance).

The following three components represent *temporal* effects:

2. Overall linear trend over years — the yearly trend in the average correlation across all colleges (2 percent of the variance).

3. College differences in linear trend — the extent to which coefficients are going up in some colleges and down in others (12 percent of the variance).

4. Nonrandom college deviations — yearly deviations about the trend line for individual colleges (6 percent of the variance).

And the remainder is:

5. Error — the expected statistical fluctuation, inversely associated with the size of the class (21 percent of the variance).

One aspect of these results is striking. That is the large amount of variation due to college differences in typical SAT validity coefficients (component 1). But the most pertinent result is the substantial variation in linear trends from college to college (component 3) — a much larger source of variation than component 2, the overall trend that was discussed in some detail in the previous section. As noted, for every two colleges where SAT coefficients were trending down in this period, there was at least one other college where the trend was up. (See Note 2-6.) Other results of Willingham and Lewis (Chapter 6) indicate that these different prediction trends in individual colleges can be highly reliable if based on multiple studies over a decade.

What are the implications of these percentages of variation in SAT coefficients that are associated with each of the five components? How would a similar analysis of the high school record compare? An accepted method (Cohen, 1988) for evaluating the size of an "effect"

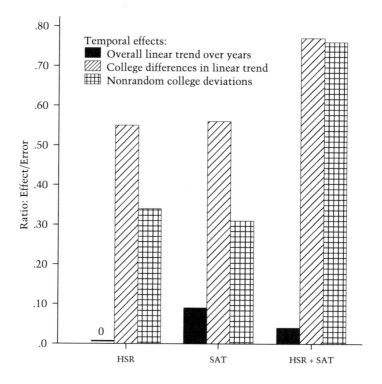

Figure 2-4

Relative Size of Three Temporal Effects in the Variation of Validity Coefficients
Based on HSR, SAT, and Both Measures Combined*

*See Willingham & Lewis, Table 6-3.

(i.e., different characteristics, experimental conditions, individual differences, etc.) is to form a ratio of the variation of interest (say, component 2, overall trend) to the error term (component 5). Figure 2-4 shows such "effect sizes" for the three temporal sources of variation for HSR, SAT, and the multiple correlation based upon both.

There are three results of particular interest. First, both of the college-based temporal variations — college differences in trend, and nonrandom college yearly deviations — are large effects in comparison to that associated with the overall trend in validity coefficients. This result shows why it would be a mistake to think of an average downward trend as characterizing institutions generally. Different colleges have experienced very different trends. Thus, the visual message of Figure 2-3 is accurate. Second, the patterns of effect sizes for SAT and HSR are very similar. Overall, SAT coefficients and HSR

33

coefficients vary in much the same way, college to college and year to year. Third, the effect sizes for the two types of temporal variation that are showing an effect (components 3 and 4) are larger in the case of the three-variable multiple correlation than in the case of either predictor separately. Taken together, these results strongly suggest that changes in validity coefficients are more likely due to changes in the institution than to changes in one of the predictors.

This analysis of institutional differences in prediction trends raises a variety of interesting questions to which we return later. But as to sample effects on validity trends, the results have two major implications. One is to suggest that these validity changes have an institutional basis, perhaps mediated through changes in the predictability of the local FGPA criterion. Willingham and Lewis (Chapter 6) discuss the possibility that institutional differences in validity trends could result from enrolling students who are progressively more or less predictable. They point out several lines of research, however, that are inconsistent with that hypothesis. Another implication is that one cannot expect consistent results when estimating an overall prediction trend with different samples of colleges — an implication that helps in understanding some of the results previously described. In the following section, we get another view of sampling variations.

Types of Institutions

Given differences in prediction trends from college to college, a question that naturally follows is whether there are differences in such trends among types of SAT users. But first, is it possible that the VSS data might be idiosyncratic? If we had the appropriate correlations from all colleges that use the SAT nationally, would the picture look any different?

Only limited non-VSS data on SAT correlations are available, particularly in earlier years, but what data there are do indicate trends within the range described. Willingham, Rock, and Pollack (Chapter 11) found that the correlation between SAT scores and college GPA was .03 lower in a national sample in 1982 than in another national sample in 1972, a period coinciding roughly with the period of decline in VSS coefficients. Fincher (1990) reported an average decline in uncorrected correlations of FGPA with SAT-V and SAT-M from 1975 to 1985 in the University System of Georgia (18 institutions) of essentially the same magnitude (.08) as the decline in corresponding VSS uncorrected coefficients (.075) over that period.

This evidence of similar trends in SAT coefficients for other databases indicates that the VSS results, properly corrected for comparability, are not likely to be giving a warped picture for SAT users overall. (See page 44 for a comment on data for ACT users.) On the other hand, results for particular types of institutions will not necessarily follow the trends observed, and indeed, that is what Morgan (1989a) found. In Chapter 4, he describes less decline in SAT correlations from 1976 to 1985 for three types of institutions: small ones, private ones, and those with a high SAT average.

Ramist and Weiss (Chapter 5) extended the Morgan analyses in several ways. They used all available VSS data (including studies based on student-reported high school rank or GPA) and did separate analyses for the 1975-85 period when correlations were declining and the prior years when correlations were increasing. In addition to control, class size, and SAT average, Ramist and Weiss used three additional institutional characteristics in their analyses: percentage of part-time students, percentage of occupational degrees, and number of remedial services. Also, these investigators did a multivariate analysis in order to help determine which college characteristics might be playing a more important role.

Ramist and Weiss found two results of interest in the early period, when the average correlation between SAT scores and FGPA was increasing. There was little difference in the amount of change in average corrected validity coefficients according to size or control, but there was a clear association between the validity trend and the SAT mean of the freshman class. Colleges with an SAT mean of 1050 or higher showed little change in the corrected SAT correlation with FGPA. In colleges with an SAT mean below 850, that correlation increased by .06.

In the subsequent span, from 1973-76 to 1985-88, the findings of Ramist and Weiss largely agreed with those of Morgan, where results could be compared. They found several types of institutions in which the corrected SAT validity coefficient dropped more than the .04 overall decline during this period. Their Table 5-10 reports the following changes in corrected coefficients from the mid-1970s to the mid-1980s:

- Public institutions, −.07;

- Institutions with one-third or more part-time students, −.09;

- Institutions with more remedial services, −.08; and

- Institutions with SAT means below 850, −.10.

The institutional characteristics associated with a decrease in SAT correlations tended to be the same as those associated with increases in the earlier period. In fact, the best indicator of correlation decrease was whether the college had an increase earlier (i.e., the early and

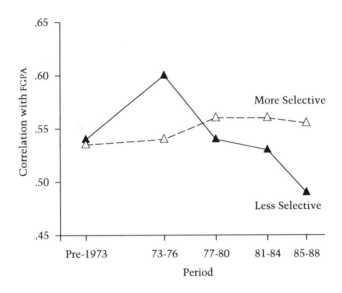

Figure 2-5

Average Corrected Correlation Between SAT Scores
and FGPA for More and Less Selective Colleges
in Five Time Periods

later slopes correlated –.24, some of which may be due to regression).
Using the six institutional characteristics, a multivariate prediction
of change in the corrected SAT correlation with FGPA gave similar results
in the early and later periods. In both instances, the trend in individual colleges was not very predictable from these nominal institutional characteristics, and the average SAT score was the only very
useful indicator of a likely increase or decrease.

Figure 2-5 shows the different trends for institutions with high and
low SAT averages.

For the 90 more selective colleges with SAT means of 1050 or above,
the average SAT validity coefficient was relatively stable from the
mid-1960s through the mid-1980s. In fact, it went up .02. For the 90
less selective colleges with SAT means below 850, the average validity
coefficient was quite unstable. The corrected coefficient increased
.06 from the late 1960s to the mid-1970s and then dropped about .10
over the next 10 years. Two other trends are worth noting. Although
both the more and less selective institutions experienced a drop in
the average SAT total score in the early period (52 and 59 points,
respectively), their experience in the next decade was different. The
more selective colleges rebounded somewhat (+9 points), but the less
selective colleges continued downward (–37 points).

Of the various differences in prediction trend associated with college type, the most notable is undoubtedly the stable level of predictive validity in the selective colleges and the substantial swing in the less selective. It is important to remember, however, that there were large institutional differences. Increasing and decreasing trends were not exclusive to the less selective colleges. By one estimate, for example, 14 percent of the colleges with below average SAT scores showed a significant decline in SAT coefficients from the mid-1970s to the mid-1980s, while nine percent of colleges with above average SAT scores showed such a change (see Note 2-7). We move now to a different aspect of possible sample effects: the students.

Demographic Differences

It is well known that there have been substantial changes in the demography of higher education over the past two decades: greater ethnic diversity, increased representation of women, more older and nontraditional students, and more foreign students (Snyder, 1987). Another familiar demographic change is the increased competition for students that many institutions have experienced in recent years (Breland, Wilder, & Robertson, 1986). It is certainly reasonable to wonder whether these changes are somehow associated with changes in the correlation of SAT scores and high school grades with FGPA.

Broadly speaking, there are two ways to investigate possible effects of such changes on predictive validity. One would be to examine the possible impact of new educational practices and programs that have come about as a result of demographic changes. We take up such possibilities later in our discussion of the criterion. Another approach, which we undertake here, is to examine the more direct effects on correlations that might result from changes in the student samples upon which validity studies are based.

First, consider sample changes due to enrollment pressure. Perhaps the institutions represented in the VSS validity studies have tended to enroll larger numbers of academically weak students. If true, that could have a direct effect on predictive validity in several ways. For example, freshman grades of such students may be intrinsically less predictable. Or their performance may be harder to differentiate if there are many additional weak students at the bottom of the class. Or perhaps the SAT works less well with such students. There is, however, no evidence of any such pileup of low-scoring students in recent years among the institutions that have participated in VSS, i.e., the colleges on which these validity data are based. Within the individual colleges studied here, there was actually a somewhat *smaller* proportion of freshmen in 1985 than in 1981 or 1978 who fell below a given "low" SAT score (i.e., the thirty-third percentile in each college for the three years combined). As shown in Figure 2-12, the proportions were .33, .34, and .31 in 1978, 1981, and 1985, respectively. (Based upon Morgan, 1990, Table 14.)

Another class of possible demographic effects concerns subgroups. That is, could a change in SAT validity coefficients result from increasing representation of women, ethnic groups, foreign students, or older students? Changes in the representation of foreign and older students do not play any direct role in these correlational trends because there were very few such students in VSS studies (see Note 2-8). These and other nontraditional students may play an indirect role, however, through modified educational programs and practices. That possibility is examined later. There are three ways in which changes in the gender or ethnic subgroups might have a direct effect on correlations between SAT scores and FGPA:

- If some subgroups have generally lower or higher test validity and have recently become more heavily represented in these colleges,

- If the SAT correlation with FGPA has increased or decreased for some subgroups in recent years, or

- If the college performance of one or more subgroups has changed so substantially in relation to their test scores as to alter the relationship between SAT and FGPA for the overall class.

Findings relevant to each of these possibilities are found in Chapter 10 by Morgan. He used student-reported high school averages in order to compare various groups of freshmen with the same type of high school record. The analyses are based on data from 198 colleges that conducted validity studies in at least two of the years 1978, 1981, and 1985.

Among the various subgroups of SAT examinees, the most obvious and statistically stable correlational difference over years was in the predictability of FGPA for males and females. The decline in SAT correlations with FGPA was twice as great for males as for females. A similar gender difference appears in other studies reported here (see Ramist & Weiss, Chapter 5, and Ramist, Lewis, & McCamley, Chapter 12). As Figure 2-6 shows, there was also a gender difference in the 1978-85 trend in the correlation between HSGPA and FGPA. For males, that correlation went down .04; for females, it did not change. Similarly, the multiple correlation based on SAT and HSGPA declined .06 for males and .01 for females.

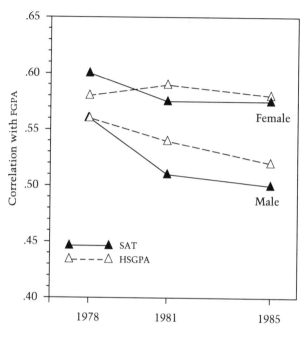

Figure 2-6

Corrected Correlation of High School GPA and SAT Scores with
FGPA for Females and Males*

*See Morgan, Chapter 10.

Thus, in these data, the decline in the predictability of college grades from 1978 to 1985 appears to be largely a male phenomenon. Because women's grades were more predictable than men's, it seems obvious that the observed decline in the predictability of FGPA is not due to the increase in the representation of women during this period. (See Note 2-9.) In fact, that demographic change would appear to have a very slight opposite effect on validity coefficients. For example, simply computing a weighted average correlation across gender groups would indicate that the two percent increase in women in this sample from 1978 to 1985 and the smaller change in validity coefficients for the women would each work to increase SAT coefficients by .001.

Nor does there appear to be any consequential effect on prediction due to changes in Asian-American, Black, and Hispanic subgroups. This conclusion stems partly from the lack of any notable trends within these groups and partly from the sparse representation of these groups in this sample of colleges. The results for the ethnic subgroups can be summarized as follows.

There was no increase in the representation of Black students in these colleges during this period, though the SAT validity did decline somewhat more for the Black than for the White students. There was a small increase in the proportion of Hispanic students. This group had lower validity than was observed for majority students, a difference not generally characteristic of this group of students (Pennock-Roman, in press). The increased representation of the Hispanic group would tend to lower overall validity slightly in this sample of studies, but that effect appears to be offset by another finding: In these data, SAT validity for Hispanic students increased from 1978 to 1985. Test validity for Asian-American students was at about the level typically observed (Sue & Abe, 1988), and this group gained in representation. Also, Asian-American students did not show any validity decline.

These findings for ethnic subgroups are based upon a limited number of colleges where at least 25 members of the subgroup were enrolled. By rough approximation (i.e., simply averaging minority and majority group correlations, weighted by group size), the Black and Hispanic subgroups likely had less than .001 influence on overall validity — trivial differences that were negative for Black students, positive for Hispanic students. The two trends noted in the data for the Asian-American students would presumably have a very slight positive effect on overall validity.

These various results cannot be viewed as precise estimates, but they do suggest that demographic changes are not directly responsible for any recent changes in correlations between SAT scores and freshman grades. The results for validity coefficients based on the HSGPA were generally similar. There is one further piece of evidence indicating that prediction trends are not the result of demographic changes. The White group showed almost exactly the same correlational trends as the total sample. That is, adding the ethnic groups to the White group neither heightened nor lessened the correlational trends observed in the White group. This result also indicates it is unlikely that correlations with FGPA have been affected by a change in the performance of subgroups or because of greater representation of subgroups that show higher or lower performance than predicted. As noted, however, there may be indirect effects on predictive validity due to institutional adjustments to demographic changes.

Summary of Results: The Sample

Principal findings regarding possible effects of changes in the sample on prediction trends were the following:

1. Analyses of Validity Study Service data from the mid-1970s to the mid-1980s revealed very large differences in the predictability of FGPA from college to college. Institutional differences in the typical level of multiple correlation based on HSR and SAT scores accounted for 64 percent of all variation in that coefficient.

2. There were large differences from college to college in the trend of validity coefficients over time. Variation in those college trends accounted for 12 percent of all variation in SAT coefficients from the mid-1970s to the mid-1980s, considerably larger than the 2 percent associated with the overall trend of SAT coefficients during this period. For every two colleges that showed a decreasing trend during this period, one college was increasing.

3. For both SAT and HSR, there were significant yearly variations in correlations at individual colleges, not random and not associated with the college trend line for these coefficients.

4. Of all institutional characteristics, the one most prominently related to predictability of FGPA, and to trends in that predictability, was the average SAT score of the freshman class. Among the more selective institutions, the average SAT validity coefficient has been quite stable for the past 20 years. Among the less selective institutions, the corrected SAT coefficient increased .06 from the mid-1960s to the mid-1970s and declined some .10 to the mid-1980s. HSR coefficients declined .05 during that latter decade in the less selective colleges.

5. Since institutional participants in the VSS are self-selected, trend analyses based upon these data are not necessarily representative of SAT users, but data from other sources indicate that the gradual decline in validity coefficients in recent years is not limited to VSS data.

6. There is a sizable gender difference in recent trends in validity coefficients. Males show at least twice the decline of females. Since validity coefficients for both SAT and HSR are higher for women, any overall downward trend in those coefficients has occurred despite, not because of, there now being more women than men in higher education.

7. Data for ethnic subgroups did not indicate any effect on validity trends, either due to changes in the mix of those groups or changes in their predictability. Majority students showed the same decline in predictability of FGPA as did total freshman classes including the ethnic subgroups.

Perhaps the most important findings concerning sample effects are the substantial variations in the trend of validity coefficients from college to college, and the association of validity change with nonselective colleges. Both of these results suggest an institutional basis for prediction trends; that is, changes in correlations with FGPA are more accurately viewed as variations in criterion predictability rather than predictor validity. While the data show no direct effects of demographic shifts on validity coefficients, there may be indirect effects on the FGPA criterion due to adjustments in curriculum and educational practices designed to serve a changing student body.

POSSIBLE CHANGES IN THE PREDICTOR

In theory, there are many possible ways in which the SAT could change over time so as to affect the relationship of scores to FGPA. These include not only how the test is constructed, but also external factors that might distort the resulting scores. For example, if predictive relationships decrease, it could be because the test has become too difficult or is measuring something different, or the scores are being warped by coaching, and so on. Most such hypotheses are testable, and the following sections summarize a variety of relevant data. It is useful, however, to ask first whether only the SAT shows some decline in correlation with FGPA or if other tests show the same trend.

The Broader Context — Other Tests

There are data available concerning trends in predictive correlations for several tests. Table 2-2 shows the findings of two studies. The top portion of the table gives the results of a pairwise trend analysis of uncorrected correlations (see Note 2-10) of FGPA with four tests in the Admissions Testing Program of the College Board. For comparison, correlations for the appropriate SAT score (i.e., SAT-Verbal or SAT-Mathematics) based on the same sample are shown in parentheses. With the exception of the Chemistry Achievement Test, which is based upon a highly selected and possibly atypical group of examinees, these tests and the SAT showed generally similar declines in correlation with FGPA from 1978 to 1985. As Morgan notes, somewhat less decline for Achievement Tests would likely result from their having received less weight than the SAT in selection and, therefore, having been less affected by increasing restriction of range during this period. (See Note 2-11.)

The lower half of Table 2-2 gives validity coefficients for three test batteries in three national samples that entered college in 1972, 1980, and 1982. The SAT and ACT data are comparable only in the sense that they presumably represent national samples of those

Table 2-2

Uncorrected Correlations Between College GPA and Various Test Scores
in Selected Years — with Comparison SAT Correlations*

From Morgan, Table 10-2	Average Yearly N	1978	1981	1985	Difference 1985-1978
College Board Tests:					
Test of Standard Written English (SAT-V)	99,931	.36 (.36)	.33 (.33)	.32 (.32)	−.04 (−.04)
English Composition (SAT-V)	35,499	.36 (.33)	.33 (.28)	.33 (.30)	−.03 (−.03)
Mathematics I (SAT-M)	27,435	.32 (.31)	.32 (.29)	.30 (.27)	−.02 (−.04)
Chemistry (SAT-V) (SAT-M)	5,586	.36 (.27) (.38)	.36 (.27) (.37)	.36 (.26) (.35)	.00 (−.01) (−.03)

From Willingham et al., Table 11-2		1972	1980	1982	Difference 1982-1972
Longitudinal Tests — Multiple R	5,553	.33	.31	.30	−.03
American College Tests — Multiple R	1,851	.39	—	.35	−.04
(SAT — Multiple R)	2,475	(.37)	(.37)	(.34)	(−.03)

* SAT correlations based on the same samples are shown in parentheses. All
criteria are freshman GPAs except for 1980 and 1982 data, in which college GPA
was based on three semesters rather than two.

respective examinees who went to college. Again, these data show
similar declines for the multiple correlations based on the three test
batteries. The decline for the longitudinal tests was larger (-.08)
when both the 1972 and 1982 samples were restricted to the same
(mostly large, public) institutions.

In general, the correlations in Table 2-2 decline somewhat less
than the changes noted in the raw coefficients in Morgan (Chapter
10) and Ramist-Weiss (Chapter 5). In the top part of the table, this
smaller decline is probably because the samples are restricted to
more able students for all of the tests save TSWE. In the bottom part of
the table, the data do not coincide with the period of maximum
decline shown in the other trend studies.

None of these data speak to the question of whether the correlation of other tests with FGPA increased in the earlier years, as suggested by SAT results. There is, however, a confirming trend in ACT data. In his report for the Committee on Ability Testing, Linn (1982) cites average ACT validity coefficients for three-year periods centering on classes that entered college in 1968, 1972, and 1974 as .47, .49, and .51, respectively. Subsequent ACT data from the same validity service indicate that by 1986 the correlation had dropped to .45. (See Note 2-12.) These trends appear similar to those of the SAT, but without benefit of an analysis that controls for yearly changes in institutional representation and range restriction, it is impossible to compare precisely the ACT and SAT trends.

These findings seem reasonably clear. Available data are largely consistent in showing that the correlation of FGPA with test scores has undergone two systematic changes in the past two decades: an increase in the late 1960s and early 1970s followed by a gradual decrease. The changes in these correlations are not large, and they are not always statistically significant, but the overall trend seems generally comparable in magnitude from test to test. These results suggest that FGPA itself may have changed to some degree in recent years, because the decline in its predictability is not limited to the SAT but seems part of a more general phenomenon. Nonetheless, it is important to examine carefully whether any changes in the test or the scores could have contributed to changes in its correlation with FGPA.

Changes in Test Characteristics

In considering possible ways in which the predictor might be implicated in any increase or decrease in predictive validity coefficients, a natural first question is whether there has been any effect due to changes in the content of the test or the way it is put together. In order to answer that question, Marco et al. (1990) undertook a detailed examination of representative forms of the SAT from 1970 to 1985, the period in which the SAT's correlation with FGPA increased and then decreased. A summary of that work is found in Chapter 7 (Marco & Crone). The purpose here is to consider only the major results and to relate those findings to other studies in this series. To that end, we consider these broad characteristics:

- Nature of the test,
- Difficulty of the task,
- Reliability of scores,

- Meaning of scores, and

- Comparability across forms.

"Nature of the test" refers to what is actually in the test and how the material is presented to examinees. The next three characteristics listed — difficulty of the task, reliability of scores, and meaning of scores — are critical statistical attributes that derive from the nature of the test. Finally, even if the first four characteristics remain constant through time, scaled scores must be rendered comparable from form-to-form and year-to-year through appropriate equating procedures. In their review of these characteristics, Marco et al. found as follows.

Nature of the test. Through its history since 1941, the SAT has been a test of developed ability in two domains: verbal comprehension and quantitative reasoning. While there have been a number of minor adjustments, the major change in the SAT during the period 1970-85 was a 1974 reduction in testing time in order to accommodate the addition of the Test of Standard Written English. This change was effected by using a larger proportion of those types of verbal and mathematical items that measure the same abilities but take less testing time. As a result, test developers were able to maintain almost the same total number of items, which is a principal determinant of the reliability of scores. At the time of these changes, and later when there were some less important adjustments within particular item types, special studies were undertaken in order to ensure no adverse effects on validity or reliability. It is important to note that changes in the correlation between SAT scores and FGPA since the mid-1970s have been gradual, year-by-year. As Table 5-5 indicates, there has been no abrupt single-year decline in validity coefficients that would seem connected to a particular test change such as the 1974 redesign. There are two deviations in that otherwise quite smooth curve: a blip up in 1971, when there were relatively few studies, and a blip down following 1985, apparently for the same reason.

Difficulty of the task. There are two ways in which the task posed to examinees might vary in difficulty. One is the difficulty of individual questions. Another is the amount of time available to answer them. Changes in the difficulty of test items can affect validity if, as a result, the test gains or loses measurement precision in those particular score ranges where most students score. There was a small deliberate reduction in test difficulty in 1974, amounting to an increase of 3 percent in correct answers. Coming in a period when test scores were declining nationally, this adjustment was intended to make the test more appropriate for the pool of examinees. If that change had any effect, it would likely have been to support or slightly enhance predictive validity.

If a test becomes difficult because it is too speeded, scores can change meaning and may also appear spuriously reliable, both effects resulting directly from the added speed component. Several factors affect speededness: time available, number of items, type of items, and ability of the group of examinees. All of these factors changed somewhat over time, rendering one of the two verbal sections slightly more speeded and both mathematics sections slightly less so. Neither portion of the test is considered to be highly speeded, and the net effect of the changes was probably a slight reduction in measurement power for high-scoring students and a slight improvement for middle- to low-scoring examinees.

Reliability of scores. Any change in a test that distorts scores or makes them less appropriate for the intended group of examinees will tend to reduce the reliability of the test. Such effects can accumulate. Furthermore, a reduction in reliability can have a direct negative impact on validity. Thus, reliability is a critical indicator of test quality. Other things being equal, the reduction in the length of sat-V in 1974 from 90 to 85 items would be expected to reduce reliability by .005. Reliability changes of this magnitude are very unlikely to result in any observed difference in validity (see Table 7-5). Marco et al. tracked sat reliability from 1970 to 1984 in order to determine what effect this change in the length of sat-V and any

Figure 2-7

Trends in the Reliability of SAT Scores—
Internal Consistency and Retest Correlations

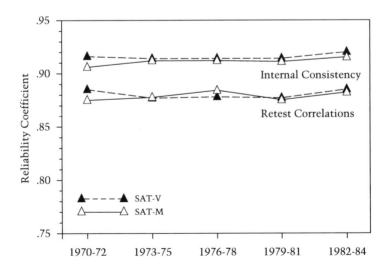

other changes — intended or unintended — might have had. Actual reliability remained quite high throughout this period and showed no noticeable change (see Figure 2-7).

Meaning of scores. While the content of test items may indicate that a test is apparently measuring the same thing over time, correlations among items and among like sections of the test provide statistical evidence as to whether that is actually the case. In this respect, the SAT appears to have been quite stable during this period. The correlation between the vocabulary and reading subscores of SAT-V remained constant, as did the relationship between corresponding sections of the verbal and mathematical parts of the SAT. As Marco et al. (1990) report, a number of correlational analyses were undertaken prior to shortening the test in 1974 in order to ensure that the meaning of the verbal and mathematical scores did not change. The correlation between verbal and mathematical scores decreased about .02 in the mid-1970s, apparently because there was less verbal material in the quantitative comparison item type introduced at that time. If that change had any effect at all, it would as likely increase as decrease predictive validity. Over that time period, the mathematical sections became somewhat more homogeneous and the verbal ones somewhat less so, but those changes were quite small compared to the dominant two-factor pattern of the test. Recent factor analyses by Dorans and Lawrence (1987) confirmed that there has been very little variation in the internal structure of the SAT, form-to-form and year-to-year.

Comparability across forms. Validity studies are normally based upon scores from different forms of the SAT, either within the same year or from one year to the next. Consequently, any significant change in the quality of score equating over time could affect validity. Accuracy of score equating receives close attention at ETS. Indices of equating quality have shown no systematic trend over time, and the most recent studies show little evidence of scale instability (Marco & Crone, Chapter 7). The only important change in equating procedure was the introduction of nonlinear IRT equating in 1982. A direct comparison showed that change had essentially no effect on validity coefficients (Chapter 7 and Marco et al., 1990).

It is useful to bear in mind that in all cases, the examination of these various characteristics of the SAT has been internal to the test and focused largely upon important but fairly obvious indices that are routinely monitored. It doesn't necessarily follow that such an investigation, even done with care, would surely identify subtle, cumulative changes in the test itself or changes in scores due to external factors. We move on to other lines of evidence that bear on such possibilities.

Validity of Old and New SATs

The previous discussion summarizes considerable evidence that the characteristics of the SAT did not change during the period 1970-85 in any consequential way likely to have affected predictive validity adversely. Nonetheless, a direct comparison of the predictive accuracy of old and new test forms would clearly be desirable. This poses a problem, however, because SAT forms are ordinarily disclosed soon after use, then retired. This means that old and new forms of the test are only administered years apart to different groups of students. Therefore, in comparing validity coefficients for old and new forms, possible effects of interest are confounded. It is impossible to know whether differences are due to the test forms or to differences in the samples, the educational programs, or the FGPA criterion.

As it happens, a special data collection involving simultaneous administration of old and new SAT forms was undertaken in 1984 in order to study the stability of the SAT scale. This database is ideal for comparing the predictive validity of old and new forms, because the same students took both forms of the test and there is no worry that the criterion is different for groups taking the two forms. In May and again in November of 1984, the two verbal and two mathematical sections of SAT forms from 1974-75 were administered in the so-called variable section of a regular national administration. In this manner, eight stratified groups of students took one old SAT section that could be compared with a corresponding new section taken by the same students. These students were subsequently traced through institutional participation in the Validity Study Service in order to obtain their freshman grade-point averages.

The results of this study are reported by Angoff, Pomplun, McHale, and Morgan in Chapter 8. Overall, the difference in the predictive validity of old and new sections was small and inconsistent — .013 on average in favor of the old form. The authors concluded that the data do not permit a clear conclusion as to whether the difference is real.

Table 2-3 summarizes validity coefficients for particular item types. These data offer a comparison of old- and new-form validity for the same types of test material in several independent groups. The overall picture does not show a consistent pattern. On the other hand, the difference between old and new forms for individual sets of items was significant in four comparisons out of 22, and results favored the old form three times. It is possible that there was something about those particular sets of items that was different between old and new forms. Consequently, a careful reexamination of the content and statistical characteristics of those item sets was

Table 2-3

Summary of Differences in Validity Coefficients (New-Old) for Particular Item Types in 1984 and 1974 Forms of the sᴀᴛ Administered to the Same Students in 1984#

Item Type	May Administration Sect. 1	Sect. 2	November Administration Sect. 1	Sect. 2
Verbal				
Antonyms	−.079**	.003	−.034	.036
Sentence Completion	−.018	.056	.031	−.030
Analogy	.024	.000	.028	.016
Reading Comprehension	−.057*	.038	.004	−.004
Mathematical				
Regular Math	−.057**	.007	−.018	−.037
Quantitative Comparison		−.008		.041*

\# From Tables 8-2 and 8-3, Angoff et al.

* P < .05

** P < .01

undertaken. Minor differences were observed, but none seemed unusual or appeared to account for a validity differential.

One other analysis is pertinent to the old-form/new-form question. In conjunction with developmental work for the Admissions Testing Program, test and other data were collected from a large group of secondary school students in spring 1989. One segment of this data collection involved administration of 1975 and 1985 forms of the sᴀᴛ to comparable stratified samples. Stricker (1990) used these data to compare the correlation of old and new test scores with academic performance in secondary school at the same time in comparable samples, undistorted by the admissions sorting process. He found that old and new sᴀᴛ scores had essentially the same correlation with self-reported grade averages. On the other hand, sᴀᴛ-V scores from the new form showed a significantly higher correlation with self-reported high school class rank than did scores from the old form (.46 vs. .39). Again, a careful examination of the high school performance scales and data for individual item types did not reveal any plausible explanation for the inconsistency.

Possible External Factors

Even assuming that there is no difference at all in the correlation of the sᴀᴛ with ꜰɢᴘᴀ when old and new forms of the test are administered at the same time to the same students, there are other possibilities to consider. External conditions were not the same in the 1980s as in the 1970s. There has been an increase in coaching; students repeat the test more; test disclosure is now a fact of life in admissions testing. Could such external factors work to distort the scores before they reach the colleges? If so, predictive validity might suffer even though the test itself remains the same.

Given the attention coaching has received in recent years, it is likely the first such external factor that comes to mind as a possible source of score distortion. One line of evidence appears to be particularly inconsistent with that hypothesis — notably, the institutional pattern of prediction trends. The most selective institutions enroll the largest proportion of coached students and would have experienced the largest increase because the least selective colleges attract relatively few such students. For this and other reasons, Baydar (1990) estimated that if increased coaching has affected SAT correlations with FGPA, the effect should be greatest in the selective colleges and least in the nonselective. But, in fact, average SAT validity coefficients have declined most in the *least* selective colleges and not at all in the most selective (see Figure 2-5).

Other evidence is inconsistent as well. As we have seen, validity has declined noticeably more for males than for females (Figure 2-6), but there is no gender difference in attendance at coaching schools (Chapter 9). Finally, the yearly trend in the level of retest reliability is relevant to possible effects of coaching. It is not unreasonable to assume that coaching would often fall between a junior-year SAT and a senior-year SAT. Any score distortion that is strong enough to affect correlations with FGPA would presumably affect junior-senior retest correlations as well, but Figure 2-7 shows no change in retest reliability through this period of declining correlations with FGPA.

Nonetheless, it is useful to estimate how much effect score changes due to coaching might possibly have on validity coefficients. Baydar (1990 and Chapter 9) simulated such coaching effects in the validity studies of four quite different institutions. She selectively added points to the SAT scores of some "coached" students and then recalculated correlations between the new scores and FGPA. The complex simulation model is described generally in Chapter 9 and in detail in a technical report (Baydar, 1990). Briefly, the model involved four steps:

- Determining hypothetical parameters for score changes on the basis of previous studies;
- Estimating, on the basis of a previous survey of coaching activity, how many and which students were most likely to have been coached;

- Specifying a statistical model for applying the score changes (e.g., assumptions used regarding individual differences in score gain); and

- Estimating effects on validity coefficients at different levels of hypothetical coaching effects and percentages of students coached.

Baydar estimated the likely cumulative effect of coaching on predictive validity at less than 1 percent change for the previous 10 years. She noted, however, that her simulations probably overrepresented the effects of coaching, because it was not possible to differentiate among three types of score gains, only one of which would be expected to reduce the correlation of SAT scores with FGPA. Thus, the model made liberal assumptions as to the possible negative effects of score gains on validity coefficients. If one assumed that the magnitude of score gains due to coaching is as stated in advertising claims of coaching schools, then larger estimates of effects on correlations would result. There is no indication in recent coaching studies, however, that such assumptions are warranted (Fraker, 1987; Smyth, 1989; Snedecor, 1989; Whitla, 1988; Zuman, 1988). Baydar's model confirms, moreover, that under an assumption of large coaching effects, one would expect to see the biggest declines in SAT correlations in the selective colleges — a result clearly contradicted by the trend data, as already indicated.

Increased coaching in recent years has been accompanied by an increase in repeat testing. Does repeat testing inflate scores and lower correlations with FGPA? There have been several studies of the effect of repeat testing on correlations with FGPA because, faced with multiple scores, colleges want to know which score is most valid. After evaluating research on the Law School Admission Test, Linn (1977) advised law schools simply to use the average score. He concluded, "The effect on the validity of the LSAT of pooling average scores for repeaters with nonrepeating scores would not be expected to be noticeable even if the proportion of repeaters increased substantially." Boldt (1986) recently studied SAT repeating and concluded that correlations with FGPA are similar regardless of which score is used, i.e., latest, highest, average. Furthermore, he found that choice of any such score was likely to be better than the first score because, for repeaters, all scores tended to underpredict actual freshman performance slightly. Thus, it seems unlikely that repeat testing has played a significant role in validity trends.

Two general types of potentially deleterious effects of test disclosure can be distinguished. On the one hand, one might worry that test quality and, therefore, correlations with FGPA could decline if many new test editions must be produced each year. ETS expressed that concern when disclosure legislation was first debated in New York State. It has not been the experience of test developers, however, that present test-disclosure mandates have had a negative effect on test quality. That appears to be confirmed by the fairly detailed tracking of test-quality indicators by Marco et al. (1990).

On the other hand, it could be argued that test disclosure may have had subtle effects on predictive validity; for example, by reducing the novelty of the test items. That is, as the test becomes more familiar, it becomes less useful as an indicator of the student's ability to cope successfully with a new intellectual challenge. That is not an unreasonable speculation, though there are also grounds for hypothesizing an opposite effect. Namely, the more familiar an examinee is with a test-item format, the less likely she or he will be led astray by irrelevant distractions, and the more likely the score will reflect true cognitive ability. In fact, in the only study that was evidently ever undertaken on the effects of familiarization and practice on the predictive validity of a new item type, the results indicated a slight increase in validity, not a decline (Powers, 1986).

It could also be argued that test disclosure facilitates test wiseness, thereby affecting scores of some students and reducing correlations with FGPA. Stricker (1982) tested that hypothesis by encouraging random groups of students who had taken the SAT to study the subsequently disclosed materials prior to any retest they might undertake. The experimental groups did no better on retest than control students, most of whom received no disclosure materials.

Despite all the foregoing, it still might be argued that some such subtle distorting effects might be cumulative and thereby have an effect on scores and their relationship with FGPA. Is it possible to determine whether the scores are stable over time using some external yardstick other than FGPA?

Stability of SAT Scores

In the three previous sections, we have examined the predictor, i.e., the test, from several points of view. Has the test itself changed? Do scores from old and new tests show any different relationship with FGPA when the sample and the criterion are held constant? Have external factors distorted the scores over time? There seems to be little evidence to support these hypotheses, and there is information that suggests in each case that the answer is negative. There is another type of analysis, however, that bears simultaneously on all three questions.

The common theme in the discussion of the predictor is whether the meaning of the test scores has changed to any consequential degree. That is, have the scores changed in the skills and knowledge they represent, or in the level of ability they imply, or in their accuracy, or in any other way that would cause them to correlate less well with freshman grades? If some such distortion of the scores were strong enough to cause a decline in the correlation with FGPA one to two years later, that is not the only relationship that would be affected. One would also expect to see a decline in the correlation of SAT-Verbal and SAT-Mathematics scores with other tests administered at about the same time and measuring generally similar constructs.

In order to determine whether there is evidence of any such trend, a search was undertaken for studies and databases that would provide correlations between SAT scores and other verbal and mathematical tests since 1970. It was possible to obtain such correlations for comparable samples in two or more years for the following 12 verbal and eight mathematical tests:

Admissions Testing Program
1. English Composition
2. Test of Standard Written English

1. Mathematics Achievement

New Jersey College Basic Skills Placement Tests
3. Reading Comprehension
4. Sentence Structure
5. Essay

2. Computation
3. Elementary Algebra

Washington Pre-College Test
6. English Usage
7. Spelling
8. Reading Comprehension
9. Vocabulary

4. Quantitative Skills
5. Applied Mathematics
6. Mathematics Achievement

National Longitudinal Study/High School and Beyond
10. Reading
11. Vocabulary

7. Mathematics

American College Test
12. English

8. Mathematics

The search yielded 70 correlations, based on samples of approximately 1,000 to 100,000, between these 20 tests and the SAT (see Appendix A-1 and Note 2-13). Summarizing the trend in those correlations from 1970 to 1985 posed somewhat the same problem as that with validity coefficients, because different tests have different characteristic correlations with SAT-V and SAT-M, and the available data came from different years. Consequently, a pairwise trend analysis was carried out for the three periods 1970-74, 1975-80, and 1981-85. The results are shown in Figure 2-8.

Figure 2-8

Trends in the Average Correlation of SAT Scores with 12 Verbal Tests
and Eight Mathematics Tests*

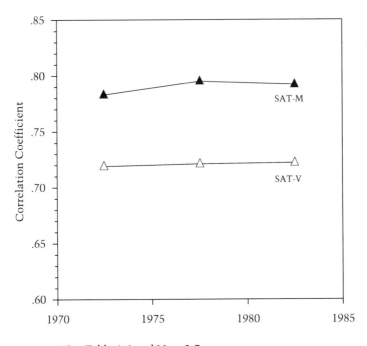

*See Table A-1 and Note 2-7.

There is no evidence of any decline in the relationship between the SAT and these other measures during this period. Compared to the SAT, any influence of external factors like coaching and test disclosure would presumably be modest with most of these tests, and with some, probably nonexistent. One might argue that the SAT scores could have been distorted in particular ways that would significantly affect their correlation with freshman grades but would not affect their correlation with other measures. That is theoretically possible, but unlikely, because there is probably little variance shared by the SAT and FGPA that is not also shared with the other tests. All in all, these results indicate strongly that the meaning of the scores has not changed.

Stability of High School Record

The pattern of correlations between SAT scores and other measures indicates that the test scores have been quite stable from 1970 to

1985. What about the copredictor — the high school record? Has it also shown a stable pattern of correlations with other measures during this period?

Table 2-4 shows correlations of HSGPA with scores of six tests for substantial samples of students in 1978 and 1985. This is the same database used by Morgan (Table 10-2). To make the 1978 and 1985 groups of students as comparable as possible, the samples here are restricted to the 87 institutions that did validity studies in both of those years. The correlations are based upon data pooled across institutions in order to avoid the significant distortions that the college selection process can introduce in correlations between predictors (Dawes, 1975). As noted earlier, colleges used different types of school records — rank or average, actual or student-reported. Even when the college computes the average from the transcript, the same scale is not always used. Therefore, high school average is here based upon student-reported grades — the only available measure of high school record that is common across all colleges.

The correlations in Table 2-4 show no difference, on average, between 1978 and 1985. In the small differences for individual tests, there is a slight tendency for verbal and mathematical tests to show

Table 2-4
Correlations Between High School GPA and Several Tests
in 1978 and 1985 *

Test	N(1000s) 1978/1985	Correlation with HSGPA		
		1978	1985	Change
CB-Mathematics Achievement	23/41	.38	.40	+.02
SAT -Math	67/77	.46	.47	+.01
CB-Chemistry Achievement	4/5	.38	.36	−.02
CB-English Composition	27/29	.36	.36	.00
SAT -Verbal	67/77	.42	.41	−.01
Test of Standard Written English	67/77	.42	.41	−.01
Average for 6 Tests		.40	.40	.00

* Correlations are based on the same data as in Morgan, Chapter 10, but the samples are pooled here, irrespective of college attended, and restricted to 87 institutions that conducted validity studies in both 1978 and 1985. HSGPA was student-reported.

a different pattern, perhaps a reflection of increased emphasis on mathematics in the secondary school curriculum. Over all, however, both SAT and HSGPA exhibit very stable relationships with other measures in recent years. The correlational trends of these two measures are also similar in a number of other ways.

Where the SAT correlations with FGPA were especially prone to decline, the HSGPA correlations declined as well. Figure 2-6, for example, showed that the average HSGPA validity coefficient went down for men but not for women from 1978 to 1985, during which time the average SAT validity coefficient dropped twice as much for men as women. Another example is provided by the sharp contrast in the validity trend for the more and less selective colleges. As Figure 2-9 illustrates, the trend for HSR has been generally similar to that for the SAT among the more and less selective colleges — generally stable in the former and declining in the latter. There is a third example. As we shall soon see, in that segment of the freshman class where the decline in the SAT correlation with FGPA has been most obvious, the corresponding correlation for high school grades declined by the same amount.

Another indication that the validity coefficients for SAT and HSR have changed in similar fashion from the mid-1970s to the mid-1980s comes from the analysis of all variations in these coefficients during that period. As mentioned earlier and described in detail in Chapter 6, there were several sources of very substantial variation for each of these coefficients. The pattern of those variations was quite similar for SAT and HSR.

These results suggest that the rising and falling prediction trends for SAT and HSR should show some correspondence in individual colleges. That is also what one would expect if the explanation for trends in validity coefficients is to be found more in the criterion than in the predictors. Indeed, at the institutional level, there is evidence of a strong correspondence between the prediction trend for SAT and the prediction trend for HSR. Willingham and Lewis (Chapter 6) found that the slopes of the lines that define these two trends correlated .55 in a group of 192 colleges. This correlation is all the more striking considering that the reliability of the institutional slopes for SAT and HSR were estimated to be .32 and .34, respectively.

Figure 2-9

Correlation of SAT Scores and HSR with Freshman GPA
for More and Less Selective Colleges*

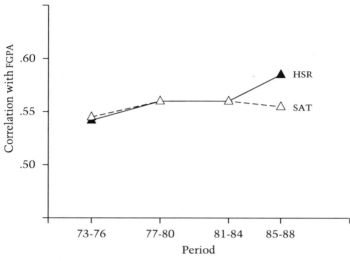

(a) More Selective Colleges

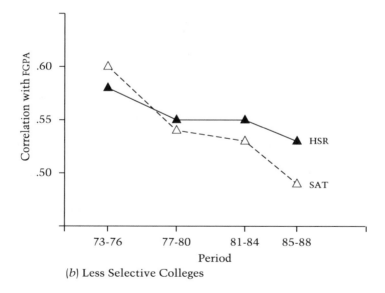

(b) Less Selective Colleges

*See Ramist & Weiss, Chapter 5.

Figure 2-10

Changes in the Prediction of Freshman GPA from
1978 to 1985 for 87 Institutions—a Comparison of
SAT and High School GPA

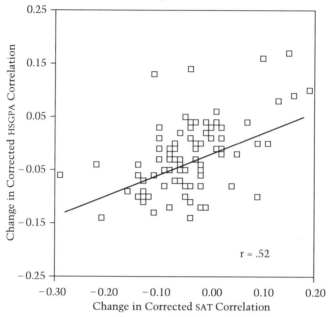

Figure 2-10 illustrates such a correlation between the two trends in a different group of colleges. Plotted here are changes in SAT correlations from 1978 to 1985 against changes in HSGPA correlations for the same 87 colleges represented in Table 2-4, just discussed. In this case, the correlation between SAT change and HSGPA change was .52. The relationship between the two trends is high partly because HSGPA and SAT validity coefficients are similarly affected by true changes in the common FGPA criterion, and partly because both are affected by the same sampling error from year to year. Taking account of the unreliability of the trends and the correlated sampling error they share, Willingham and Lewis (Chapter 6) estimated the "true" correlation between SAT trend and HSR trend to be .87 (see page 148 and Note 6-3). This result indicates that changes in the criterion are very likely the major factor in determining trends in the validity coefficients for both the school record and the SAT.

Summary of Results: The Predictor

Principal findings regarding possible effects of changes in the predictor on prediction trends were the following:

1. There were several tests for which correlations with FGPA could be evaluated on the basis of comparable samples in different years over the past two decades. The pattern of changes in validity coefficients was, in most cases, quite similar to that of the SAT.

2. A detailed examination of the characteristics of the SAT — content, difficulty, reliability, meaning of scores, comparability of forms — did not reveal any changes in the test from 1970 to 1985 that were plausibly related to any significant change in predictive validity.

3. When old and new forms of the SAT were administered to the same students at the same time, differences in predictive validity were small and inconsistent. Overall, there was a slight edge to the old form, but it was not clear whether the difference was statistically significant.

4. Results of a simulation study of possible coaching effects indicated that, with research-based estimates of coaching incidence and resulting score gain, and with liberal assumptions as to the possible negative effects of any such score gains on correlations with FGPA, changes in SAT validity coefficients would likely be less than one percent. Coaching also seems unlikely to have affected validity coefficients because the pattern of validity change (as to college selectivity and gender) is inconsistent with the pattern of attendance at coaching schools.

5. Results of pertinent previous research do not support the hypothesis that test disclosure or changes in the incidence of repeat testing have affected the correlation of SAT scores with FGPA.

6. If SAT scores reported to colleges were more likely to be in error in recent years for whatever reason, the scores would be expected to show a pattern of lower correlations with other measures generally, not just with FGPA. A large quantity of data showed quite stable relationships between SAT-V and SAT-M scores and 20 other tests during the period 1970 to 1985.

7. The two predictors, SAT and HSGPA, have shown a close correspondence in several respects. Correlations of the HSGPA with the SAT and with other tests appear to have been quite stable from the mid-1970s to the mid-1980s. Where SAT validity coefficients have been more prone to drop (e.g., for nonselective colleges, and for males), the average HSGPA coefficient has also dropped. Among colleges, the extent of yearly deviation as well as long-term variation in the two validity coefficients was the same. Finally, in individual colleges the trend in validity coefficients for HSGPA was strongly correlated with the trend in SAT validity coefficients.

The two most important findings in this section were the stability of the SAT and the generality of validity changes. There seems to be little likelihood that changes in the SAT could account for changes in validity coefficients to any consequential degree. Evidence for the stability of the scores and the test itself is reasonably strong. Also, observed trends in validity coefficients are not unique to the SAT; other tests show similar trends. Moreover, among the colleges, variations in SAT validity and HSR validity are remarkably similar. These results, like those of the previous section on sample effects, suggest that changes over time in average correlations of predictors with FGPA are more accurately viewed as variations in criterion predictability than predictor validity.

POSSIBLE CHANGES IN THE CRITERION

We have now examined two broad classes of possible causes for fluctuations in the predictability of FGPA: changes in the predictors and changes in the sample on which correlations are based. Analysis of the predictors suggests that they have been stable. Analysis of sample effects indicates that there are significant differences in validity trends from institution to institution, and that declining predictability is particularly associated with less selective institutions. These findings suggest a careful examination of possible instability or change in FGPA.

Looking at the educational system broadly, there have been a variety of changes over the past 15 years that might have had some influence — direct or indirect — on the nature of FGPA. The major trends are well known and require no elaboration. Demographic shifts have diversified the clientele of higher education and intensified the competition for students, as the annual cohort of 18-year-olds has declined (Hodgkinson, 1983). Simultaneously, there has been increasing concern and debate regarding quality of education and standards of performance (see for example, *A Nation at Risk*, the National Commission on Excellence in Education, 1983). These social trends have presented institutions with urgent goals, not always fully compatible: enhancing educational opportunity, improving enrollment management, increasing retention, raising standards. In turn, much attention has been directed to reforming the curriculum, improving instructional programs, assessing educational outcomes. Programs intended to aid first-year students have received particular attention: more remedial courses (College Board, 1986; Tomlinson, 1989); greatly increased use of the Advanced Placement Program (College Board, 1988); plus a spate of conferences on the "freshman-year experience."

In this complex mix of new pressures on institutions, as well as new goals and new practices, one might speculate about a wide range of possible changes that could have subtly influenced the FGPA. It is important to pause and recognize, however, that FGPA is not a single scale or entity like a test. Measurement specialists periodically marvel at the interesting history and enormous variety of grading practices (Thorndike, 1969; Cureton, 1971). FGPAs are based on grades assigned in thousands of programs and colleges by many thousands of instructors, each exercising his or her own professional judgment regarding a student's level of accomplishment in a particular course. This leaves plenty of room for diversity, and factors affecting one student's FGPA obviously will not necessarily be the same as those that affect another's. Furthermore, as noted, there are significant institutional differences in validity trends — some going up, some down. If a gradual downward trend in predictability is due to changes in the nature of FGPA, we are likely witnessing the net effect of several factors that apply selectively in different courses, colleges, time periods, etc.

Finally, it is one thing to speculate about complex social and educational dynamics (e.g., "Maybe some students and professors don't take grades as seriously as they used to"); it is quite another thing (and a necessary step) to find concrete ways of connecting changes in FGPA to changes in its correlation with preadmission predictors. What types of instability or change in FGPA might alter its predictability? Several possibilities come quickly to mind:

- More or less rigor in the examining process,

- More or less grade inflation,

- Variation in the reliability of grades,

- Variation in grading standards across courses,

- Higher or lower incidence of remedial and advanced coursework,

- More or less diversity in the freshman curriculum,

- Changes in the basis of grading (i.e., what is rewarded),

- Changes in the competences required of students, and

- Changes in program enrollment.

These hypotheses overlap, and some are more amenable to empirical test than others. For purposes of this discussion, we will examine these potential changes in FGPA under three broad headings: The possibility that grades now carry a somewhat different *meaning*, a possible shift in the *accuracy* of grades, and a possible change in the *comparability* of grades across courses and departments. These topics are addressed in subsequent sections, but first it will be useful to see if the tendency toward a somewhat less predictable FGPA is characteristic of the whole freshman class or if it can be narrowed somewhat. More specifically, are similar correlational trends observed among the more and less able students in a given freshman class?

Predictability Within the Freshman Class

Two observations suggest that institutional changes in the predictability of FGPA — particularly a decline in correlations — might not show the same pattern for students at higher and lower ability levels within a given institution. First, as we have noted, there is the greater institutional emphasis on remediation, placement, and retention programs. These efforts are directed to improving institutional effectiveness in a more competitive era. If they have resulted in any change in FGPA and its predictability, the effects might well be greater among those freshmen who tend to be more at risk. This is because if such programs succeed, one outcome should be better performance (i.e., FGPA) by academically weaker freshmen, the likely effect of which would be to weaken the relationship of predictors to the criterion. A second observation, seemingly consistent with that hypothesis, is the fact that the less selective institutions and those with more remedial programs and more part-time students have experienced more decline in predictability (Ramist & Weiss, Chapter 5). Thus, it is useful to determine whether predictability has changed more in the lower than in the upper half of the class.

Morgan (Chapter 10 and 1990) examined this question as follows. Using data on 1978, 1981, and 1985 freshmen, he segmented the freshmen of each college into low, middle, and high thirds on the basis of SAT total scores, and then predicted grades from test scores within each third for each college. In this analysis, the raw regression weights for SAT-V and SAT-M show how grades are related to scores in these three segments of the class. The changes in regression from 1978 to 1985 are illustrated in Figure 2-11 in the following manner: The regression slope for each of the three years is started at the same arbitrary point at the upper right; then the slopes for the middle and lower thirds of the class are simply tacked on to illustrate the changing relationship.

For both verbal and mathematical scores, the relationship between the SAT and the FGPA showed little difference from the low to middle to high third of the class in 1978. In 1981, the regression line in the low third of the class showed some sign of flattening. That tendency

Figure 2-11

A Schematic Representation of the Relationship Between
FGPA and SAT Scores in High, Middle, and Low Thirds
of the Freshman Class—Based upon
Average Raw Score Regression Weights*

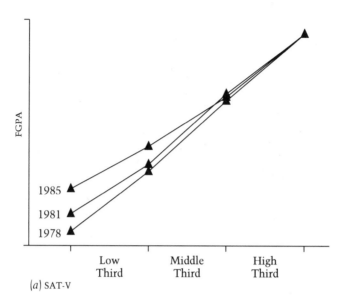

(a) SAT-V

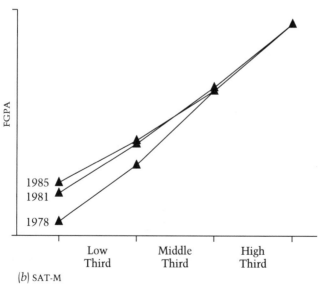

(b) SAT-M

*See Morgan, Table 10-6.

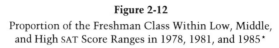

Figure 2-12

Proportion of the Freshman Class Within Low, Middle,
and High SAT Score Ranges in 1978, 1981, and 1985*

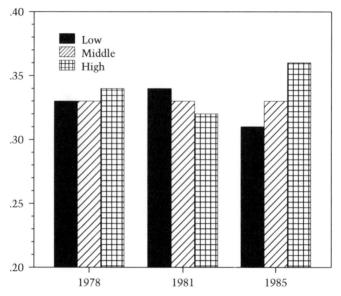

*Variable score ranges by college but consistent each year.

was more noticeable in 1985. In the low third of the class, the 1985 regression weights for SAT-V and SAT-M are some 70 to 75 percent of the size of the 1978 weights. The middle third showed a similar pattern. In the high third of the class, however, there was little if any change in the degree of relationship between test scores and FGPA.

Why would such a change occur? There are a number of possible explanations. One reason might be a pile up of low test scores. If these colleges were admitting more students with low SAT scores in 1985 than in 1978, faculties might not react with lower grades, or they might not be able to differentiate well among those students, in which case the regression slopes might change as in Figure 2-11. Figure 2-12 indicates, however, that no such change occurred in the admission pattern in these particular institutions. In this figure, the low, middle, and high groups were defined on the basis of total SAT scores at the thirty-third and sixty-sixth percentiles in each college (for 1978, 1981, and 1985 combined). Relative to their own norms, these institutions enrolled somewhat *fewer* students with low SAT scores in 1985 than was true in 1978 or 1981.

Another possible explanation is some change in the test. If the SAT were getting too difficult for the examinees it would tend to measure less well at low score levels, and might show a lower relationship with FGPA. The data in Chapter 7 do not support that hypothesis. The only change in test difficulty since 1970 was to make the SAT slightly *less* difficult in 1974. Nonetheless, it is useful to examine the possibility that the change in prediction in the lower half of the class is due to a change in the test.

If the smaller regression coefficients for the lower and middle thirds of the class in 1985 were due to a difference in the 1985 test, then one would expect to see a difference in the results for old and new test forms when they are administered at the same time. That is, the new form would show the lower relationship but the old form would not. Angoff, Pomplun, McHale, and Morgan (Chapter 8) made that comparison and found that the 1974 and 1984 test forms gave similar results when administered in 1984; i.e., both the old and new forms were clearly better predictors in the high than in the low third of the class. This contrast between the Morgan and Angoff findings regarding the older form suggests that the effect is due not to a change in the test, but to when the criterion data were obtained.

Another possibility is that some change in the population of students or in the college curriculum has made the SAT less appropriate for students in the bottom half of the class. That hypothesis raises this question: Has the high school record held up better as a predictor of FGPA for students in the lower half? Morgan (Chapter 10) addressed that point. He found that in the low third of the class *both* HSGPA and SAT correlated .05 lower with FGPA in 1985 than in 1978. In other words, whatever caused the recently lower correlations in the low third equally affected SAT and HSGPA.

Both Morgan (Chapter 10) and Ramist, Lewis, and McCamley (Chapter 12) uncovered an apparently unappreciated difference in the validity of HSGPA and SAT in different segments of the freshman class. In both of these studies, the grades of students in the low third of the class were less predictable than those of students in the high third, but the fall off in prediction for the less able students was much sharper for the HSGPA. The relationship is illustrated in Figure 2-13, which shows the SAT to be a slightly better predictor than HSGPA in the low third of the class. As a corollary, the incremental validity of the test is greatest for those students. According to conventional wisdom, in order to identify academic promise among weaker students, one should look not to a test score, but to prior performance and other evidence. A test score alone is certainly not an adequate basis to judge any student, but these results suggest that it is better than imagined in assessing academic capabilities of weaker students.

Figure 2-13

Relative Level of Corrected Validity Coefficients for Students
in the Low, Middle, and High Thirds of the Freshman
Class on Overall Academic Ability*

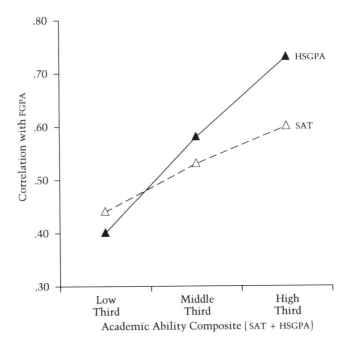

Academic Ability Composite (SAT + HSGPA)

*See Ramist, Lewis, & McCamley, Table 12-9.

These various results concerning correlations in different segments of the freshman class suggest again that the lower validity
coefficients in recent years reflect a change in the predictability of
the FGPA rather than a change in the predictors. That conclusion is
based upon several considerations: The relatively lower test validity
in the lower freshman-class segments is evidently recent; old forms
of the SAT show relatively lower freshman-class validity in lower
freshman-class segments only if correlated with recent FGPAS; the HSGPA
has shown the same decline in validity in lower class segments in
recent years. These results appear to be consistent with the hypothesis
that institutional adjustments to recent pressures for better retention and more effective education for a more diverse freshman class
would more likely affect predictor-criterion relationships in the
lower half than in the upper half of the freshman class. We move now
to consideration of what factors might cause a change in the predictability of FGPA.

Meaning of Freshman GPA

What does FGPA mean as to the *type* of academic performance represented — that is, the cognitive or substantive meaning of grades, as distinct from the scale value of an A or a B? Might correlations with FGPA have declined because that meaning has shifted in recent years? Presumably, whether students generally have high or low FGPAS depends upon a mix of abilities, knowledge, class behavior, etc., because the demands of different instructors and courses vary. Should that mix change in any systematic way in higher education overall, somewhat different tests and other information might be called for in the admissions process.

There are various ways one can think about possible changes that might give FGPA a different meaning. For example, the content of the "average" freshman-year curriculum may have shifted so as to give somewhat more emphasis to particular subject areas or to the academic skills required. The instructional process may have changed in ways that place more stress either upon acquisition of specific skills and knowledge, or upon more complex performance; i.e., learning that requires selective use of a range of information and talents, adaptation to a particular audience or context, and so on. Or faculty values may be changing with regard to the types of student talent and behavior that tend to get rewarded.

It is also true that the meaning of grades can be readily affected by the grading process. For example, the meaning of FGPA may depend partly upon the types of examinations used (essay, objective, oral, product, or performance), factors considered in grading (class participation, attendance, completion of work assignments), and the nature of the grading standard (an expected level of proficiency versus effort or improvement). Lewis, Dexter, and Smith (1978) report that teachers consider a broad range of such factors in grading, and opinions differ widely as to their appropriateness. In an extensive study of grades in secondary school, Ekstrom (in preparation) found that a variety of student attitudes and behaviors were significantly related to grades earned and to teacher attitudes about individual students.

How might one determine whether any changes in substance or process have significantly changed the meaning of FGPA? Prediction studies probably constitute the preponderance of systematic research that would seemingly have some bearing on the meaning of the FGPA. Although this literature is quite extensive (for reviews see Fishman & Pasanella, 1960; Breland, 1981), it is not particularly useful for the question at hand, partly because prediction research has a limited focus on measures that might be practical to employ in admissions. The main problem, however, is that prediction studies are not designed to answer the question posed: Does FGPA show a similar pattern of relationships with a diverse set of measures administered to representative groups of college students at different times? There has been no such study, nor is one likely, due to the time it would require of students and the considerable expense it would entail for little apparent practical benefit.

In the absence of the data one would like to have, what information is available that might give some clue? One line of evidence lies in the types of courses freshmen are taking. For example, in some colleges more freshmen may now take lower level courses that are more likely to emphasize acquisition of discrete knowledge and skill (e.g., remedial writing or mathematics). If so, this could cause a decline in the correlation between SAT-M and FGPA, because SAT-M places special emphasis on higher level analytic reasoning. Or an increasing enrollment in fine arts courses might cause SAT-FGPA correlations to decline because performance in the arts likely calls for aptitudes different from those required in most academic courses. In fact Ramist, Lewis, and McCamley (Chapter 12) do report that colleges with a large decline in SAT validity coefficients from 1982 to 1985 were prone to show certain patterns of course shifts that would lower SAT correlations; e.g., fewer students taking courses that tend to have high SAT correlations such as introductory economics and computer science, and more students taking courses that tend to have low SAT correlations, such as foreign language, art, music, and education.

One could count the number of students taking different types of courses and determine whether the pattern had changed, but the results would be hard to interpret because it is not obvious what effect a given configuration of courses would actually have on validity. In their study of 38 institutions, Ramist, Lewis, and McCamley estimated directly the overall effect of course volume shifts on validity coefficients.

They computed the average correlation of SAT with course grade across courses for 1982 and 1985 by weighting the correlations in two ways: (1) using the actual number of students taking the course in the year (i.e., not controlling for course volume change), and (2) using the sum of the numbers of students taking the course in 1982 and 1985 (i.e., controlling for course volume change). Validity coefficients of SAT and HSGPA dropped .004 more with the former weighting than the latter. Thus, the shifting volume of students in different courses had only a small effect on validity coefficients. Even the small differences observed may be due as much to variations in the accuracy of grades in different courses as to variations in the meaning of grades. This result pertains to a limited time span, but the sample is large. Course shifts may well have affected coefficients in some institutions, but it seems unlikely that predictability of FGPA overall has changed significantly because students take a somewhat different mix of courses from year to year.

A study by Pomplun, Burton, and Lewis (Chapter 13) provides another view of possible changes in the meaning of FGPA. These researchers took advantage of the fact that there is a variety of test information in ETS files that is useful even though it may not represent nearly the breadth of information one would prefer. From Admissions Testing Program files, they pulled all available information on comparable tests for comparable samples of students over the widest possible time span. As a result, they examined samples of students who entered college in 1978, the earliest year for which student response data for individual items were still on file, and 1985, the latest year for which sufficient criterion data were available. By examining different tests and scores based on different parcels of test items, it was possible to estimate (through LISREL modeling) whether there had been any change from 1978 to 1985 in the pattern of relationships between FGPA and several types of skills and abilities:

- Verbal and quantitative ability,

- Level of cognitive functioning represented in different types of test items (e.g., reproduction, evaluation, inference),

- Reading and writing skills as represented by an SAT-V subscore and the Test of Standard Written English score, respectively, and

- Achievement in particular subject areas (English composition, foreign languages, history, mathematics, science).

The question of primary interest in this analysis was whether there was evidence of any shift in the statistical weight (i.e., importance) of these various types of measures in predicting FGPA in 1985 as compared to 1978. Results for the two years were quite similar. The only difference not within sampling error was a somewhat weaker contribution of the History Achievement Test to prediction of FGPA in 1985 than in 1978.

Failure to find differences does not mean that they are not there, of course, waiting to be detected by other means or other measures. The principal shortcoming of the two analyses reported here is the fact that they are based on available measures and cannot address the possibility that quite different measures of student ability or accomplishment might show differences in the meaning of grades now assigned to freshmen as compared to a decade earlier. Nevertheless, the analysis by Pomplun, Burton, and Lewis provides a number of opportunities for plausible changes to show themselves and, in general, the findings give no indication of any significant shift in the meaning of the grade criterion as to the types of knowledge or competence it tends to represent.

Figure 2-14

Average SAT Score and Average FGPA Within Colleges, by Period*

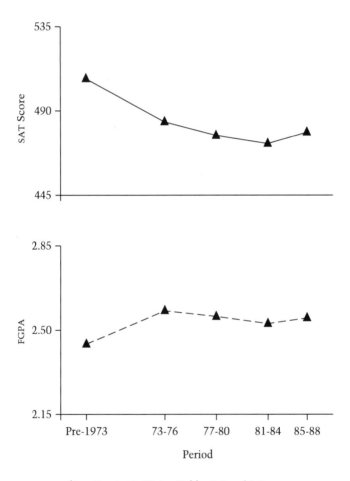

*See Ramist & Weiss, Tables 5-1 and 5-3.

Accuracy of Freshman GPA

If grades become less accurate in representing actual performance of students, FGPA will necessarily be less predictable. The accuracy of grading can vary in many ways. For discussion purposes, these can be grouped roughly in the same manner that one might evaluate the characteristics of a test: difficulty, scaling, reliability, and equating. It should be recognized, however, that while there is a vast amount of research literature on these technical aspects of test quality, the corresponding literature on grading is relatively sparse.

Perhaps the most commonly suspected inaccuracy in grading is grade inflation, which is akin to a drift in the *difficulty* of grading; i.e., "An A is not what it used to be." In the late 1950s and early 1960s it was commonly observed that, as many institutions became more selective and the average SAT scores of their freshmen increased, their average FGPA showed little corresponding change (Webb, 1959; Aiken, 1963; Willingham, 1963; Hills, 1964). In subsequent years a reverse trend took over: grade inflation. An interesting finding by Ramist and Weiss (Chapter 5) was that the *increase* in the relationship of SAT scores to FGPA (early 1970s) came in such an inflationary period.

That effect is illustrated in Figure 2-14. While the average SAT score and average FGPA are shown on scales that are roughly comparable as to range, the elevation of the two trend lines is largely arbitrary and not critical. The important fact indicated here is the significant increase in FGPA at a time when SAT scores were going down in these institutions and also nationally (College Board, 1988b). Moreover, grades were becoming inflated — an apparent decrease in grading standards overall — while the mean SAT validity coefficient was going up (see Figure 2-1). From the mid-1970s to the mid-1980s, mean validity coefficients were declining, but there was little indication of any change in grading standards. These data belie a common misconception: that grade inflation will necessarily make the GPA less predictable. (See Bejar & Blew, 1981, for an earlier demonstration of this point.)

From a technical standpoint, there is actually little reason to expect that moderate overall shifts in the grading level, such as have been observed over the years, would have much effect on validity coefficients. A more likely basis for a negative effect of grade inflation on validity coefficients would be differential inflation, that is, a tendency for grades to be disproportionately high in some courses or fields. We examine that possibility in the following section on comparability.

Some changes in the *scaling* of grades (as opposed to the level) could easily affect predictability of FGPA. For example, if the scale is restricted so that the full range is not used, FGPA would likely be less predictable, because true performance differences are less well identified. The best example is perhaps the preponderance of A's and B's in many graduate programs. At the undergraduate level, such scale restriction could show up as faculty reluctance to assign F's, perhaps as a result of intensified institutional efforts in recent years to retain more students.

There is no evidence of any general tendency toward restriction of the freshman grade scale. Among the 650,000 grades analyzed by Ramist, Lewis, and McCamley (Chapter 12), there was no consistent pattern of fewer F's in 1985 compared to 1982. Furthermore, Ramist and Weiss's data from the Validity Study Service indicate that the standard deviation of FGPA within those institutions was quite stable from the mid-1970s to the mid-1980s (specifically, a drop of .01; see Table 5-3). It is possible that grades in individual courses or areas could be differentially restricted to a greater degree than was the case in earlier years, i.e., mainly low grades in some courses and mainly high grades in others.

Fincher (1990) does describe, however, a particular case of FGPA restriction that is interesting. He reports that institutions within the University System of Georgia often have a significant freshman enrollment in developmental studies programs. These programs do not award degree credit, and it is the policy of the Georgia system not to include students in validity studies who have completed fewer than 25 credit hours. Fincher reports (1990, p. 15) that the most impressive effect of this limitation was a substantial drop of .15 to .20 in the standard deviation of FGPA — a decrease in the variability of FGPA that "may have the most telling effect on the observed reduction in validity coefficients." The standard deviation of FGPA averages about .70 across colleges generally (Ramist & Weiss, Chapter 5).

A third aspect of accuracy is *reliability*, akin to the consistency of individual scores. A major determinant of the reliability of FGPA is the quality of the examining or assessment process in individual classrooms. From a practical standpoint, it is almost impossible to determine whether there has been any significant change in classroom assessment in recent years. Another determinant of reliability, which can be examined, is the number of courses on which FGPA is based. Involvement of more courses normally implies greater reliability. Results reported by Ramist, Lewis, and McCamley indicated that the average number of courses in the FGPA was somewhat useful in accounting for institutional variations in the predictability of FGPA. On the other hand, that average over all colleges changed little from 1982 to 1985, and it was not useful in predicting change in validity coefficients.

The most common method of estimating the reliability of grade averages is to correlate them for successive terms or on the basis of "odd and even" courses within a marking period (Humphreys, 1968; Werts, Linn, & Jöreskog, 1978; Wilson, 1983). It is well established in psychometric theory and practice that the validity of any test or measure is affected negatively by a decrease in reliability and positively by an increase. (See Table 7-5 and accompanying discussion in Chapter 7.) That principle assumes, of course, that reliability estimates are based upon everyone taking either the same test or test forms made comparable through test equating.

With the GPA, that is almost routinely not the case. Students take different programs and different courses in which, as we shall soon see, grades are far from comparable. There may be quite different effects on reliability and validity from the addition of this "correlated error," as the measurement specialists call it. Assume, for example, that students in a given major receive grades that are routinely and arbitrarily a letter-grade higher than is typical in their college. A grading difference of this sort can render the GPAs of the total class less predictable, but actually increase the correlation between grade averages in successive terms (i.e., an apparent increase in the reliability of GPA).

What is the implication for the present topic? That the reliability of FGPA, as conventionally estimated, is not likely to be useful for understanding validity changes, because it is confounded with comparability of grades across courses and fields. That confounding shows up in inconsistent relationships between reliability and validity in the analysis of Ramist, Lewis, and McCamley in Chapter 12. Measures of the comparability of grades, on the other hand, show surprisingly strong and consistent relationships to validity and changes in validity. This gets us to the fourth and most important type of grade accuracy.

Comparability of Freshman GPA

Some time ago, Starch and Elliott (1913) demonstrated that a grade of B from one instructor does not necessarily mean the same thing as a B from another instructor. Decades later, the research director of the College Board (Fishman, 1958) observed, "the unreliability of grades *within* departments and the variability of grading standards *across* departments is apparent to all who have looked into these matters." Recent work indicates that it is still appropriate to question whether the FGPA criterion is comparable from student to student. Potentially, there are several types of noncomparability. Instructors may not grade different sections in a comparable manner. Different instructors teaching the same course may use different standards. Grades may not be comparable from course to course or from one department to another. The only types of noncomparability that have been studied in any detail are differences across courses or majors, but this research has yielded interesting results.

Several studies have documented the lack of comparability of grades across course areas, whether one judges comparability by comparing average grades with average preadmission measures or by comparing grades earned by the same students in different courses (Juola, 1968; Goldman, Schmidt, Hewitt, & Fisher, 1974; Goldman & Widawski, 1976; Willingham, 1985; Strenta & Elliott, 1987). Indices of the relative level of grades in particular course areas correlate substantially from institution to institution and study to study (Elliott & Strenta, 1988). The typical pattern is to find that students in more technically oriented areas like mathematics and natural science tend to have better-than-average test scores and high school grades, but that their college grades are not correspondingly high. Similarly, when comparing students of comparable ability, one finds that college grades tend to run higher in less technical areas like education and sociology.

Previous studies have also demonstrated that noncomparability of college grades is a significant factor in lowering predictability, and that validity of predictors is enhanced by adjusting grades to make them more comparable (Elliott & Strenta, 1988; Goldman & Slaughter, 1976; Young, 1990a). Comparability of grades has also been found to have little impact on predictive validity when there is a strong core curriculum (Willingham, 1963; Butler & McCauley, 1987) and more impact when students freely select courses across areas or specialize in different majors in the upper division (Willingham, 1985; Strenta & Elliott, 1987; Elliott & Strenta, 1988).

Comparability of grades has been shown to be partly, if not largely, responsible for two validity anomalies: the underprediction of women's grades (Elliott & Strenta, 1988; McCornack & McLeod, 1988; Young, 1990b) and the tendency for successive yearly college GPAs to become less predictable (Willingham, 1985; Elliott & Strenta, 1988). Finally, results of these last two studies also suggested that criterion noncomparability has more effect on the correlation of college GPA with test scores than with high school grades.

These results show that the predictability of college performance can be significantly affected by the extent to which it is based upon a comparable standard — and it is clear that the FGPA standard is often not comparable. Thus, there is much more indication in previous research that noncomparability is likely to be a source of criterion instability than was the case with other aspects of grading accuracy.

Evidence concerning the effects of that instability on the predict-ability of FGPA comes from an extensive study of college grading reported by Ramist, Lewis, and McCamley in Chapter 12. These authors analyzed individual course grades of some 80,000 freshmen from 4,680 courses in 38 institutions in 1982 and 1985. Their analyses showed that grade variations from course to course are quite common. One view of comparable standards comes from noting differences — sometimes substantial — between average grades assigned in a course and the average predicted FGPA of students enrolled in the course. Across the 38 institutions, the average differ-ences between actual course grades and predicted FGPA are shown below for two groups of courses: those in which grades had the highest and lowest average corrected correlations with SAT scores (from Table 12-13):

Courses with the Highest SAT Correlations	Average SAT Correlation	Average Course Grade Minus Average Predicted FGPA
Biology — nonmajors	.61	−.07
Advanced physical science & engineering	.60	−.06
Advanced biology	.60	−.04
Economics	.58	−.17
Biology — lab/majors	.58	−.35
Advanced mathematics	.57	−.06
Courses with the Lowest SAT Correlations		
Physical education	.21	+.78
Remedial English	.25	+.42
Trade/vocational	.27	+.30
Art/music/theater — studio	.32	+.56
Remedial reading/literature	.33	+.28
Military science	.33	+.45

The courses with high correlations (i.e., the most predictable grades) were quantitative or scientific in nature, and the average grade was consistently lower than the predicted FGPA of the students enrolled. The courses with low correlations (i.e., the least predictable grades) were nonquantitative and less traditionally academic, and the average grade was typically much higher than the predicted FGPA of students enrolled. This grade pattern is quite similar to that previously described by Elliott and Strenta (1988).

Another view of comparable standards is the appropriateness of the average grade assigned in individual courses — a measure of which is provided by the correlation between the average course grade and the average SAT score across all courses taken by freshmen. Such a correlation can be computed for each college. As reported in Chapter 12, it was typically very low, .10 on average for 38 institutions. When computed for each college, this correlation provides a measure for investigating the relationship between changes in comparability and changes in predictability.

Another comparability measure developed by Ramist, Lewis, and McCamley was course-taking variety, as indicated by the number of courses required to account for 50 percent of all freshman credits at an institution in a given year. The more variety, the less FGPA reflects a core curriculum and, presumably, the more opportunity there is for noncomparable standards among courses to reduce validity coefficients. In these 38 colleges, the average number of courses required to account for 50 percent of freshman credits increased from 14 in 1982 to 16 in 1985. Among those colleges where SAT coefficients declined most, the average number of courses increased from 14 to 18.

The next step was to examine the relationship of these measures and several others with variations in 1982-1985 trends in the predictability of grades at the 38 colleges. To a striking degree, it was possible to account for institutional gains or losses in the predictability of FGPA. The obtained multiple correlations were .70 (corrected for shrinkage) when the focus was on predicting trends in SAT validity coefficients and .51 when the goal was predicting trends in HSGPA validity coefficients. In order of importance, these three variables were associated with a decline in SAT coefficients:

- An increase in course-taking variety,

- A low SAT mean for the freshman class, and

- A decrease in the correlation of course-grade average and SAT average.

In order of importance, these three variables were associated with a decline in HSGPA coefficients:

- A decrease in the correlation of course-grade average and SAT average,

- An increase in the percentage of credits in advanced courses, and

- An increase in the percentage of credits in remedial courses.

With the exception of "SAT mean for the freshman class," all of these measures are connected in one way or another with criterion comparability. Noncomparability is clearly more of a possibility when more students are taking advanced or remedial courses instead of the "regular" freshman course in a subject area. Figure 2-15 illustrates the role of "course-taking variety" and the "correlation of course-grade average and SAT average" in 1982 data from one institution. Because freshmen typically take a great variety of courses (242 in this institution), courses are grouped into categories here in order to provide an interpretable picture. A glance at this plot quickly causes one to question whether grades in these 27 course categories represent comparable standards. Overall, there appears to be little relationship between average grade and average ability level. This particular institution presents a typical picture in this regard.

It is useful to distinguish two possible interpretations of "comparable standard" that may have quite different educational implications. Standard can refer to a *grading* standard employed by the instructor or a *performance* standard achieved by the student. In research reports on this topic, the more common interpretation is that the grading is different, unconsciously if not by design. "Adaptation theory" is one explanation offered: Students who are more (or less) academically talented tend to congregate in different areas, and instructors come to adapt their grade expectations accordingly (Goldman & Hewitt, 1975).

There may be other, more educationally relevant hypotheses as to why students make higher grades in some courses than others. Students who elect to take a given course may be more interested and work harder, or they may have special talents useful in that course. Students may deserve high grades in some courses or areas because the instruction is better and they learn more. One must look to other evidence in order to judge the plausibility of these rival hypotheses. For example, we might seek to determine whether grade averages show revealing patterns from year to year or college to college, whether there is external evidence of superior instruction or student performance, whether students always make high grades in self-selected academic courses or programs, and so on.

In some instances, unusually high grades may be readily explained in terms of unusual interest or special abilities. In Figure 2-15, that may well be the case for the much higher grades in studio art and music than in other art and music courses for students who have similar test scores. But this explanation does not account for the generally low grades in some other courses that are presumably chosen, in part, because of special interest and ability (e.g., computer science, regular writing, physical science).

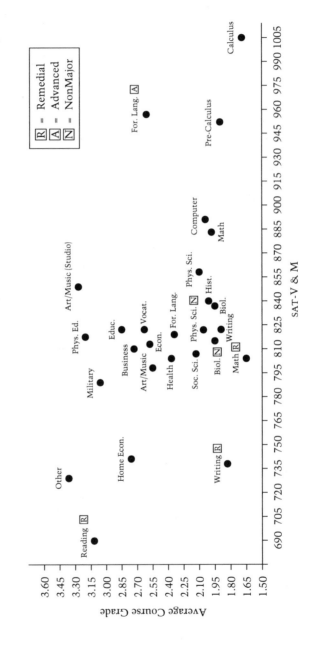

Figure 2-15

Course-Grade Averages and SAT Score Averages for 27 Course Categories—
an Illustration of Grade Variations at One Institution

78

One might argue that students in remedial reading deserve high grades because the superior instruction results in high performance. If so, it is not clear why instruction in remedial writing is evidently so much less successful. It may not seem inappropriate that grades run low in remedial mathematics because this is a less able and less well-prepared group of students, but it is not clear why the grade average in calculus should be approximately the same — particularly since this was the most able group of freshmen in the class, judging from their SAT scores. Whatever the explanation, these disjunctions between average test-score level and average grade level in different courses reduce the relationship between scores and FGPA computed for the whole class.

The same principle applies to changes in such correlations if the disjunctions become more severe from one year to the next. Such a situation is illustrated in Figure 2-16, based on a comparison with the freshman class in the same institution three years later. Even though the course categories are broad groupings, in nine of the 27 instances there were substantial shifts in either the average test score or the average grade assigned — at least one-half of a standard deviation in each case from 1982 to 1985. In this institution, shifts over all courses, such as those illustrated in Figure 2-16, resulted in lowering the correlation between SAT average and course-grade average from +.12 to -.10. The SAT validity coefficient dropped .05 during that period. Among the 13 colleges with the largest SAT validity declines, this correlation dropped an average of .10.

If lack of criterion comparability across courses lowers correlations between predictors and FGPA, then validity coefficients within courses should be stronger than one would expect for a single course grade. Goldman and Slaughter (1976) first demonstrated such a relationship. If such noncomparability of course grades is partly the cause of a lower average predictability, then there should be less decline in correlations with course grades than is the case with overall GPA. These results were confirmed in the analysis of Ramist, Lewis, and McCamley. Table 2-5 shows their key findings, which give rise to the following observations:

- The SAT is routinely described by sponsors and users as having somewhat lower predictive validity than high school grades. That appears to be true for FGPA (here, .54 and .57, respectively) but not for course grades where the criterion is the same for all students (.49 vs. .46). The SAT increment was also substantially larger with course grade rather than FGPA as the criterion.

- The decline in predictive validity of the SAT was noticeably diminished when predictions were based on course grades instead

Figure 2-16

An Illustration of Shifts in Average Grades Relative to Average Test Scores—
for Nine Course Categories That Changed by One-half Standard Deviation
on Either Measure from 1982 to 1985

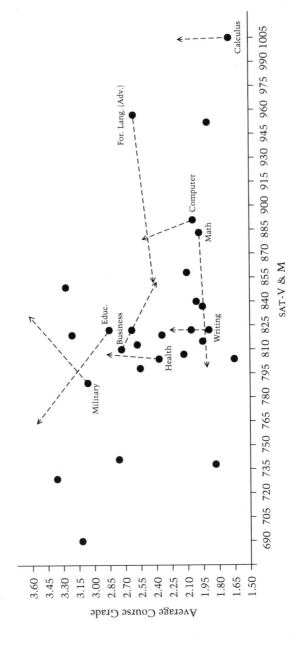

Table 2-5

Prediction of Overall Freshman GPA and Grades Within
Individual Courses — Average Results For 38 Institutions#

| | Corrected Correlation with: | |
	Course Grade	Freshman GPA
1985		
SAT	.49	.54
HSGPA	.46	.57
SAT Increment*	.11	.07
Change, 1982 to 1985		
SAT	−.018	−.030
HSGPA	−.009	−.015
SAT Increment*	−.007	−.011

* Difference between the HSGPA validity coefficient and the
multiple correlation based on HSGPA and SAT.

From Ramist, Lewis, & McCamley, Chapter 12.

of FGPA — from -.030 to -.018. This result demonstrates the relationship between noncomparability and lower predictability of FGPA.

- The within-course correlations are quite high, considering that they are based upon only one course grade. In fact, the SAT is correlated only .05 higher with FGPA than with a single course grade (.54 vs. .49). As Goldman and Slaughter (1976) have pointed out, if the course grades were comparable, their accumulation into a much more reliable FGPA should yield a much higher correlation — in this case, .75 (see page 279 and Note 12-6).

- These results also indicate that grade variation across courses has a larger effect on the predictive validity of SAT than of HSGPA. While the SAT correlated .05 higher with FGPA than with course grade, the HSGPA correlated .11 higher with FGPA than with course grades (.57 vs. .46, but not as high as the .71 that would be expected if course grades were comparable). This differential effect of grade comparability on SAT and HSGPA correlations may have produced somewhat more decline in average SAT correlations.

The HSGPA used in this study was self-reported, which often yields correlations somewhat lower than a transcript HSGPA (Morgan, 1990; Freeberg, Rock, & Pollack, 1989). As a further check, the analysis of Table 2-5 was repeated for 27 institutions that had provided transcript-based high school rank or GPA. In general, the results were quite similar to those shown in Table 2-5. For the two years and the two types of college criteria, the validity of the college-reported school record was typically about .01 higher than the student-reported record. The increment in course-grade prediction, which came from adding SAT to college-reported school rank or GPA, was .12, twice as large as the .06 increment for the FGPA criterion. In all but three of 25 course categories, the SAT coefficient was equal to or higher than that of the college-reported school record. In every course category the SAT increment was higher with course grade as the criterion than with FGPA.

Presumably, one of the mechanisms that produces noncomparable FGPAs is differential course selection, e.g., a tendency for weaker students to take courses where grades are relatively high. Ramist, Lewis, and McCamley tested that hypothesis by defining "leniently graded" or "strictly graded" courses on the basis of the difference between the average course grade and the average predicted FGPA (from SAT and HSGPA) of students enrolled. Then each freshman class was sorted into lower, middle, and upper thirds on high school grades and SAT scores. The course selection hypothesis was confirmed by the fact that among students in the low third of their class on both SAT and HSGPA, the ratio of lenient to strict courses was 1.33, while the ratio for students in both higher thirds was .86.

Summary of Results: The Criterion

Principal findings regarding the possible effects of changes in the criterion on prediction trends were the following:

1. Lower predictability of freshman GPA in recent years is especially characteristic of lower ability students within the freshman classes of individual colleges. Students in the top third showed little, if any, change in corrected validity coefficients.

2. Freshmen who ranked in the low third of their class on SAT scores showed the same decline in corrected validity coefficients from 1978 to 1985 for SAT and for high school GPA. Grades of students in the low third tended to be less predictable than those of students in the top third. In all years examined, however, the SAT was a better predictor of grades for less able students than was the HSGPA.

3. In one study, the types of courses taken by students in 1982 and 1985 were analyzed in detail. In another study, the pattern of weights indicating the usefulness of different types of skills and abilities in predicting FGPA was analyzed for 1978 and 1985. Neither analysis suggested that there had been any significant change in predictability of FGPA due to change in course content or

substantive meaning of FGPA, though that may have occurred in some colleges.

4. Several aspects of the accuracy of FGPA were examined: grade inflation, grade-scale restriction, reliability of GPA. These were found to be largely unchanged from the mid-1970s to the mid-1980s and, in any event, not necessarily related to validity change.

5. A fourth type of criterion accuracy — comparability of grades from course to course — was found to be strongly related to predictive validity and to validity change. Consistent with other studies in recent years, results from an analysis of grades of some 80,000 students in 38 institutions indicated large differences in average grade from course to course in relation to average ability of students enrolled (based on HSGPA and SAT). Grades were lowest relative to ability in scientific and quantitative courses. Because of such differences among courses, the correlation between average course grade and average SAT score was .10 for some 4,600 courses studied.

6. In these 38 colleges, the freshman curriculum became somewhat more diverse from 1982 to 1985. The number of courses required to account for 50 percent of all freshman credits increased from 14 to 16. The increase in those institutions that showed more decline in validity coefficients during this period was 14 to 18.

7. These two indicators of grade comparability — diverse course selection and low relationship between mean course grade and mean test score — plus several other measures, such as percentages of remedial and advanced coursework, were used to predict changes in predictability of FGPA in these 38 colleges. The multiple correlation for predicting such change was .70 for SAT coefficients and .51 for HSGPA coefficients. Smaller declines in correlations with course grades than with overall FGPA (e.g., -.018 vs. -.030 for the SAT) confirmed that noncomparable grades from course to course accounted for a significant portion of changes in validity coefficients in these institutions.

8. Within individual courses, where noncomparability of grades is considerably reduced, SAT validity was higher than that of HSGPA overall. SAT correlations with course grades were equal to or higher than HSGPA correlations in all but three of 25 course categories. In predicting the composite FGPA, the effect of combining noncomparable course grades was greater on SAT validity coefficients than on HSGPA coefficients. That differential effect was reflected in another important finding: The incremental validity

of the SAT was much greater with course grade as the criterion (.11 to .12) than as that increment is traditionally estimated, with FGPA criterion (.06 to .07).

One impression from these results is that a simple overall analysis of the relationship between FGPA and scores on preadmission predictors conceals almost as much as it reveals. When the composite FGPA criterion is unbundled, it is clear that there are substantial variations in grading patterns and in the predictability of grades across courses and academic areas. Because course grades are not comparable, averaging them together yields an FGPA that is not comparable from student to student. Consequently, there are important differences in the pattern of validity coefficients and in trends in those coefficients over time, depending upon the criterion one uses — FGPA or course grade, the more accurate measure unit for unit. As a final complication, the predictability of FGPA has evidently declined mainly for students in the lower half of the freshman class.

In the previous section on possible changes in the predictor, results indicated stability in the SAT and the high school record and close correspondence in the correlational patterns for those two measures from the mid-1970s to the mid-1980s. In the earlier section on possible changes in the sample, results indicated substantial institutional differences in validity trends. In both cases, the findings suggested that changes in the predictability of the FGPA criterion are the most likely source of change in validity coefficients over time. Results summarized in this final section confirm that such changes in predictability do occur and that they are strongly related to changes in educational practices or grading patterns within individual colleges. In the following chapter, we take up several important implications of these findings.

CHAPTER 3

Conclusions and Implications

WARREN W. WILLINGHAM*

The previous chapter brought together a variety of research results relevant to the question of why average correlations between freshman GPA and preadmission measures (SAT scores and high school record) vary from year to year. In addition to estimating trends over two decades, a number of potential causes of such trends were examined: possible changes in the samples of students or colleges, possible changes in the predictors, and possible changes in the FGPA criterion. This chapter summarizes the principal conclusions and considers some implications of the findings.

Principal Conclusions

1. *From the mid-1960s to the mid-1970s* SAT *correlations with* FGPA *tended to go up while high school record (*HSR*) correlations tended to go down, but there was little change in overall predictability of* FGPA. *From the mid-1970s to the mid-1980s there was a gradual decline in predictability of* FGPA, *reflected somewhat more in* SAT *scores than in* HSR.

In estimating trends in the average correlations between predictors and the FGPA criterion, considerable attention was given to ways of insuring that yearly data were as comparable as possible. Correlations were corrected for restriction of range in order to avoid one important source of noncomparability. Estimates of correlational trends are inherently imprecise, however, because each year different groups of colleges choose to do validity studies and statistical methods of handling that problem are not entirely satisfactory. Trends must be interpreted with those important caveats in mind.

There is no indication that overall predictability of FGPA (i.e., the corrected multiple correlation based on SAT and HSR) changed to any significant degree from the mid-1960s to the mid-1970s. On the other hand, there is fairly clear evidence that SAT correlations and HSR correlations were on different trends during this early period — the SAT going up and the HSR going down. At the same time, the contribution of the SAT-Mathematics score in predicting FGPA increased relative to the SAT-Verbal score, traditionally the better predictor.

---

*I am grateful to Nancy Cole for her useful review of this chapter.

In the next decade — from the mid-1970s to the mid-1980s — the overall predictability of FGPA did decline somewhat. During this period, the average multiple correlation (based on SAT and HSR and corrected for range restriction) dropped about .02. This change was evidently reflected more in the SAT (-.03 to -.05) than the HSR (.00 to -.03). The most obvious difference between the first and second decade was in the trend of the SAT correlations: increasing until 1974 and then decreasing. In the second decade, there was a tendency for the SAT correlation to decrease in those colleges where it had earlier increased. As a result of these trends, the increment to the multiple correlation (i.e., due to the addition of the SAT to the HSR) increased slightly in the first decade, then decreased similarly.

2. *Substantial differences in prediction trends from college to college indicate that such trends represent an institution-based phenomenon.*

Averages present an incomplete picture. While the average corrected correlation of SAT scores with FGPA declined some .03 to .05 from the mid-1970s to the mid-1980s, the experience of individual institutions varied a great deal. For every two colleges with declining SAT correlations during this period, there was one college with increasing correlations. More detailed analysis indicated several differences in validity data from college to college. The typical level of corrected multiple correlation based on SAT and HSR (i.e., the overall predictability of FGPA) varied widely. For some colleges that correlation hovered in the .30s, in others in the .70s. Colleges showed more yearly fluctuations above and below their typical correlational level than would be expected by chance. This was equally true of the relationship of HSR and SAT scores to FGPA.

In individual colleges, corrected SAT and HSR validity coefficients show characteristic long-term trends that, with enough studies, are quite stable. While there were substantial institutional differences in these prediction trends, the HSR trend and the SAT trend were strongly related from college to college. From the mid-1970s to the mid-1980s, the proportion of total variation in SAT correlations due to *differences* in trends from college to college was six times as large as the variation due to the declining trend in the average correlation overall.

These substantial differences from college to college indicate that trends in correlations are much less likely due to changes in predictors than to changes within some institutions. Which institutions? Most nominal characteristics of colleges (e.g., size and control) show only small relationships to such correlational trends. Institutional selectivity (i.e., average SAT score) appears to differentiate best among colleges that do and do not show systematic fluctuations in correlations over time. As a group, the least selective colleges showed the widest swings in predictability of FGPA — up from the mid-1960s to the mid-1970s, and down thereafter. For the most selective colleges, the average corrected SAT validity coefficient was stable throughout this 20-year period. In both types of institutions, however, there were large differences in prediction trends from college to college.

3. *While correlations with* FGPA *have drifted up or down at many institutions, there is no evidence of any consequential change in the* SAT *that would have affected those correlations.*

Several studies were undertaken in order to determine whether any changes in the SAT might cause or contribute to a pre-1974 increase and subsequent decrease in average correlations with FGPA. An extensive examination of all important characteristics of the test — content, difficulty, reliability, meaning of scores, scale comparability — did not reveal any changes in the test from 1970 to 1985 that were plausibly related to any significant change in prediction of FGPA. As a further check, old and new forms of the test were administered to the same students at the same times. Differences in validity coefficients for various corresponding segments of old and new forms were small and inconsistent.

Results of recent studies suggest it is unlikely that external factors like repeat testing or test disclosure have affected the correlation of SAT scores with FGPA. It is also unlikely that coaching has had any significant effect on the predictive validity of SAT scores, because the pattern of correlational trends in recent years (e.g., more decline for nonselective colleges and males) is inconsistent with the pattern of attendance at coaching schools. Furthermore, a special study simulating possible influences of coaching indicated that, even with liberal estimates regarding such effects, any change in validity coefficients would be less than one percent over 10 years.

If SAT scores were to become distorted and less dependable for whatever cause, there is no reason to expect that only their correlation with FGPA would be affected. Another important check on the stability of those scores as a measure of developed academic ability is whether there has been any change in recent years in the relationship of SAT scores to similar measures with which they are normally well correlated. An analysis of considerable correlational data showed no change in such relationships.

4. *Different predictors show similar correlational trends with* FGPA — *further indication that these trends represent variations in the predictability of the criterion rather than changes in the* SAT.

If correlations between a predictor and FGPA change over time, one clue as to whether that trend is due to changes in the predictor or changes in the criterion is whether or not correlational patterns for different predictors are similar. Two types of evidence show similar correlational patterns for different predictors in recent years.

One line of evidence is the trend in validity coefficients for tests other than the SAT. There were several tests for which correlations with FGPA could be evaluated on the basis of generally comparable samples in different years over the past two decades. The trends in those coefficients were, in most cases, quite similar to that of the SAT.

Another line of evidence is the degree of similarity in the correlational patterns for HSR and SAT based upon the same institutions or groups of students. From the mid-1970s to the mid-1980s, those patterns could be compared in a number of ways, and overall, they were remarkably similar. In each of those instances where SAT coefficients were likely to decline, HSR coefficients declined as well (i.e., in nonselective colleges, among males, among students in the lower half of the class). Also, as noted, patterns of variation in HSR and SAT validity coefficients across colleges and years were highly similar, and long-term trends in the two were strongly related in individual colleges.

5. There is little evidence that demographic changes have had any direct effect on validity coefficients in recent years.

There are two obvious ways in which demographic changes might affect trends in predictive correlations: a change in representation of a subgroup whose grades are more or less predictable than students generally, or a change in the predictability of a group. Potentially, the largest subgroup effect on correlational trends would be that of gender, because both gender groups are large. There was a clear gender difference in prediction trends. From the mid-1970s to the mid-1980s, males showed twice as much decline in validity coefficients as did females. Thus, increasing representation of women would tend slightly to increase, not decrease, validity coefficients. Furthermore, both HSR and SAT coefficients are higher for women. Again, more women would tend to increase the correlation slightly. In sum, any overall downward trend in these coefficients has occurred despite — not because of — the fact that there are now more women in higher education than was true earlier.

Predictive data were analyzed for three ethnic subgroups: Black, Hispanic, and Asian-American students. These trend analyses did not indicate any significant subgroup effects on validity coefficients, due either to changes in the mix of those groups or to changes in their predictability. Majority students showed the same decline in predictability of FGPA as did total classes including the ethnic subgroups.

While many institutions may have experienced enrollment pressures in recent years, there is no indication that a decline in the predictability of FGPA is due simply to the enrollment of larger numbers of weaker students whose grades may be less predictable. Within the individual institutions studied here, there was actually a somewhat smaller proportion of freshmen with low SAT scores in 1985 relative to earlier classes in those colleges. Also, the increasing representation of older students and foreign students had little if any direct effect on trends in validity coefficients, because very few such students were included in these studies.

While there is no evidence of consequential direct effects of demographic shifts (i.e., no statistical effects because of smaller or larger representation of particular types of students in validity studies), the possibility of indirect educational effects is an open question. For example, some colleges may have undertaken special efforts to improve retention or to diversify offerings in order to attract a broader clientele. In that manner, real or potential demographic shifts may have encouraged changes in educational programs or practices that could alter the nature of the FGPA criterion. That possibility is suggested by the finding that the predictability of the FGPA has declined more in the low third than in the high third of a given freshman class, even though there has been no increase in low SAT scores in the low third.

That finding does not appear to result from a change in the SAT or its usefulness with the less able students in the class. Old forms of the test also showed such weaker predictive relationships in the low third of the class, but only when the test was administered to students in a recent class. Furthermore, validity coefficients for the high school record have shown a very similar pattern — more decline for the less able students in the class. SAT scores provided a slightly better prediction of FGPA for students in the low third of the class than did the HSR. This is contrary to the usual assumption that performance in high school gives a much better indication of academic promise than does the SAT for students who are in the gray area of an institution's applicant selection range.

6. *The nature of the FGPA varies from student to student and from year to year within a given institution. Such variation in the comparability of FGPA is strongly related to its predictability.*

One could hypothesize several types of changes in the freshman grade criterion that might cause variation in its predictability. For some such hypothetical changes, we find no supporting evidence. For example, available evidence does not seem to indicate much if any overall change in the meaning of FGPA, i.e., the types of academic competence and accomplishment it generally represents. Also, some types of grading accuracy, like overall grade inflation, are not likely to have had any effect on the predictability of FGPA. Other aspects of grading accuracy, like the reliability of classroom testing procedures, could not be evaluated with available data.

The comparability of course grades, on the other hand, is one type of grading accuracy that could be evaluated, in part, and lack of comparability appears to cause significant fluctuations in the predictability of FGPA. In a typical institution, freshmen are enrolled in a very wide variety of courses ranging from remedial to upper division. The average SAT scores of students in these different courses also vary widely — with, for example, higher SAT scores associated with more advanced courses and lower scores with remedial courses — but the average grade earned is often similar across a wide range of courses. Furthermore, weaker students are more likely to enroll in courses where high grades are easier to obtain. These educational dynamics concerning course selection and grade patterns vary from college to college and from year to year within the same college.

Variations in the predictability of FGPA were examined in relation to several likely indicators of grade comparability, e.g., course diversity, differences in course grade levels, proportion of remedial or advanced courses, etc. Not only did such measures account for differences in validity coefficients from college to college, but they were also strongly related to changes in those coefficients from year to year. It was not possible to examine the extent to which predictability of FGPA may also be affected by grade variations among sections or among instructors teaching the same course.

7. *Using individual course grades as the criterion presents a very different picture of predictive validity and a substantially larger contribution by the* SAT *than when* FGPA *is the criterion.*

The SAT is intended to provide a standard and objective measure of how well a student is likely to do academically. Course grades, representing teacher judgment of performance in a particular class, are a natural starting point for judging how the test relates to academic performance. However, grades in individual courses are relatively less reliable than grade composites (grades combined from several courses). On the other hand, if grades in different courses are based on different standards or have different meanings, their combination into a composite FGPA is less appropriate as a criterion measure.

The possibility that tests and high school record predict very well in individual courses but less well when disparate courses are averaged was examined. It was found that the relationship between predictors and course grades varies considerably, depending on the nature of the course. High correlations are more likely to be found in courses where it is difficult to obtain high grades (e.g., biology, physical science, advanced mathematics). Low correlations are more likely to be found in courses where the high grades are easier to obtain (e.g., physical education, art, music, remedial English, military science).

That combining noncomparable course grades has a negative effect on the predictability of FGPA is illustrated by comparing the validity declines when first FGPA, then course grade was the criterion. Using course grade rather than FGPA reduced the decline in correlations by almost half. The fact that noncomparability of grades has a somewhat smaller effect on HSR correlations with FGPA than on SAT correlations with FGPA may account for the fact that the HSR correlations declined somewhat less in recent years.

Contrary to popular conception, data presented here indicate that, with some consistency, SAT scores are more highly related to course grades than is the high school record. The SAT correlation with course grade equaled or exceeded that of HSR in all but three of 26 categories of courses analyzed. Also, with course grade as the criterion, the incremental validity due to the SAT was considerably higher (.11 to .12) than when estimated, as it traditionally has been, on the basis of correlations with the FGPA criterion (in these data, .06 to .07). For every category of courses, the SAT increment was higher for predicting course grade than for predicting FGPA.

When this series of studies was started, we assumed first that observed trends in the average correlation between preadmission measures and freshman GPA resulted from the data not being comparable from year to year; in other words, due to statistical artifacts. That was partly an accurate assumption. But when the data were made as comparable as possible from year to year, some trends did persist — not large, not consistent, and not amenable to very precise estimation, but clearly detectable trends, nonetheless.

In ensuing studies much attention was directed to the SAT. There were some obvious hunches as to why the correlation between SAT scores and freshman GPA might change over time: Perhaps the test had changed in subtle ways; or the scores were being distorted by coaching or other external factors; or the test was not as predictive for ethnic groups, women, or other new students entering higher education in greater numbers; or demands now placed on students required somewhat different abilities than those represented in the SAT. None of these hypotheses has proven useful in understanding trends in validity coefficients.

On the other hand, several findings do seem particularly significant. All were somewhat unexpected; all pertain in one way or another to the freshman grade criterion. First, institutional differences in the predictability of freshman GPA play a larger role than expected. The findings clearly indicate that trends in the predictability of freshman GPA are associated with individual colleges, not individual predictors. Another surprising finding is that the level and trend in the predictability of FGPA in individual colleges is directly connected with educational practices such as course offerings, course selection, and grading. Finally, a particularly interesting perspective on predictive validity comes from looking beyond overall prediction of FGPA — from unbundling that prediction, so to speak. One can unbundle by using individual course grades as the criterion, or by predicting FGPA for different segments of the class. In both cases, the results provide a better understanding of SAT predictive capability and what the test contributes to HSR in identifying students who are likely to do well in college. This picture raises several general issues that deserve comment. In particular, it is useful to ask what these findings mean for the SAT; how prediction studies can be better conducted, interpreted, and used; and what important questions remain.

SAT Scores and Their Use

Is the SAT still working? Results of these studies certainly indicate that SAT scores remain a useful indicator of academic performance in college — more useful, in some significant respects, than was previously recognized. There is no evidence of any consequential change in the test. It measures the same skills of verbal and quantitative reasoning as in the past, and these skills apparently remain important to success in a wide range of academic work. Data reported here illustrate, however, that it is in the more traditional academic courses with apparently rigorous grading that SAT scores tend to show the strongest relationship with academic performance in college.

For many years, it has been assumed that college grades are more accurately forecast by the high school record than by test scores. Apparently, that is not actually the case. FGPA does show higher correlations with HSR than with SAT scores, but only because combining noncomparable course grades into the FGPA restricts the SAT correlation more than the HSR correlation. When course grade is the criterion, the SAT shows particularly strong incremental validity and is typically a better predictor than HSR. That is, the test is demonstrably more useful if the performance criterion is not distorted by combining noncomparable grades. Given all the discussion in recent years as to whether the SAT adds significantly to HSR in predicting grades, these are striking results.

What about an institution that has experienced a decline in the correlation of SAT scores with FGPA? Should such an institution stop using the test or give it less weight? As has always been the case, colleges should require admission tests only if the scores are useful. That question can only be answered by individual colleges, but several of the findings here are pertinent. There is a fairly strong tendency for HSR validity coefficients to move in the same direction as SAT coefficients. That is, the problem is more likely to be a loss in predictability of FGPA, rather than a lower validity coefficient for SAT or HSR alone. If that is the case, the second predictor is probably needed more, not less. Furthermore, the availability of a standard measure like the SAT is the best hope for understanding the causes and the educational implications of a sharp change in the predictability of grades.

As to how much weight test scores should have in selection, there are other important considerations. Colleges have multiple goals. In addition to attracting freshmen who show academic promise, recruitment and selection priorities require appropriate weight on a variety of student talents, interests, and background characteristics. On the specific question of predicting grades, results here indicate that in the low third of the freshman class — the HSR and SAT levels where most selection decisions are made — the SAT is actually a marginally better predictor of FGPA than is HSR. Thus, if accurate prediction of FGPA is important but becomes more problematic over time, putting less weight on test scores in selection may be counterproductive. These considerations argue all the more that colleges should inform their policy and practice regarding test use with results of local validity studies.

Would some change in the SAT make it a better predictor? There may well be ways to improve the SAT, but this series of studies does not speak to that question in any clear and useful way. There is no indication in these findings of any particular change in the test (e.g., more emphasis on subject knowledge, a different mix of item types, a higher or lower cognitive level, etc.) that would increase correlations with FGPA. It seems reasonably clear that variations in predictability of FGPA result from changes in the grade criterion in some colleges. The nature of such changes is perhaps the most interesting aspect of this topic.

Why Does Grade Prediction Vary?

Have students generally become somewhat less predictable in recent years? That seems unlikely for several reasons. The observed decline in predictability of FGPA is particularly characteristic of the lower half of the freshman class within these individual colleges, and judging from their SAT scores, these students are not any less academically competent than in previous years. A decline in predictability is more characteristic of less selective institutions, but there are large institutional differences in such prediction trends. Downward trends are more frequent in recent years, but a substantial proportion of colleges shows upward trends. Taken together, these results indicate that change in predictability is a college phenomenon, not a change in students generally.

If a college observes a change in validity coefficients over time — particularly a progressive decline — what might explain the trend? The research reported here suggests some of the factors that may be operating, though it is important to recognize that these results, for a limited group of colleges, do not necessarily reflect higher education generally or what goes on in a particular college.

A progressive decline in validity coefficients could indicate that the college is doing a better and better job of bringing weak students up to speed — proving predictions wrong, so to speak. If that is the case, it would be an exciting outcome — a success story worth understanding in detail and transporting to other colleges. On the other hand, the same prediction trend could result from a progressively weaker core curriculum, more diverse coursework in which grading standards vary, more opportunity for students to seek out more demanding or less demanding courses or instructors.

There are other possibilities. A given college might show a decline in the predictability of freshman grades because of systematic changes in the courses offered; e.g., more courses in which grades tend to be less dependent on traditional academic abilities, or breaking up key courses taken by many students in favor of differentiated courses where grades have different meanings. Finally, in a college experiencing such a decline in predictability, classroom assessment may have changed over time, from emphasis on frequent examinations to a more subjective or less rigorous assessment.

While a progressive change in validity coefficients is not automatically good or bad, it may be an important sign for the institution. One implication is clear: Colleges should do prediction studies on a regular basis, because trends in prediction results may signal significant educational changes in addition to a possible need for modifications in the way tests and other predictors are used. In order to serve both functions, however, prediction studies need to be augmented somewhat.

Making Prediction Studies More Useful

Findings reported here challenge conventional wisdom about predictive validity studies. The overall grade-point average is not a sufficient criterion for understanding the relationship between pre-admission measures and academic performance. Prediction results at individual colleges change more than had been appreciated, over the short term as well as the long term. Changes in prediction results are closely related to changes in educational practices. And in a given study, prediction results vary in significant ways, depending upon what segment of the class one focuses upon.

There is certainly not yet the basis for a well-constructed theory as to how and why prediction results vary as much as they do. Nevertheless, it seems likely that institutions could learn much about the dynamics of their educational programs if prediction studies had a few added features. Some types of analysis might be more efficiently conducted through local studies, others through a centralized service like VSS. Findings reported here suggest several possibilities:

- A supplementary analysis of students in the low third of the class may often yield different predictor weights and more effective identification of which marginal applicants are more likely to earn a passing FGPA.

- Supplementary analyses using individual course grades or a standard set of course grades as a criterion could provide more realistic predictions of individual performance and more accurate estimates from year to year of the effectiveness of prediction overall than does a traditional study using only FGPA, based on whatever courses students happen to select.

- Prediction of performance differentials for different groups of students in different areas of academic concentration could provide information useful for advising students and evaluating academic progress and programs. Such analyses are to be contrasted with placement studies that focus on particular course sequences and employ achievement tests most relevant to those courses.

- Analyses that track average grade levels in key courses — in relation to indications of the ability of students in those courses — could provide useful information for the benefit of faculty who offer the courses and deans who are concerned with maintaining consistent and reasonable standards.

- Presenting results in ways that may differentiate possible causes of a progressive increase or decrease in the predictability of freshman grades could be useful to colleges experiencing such trends.

- Prediction of additional criteria that supplement freshman grades (e.g., long-term GPA, academic honors, other outstanding accomplishments in college, outcomes assessments) could help many colleges in developing sound admissions policies and possibly broadening their applicant pool.

Tracking Prediction Trends

There are three reasons why it is important to collect systematic data on summary prediction trends relevant to the SAT and its use. Those who sponsor and develop the test need accurate information regarding any changes that might call for modification in the test. It is also desirable to have information on progressive changes in the nature of the freshman grade criterion in different types of colleges because of possible implications that such changes may have for educational practice and policy generally. Changing relationships between student performance and a standard measure of academic ability provide one valuable source of such information. Finally, individual colleges can better interpret their own prediction studies if reliable trend data are available for like institutions.

One thing we have surely discovered in the course of this work is that useful trend analysis is severely hampered by inconsistencies in the prediction studies that are normally available. The Validity Study Service is designed to serve institutions. The content, design, and timing of studies varies according to institutional interests and needs. While that flexibility is desirable for the colleges, it limits the accuracy and usefulness of any summary that could otherwise be helpful in interpreting results. The common benefit that can be derived from accumulated prediction data would be greatly improved by working toward data collection that is more comparable from year to year — particularly as to the representativeness of the institutions participating and the types of common data included in studies.

There may be merit in organizing a panel or core group of colleges that would participate in a cooperative program of prediction studies on some regular schedule. Periodic summary analyses of relationships among key predictors and types of academic criteria for different groups of institutions could be of considerable added value to the participants and to colleges generally. The associational structure of the College Board is well suited to consultation among participants as to data collection, interpretation of summary results, and possibly other cooperative studies of special interest.

Questions Outstanding

Like any close examination of a complex issue, this analysis has answered some questions and raised others. A general impression, however, is that several important topics deserve much more attention than they commonly receive.

First, there should be more research and informed discussion about grades, grading, and the basis upon which student performance is judged. The grade-point average may well be an administrative necessity, and it is certainly a convenience for research and other purposes. But the GPA is certainly not ideal, either for validating admissions measures or for indicating what students have learned in college. Lack of confidence in the GPA as a measure of achievement in college has no doubt helped fuel interest in outcomes assessment. Accurate accounting of the outcomes of undergraduate education is important for many reasons — educational, social, political — and the first key step in improving that process should certainly be strengthening faculty assessment procedures wherever possible.

There have been some useful studies in recent years concerning grading practices, departmental variations, alternate criteria, assessing performance over the full four years of college, and so on. Our findings suggest, however, that there is still much to learn about how assessment actually works in classrooms, differences in examining procedures, how they might be improved, variations from one instructor to another, and how these dynamics vary over time and across programs. Given the intense public scrutiny of admissions testing and the enormous amount of research devoted to these tests, it is remarkable that school and college grading has attracted so little formal examination. The accuracy of grades and how well they represent student performance has a lot to do with the equity of assessment, the meaning of academic standards, and also how well the GPA can be predicted with preadmission measures.

A related second question is why college grade-prediction results vary as much as they do — college to college and year to year. It has been argued on theoretical grounds, and observed in some contexts, that predictor-criterion relationships do not vary significantly across generally similar sites. Findings reported here not only show substantial differences in validity coefficients from college to college, but more surprising, significant yearly deviations as well as shifting long-term trends within the same college. Furthermore, our results suggest the real possibility of identifying systematic changes in the criterion that can help to account for such variations in correlational results. That prospect presents a new challenge to validity theory and a new tool for prediction practice. In fact, one of the more promising implications of our findings is that many colleges, through added attention to the soundness of assessment procedures, may be able to improve substantially the accuracy of grade prediction.

A third topic of general interest and potential educational significance is the pattern of predictive relationships for students in the low, middle, and high thirds of the freshman class. Not only is the FGPA less predictable (with either SAT or HSR) for less able students, it is mainly for these students that predictability has declined in recent years. Why is this so? Are some colleges learning how to salvage weaker students so that they not only do better than predicted in the freshman year, but also tend, in subsequent years, to catch up with better prepared peers? Or do these different predictive relationships at the low and high ends of the class simply reflect different patterns of course selection and differential grading standards?

These three topics are complex and overlapping. There are other, more specific questions that deserve research attention, but are no less challenging:

- Why are grades in apparently difficult courses more predictable than grades in apparently less difficult courses?

- Why has predictability of FGPA declined more for males than for females?

- Are there different criterion dynamics that explain yearly fluctuations versus long-term trends in predictability?

- Why is the high school record a weaker predictor when it counts the most, i.e., with less able students who are most likely to be in the gray area when applicants are selected and most likely to be at risk in the freshman year?

- Are there other types of academic performance, not specifically examined here, that are now more important in the eyes of faculty?

To recapitulate briefly, there are two general implications of the preceding discussion. The first is that colleges should do validity studies on a more regular basis. Overall, our findings present contrasting arguments as to how much weight to place on test scores and high school record in judging whether a student is likely to do well in a particular academic program. Because results vary considerably from college to college, it is important that use of HSR and SAT scores be guided by local studies. Because results in a given college may change over time, it is important that studies be repeated periodically. Changes in results may call for modifications in admissions criteria or signal institutional changes that deserve attention. Also, a more regular program of validity studies by SAT users should include steps to improve the representativeness of participating colleges year by year so that trend data will be more accurate and more useful to the institutions.

A second implication is that prediction research needs to be reformulated so that it is more effectively connected to the educational process. The SAT serves a limited but important function in the transition of students from school to college — helping students to select colleges and programs where they are likely to do well, and helping colleges recruit and select students appropriate to their programs. Validity studies have supported that process, and with improvements in the criterion, there are excellent prospects of making grade predictions more accurate. With some additions and modifications such as those suggested, these same studies could better serve their primary purpose, and also provide colleges with a much richer base of information. Extending prediction research beyond its traditional statistical emphasis to more substantive educational issues could broaden the usefulness of such work and assist colleges in gauging student progress and judging how well programs are working.

PART II
PROJECT REPORTS

Analyses of the Predictive Validity of the SAT and High School Grades from 1976 to 1985

RICK MORGAN

Many colleges conduct studies to determine the extent to which measures used in admissions predict college performance. Beginning with the enrolling class of 1964, the College Board established the Validity Study Service (vss), to which colleges may send data for an analysis of the predictive validity of college admissions measures. The analysis of the data provides least-squares regression estimates for sets of predictors of freshman grade-point average (FGPA). Following the completion of all the requests for data analysis for an enrolling year, average multiple correlations of SAT scores and high school grade information with FGPA are computed for all studies in which SAT-Verbal, SAT-Mathematical, and a measure of high school record were used to predict FGPA for the entire freshman class. These average correlations are the estimates of predictive validity for each enrolling year.

Two major problems with drawing conclusions about trends in predictive validity using these yearly averages are that the group of academic institutions conducting validity studies in any given year may not be representative and that the composition of this group changes from year to year. Consequently, yearly fluctuations in the average validity coefficients could result from different colleges choosing to participate in different years, as well as from several other factors. These other factors include changes in:

- The characteristics of students choosing to attend college,

- College admissions practices,

- The test, and

- Grading practices or the meaning of the criterion.

Yearly average vss validity data taken from Ramist (1984) and more recent data made available by the vss program are summarized in Table 4-1. The table shows the size of the average yearly multiple correlation of SAT-V, SAT-M, and high school record (HSR) with FGPA, the average yearly multiple correlation of SAT-V and SAT-M with FGPA, and

Table 4-1

Average Correlations of SAT Scores and High School Record with FGPA*

	All Available VSS Data**			Studies Using Actual HSR		
Year	Multiple Correlation	SAT Correlation	HSR Correlation	Multiple Correlation	SAT Correlation	HSR Correlation
1964	.60	.44	.52	.60	.44	.52
1965	.60	.40	.54	.60	.40	.54
1966	.58	.39	.52	.58	.39	.52
1967	.57	.40	.52	.57	.40	.52
1968	.59	.42	.52	.59	.42	.52
1969	.57	.41	.51	.57	.41	.51
1970	.55	.39	.49	.55	.39	.49
1971	.54	.38	.48	.54	.38	.48
1972	.56	.41	.49	.56	.41	.49
1973	.57	.43	.49	.56	.43	.49
1974	.58	.47	.50	.58	.46	.50
1975	.56	.44	.48	.56	.45	.48
1976	.56	.45	.47	.57	.45	.50
1977	.56	.44	.49	.56	.43	.49
1978	.54	.42	.46	.56	.42	.49
1979	.55	.42	.47	.57	.42	.50
1980	.54	.41	.46	.56	.42	.48
1981	.54	.38	.47	.56	.39	.50
1982	.54	.40	.47	.58	.41	.52
1983	.53	.39	.46	.55	.40	.49
1984	.51	.37	.45	.54	.38	.48
1985	.52	.37	.47	.56	.38	.50

* From Ramist (1984)

** "SAT correlation" refers to a multiple based on SAT-V and SAT-M; "multiple correlation" is based on those two scores plus HSR.

the average correlation of high school academic record with FGPA for the enrolling classes of 1964 through 1985. The observed data suggest a steady gradual decline in the predictability of college performance from the optimal weighting of HSR and SAT scores (the multiple correlation). The trend in average yearly correlations for HSR with freshman grades is generally parallel to the multiple correlation. However, it does not necessarily follow that these observed data represent true changes in predictive validity, because the participating colleges change each year. Also, one cause for these trends can be traced to the 1972 introduction of the option of using student-reported high school data from the Student Descriptive Questionnaire. Prior to 1972, colleges provided actual high school record information. Because self-reported data generally have lower correlations, averages based solely on the studies supplying actual HSR information are also listed in Table 4-1. As expected, correlations involving college-reported HSR are higher, with the aforementioned declines leveling off in the last 10 years.

Two distinct trends in the average yearly correlation of SAT scores with freshman grades are present in Table 4-1. Beginning in the early 1970s and continuing to the mid-1970s, the average correlations of SAT scores with freshman grades increased. In subsequent years, this relationship returned to levels approximating those of the mid-1960s. In assessing all the correlations, it should be noted that the average number of studies on which the yearly averages are based has increased. From 1964 to 1969, the correlations are based on an average of 53 studies per year, while the average number of studies is 96 for the period from 1970 to 1975, and 165 for the years after that. The effect of the increase in the number of colleges on the correlations is not known.

Because the fluctuations in college participation in the VSS could be influencing the trends in average correlations presented in Table 4-1, this study was designed to explore these trends after removing effects resulting from differential college participation. Specifically, this study investigates the predictive validity of the SAT and measures of high school record from 1976 to 1985. This 10-year period begins with data from the peak years for the average correlation of SAT scores with FGPA and ends with the most current set of data. (See Note 2-4.) Most of the emphasis in this study is on the SAT, although an understanding of overall predictive validity trends requires analysis of the trends involving HSR as a predictor of FGPA. In order to analyze within-college trends, the study uses data from colleges that conducted more than one predictive validity analysis in the 10-year period. In the first part of the study, a pairwise difference estimation technique is used to provide estimates of trends in several measures of predictive validity. In the second part, the same analysis is applied to groups of colleges defined by various characteristics in order to investigate whether the predictive validity trends are related to characteristics of the colleges involved.

As a result of the pairwise estimation technique, differential yearly participation in VSS is much better controlled than the observed data found in Table 4-1. The pairwise difference estimation technique, however, cannot account for fluctuations in correlations that may result from other factors, such as changes in the composition of students attending participating colleges or in the grading or composition of courses taken by the students during their freshman year. Nor can the results of the study be generalized to colleges that did not participate in VSS.

PROCEDURE

Population

Because the study focuses on within-college trends, the data set included only colleges that conducted analyses in at least two of the 10 years under study. The study sample included only analyses based on at least 75 complete student records from a college's entire freshman class (rather than a subset based on gender, ethnicity, or major). The selected studies utilized SAT-V, SAT-M, and one of two college-reported measures of HSR (high school grades on a 0-4 scale and high school class ranks) to predict FGPA, which was also limited to colleges using a 0-4 scale. In order not to underestimate the relationship of FGPA with HSR, the data set excluded self-reported high school information. These constraints on the data permitted a more accurate analysis of change in predictive validity over time than was provided in Table 4-1. The sample includes 222 colleges that conducted 778 different validity studies over the 10-year period.

For each of the 778 analyses included in this study, the mean, standard deviation, and correlations among the three predictor variables and FGPA were extracted from the VSS database. These data were merged with college demographic information concerning freshman class size and type of college (public or private).

Method of Analysis

One way of estimating trends in predictive validity would be to examine only those colleges that had conducted analyses in each of the 10 years under study. However, the number of such colleges was too small to produce meaningful validity estimates. An alternative would be to examine changes over time in the results of colleges with multiple analyses. In this study, the repeated measures estimation procedure found in Goldman and Widawski (1976) was used to produce estimates for each of the 10 years, based on pairwise estimates of change. (See Note 4-1.)

The pairwise difference estimation technique produced yearly estimates of the means and standard deviations of the predictor variables and FGPA, permitting an examination of the trends of these measures on predictive validity results. Correlations corrected for the multivariate restriction of range of SAT-V, SAT-M, and HSR (see Note 4-2) were also estimated.

Grouping Variables

The second part of the study examined predictive validity for different types of colleges. Validity estimates using the repeated measures procedure were derived for the following categories:

- Type of college control: Public colleges
                             Private colleges

- Selectivity: Colleges with average SAT total score at or above 950
                             Colleges with average SAT total score below 950

- Freshman class size: Colleges with 750 or more freshmen
                             Colleges with fewer than 750 freshmen.

RESULTS

The tables that follow present estimates of validity-related measures for each of the 10 years. The standard errors, which provide measures of the precision of these estimates, are shown in parentheses. The focus of the data interpretation is primarily on the linear trends provided by slope coefficients. These slopes refer to the linear regression lines characterizing year-to-year change. The size of a slope's standard error provides a measure of its precision. The absolute size of the slope is important, with slopes close to zero indicating little or no trend. Slopes that differ from zero by a few standard errors and have values representing meaningful change are interpreted as suggesting a trend. Slopes that differ from zero by less than a standard error and have values representing minimal change are interpreted as representing no systematic trend. Slopes that meet neither criterion are interpreted with caution. Multiplying the slope coefficient by nine provides an estimate of the amount of change in a measure for the 10-year period.

Table 4-2 shows the yearly averages of the within-college standard deviations for SAT-V, SAT-M, high school rank, high school GPA, and FGPA. The negative slopes for the within-college standard deviation estimates of SAT-V, SAT-M, and FGPA indicate lower standard deviations for the mid-1980s than for the mid-1970s. Little systematic change occurred in the standard deviations in either of the two measures of HSR. The reduction in the average standard deviation for SAT-V and SAT-M would be expected to result in lower correlations of SAT scores with FGPA. The increased homogeneity, with regard to SAT scores of the students within the colleges in this study, has not resulted from increased homogeneity in the total test-taking population. Based on

Table 4-2

Estimates of the Yearly Standard Deviations with
Associated Standard Errors and Slopes of the Best-Fitting Lines
of the Standard Deviations for Predictor and Criterion Variables

Year	SAT-V	SAT-M	High School Rank	High School GPA	FGPA
1976	89 (.91)	93(1.25)	7.5(.10)	.51(.01)	.73(.01)
1977	88 (.91)	91 (.89)	7.3(.13)	.52(.02)	.73(.01)
1978	86 (.86)	89 (.95)	7.4(.11)	.52(.02)	.71(.01)
1979	87(1.13)	90 (.98)	7.5(.14)	.53(.02)	.71(.01)
1980	86 (.95)	89(1.02)	7.5(.12)	.52(.02)	.70(.01)
1981	85 (.86)	88 (.99)	7.3(.16)	.50(.01)	.69(.01)
1982	85 (.85)	88(1.25)	7.5(.15)	.51(.01)	.68(.01)
1983	85 (.84)	89 (.86)	7.5(.12)	.52(.01)	.70(.01)
1984	86 (.99)	89 (.94)	7.4(.12)	.52(.02)	.71(.01)
1985	86 (.97)	89(1.20)	7.5(.15)	.51(.01)	.69(.01)
Slope	−.33	−.35	.002	−.000	−.004
S. E. Slope	.08	.11	.015	.002	.001

data from the College Board (1984, 1985), in the population of SAT examinees, the standard deviation of SAT-V increased from 110 to 111, while the standard deviation of SAT-M decreased from 120 to 119 between 1976 and 1985. The reduction of the standard deviations for the colleges in this study might be a result of different recruitment practices that identify a more homogeneous group of applicants, increased emphasis on the SAT in college admissions, or self-selection in the colleges that students apply to and choose to enroll in. Reductions in the standard deviation of FGPA could result in lower correlations of any variable with FGPA.

The yearly estimates for the correlations adjusted for restriction of range are presented in Table 4-3. The restriction of range adjustment controls for year-to-year changes in the distributions of SAT scores and high school records for the colleges being studied. The restriction-of-range adjustment also makes colleges with different degrees of selectivity more comparable, so that averages over colleges are more meaningful. The table indicates no systematic trends in the multiple correlation of SAT scores and HSR with FGPA or in the correlation of HSR with FGPA. The multiple SAT correlation has a negative slope of −.0040. SAT-M has a slope of −.0033, while SAT-V has a slope of −.0038. For nine of the 10 years, the SAT-M correlation with FGPA is slightly higher than the SAT-V correlation with FGPA.

Table 4-3

Estimates of the Yearly Correlations for SAT Scores and HSR
after Multivariate Correction for Restriction of Range of
SAT-V, SAT-M, and HSR with Associated Standard Errors and Slopes
of the Best-Fitting Lines for the Correlations

Year	SAT-V	SAT-M	Multiple SAT	HSR	Multiple Correlation
1976	.45(.01)	.46(.01)	.51(.01)	.57(.01)	.64(.01)
1977	.45(.01)	.46(.01)	.51(.01)	.57(.01)	.64(.01)
1978	.45(.01)	.46(.01)	.51(.01)	.56(.01)	.64(.01)
1979	.43(.01)	.44(.01)	.49(.01)	.56(.01)	.62(.01)
1980	.44(.01)	.46(.01)	.50(.01)	.55(.01)	.63(.01)
1981	.44(.01)	.44(.01)	.49(.01)	.58(.01)	.65(.01)
1982	.44(.01)	.45(.01)	.50(.01)	.58(.01)	.65(.01)
1983	.43(.01)	.44(.01)	.49(.01)	.56(.01)	.63(.01)
1984	.42(.01)	.44(.01)	.48(.01)	.56(.02)	.63(.01)
1985	.41(.01)	.42(.01)	.47(.01)	.58(.01)	.64(.01)
Slope	−.0038	−.0033	−.0040	−.0005	−.0010
S. E. Slope	.0013	.0010	.0012	.0015	.0011

Figure 4-1 indicates that after controlling for institutional variation in VSS studies and internal variation of SAT scores and high school records, the multiple SAT correlation with FGPA declines by .04 from 1976 to 1985, rather than the .08 indicated in Table 4-1. The figure also provides vertical line segments to indicate bounds of one standard error for each yearly estimate.

The repeated measures estimates of change after correcting for restriction of range produced estimates that show considerably less decline than those in Table 4-1. This finding suggests that a large part of the overall decline in correlations can be attributed to increased within-college restriction of range of the predictor variables and to differential college participation in the VSS.

Types of Colleges

Categorizing the colleges revealed that 81 were public and 141 were private, that 143 enrolled fewer than 750 freshmen and 79 enrolled at least 750, and that 119 colleges had mean SAT total scores of less than 950 and 108 had mean scores of at least 950 (five colleges had means in both categories in different years). The grouping of the data based on type of college control, freshman class size, and average total SAT score resulted in smaller numbers of colleges providing pairwise

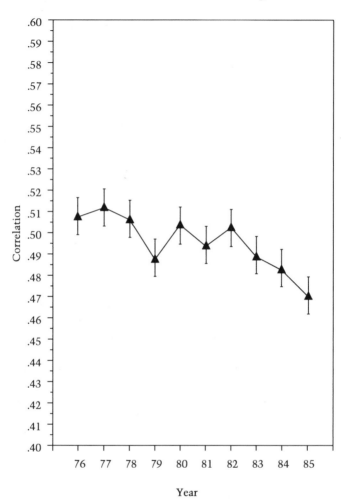

Figure 4-1

Ten–Year Estimates of the Correlation of SAT Scores with FGPA
Corrected for Restriction of Range

Year

estimates for the categories. As a result, the standard errors for estimates of both the slope and the yearly correlations are larger.

Table 4-4 provides the yearly estimates of the multiple correlation of HSGPA and SAT scores with FGPA corrected for restriction of range. Public colleges have the largest decline in the correlation with a slope of −.0030. However, this slope, like the other five, is not large enough to be judged different from zero.

Table 4-4

Yearly Estimates Within College Categories of Multiple Correlation of SAT Scores and HSR with FGPA after Multivariate Correction for Restriction of Range with Associated Standard Errors and Slopes of the Best-Fitting Lines for the Corrected Correlations

Year	Private Colleges	Public Colleges	Fewer than 750 Freshmen	750+ Freshmen	Less than 950 SAT V + M	950+ SAT V + M
1976	.65(.02)	.64(.01)	.66(.01)	.61(.02)	.67(.01)	.62(.02)
1977	.65(.01)	.62(.01)	.66(.01)	.61(.01)	.65(.01)	.63(.02)
1978	.65(.01)	.61(.01)	.66(.01)	.58(.02)	.64(.01)	.63(.01)
1979	.64(.01)	.59(.02)	.64(.01)	.58(.01)	.65(.01)	.59(.02)
1980	.64(.01)	.61(.02)	.65(.01)	.60(.02)	.64(.02)	.62(.01)
1981	.65(.01)	.63(.01)	.66(.01)	.61(.01)	.66(.01)	.63(.01)
1982	.66(.01)	.62(.02)	.66(.01)	.61(.02)	.66(.01)	.63(.01)
1983	.65(.01)	.59(.02)	.65(.01)	.59(.02)	.63(.02)	.62(.01)
1984	.63(.01)	.62(.02)	.65(.01)	.59(.02)	.65(.02)	.61(.02)
1985	.66(.01)	.58(.02)	.65(.01)	.60(.02)	.64(.02)	.63(.01)
Slope	−.0003	−.0030	−.0009	−.0012	−.0017	.0000
S.E.	.0014	.0016	.0013	.0017	.0016	.0019

Figure 4-2 displays the yearly estimates and accompanying standard error bands for the corrected correlation of the SAT with FGPA for public and private colleges. The figure shows that the correlation is higher for private colleges and that the difference between the average correlations has widened from 1976 to 1985. The slope of the line for private colleges (−.0024) is less than a third the slope for public colleges (−.0090). The large drop in the public college line in 1985 is due in part to the small sample sizes for that year's pairwise estimates. The standard error for public colleges in 1985 is twice as large as any other standard error associated with the estimates in the figure.

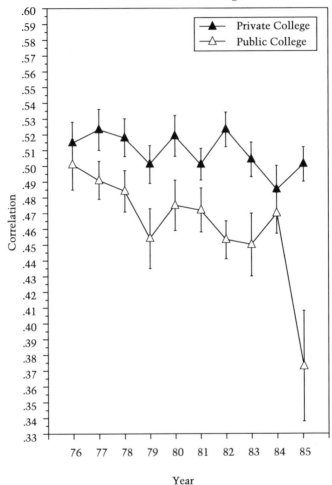

Figure 4-2

Ten–Year Estimates of the Correlation of SAT Scores with FGPA
Corrected for Restriction of Range for
Private and Public Colleges

Figure 4-3 displays the yearly SAT correlations according to the size
of the freshman class. Smaller colleges have consistently higher SAT
correlations, and there is less decline in the correlation for these
colleges, with the slope of their line (–.0032) being less than half the
slope for larger colleges (–.0066).

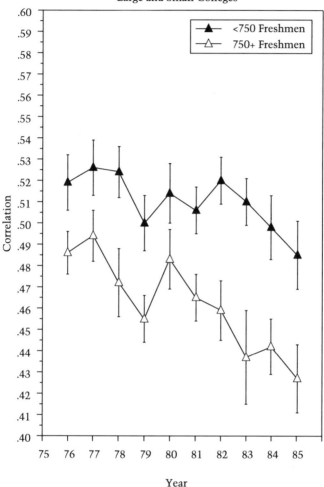

Figure 4-3

Ten–Year Estimates of the Correlation of SAT Scores with FGPA
Corrected for Restriction of Range for
Large and Small Colleges

Figure 4-4 displays the yearly SAT correlations for colleges grouped by average SAT total score. For nine of the 10 years studied, the multiple SAT correlation is higher for more selective colleges than for less selective ones. A sharper multiple correlation decline is also

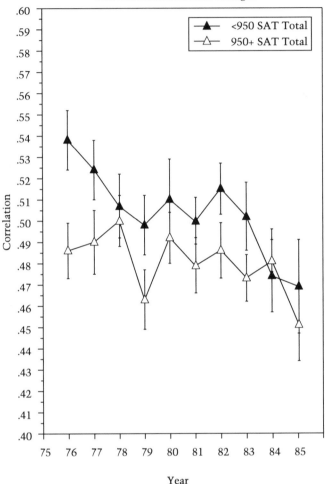

Figure 4-4

Ten–Year Estimates of the Correlation of SAT Scores with FGPA
Corrected for Restriction of Range for
More and Less Selective Colleges

present for less selective colleges. The slope of the line is –.0058 for them and –.0024 for more selective colleges.

The figures show that some decline in predictive validity occurred for all the categorizations of the data. It is clear that the declines varied among these nominal college characteristics, even though the characteristics have no obvious relationship to the factors that might cause a change in predictive validity. This finding suggests that further study of more relevant factors is needed to understand the observed declines more fully.

CONCLUSIONS

The analyses of colleges conducting multiple studies found that the estimates of change in the correlation of SAT scores with FGPA were smaller than the initial yearly averages indicated. Two factors appear to have exaggerated the amount of change. First, in the period from 1976 through 1985, students within colleges became more homogeneous with respect to SAT scores. Second, the decline resulted, in part, from differential college participation in VSS. Thus, when yearly average correlations were computed to account for these two spurious factors, the decline in the predictive validity became approximately half the decline suggested by the raw VSS yearly correlation averages.

The analyses based on college categorizations indicated that the decline in the correlation of SAT scores with FGPA was not limited to a specific type of college. The data suggest that private colleges, smaller colleges, and more selective colleges had smaller changes in predictive validity than public, larger, and less selective colleges. However, these data do not indicate why predictive validity changed from 1976 to 1985. Analyses of other characteristics, such as changes in curriculum or grading practices, would be more likely to help clarify why the relationship between SAT scores and FGPA has declined.

In conclusion, the repeated measures analyses detected a decline in the predictive validity of SAT scores. The degree to which the decline results from changes in the composition of first-year college students, changes in the SAT, changes in the courses contributing to FGPA, or changes in the real relationship of SAT scores with FGPA is uncertain. What is certain from these analyses is that the decline is not well characterized by simple comparisons of average correlations based on the total self-selected population of colleges participating in the VSS from one year to another.

CHAPTER 5

The Predictive Validity of the SAT, 1964 to 1988

LEONARD RAMIST & GLORIA WEISS*

Since 1964, the College Board's Validity Study Service (vss) has assisted colleges and universities in evaluating the validity of Scholastic Aptitude Test (SAT) scores, measures of high school performance, Achievement Tests, or other institutionally supplied variables as predictors of college performance for their enrolled freshman classes. Most colleges use freshman grade-point average (FGPA) analyses of all students, males and females. The analysis consists of least-squares regression estimates computed for the series of predictors.

Colleges initiate a validity study when they send data to ETS for processing. They may supply all predictor, criterion, and subgroup-identifying information. In addition, they may use Admissions Testing Program (ATP) test scores as well as sex-identifying and Student Descriptive Questionnaire (SDQ) data from the ATP database. SDQ data are used to identify subgroups or to define student-supplied measures, either high school grade-point average (HSGPA) or class rank. For validity studies on 1986 and 1987 classes, the ATP database was inaccessible because changes were being made to the system in order to accommodate the new SDQ and other new ATP file structures; consequently, the volume of studies on these classes was small.

The last major summary of SAT validity data, encompassing studies through the 1982 entering class, was published in *The College Board Technical Handbook for the Scholastic Aptitude Test and Achievement Tests*, Chapter VIII, "Predictive Validity of the ATP Tests" (Donlon, 1984a). The summary presented results uncorrected and corrected for restriction of range, overall and by college type, by student group, and by entering class year. Generally, colleges with

---

* The authors wish to acknowledge the work of Mitchell Rosen in designing and programming the computer analyses necessary to accomplish the pairwise matching of the validity study data. We are also indebted to Karen Carroll and Laura McCamley for refining and extending the analyses, to Bruce Kaplan for supplementary analysis, and to Nancy Feryok and Rick Morgan for creating the input data file. We are grateful for the excellent advice that we received from Charles Lewis and Warren Willingham, in addition to reviews by Ann Jungeblut, Bob Linn, Sam Messick, Lorrie Shepard, and Howard Wainer.

students who have a wide range of levels of academic preparedness (little restriction of the range of test scores) and who tend to take the same freshman courses show higher uncorrected correlations between the SAT and FGPA; colleges with students who have similar test scores and tend to take a wide variety of courses show lower uncorrected correlations. Correction for restriction of range eliminates the reduction in correlation due to lack of variability of test scores, but the reduction due to lack of criterion comparability cannot be corrected by any known method.

Average validity results for studies through the 1982 entering class showed no systematic change in the uncorrected and corrected correlations in the 1960s, a rapid increase for both in the early 1970s, and a gradual decline for both in the late 1970s that leveled off between 1981 and 1982. These comparisons, however, are tenuous, because the timing and frequency of validity studies are matters of college choice. The samples of colleges requesting studies differ from year to year and are not likely to be representative of the universe of institutions. A better method than merely averaging validity results is necessary to obtain estimates of changes in and levels of SAT validity.

METHODOLOGY

Pairwise Matching

A reasonable method of comparing correlations from one year to the next, or determining an overall correlation level, is to match earlier and later studies for the same institution. Morgan (1989a) used this method to obtain estimates of average yearly correlations for entering classes 1976-1985 (see Chapter 4).

This current study extends the Morgan analysis to encompass all validity studies in the VSS database that use SAT scores and a measure of high school record to predict FGPA, thereby increasing the number of yearly pairwise matches from 704 to 6,356, and examines other variables potentially related to validity. The analysis includes:

- Studies conducted on entering classes from 1964 to 1988 (plus a few studies on classes from 1960 to 1963);

- Combined results from studies in which males and females were analyzed separately;

- Studies using either a student-reported or a college-reported measure of high school record;

- Additional validity-related variables from each study;

- Additional college characteristics: percentage of students who are part-time, number of remedial services offered, percentage of degrees that are occupational, SAT standard deviation, and College Board geographical region;

- Separate analyses for males and females;

- Multivariate analysis of the factors related to major SAT validity trends.

Specifications for selecting studies from the VSS database were:

- Use of SAT scores and a measure of high school record to predict FGPA;

- At least 75 complete student records;

- Use of the analysis with the largest number of complete student records where multiple analyses were based on the same measure of high school record.

Matching by Years

The pairwise matching technique was used to make comparisons by years and by groups of years, hereafter referred to as periods. The yearly analysis covered entering classes from 1970 through 1988, grouping the classes of 1986-1988 together as one year and excluding classes prior to 1970 because of smaller numbers of participating colleges. This approach yielded 2,590 studies for 657 colleges, which generated 6,356 yearly matches (each match is in two years). Excluding years prior to 1970 eliminated 71 colleges that only did studies prior to 1970. Of the 657 colleges with studies of classes after 1969, 477 were included in the pairwise matching; 180 were excluded, because each had data for only one year.

Matching by Periods of Years

To make tabulation efficient and interpretation manageable, data for all colleges were combined by year, and the years were grouped into five periods: pre-1973; 1973-1976; 1977-1980; 1981-1984; and 1985-1988. Within each period, colleges conducting multiple studies over the years were combined using averages weighted by the number of student records.

Colleges may have used any of four measures of high school record: college-reported GPA, college-reported rank, student-reported GPA, and student-reported rank. Pairwise matching of periods without respect to the measure used yielded data for 728 colleges, of which

466 were in more than one period and generated 1,636 unique matches, ranging from 448 for 1985-88 to 794 for 1977-1980, an average of 3.5 per college. Results from these matches were used to generate validity data about the SAT.

To obtain validity data about HSGPA or class rank (with comparable SAT data), pairwise matching results were also obtained for each of the four high school measures separately and for the aggregate of the matches from one period to another. The aggregate includes only matches for which the same high school measure was used in both periods. This process yielded the following data:

Measure	Number of Colleges	Number of Colleges in More than One Period	Number of Matches
College-reported GPA	257	118	331
College-reported Rank	471	232	686
Student-reported GPA	213	74	166
Student-reported Rank	154	43	62
Total Across Measures	1,095*	467*	1,245*

*Some of the colleges had matches for more than one high school measure.

College Characteristics

Descriptive data on each college's programs, admissions requirements, and student body demographics, compiled for the College Board's Annual Survey of Colleges (1987), were appended to each validity study record. Morgan (1989a) reported on separate pairwise analyses of two characteristics from the annual survey — college control (public and private) and freshman class size — and on one obtained from the validity studies — SAT-Verbal plus -Mathematical mean score, which was used as an index of selectivity. The current study includes these plus four more characteristics from the annual survey — percentage of enrollment that is part-time, number of remedial services, percentage of degrees that are occupational, and College Board geographical region — as well as another characteristic, SAT standard deviation, from the validity studies. In all, these college characteristics generated 30 analyses, plus one on all colleges.

Data Elements

Each pairwise match, by year and by period of years, across all colleges and college characteristics, included all means, standard deviations, raw regression weights and intercept, standardized regression weights, uncorrected single and multiple correlations, SAT correlation increment, SAT partial correlation, correlations corrected for restriction of range, and standard error for the SAT-Verbal and SAT-Mathematical scores, a measure of high school record (HSR), and FGPA. Correlations were computed for all matches. FGPA means, standard deviations, and standard errors were computed only for FGPA on a 0-4 scale. Means, standard deviations, and raw regression weights were computed separately for each type of HSR — college-reported HSGPA (on a 0-4 scale), college-reported class rank (converted to a 20-80 scale; see Note 5-1), student-reported HSGPA (on a 0-4 scale), and student-reported class rank (converted to a 20-80 scale; see Note 5-1).

Correlations were corrected for restriction of range in order to make them comparable from year to year. Corrections were based on a model of three-variable restriction — HSR, SAT-Verbal score, and SAT-Mathematical score. The model assumes restriction of range either by student self-selection, in applying or in accepting an offer of enrollment, or by institutional selection, in offering admission. In order to estimate what the correlations between the predictors and the criterion would have been if all or a cross-section of the test-taking group had enrolled at the college, corrections for observed correlations based on enrolling data utilize best estimates of standard deviations of, and correlations among, the predictors for all SAT takers. (See Note 5-2.)

Multivariate Analysis of Major Correlation Trends

The data showed an increase in the matched corrected correlations of SAT scores with FGPA from the pre-1973 period to the 1973-1976 period, and a decrease from the 1973-1976 period to the 1985-1988 period. Two series of multiple regression analyses were undertaken to investigate these trends. The first series used the correlation increase from the pre-1973 period to the 1973-1976 period as the dependent variable. The second series used the slope of the correlation decline from the 1973-1976 period to the 1985-1988 period as the dependent variable. In both series, college control, freshman class size, percentage of students who are part-time, number of remedial courses, percentage of degrees that are occupational, and SAT-Verbal plus -Mathematical mean scores were used as independent variables.

OVERALL TRENDS

SAT Scores

Table 5-1 indicates the results of pairwise matching by period of the SAT-Verbal, SAT-Mathematical, and total SAT means and standard deviations for all 466 colleges with at least one match. There was a

Table 5-1

SAT Mean and Standard Deviation Trends by Period

Period	SAT *Means*			SAT *Standard Deviations*		
	SAT-V	SAT-M	SAT *Total*	SAT-V	SAT-M	SAT *Total*
Pre-1973	496	522	1018	82	83	140
1973-1976	466	502	968	88	91	156
1977-1980	454	492	946	87	90	153
1981-1984	450	489	939	85	89	150
1985-1988	456	497	953	85	88	149
*Slope (with SE) from Period to Period**						
1 Period: Pre-1973 to 1973-1976	–30(2)	–20(2)	–50	+6(1)	+8(1)	+16
3 Periods: 1973-1976 to 1985-1988	–4(1)	–2(1)	–6	–1(0)	–1(0)	–2

*The one-period slope is merely the difference between pre-1973 and 1973-1976 periods. The three-period slope is the slope through the four points, for periods 1973-1976, 1977-1980, 1981-1984, and 1985-1988. For this purpose, it treats the periods as if studies were uniformly distributed within each period. The standard errors of the slopes are in parentheses. For a description of how the standard errors were calculated, see Note 4-1.

decline of 50 total points (30 verbal and 20 mathematical) from pre-1973 to 1973-1976, a further decline of 29 points (16 verbal and 13 mathematical) to 1981-1984, and then a mild reversal of 14 points (6 verbal and 8 mathematical) to 1985-1988.

As SAT means decreased substantially from pre-1973 to 1973-1976, SAT standard deviations increased substantially, suggesting a reduction of restriction of range. Although SAT means continued to decline slowly after 1973-1976, SAT standard deviations lost about half of the gain that took place prior to 1973-1976, thereby suggesting increasing restriction of range.

High School Record

Table 5-2 displays the results of pairwise matching by period of HSR means and standard deviations, both college-reported and student-reported. Changes were minimal.

Freshman GPA

In determining the level and variability of FGPA over time, 25 of 466 colleges with matches were excluded because FGPA was not on a 0-4 scale. As displayed in Table 5-3, pairwise matching by period of FGPA means for the remaining 441 colleges shows a large increase from 2.43 for pre-1973 to 2.61 for 1973-1976. Coupled with the 49-point

Table 5-2

High School GPA and Rank Mean and Standard Deviation Trends by Period

| | High School Means | | | | High School Standard Deviations | | | |
| | College-Reported | | Student-Reported | | College-Reported | | Student-Reported | |
Period	GPA	Rank	GPA	Rank	GPA	Rank	GPA	Rank
Pre-1973	2.9	58	NA*	NA*	.52	7.2	NA*	NA*
1973-1976	3.0	58	3.1	58	.52	7.6	.53	5.3
1977-1980	3.0	58	3.1	58	.53	7.4	.51	5.4
1981-1984	3.0	58	3.1	57	.51	7.4	.50	5.5
1985-1988	3.0	58	3.1	57	.51	7.3	.49	5.7

*Slope (with SE) from
Period to Period*

1 Period: Pre-1973 to								
1973-1976	+0.1	0	NA*	NA*	.00	+0.4	NA*	NA*
	(0.0)	(0)	NA*	NA*	(.00)	(0.1)	NA*	NA*
3 Periods: 1973-1976 to								
1985-1988	0.0	0	0.0	0	.00	−0.1	−.01	+0.1
	(0.0)	(0)	(0.0)	(0)	(.00)	(0.0)	(.00)	(0.1)

Number of Colleges

With a Study	257	471	213	154	257	471	213	154
With a Match	118	232	74	43	118	232	74	43

*The number of colleges doing pre-1973 studies using SDQ high school measures
was too low because the SDQ was introduced in 1972.

SAT decrease from pre-1973 to 1973-1976 (Table 5-1), the data appear
to be strongly indicative of grade inflation. The declines in FGPA in 1977-
1980 and in 1981-1984 were consistent with continued SAT mean
declines. The leveling of FGPA in 1985-1988 (+.01) as SAT scores were
increasing (+14 points) may indicate a slight reversal of grade inflation.

Assuming grade inflation, one might expect restriction of range in
the criterion. Table 5-3 shows that this was not the case. The FGPA
standard deviation paralleled changes in both the FGPA mean and the
SAT standard deviation: increasing rapidly from pre-1973 to 1973-
1976, and decreasing slowly thereafter.

Table 5-3

Freshman GPA Trend by Period

Period	FGPA Mean	FGPA Standard Deviation
Pre-1973	2.43	.68
1973-1976	2.61	.71
1977-1980	2.57	.72
1981-1984	2.54	.71
1985-1988	2.55	.70
Slope (with SE) from Period to Period		
1 Period: Pre-1973 to 1973-1976	+.18(.01)	+.032 (.009)
3 Periods:1973-1976 to 1985-1988	−.02(.01)	−.004 (.003)

SAT Correlations with FGPA

The results of pairwise matching of uncorrected and corrected SAT correlations with FGPA are displayed in Table 5-4. The uncorrected correlations showed increases from pre-1973 to 1973-1976, especially for the SAT-Mathematical correlation, followed by gradual decreases thereafter. In the pre-1973 period, the uncorrected correlation for the SAT-Verbal score was .05 higher than the uncorrected correlation for the SAT-Mathematical score; in 1973-1976, the former increased by .05 and the latter increased by almost .10. In the periods thereafter, the correlations declined together; they were equal or .01 apart from 1973-1976 to 1985-1988. The uncorrected SAT multiple correlation increased from .38 in the pre-1973 period to .45 in 1973-1976, and then decreased by an average of .026 per period to .37 in 1985-1988.

The uncorrected SAT correlation increases and decreases shown in Table 5-4 are similar to the SAT standard deviation increases and decreases shown in Table 5-1. Typically, correlations do vary with the predictor's standard deviations. When colleges were classified by the average of their SAT-Verbal and -Mathematical standard deviations, the average uncorrected correlations in, for example, the 1985-1988 period, ranged from .33 for colleges with average standard deviations below 80 to .43 for colleges with average standard deviations of 100 or above.

Statistical correction eliminates the artificial reduction in correlation due to restriction of range and reveals a more accurate estimate of the trend. The three-variable correction described earlier in this chapter was applied to these correlations to determine the levels of correlation that would have been observed if a cross-section of the full test-taking population had enrolled at each college. After correction, in the period 1973-1976, for example, the six average corrected correlations for six categories of colleges — with average standard deviations below 80, 80 up to 85, 85 up to 90, 90 up to 95, 95 up to 100, and 100 or higher — were all .55 or .56, compared with uncorrected correlations ranging from .40 to .51.

The pairwise matching of corrected correlations by period in Table 5-4 and Figure 5-1 shows that the increase and decrease in average SAT standard deviations partially explained the increase and decrease in average SAT correlations with FGPA. A reduction of restriction of range explained 61 percent of the increase in average SAT multiple correlation from pre-1973 to 1973-1976; correction reduced the increase from +.070 to +.027. An increase in restriction of range explained 42 percent of the decrease in average SAT multiple correlations from 1973-1976 to 1985-1988; the slope from one four-year period to the next was –.026 without correction and –.015 with correction.

The average change in SAT corrected multiple correlation from pre-1973 to 1973-1976 was +.026. Changes for the 182 colleges with data in both periods ranged from –.27 to +.40; 59 percent of the colleges experienced increases, and 41 percent experienced decreases.

Table 5-4

SAT Correlations with FGPA by Period

Period	Uncorrected SAT Correlations			Corrected SAT Correlations		
	SAT-V	SAT-M	SAT Multiple	SAT-V	SAT-M	SAT Multiple
Pre-1973	.34	.29	.38	.49	.48	.53
1973-1976	.39	.38	.45	.50	.51	.56
1977-1980	.36	.36	.42	.49	.50	.55
1981-1984	.34	.34	.40	.48	.49	.53
1985-1988	.32	.31	.37	.46	.47	.52
Slope (with SE) from Period to Period						
1 Period: Pre-1973 to 1973-1976	+.054 (.007)	+.096 (.007)	+.070 (.007)	+.016 (.006)	+.034 (.007)	+.027 (.006)
3 Periods: 1973-1976 to 1985-1988	–.024 (.003)	–.024 (.003)	–.026 (.003)	–.013 (.003)	–.014 (.003)	–.015 (.002)

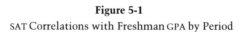

Figure 5-1

SAT Correlations with Freshman GPA by Period

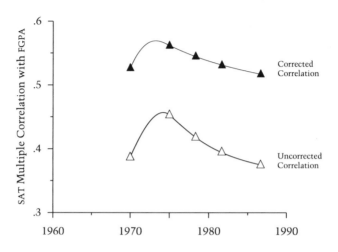

The slope per period from 1973-1976 to 1985-1988 indicates an average per-period change in SAT corrected multiple correlation of −.015. Changes for the 381 colleges with sufficient data to compute a slope from 1973-1976 to 1985-1988 ranged from −.40 to +.29; 62 percent of the colleges experienced decreases, and 38 percent experienced increases.

Table 5-5 displays the results of pairwise matching of corrected correlations by entering class year from 1970 to 1988, with 1986-1988 grouped. It shows that 1974 had the highest correlations (.51 for the verbal score, .53 for the mathematical score, and .57 for the multiple correlation) and 1986-1988 (treated as one year) had the lowest correlations (.44 for the verbal score, .43 for the mathematical score, and .49 for the multiple correlation).

HSR Correlations with FGPA

As described earlier in this chapter, studies were matched by type of HSR: college-reported GPA, college-reported rank, student-reported GPA, and student-reported rank. Table 5-6 shows results for pairwise matching by period of corrected correlations for each measure separately and of uncorrected and corrected correlations across all measures, with corresponding SAT data for the studies that were matched by type of HSR. The SAT correlations and slopes are identical to those in Table 5-4 (with only a very slight difference in one of the slopes), in

Table 5-5

Corrected SAT Correlations with FGPA by Year

Entering Class Year	Number of Matches	Corrected SAT Correlations with FGPA		
		Verbal	Mathematical	SAT Multiple
1970	455	.48	.46	.52
1971	165	.50	.51	.56
1972	543	.48	.47	.52
1973	455	.50	.50	.55
1974	603	.51	.53	.57
1975	637	.49	.51	.56
1976	798	.51	.51	.56
1977	848	.50	.51	.56
1978	994	.49	.50	.55
1979	1,064	.48	.49	.53
1980	1,101	.48	.50	.54
1981	1,034	.48	.49	.54
1982	1,058	.49	.50	.54
1983	957	.48	.49	.53
1984	955	.46	.48	.52
1985	862	.47	.47	.52
1986-1988	183	.44	.43	.49
TOTAL	12,712*			

Slope (with SE) Per Year

| 12 years: 1974 to 1986-1988 | | $-.004(.0009)$ | $-.005(.0009)$ | $-.005(.0010)$ |

*The number of unique matches is 6,356, because each match consists of two years.

which studies were matched pairwise by college without requiring a high school measure match.

Whereas SAT correlations showed very large increases and decreases in uncorrected correlations, and reduced but still fairly large increases and decreases in corrected correlations before and after the 1973-1976 period, HSR correlations showed little change. Uncorrected, they increased and then decreased slightly before and after 1973-1976. But after correction, the overall HSR correlation was the same (.58) from 1973-1976 to 1985-1988, while the SAT correlation declined from .56 to .52.

Generally, after correction, correlations for college-reported GPA were somewhat higher than those for college-reported rank, which in turn

Table 5-6

High School GPA or Rank Correlations with FGPA by Period

Period	Corrected for Each Measure				All Measures Combined			
	College-Reported		Student-Reported		HSR		SAT	
	GPA*	Rank	GPA	Rank	Uncorrected	Corrected*	Uncorrected	Corrected
Pre-1973	.61	.59	NA**	NA**	.48	.59	.38	.54
1973-1976	.62	.57	.55	.58	.50	.58	.45	.56
1977-1980	.60	.58	.52	.56	.49	.58	.42	.55
1981-1984	.61	.58	.52	.55	.48	.58	.40	.53
1985-1988	.62	.59	.53	.55	.48	.58	.38	.52
Slope (with SE) from Period to Period								
1 Period: Pre-1973 to 1973-1976	+.001 (.011)	-.018 (.009)	NA**	NA**	+.012 (.008)	-.013 (.001)	+.066 (.008)	+.020 (.008)
3 Periods:1973-1976 to 1985-1988	+.002 (.004)	+.004 (.003)	-.006 (.008)	-.009 (.012)	-.004 (.000)	+.002 (.001)	-.025 (.001)	-.014 (.001)
Number of Colleges								
With a Study	257	471	213	154	1,095	1,095	1,095	1,095
With a Match	118	232	74	43	423	423	423	423

* College-reported HSGPAs with a range other than 0-4 were not corrected for restriction of range (44 colleges with at least one match).

** The number of colleges doing pre-1973 studies using SDQ high school measures was too low because the SDQ was introduced in 1972.

were somewhat higher than correlations for student-reported rank, and correlations for student-reported GPA were the lowest. Correlations for both student-reported measures decreased slightly from 1973-1976 to 1985-88, but neither of the college-reported measures displayed this trend.

Proportional Contributions of SAT Scores and HSR to the Prediction of FGPA

Least-squares regression weights for SAT-Verbal and -Mathematical scores and HSR were standardized and pairwise matched by period. For each period, the absolute values of the three pairwise-matched weights were summed, and the proportion of each weight to the total was determined. The resulting proportional contributions of the predictors are displayed in Table 5-7.

Pre-1973 contributions were 59 percent for HSR and 41 percent for SAT scores, of which about two-thirds was for the SAT-Verbal score and one-third was for the SAT-Mathematical score. From pre-1973 to 1973-1976, a shift of 5 percentage points from HSR to the SAT-Mathematical score helped increase the contribution of the latter by half, from 14 to 21 percent, and the contribution of total SAT scores from 41 to 46 percent. Thereafter, there was a gradual shift from SAT scores back to HSR so that the 1981-84 contributions were the same as the pre-1973 contributions, and the 1985-1988 contributions were 61 percent for HSR and 39 percent for SAT scores. These trends are consistent with both uncorrected and corrected SAT correlations (Table 5-4).

Multiple Correlation of SAT Scores and HSR in Predicting FGPA, with Unique SAT Contribution

Table 5-8 displays uncorrected and corrected multiple correlations that were pairwise matched by period. It shows relatively small increases from pre-1973 to 1973-1976 and relatively small decreases from 1973-1976 to 1985-1988.

Table 5-7

Proportional Contributions of SAT Scores and HSR in the Prediction of FGPA by Period

Period	SAT-Verbal	SAT-Mathematical	HSR	Total SAT
Pre-1973	26%	14%	59%	41%
1973-1976	25%	21%	54%	46%
1977-1980	25%	20%	55%	45%
1981-1984	23%	18%	59%	41%
1985-1988	23%	16%	61%	39%

Two statistics that can be used to indicate the SAT's unique contribution to the prediction are:

- The SAT increment to the multiple correlation after HSR, and
- The partial correlation using the SAT to predict FGPA holding HSR constant.

These data were also pairwise matched by period and are displayed in Table 5-8, both uncorrected and corrected for restriction of range. They show the same pattern of increase from pre-1973 to 1973-1976 and decrease to 1985-1988 as correlations for SAT scores (Table 5-4).

Correlations Among Predictors and Criterion

In examining correlations among the SAT-Verbal score, the SAT-Mathematical score, HSR, and FGPA, all uncorrected correlations increased from pre-1973 to 1973-1976 and then decreased from 1973-1976 to 1985-1988. The three correlations involving the SAT-Mathematical score increased the most and were the only correlations that decreased less (.04–.07) than they had increased (.08–.10), so that 1985-1988 levels were higher than pre-1973 levels (by .03–.06), especially for the SAT-Mathematical correlation with HSR (.06).

Correlations for Females and Males

Of the 466 colleges with a match, 253 (55 percent) identified males for separate analysis in at least two periods and 259 (56 percent)

Table 5-8

SAT Contribution to Multiple Correlation of SAT Scores
and HSR in Predicting FGPA, by Period

Period	Multiple Correlation		Partial Correlation		SAT Increment	
	Uncorrected	Corrected	Uncorrected	Corrected	Uncorrected	Corrected
Pre-1973	.55	.66	.27	.35	.064	.067
1973-1976	.57	.66	.31	.38	.072	.080
1977-1980	.56	.65	.30	.37	.070	.075
1981-1984	.54	.64	.27	.34	.061	.066
1985-1988	.54	.64	.25	.32	.057	.060
Slope (with SE) from Period to Period						
1 Period: Pre-1973 to 1973-1976	+.022 (.007)	+.001 (.006)	+.039 (.01)	+.031 (.01)	+.008 (.005)	+.013 (.003)
3 Periods: 1973-1976 to 1985-1988	–.010 (.003)	–.005 (.003)	–.019 (.00)	–.020 (.00)	–.006 (.000)	–.007 (.000)

identified females. These colleges were the basis of pairwise matching by sex of corrected correlations in Table 5-9.

Over all periods, for the SAT, HSR, and the SAT increment, female correlations were substantially higher than male correlations. SAT correlations for females were quite stable across all periods. Males had most of the large increase in the SAT correlation from pre-1973 to 1973-1976 (+.044 compared to +.008 for females) and also most of the large decrease from 1973-1976 to 1985-1988 (slope of –.012 compared to –.006 for females).

For the HSR correlation, males were quite stable across all periods. Females had a large decrease in HSR correlation from pre-1973 to 1973-1976 (–.036 compared to +.002 for males) when the SAT correlation was increasing, and a large increase from 1973-1976 to 1985-1988 (slope of +.008 compared to +.002 for males) when the SAT correlation was decreasing. The SAT increment increased for both males (slope of +.022) and females (slope of +.009) from pre-1973 to 1973-1976 and decreased for both from 1973-1976 to 1985-1988 (slope of –.004 for males and –.005 for females).

COLLEGE CHARACTERISTICS

As described earlier in this chapter, separate pairwise matching analyses were performed for 30 categories of colleges based on control, freshman-class size, percentage of students attending part-time, number of remedial services, percentage of degrees that are

Table 5-9

Corrected Correlations with FGPA by Sex and by Period for
the SAT, HSR, and SAT Increment

Period	SAT		HSR		SAT Increment	
	Males	Females	Males	Females	Males	Females
Pre-1973	.51	.58	.55	.61	.064	.085
1973-1976	.55	.59	.56	.57	.086	.094
1977-1980	.52	.57	.55	.58	.072	.084
1981-1984	.53	.56	.56	.59	.072	.080
1985-1988	.51	.57	.55	.60	.072	.080
Slope (with SE) from Period to Period						
1 Period: Pre-1973 to 1973-1976	+.044 (.013)	+.008 (.009)	+.002 (.009)	–.036 (.009)	+.022 (.005)	+.009 (.005)
3 Periods: 1973-1976 to 1985-1988	–.012 (.006)	–.006 (.004)	–.002 (.003)	+.008 (.003)	–.004 (.002)	–.005 (.002)

Table 5-10

Changes in SAT Multiple Correlation with FGPA by College Characteristic, Corrected for Restriction of Range

	Number of Colleges with at Least One Match (Two or More Studies)*	Pre-1973 to 1973-1976 Change in Corrected SAT Correlation	1973-1976 to 1985-1988 Change in Corrected SAT Correlation	1985-1988 Corrected SAT Correlation
TOTAL	466	+.027	−.044	.52
CONTROL				
Four-year public	139	+.017	−.068	.48
Four-year private	270	+.027	−.025	.54
Other	37	+.019	−.086	.46
FRESHMAN-CLASS SIZE				
Fewer than 500	205	+.027	−.032	.54
500 up to 1500	164	+.037	−.061	.50
1500 or more	95	+.004	−.043	.49
PART-TIME STUDENTS				
Less than 1/3	325	+.023	−.029	.53
1/3 to 2/3	30	+.031	−.104	.45
2/3 or more	27	+.033	−.070	.48
NUMBER OF REMEDIAL SERVICES				
0-2	39	+.076	−.029	.56
3-5	216	+.009	−.019	.53
6-8	211	+.036	−.078	.49
OCCUPATIONAL DEGREES**				
Less than 10%	166	+.023	−.048	.50
10% to 50%	80	+.024	−.030	.53
50% or more	220	+.031	−.046	.52
SAT TOTAL MEAN				
Less than 850	90	+.058	−.103	.49
850 to 1050	286	+.028	−.051	.51
1050 or higher	90	+.008	+.011	.56
SAT AVERAGE STANDARD DEVIATION				
Less than 80	117	+.011	−.020	.54
80 up to 85	79	+.039	−.041	.52
85 up to 90	84	+.025	−.037	.52
90 up to 95	77	+.031	−.082	.47
95 up to 100	54	+.040	−.058	.50
100 or higher	55	+.039	−.059	.50
COLLEGE BOARD REGION				
New England	66	+.036	−.035	.49
Middle States	117	+.014	−.049	.51
South	115	+.024	−.037	.55
Midwest	87	+.032	−.044	.53
Southwest	27	+.050	−.108	.48
West	54	+.022	−.026	.50

* For some characteristics, especially percentage of part-time students, information was not available for some of the colleges.

** Occupational degrees are in agriculture, architecture and environmental design, business and management, business and office/marketing, communications, computer and information science, education, teacher education, engineering, engineering technologies, health science, allied health, home economics, law, library and archival science, military science, parks/recreation/public affairs, and trade/industrial.

occupational, SAT total mean, SAT average standard deviation, and College Board geographical region. Table 5-10 displays the pre-1973 to 1973-1976 change and the 1973-1976 to 1985-1988 change in the corrected SAT multiple correlation with FGPA for each of the categories of colleges.

Pre-1973 to 1973-1976: Increasing SAT Correlations

Across all colleges, there was an increase of .027 from pre-1973 to 1973-1976. The main discriminating characteristic appeared to be the SAT total mean; colleges with a mean below 850 (less selective colleges) increased by +.058, colleges with a mean from 850 to 1050 increased by +.028, and colleges with a mean of 1050 or higher (more selective colleges) increased by only +.008. Large colleges of 1,500 or more freshmen also showed very little increase, +.004, whereas medium-size and small colleges had above-average or average increases. The only regional changes that were atypical were the large increase of +.050 in the Southwest (with only 27 colleges with a match) and the small increase of +.014 in the Middle States region. Both the 39 colleges with few remedial services (0-2) and the 211 colleges with a large number of remedial services (6-8) had large increases (+.076 and +.036, respectively), but the 216 colleges with an average number of remedial services (3-5) had a small increase (+.009).

To determine which college-characteristic variables are directly related to the increase in corrected SAT correlation, the change in corrected SAT correlation was used as the dependent variable in a stepwise multiple-regression analysis. Independent variables were control, freshman-class size, proportion of students part-time, number of remedial services, percentage of degrees that are occupational, and SAT total mean. (See Note 5-3.)

The only variable contributing at least .01 to the multiple correlation was the SAT total mean. The correlation between the SAT total mean and the corrected correlation increase was −.11. Low remediation and small freshman-class size had a marginal effect, raising the multiple correlation to .16.

1973-1976 to 1985-1988: Decreasing SAT Correlations

As shown in Table 5-10, across all colleges there was a corrected SAT correlation decline of −.044 from 1973-1976 to 1985-1988. As with the SAT correlation increase from pre-1973 to 1973-1976, the main discriminating characteristic appeared to be the SAT total mean. Colleges with a mean below 850 (less selective colleges) had a decline of –.103; colleges with a mean from 850 to 1050 declined –.051; and colleges with a mean of 1050 or higher (more selective colleges) were the only group with an increase, which was +.011, greater than the increase from pre-1973 to 1973-1976 (+.008).

Four-year private colleges declined less (–.025) than four-year public colleges (–.068). Colleges with medium and high levels of part-time students declined more (–.104 and –.070, respectively) than colleges with lower part-time percentages (–.029). The decline of –.108 for Southwestern colleges is likely due both to the small number of colleges with a match (27) and to their relatively low SAT mean. The 54 colleges in the West declined by only –.026. Colleges in all other regions declined by between –.035 and –.049.

The highest 1985-1988 SAT correlation level of .56 was at more selective colleges and at colleges offering few remedial services. The lowest level (.45) was at colleges with between one-third and two-thirds part-time students.

To determine which college-characteristic variables are directly related to the decrease in corrected SAT correlation, the three-period slope of corrected SAT correlations was used as the dependent variable in a stepwise multiple-regression analysis. Analysis of the SAT correlation decrease was based on 388 colleges that had data in at least two of the four periods (1973-1976, 1977-1980, 1981-1984, and 1985-1988).

Beyond observing that the SAT correlation increase from pre-1973 to 1973-1976 predicts the SAT correlation decrease from 1973-1976 to 1985-1988, and vice versa, the analysis of college characteristics shows that SAT mean level is the most important predictor of both the correlation increase and the correlation decrease. As with the correlation increase, the only variable contributing at least .01 to the multiple correlation was the SAT total mean. Whereas the correlation was –.11 between the SAT total mean and the corrected correlation increase, it was +.11 between the mean and the correlation decrease. Low percentage of occupational degrees and low percentage of part-time students had marginal effects, raising the correlation to .15. Note that when limited to the 151 colleges with sufficient data to calculate both a pre-1973 to 1973-1976 change and a 1973-1976 to 1985-1988 slope, the pre-1973 to 1973-1976 change was the best predictor of the 1973-1976 to 1985-1988 slope, yielding a correlation of –.43. (See Note 5-4.) For this same group of colleges, the correlation for the SAT mean in predicting the 1973-1976 to 1985-1988 slope was +.28.

LESS SELECTIVE AND MORE SELECTIVE COLLEGES

Because they differ in validity trends, and because the SAT mean was the variable most related to both the increase and the decrease in SAT correlation, it is useful to examine more closely the contrasting trends for the 90 more selective colleges (total SAT score of 1050 or higher) and the 90 less selective colleges (total SAT score below 850).

SAT Scores

For both less selective and more selective colleges, there was a decline in the SAT total mean from pre-1973 to 1973-1976 (59 and 52 points, respectively). After 1973-1976, the means went in different directions; less selective colleges experienced an additional decline (–37), while more selective colleges experienced an increase (+9) and thereby offset about one-sixth of the earlier decline. Across all years, less selective colleges experienced declines of similar magnitude between verbal (–51) and mathematical (–45) scores, but for more selective colleges the mathematical mean decline (–12) was much smaller than the verbal mean decline (–31).

Both less selective and more selective colleges experienced increasing SAT standard deviations from pre-1973 to 1973-1976 (+8 and +11, respectively) and decreasing SAT standard deviations from 1973-1976 to 1985-1988 (-6 and -11, respectively). The 1985-1988 SAT standard deviation is somewhat higher for less selective colleges (146) than for more selective colleges (135).

Freshman GPA

From pre-1973 to 1973-1976, concurrent with sharply reduced SAT scores, the increase in mean FGPAS was evidence of grade inflation at both less selective and more selective colleges (both +.17). After 1973-1976, grades were more consistent with the changes in SAT score levels — sharply lower at less selective colleges (–.16) and higher at more selective colleges (+.03). The 1985-1988 FGPA standard deviation is higher for less selective colleges (.78) than for more selective colleges (.60).

SAT Correlations with FGPA

In pre-1973 studies, the corrected SAT correlation with FGPA was the same (.54) for both less selective and more selective colleges. For less selective colleges, it increased .06 from pre-1973 (.54) to 1973-1976 (.60) and became the highest of any group based on selectivity, but from then to 1985-1988, it decreased .10 (to .49 after rounding) and became the lowest of any group based on selectivity. For more selective colleges, the corrected SAT correlation with FGPA increased slightly, from .54 in the pre-1973 and 1973-1976 periods to .56 in 1977-1980 and since then.

HSR Correlations with FGPA

In pre-1973 studies, the corrected HSR correlation with FGPA also was the same (.58) for both less selective and more selective colleges. For less selective colleges, HSR displayed more attenuated corrected correlation movements (no change up to 1973-1976 and –.05 since 1973-1976) compared to the SAT (+.06 to 1973-1976 and –.10 since then). The substantial decline of both correlations at less selective colleges implies that the FGPA criterion is changing at these colleges. For more selective colleges, while the SAT corrected correlation remained relatively steady (at .54–.56), the HSR corrected correlation decreased by .04 from pre-1973 to 1973-1976 and then increased by .04 from 1973-1976 to 1985-1988.

Unique SAT Contribution to Prediction

The corrected SAT increment and the partial correlation increased more from pre-1973 to 1973-1976 and decreased more from 1973-1976 to 1985-1988 for less selective colleges. For them, the 1985-1988 levels are lower (.066 SAT increment and .32 partial correlation) than the pre-1973 levels (.067 and .34). For more selective colleges, the 1985-1988 levels are higher (.076 SAT increment and .37 partial correlation) than the pre-1973 levels (.072 and .35).

Correlations Among Predictors and the Criterion

SAT scores have become more correlated with HSR over time for the students of less selective colleges (by 1985-1988, .31 for the verbal score and .33 for the mathematical score) than for the students of more selective colleges (.21 and .27, respectively). SAT-Verbal and –Mathematical scores also have become increasingly more correlated with each other over time for the students of less selective colleges (in 1985-1988, .53) than for more selective colleges (.39).

SUMMARY

A pairwise matching of SAT validity studies was done for 728 colleges that had performed studies through the Validity Study Service on entering classes from 1964 to 1988. Matches were done by years, generating 6,356 unique matches for 477 colleges, and by periods of years, generating 1,636 unique matches for 466 colleges.

The overall trend clearly indicates two mirror-image occurrences:

increasing SAT correlations from pre-1973 (1964-1972) to 1973-1976, and decreasing SAT correlations from 1973-1976 to 1985-88.

Pre-1973 to 1973-1976: Increasing SAT Correlations

1. The SAT *total mean decreased* 50 points, 30 on the verbal score and 20 on the mathematical score, which was about one-third of a standard deviation (Table 5-1).

2. The SAT *total standard deviation increased* 16 points, almost a one-quarter increase in variance, suggesting a substantial reduction in restriction of range (Table 5-1).

3. In contrast to the SAT, for college-reported measures of HSR, there was *no decline in means* for SAT takers and *little change in standard deviations* (Table 5-2).

4. There was evidence of *grade inflation:* While the SAT mean decreased by 50 points, the FGPA mean increased by almost one-fifth of a grade, more than one-quarter of a standard deviation (Table 5-3).

5. Higher freshman grades *increased* rather than restricted the *variability of grades;* the FGPA standard deviation increased by .03, which was almost a one-tenth increase in variance, proportionally smaller than the increase in SAT variance (Table 5-3).

6. *Uncorrected SAT correlations* with FGPA *increased,* especially for the mathematical score: .054 for the verbal score, .096 for the mathematical score, and .070 for the SAT multiple correlation (Table 5-4 and Figure 5-1).

7. Because of the increase in the variability of SAT scores at a typical college, *correction for restriction of range eliminated most of the correlation increase* — 70 percent for the verbal score, 65 percent for the mathematical score, and *61 percent for the SAT multiple correlation* — leaving corrected correlation increases of .016 for the verbal score, .034 for the mathematical score, and .027 for the SAT multiple correlation (Table 5-4).

8. The overall uncorrected *HSR correlation* with FGPA increased (by .012), but after correction for restriction of range *decreased* (by .013, as shown in Table 5-6).

9. While the proportional contribution of the SAT-Verbal score to the optimal prediction equation decreased (from 26 to 25 percent), the *contribution of the SAT-Mathematical score increased* by half

(from 14 to 21 percent) and the contribution of HSR decreased (from 59 to 54 percent, as shown in Table 5-7).

10. The *SAT increment* to prediction *increased* by .008 uncorrected and .013 corrected, and the *partial correlation of the SAT* (for a given HSR) *increased* by .04 uncorrected and .03 corrected (Table 5-8).

11. Averaging the changes for all colleges, *all correlations among the SAT scores, HSR, and FGPA increased,* but the increases were greatest (+.08 to +.10) for the correlations involving the SAT-Mathematical score, and larger for less selective colleges (+.03 to +.13) than for more selective colleges (−.04 to +.06).

12. The *increase in corrected SAT correlation* was *greater for males* (+.04) than for females (+.01), while the corrected HSR correlation decreased for females (−.04) compared with a small increase for males (+.01, as shown in Table 5-9).

13. The only *college characteristic* significantly *related to the SAT correlation increase* was *low SAT mean;* the corrected SAT correlation increased by .06 for less selective colleges, but only by .01 for more selective colleges (Table 5-10).

1973-76 to 1985-1988: Decreasing SAT Correlations

1. From 1973-1976 to 1981-1984, the *SAT total mean decreased* 29 points, 16 on the verbal scale and 13 on the mathematical scale, but then reversed itself and recouped 14 (6 verbal and 8 mathematical) of the 29 points from 1981-1984 to 1985-1988; the net decline was 15 points (10 verbal and 5 mathematical), about one-tenth of a standard deviation (Table 5-1).

2. *SAT total standard deviation decreased* 7 points, and the individual verbal and mathematical standard deviations each decreased 3 points; the standard deviation declined when the mean decreased and also when the mean increased (Table 5-1).

3. While the SAT mean decreased and then increased and the SAT standard deviation decreased, *the HSR means and standard deviations* of SAT takers *remained stable* (Table 5-2).

4. The *FGPA mean decrease* of .06 was consistent with the SAT mean decrease: Both were about one-tenth of a standard deviation (Table 5-3). More selective colleges did not experience a decrease in the mean FGPA.

5. The *FGPA* *standard* *deviation* *decreased* very slightly, by .01 (Table 5-3).

6. *Uncorrected* *SAT* *correlations* with *FGPA* *decreased* by .07 for the verbal score, by .07 for the mathematical score, and by .08 for the multiple correlation (Table 5-4 and Figure 5-1).

7. Because the variability of SAT scores at a typical college decreased, *correction for restriction of range eliminated about half of the correlation decrease* — 43 percent for the verbal score, 43 percent for the mathematical score, and *50 percent for the* *SAT* *multiple correlation* — leaving corrected correlation decreases of .04 for the verbal score, the mathematical score, and the SAT multiple correlation (Table 5-4). For more selective colleges, correction eliminated all of the uncorrected SAT correlation decrease (−.03) and converted the change to a small increase (+.01).

8. The overall uncorrected *HSR correlation* with *FGPA* decreased by .02, but after correction for restriction of range, it *was unchanged* (Table 5-6).

9. The *proportional contribution of HSR* to the optimal prediction equation *increased* from 54 to 61 percent, while the contribution of the SAT-Verbal score decreased from 25 to 23 percent and the contribution of the SAT-Mathematical score decreased from 21 to 16 percent, making the verbal-to-mathematical ratio of weights 1.4 in 1985-1988, the highest it has been since it was sharply reduced from 1.9 to 1.2 in the 1973-1976 period (Table 5-7).

10. The *SAT increment* to prediction *decreased* by .015 uncorrected and by .020 corrected, and the *partial correlation decreased* by .06 uncorrected and corrected (Table 5-8).

11. Averaging the changes for all colleges, *all correlations among the* *SAT scores, HSR, and FGPA decreased.*

12. The *decrease in corrected SAT correlation* was *twice as great for males* (−.04) as for females (−.02), and only for females was there an increase (+.03) in corrected HSR correlation (compared with −.01 for males, as shown in Table 5-9).

13. The only *college characteristic* significantly related to the SAT *correlation decrease* was *low SAT means;* the corrected SAT correlation decreased by −.10 for less selective colleges, but increased by +.01 for more selective colleges (Table 5-10).

Overall Findings

The results showed a sharp increase in SAT correlations with FGPA from the pre-1973 period to the 1973-1976 period, and a slower and steady decrease from 1973-1976 to 1985-1988. From the pre-1973 period to the 1973-1976 period, the average corrected correlation increase was .03 (with 59 percent of the colleges increasing). Subsequently, the average corrected correlation decrease was .04 (with 62 percent of the colleges decreasing). Both the increase and the decrease were substantially greater for males than for females. The increase in correlation from pre-1973 to 1973-1976 for the mathematical score greatly exceeded the increase for the verbal score and placed the two correlations at about the same level in 1973-1976; from then on, they declined equally. HSR experienced a much smaller corresponding correlation increase and decrease, both of which were eliminated completely and slightly reversed after correction for restriction of range. The proportional contribution of the least-squares weights for SAT scores increased from 41 percent prior to 1973 to 46 percent in 1973-1976, and then decreased to 39 percent in 1985-1988.

The college characteristic that was the best predictor of change in the SAT correlation was the SAT mean level. Colleges with an SAT mean below 850 (the bottom quintile) averaged a larger SAT correlation increase from pre-1973 to 1973-1976 (+.06), compared with no change for the HSR correlation, and also a larger SAT correlation decrease from 1973-1976 to 1985-1988 (–.10), compared with a decrease of .05 for the HSR correlation. For colleges with an SAT mean of 1050 or higher (the top quintile), the corrected SAT correlation remained essentially unchanged at about .55 throughout the 25-year period, while the corrected HSR correlation declined by .04 from pre-1973 (.58) to 1973-1976 (.54) and then increased by .04 from 1973-1976 to 1985-1988 (.58).

CHAPTER 6

Institutional Differences in Prediction Trends

WARREN W. WILLINGHAM & CHARLES LEWIS*

Trends in the correlation of SAT scores with freshman grade-point average (FGPA) vary from college to college. Whereas this correlation has declined on average — about .04 to .05 from 1974 through the mid-1980s — one college in three showed an increase (Ramist & Weiss, Chapter 5). Do such variations represent real differences in the trends in validity coefficients from college to college or simply random fluctuations around a general tendency to decline?

The question is significant for several reasons. First, if institutional differences in trend are real, then the sample of institutions available for study becomes an important consideration in estimating prediction trends. Second, appreciation of the role of institutional variations may help in understanding the underlying reason for prediction trends — in particular, whether such trends are better conceived as changes in test validity or in criterion predictability. An absence of significant institutional differences in trend would suggest that changes in the predictor had caused its predictive validity to drift downward, though some colleges could show an increase by chance. On the other hand, significant institutional differences in trends would be more readily explained by changes in the sample of students or in the criterion than by changes in the predictor — mainly because the predictor is standard for all students while the sample and the criterion can easily vary from college to college and year to year. All correlations in this study were corrected for range restriction in order to control for a major source of sample differences.

Thus, a pattern of significant college differences could speak to both the locus and the cause of changes in validity coefficients. A third and less obvious reason for examining such institutional differences is methodological. If trends do vary from college to college, then trend analyses can yield different results, depending on how one weights multiple validity studies from the same college.

In the course of the research reported in this volume, two lines of evidence pointed to the likelihood of important institutional differ-

* The authors express appreciation to Leonard Ramist and Gloria Weiss for use of the VSS database prepared for their analyses reported in Chapter 5.

ences in these correlational trends. The study by Morgan (1989a, and Chapter 4 of this volume) and the subsequent study by Ramist and Weiss (Chapter 5) both found that some types of institutions showed more change in validity coefficients than others. Furthermore, prediction trends in individual institutions have proven to be predictable to a surprising degree in some analyses (see Chapter 12). The purpose of the present study was to investigate directly whether there are reliable institutional differences in prediction trends. This analysis focused upon the years 1974 to 1988 because there were insufficient data for effective analyses of the reliability of institutional trends in the early years of VSS. Moreover, the recent period is of more interest because of the consistent trend.

We are concerned with several related questions: Is the *prediction trend* (i.e., whether validity coefficients are going up or down) a consistent characteristic of a college? What factors determine whether the college prediction trend is stable or unstable? How much do validity coefficients change from year to year, compared to longer periods? Does a change in the SAT validity coefficient at a given college tend to be accompanied by a change in the validity coefficient for high school record (HSR)? We take up these questions first. Finding considerable evidence of real institutional differences, we examine in a subsequent section the possible methodological implications for trend analysis.

CONSISTENCY OF INSTITUTIONAL PREDICTION TRENDS

Figure 6-1 shows an illustrative series of six validity coefficients for a given college. The least-squares line through the six points describes the *prediction trend* for this college. *Slope t* of that line provides an index of the extent to which the validity coefficient at this college is increasing or decreasing (e.g., for a college with validity coefficients of .45 and .45 in successive years, slope t = 0, no change). There are two useful ways of evaluating the consistency of such institutional prediction trends.

One indication of consistent institutional trends is given by the reliability of slope t; i.e., the extent to which slope t differentiates among institutions — validity going up in some, down in others. A second, complementary indicator would be the stability of slope t for a given institution. The reliability of slope t is the first interest because it is more directly relevant to understanding the nature of changes in validity coefficients. But the stability of slope t is also interesting, partly because it heavily influences the reliability of slope t, and partly because the institution, the user of validity information, is especially concerned with the future course of its own trend line.

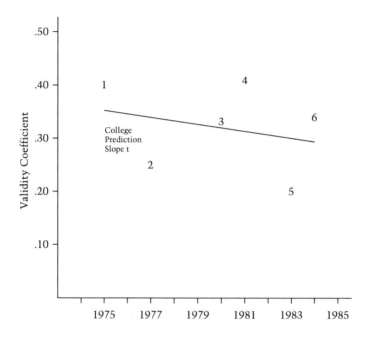

Figure 6-1

Illustration of a College Prediction Slope t Defined
by Six Validity Studies over 10 Years

Reliability of the Prediction Trend

Data used in the analyses reported here came from the Ramist-Weiss
database developed from results of studies carried out through the
Validity Study Service (VSS) and described in Chapter 5. Split-half
reliability estimates for the institutional trends during this period
were based upon the correlation between two slopes computed
separately for the odd- and even-numbered validity studies of each
college. In Figure 6-1, for example, the two split-half slopes, for
purposes of estimating reliability, would be based upon studies 1,3,5
and studies 2,4,6. Accordingly, the sample of institutions was
restricted to those that: (a) did at least four studies during this period,
and (b) used a consistent measure of high school performance in
those studies. Of 574 colleges that did VSS studies in these years, 192
met both these criteria. For this group of colleges, SAT validity coefficients increased for one-third and decreased for two-thirds during
this period. The colleges did an average of 5.9 studies. All correlations were corrected for restriction of range of SAT-V, SAT-M, and HSR.

Split-half correlations (in parentheses) and Spearman-Brown reliabilities for the slopes of the predictors of interest were:

- SAT (multiple correlations for V,M)   (.19)   .32
- HSR   (.21)   .34
- SAT and HSR   (.27)   .43

These results indicate, in each case, substantial institutional differences in the prediction trends for this group of 192 colleges in these years. It is impossible to know what results might have been obtained in the large group of colleges that did only one or two validity studies. Also, the pattern of studies varied widely among the 192 colleges that are included. The numbers of studies ranged from four to 13; the period over which they were done ranged from four to 15 years. What level of reliability might one expect if each college did a study each year? Is slope t likely to be a more reliable institutional characteristic over a limited period of time while conditions remain reasonably constant, or over a longer period of time when the prediction trend can become better anchored? How important is the number of studies to the reliability of slope t?

Some additional analyses were suggestive. When the span of years was restricted to either four or six, the split-half reliability of the slope t for SAT coefficients tended to be smaller than that based on all 192 colleges over the full period (.27 vs. .32). This result implies that a wider span of years yields a more reliable slope. A different method of estimating the reliability of slope t may shed some light on the effect of a larger number of studies. In the usual formula

$$\text{Reliability} = 1 - (\text{Error Variance})/\text{Total Variance} \tag{1}$$

the total variance of the slope t is

$$\text{Total Var}(t) = \sum (t_i - \Sigma t_i / N)^2 / N \tag{2}$$

The error component of (1) is represented by the error variance of institutional slopes averaged across institutions; that is

$$\text{Error Var}(t) = \Sigma se^2(t_i) / N \tag{3}$$

So computed, the reliability of slope t for the SAT was .35, similar to the stepped-up split-half estimate of .32. But when the error variance was estimated by pooling the squared deviations from slopes for each institution, the reliability increased to .42. Because this method of computation places weight on institutional data in proportion to the number of studies done by each, the implication of this result is that more validity studies should yield a slope t of higher reliability. A more elementary reason for such a relationship is illustrated by

$$se^2(t) = \frac{\sigma_e^2}{(K)s_y^2} \tag{4}$$

which shows the standard error of slope t to vary directly with the dispersion of the points around the line as in Figure 6-1 (σ_e^2), and inversely with the number of studies (K) and the variance of the years (s_y^2). Hence, the more studies colleges conduct over longer time spans, the smaller the standard errors of the slopes and the higher the reliability.

It is almost impossible with the data in hand to determine empirically what effect the number of studies and the span of years might have on reliability of college trends, i.e., the slopes. Number of studies is confounded with span of years, and the available data matrix of colleges by years is very incomplete. Those problems can be largely surmounted, however, by evaluating what effect the three factors on the right side of equation 4 have on the stability of the slope for individual colleges.

Stability of the Prediction Trend

Stability of slope t refers to the consistency of the prediction trend line for an individual institution. It is conveniently indexed by the standard error of the line in Figure 6-1 that has an institutional slope t_i. Since the average of these squared standard errors constitutes the error term (equation 3 above) in the computation of slope reliability, the two are intimately related. Reliability is a characteristic of a set of colleges, while slope stability and its determinants — number of studies, years, class size — vary from college to college. For any given amount of diversity among colleges as to prediction trends, greater slope stability will yield higher slope reliability.

The institution has a practical interest in slope stability. If the results of its validity studies show an uncharacteristic change over time, at what point does that change cease being a random fluctuation and become a trend worth closer examination? A comparison of the observed prediction slope with its standard error can inform that interest. How often should institutions do validity studies in order to be assured that reasonably stable slopes will correctly signal significant trends in prediction? This brings us back to the question of what determines slope stability.

A great advantage of slope stability as an indicator of consistency in validity trends is that stability (i.e., the inverse of the standard error of t_i) can be estimated for individual institutions and correlated with other measures that may affect it. As we have noted, the three measures one would assume to have a bearing on se t_i are the number of studies an institution has done, the spread (i.e., variance) of years over which the studies were done, and the size of the samples (i.e., freshman classes). An examination of plots indicated that these measures, expressed in $\log_e$ form, were linearly and inversely related to $\log_e$ se t_i, and hence directly related to slope stability.

The results of multiple regression analyses for the three criteria of principal interest (i.e., slopes for different predictors) are shown in Table 6-1. In each case, the stability of the slope is highly predictable. The three measures show a similar pattern of correlations for the different slopes. The dominant factor is the degree to which the slope is anchored, i.e., the variance of the yearly distribution of studies. Since this measure is expressed in $\log_e$ form, one might wonder whether, with an increasing range of years, the S.E. of the slope might show some tendency to increase — possibly because slopes change direction in time. While that would seem to be a reasonable assumption, closer analysis did not reveal any such tendency. (See Note 6-1.) In any event, an implication of these findings is that a

Table 6-1

Determinants of the Stability of Institutional Prediction Slopes (N=192)

	Dependent Variable — Standard Error of Slope for Validity Coefficients Based on:		
	HSR	SAT(V,M)	HSR, SAT
	(r) wt.	(r) wt.	(r) wt.
Variable:*			
Number of Validity Studies	(.32) .02	(.38) .15	(.32) .03
Variance of Years	(.64) .62	(.65) .59	(.62) .61
Size of Class	(.27) .19	(.43) .33	(.29) .21
Multiple Correlation	.67	.74	.66

*All variables expressed as $\log_e$. All r's and weights negative, signs omitted.

146

continuing program of validity studies every few years would be a more cost-effective way for a college to monitor prediction trends than annual studies would be.

With this basis for understanding the stability of institutional prediction slopes, it becomes possible to estimate what reliability of slopes might be expected under different conditions. For example, if one assumes that the observed diversity among institutional slopes is a constant (in this case, an estimated true slope standard deviation of about .01), then reliability would be .17 for a group of small colleges (classes of 300) that did four studies in four years. The slope reliability would be .85 for a group of large colleges (classes of 1,000) that did 10 studies in 10 years. Corresponding figures for HSR would be .14 and .74. (See Note 6-2.)

Relationships among Prediction Slopes

The foregoing analysis of the reliability and stability of prediction slopes provides discriminant evidence of institutional differences regarding changes in predictability, that is, evidence that the slopes actually differ. Other studies have shown some association of prediction slopes with nominal characteristics of colleges, like size and selectivity (Morgan, Chapter 4; Ramist & Weiss, Chapter 5), and also with educational dynamics, like diversity of course selection and proportion of freshmen placed in special courses (Ramist, Lewis, & McCamley, Chapter 12). Such findings can be viewed as convergent evidence of institutional differences. Another form of convergent evidence would be the relationship among prediction slopes based upon different predictors. In these 192 colleges the correlations were as follows for slopes based on HSR, SAT-V,M, and all three variables (3 Var.):

- Slope (HSR) vs. Slope (SAT) — .55
- Slope (HSR) vs. Slope (3 Var.) — .89
- Slope (SAT) vs. Slope (3 Var.) — .86

These correlations are strikingly high, though the .86 and .89 involve a part-whole dependency that is difficult to evaluate. In a sense, the correlation of .55 between the slopes for HSR and SAT is even more surprising, because it presents the anomaly of a correlation between two measures being substantially greater than the reliability of either (.34 and .32, respectively). There is no reason to expect any relationship between these two slopes if prediction trends are due to changes in either predictor. On the other hand, if prediction trends are due to changes in the criterion, such changes would have a similar effect on the validity of both HSR and SAT. This dependency would build in a relationship between the two prediction slopes.

There are two types of dependency. One is real in the sense that any factors that work over time to increase or decrease the accuracy or predictability of the criterion will likely affect the validity of both high school record (HSR) and SAT and drive up the correlation between their prediction slopes. Another type of dependency is correlated error. The reason the .55 correlation between the two prediction slopes is higher than their reliabilities is that the correlation includes correlated error and the reliabilities do not. This comes about as follows.

In deriving the reliability estimates, all yearly deviations in validity coefficients are treated as error. As we shall see, there is a substantial amount of such yearly variation, some random and some nonrandom. To the extent that those deviations are correlated for HSR and SAT, the resulting correlated error raises the correlation between the prediction slopes for HSR and SAT. If, in effect, we remove the correlated error and correct for unreliability, the resulting "true" correlation is .87 — a more accurate representation of the underlying relationship between the trend in HSR validity and the trend in SAT validity. (See Note 6-3.)

This result indicates that changes in the predictive validity of HSR and SAT go hand in hand and are tightly linked through the criterion, FGPA. It would seem reasonable to assume that this very strong relationship in the validity trend for the two predictors is due to progressive changes in the predictability of the criterion in different colleges. One cannot rule out the possibility that academic performance is progressively more or less predictable for successive samples of freshmen entering individual colleges; however, research evidence offers little support for that hypothesis.

There was a flurry of research on "moderator variables" and "predicting predictability" some years ago. Although theoretically interesting, that work achieved little practical result because, in large measure, it did not succeed in finding any personal characteristics that could reliably identify which individuals are more or less predictable (French, 1961; Ghiselli, 1963; Stricker, 1966). Results reported here also indicate that student sample effects do not explain validity changes. For example, the clearest difference in predictability for subgroups is due to gender, and yet women, whose performance is more predictable than men's, have gained representation in these colleges (Morgan, Chapter 10). Also Ramist, Lewis, and McCamley (Chapter 12) did not find the percentage of women in the freshman class to be a useful predictor of change in SAT validity coefficients. On the other hand, there is considerable evidence of changes in validity due to changes in the criterion, both in previous research (see Chapter 2 for an overview) and in the study by Ramist, Lewis, and McCamley (Chapter 12).

Yearly Fluctuation

Up to now we have focused on relatively long-term prediction trends, typically over five to 10 years. Yearly fluctuations in validity coefficients offer a somewhat different view of prediction trends. Such changes are trends, to be sure, but very short-term and presumably quite unstable, if not wholly random. Yearly fluctuations deserve more than passing attention, however, if for no other reason than the curiosity they often provoke among test users, along with legitimate speculation as to whether there is some "cause" for the changes that ought to be investigated. Why do an institution's validity coefficients change from one year to the next? "Mostly sampling variations" would be a traditional answer. Given the institutional differences in prediction trends just described, a better answer might be, "Whatever trend the college is experiencing, plus sampling fluctuations."

There is another possibility: real institutional changes resulting in real validity shifts that may not be at all stable. Examples include a change in policy regarding advanced placement, assignment of a substantial number of freshmen to noncredit remedial programs, a momentary but significant change in grading in some courses, a temporary change in scheduling some freshmen for notably tough required courses, a relaxation of end-of-course examination policies, a change in grade-reporting policies or in rules governing academic standing. Such educational changes are real enough, even if temporary. Depending on the circumstances, they may or may not be intentional or viewed as wholly beneficial. Should such a change in policy or practice affect validity coefficients through changes in the FGPA criterion, the effect can hardly be viewed as a sampling fluctuation, nor would it necessarily be part of any long-term trend.

There are two possible benefits to an analysis of year-to-year changes in validity coefficients. One is to determine how often institutions obtain prediction results that are significantly different from studies the previous year. Another advantage is that the extent of such fluctuations can be compared in different periods, as a possible indication of change in the consistency of prediction results, say, from the 1970s to the 1980s. Table 6-2 shows the results of an analysis to that end. Among the 192 colleges in our database, there were 88 instances of paired studies in consecutive years in the period

Table 6-2

Changes in Validity Coefficients When Colleges
Repeat Studies in Consecutive Years

	88 Pairs of Studies, 1974-77			227 Pairs of Studies, 1982-85		
	HSR	SAT	HSR, SAT	HSR	SAT	HSR, SAT
Change in validity coefficient						
Mean difference	−.007	−.007	−.003	.001	−.003	.000
Mean absolute difference	.056	.053	.051	.062	.064	.062
Mean standard error of diff.*	.047	.051	.040	.048	.051	.042
Proportion of differences where |t| exceeds:						
nominal 5% level	.22	.09	.22	.24	.24	.28
nominal 1% level	.10	.03	.14	.13	.16	.16

* See Note 6-4.

1974-77 and 227 such paired studies in the period 1982-85 (some studies/colleges appear more than once). In this analysis a standard error based on the size of the study samples was used to evaluate differences in corrected validity coefficients between studies in consecutive years. (See Note 6-4.)

In the more recent period, 1982 to 1985, Table 6-2 indicates that the mean absolute differences in yearly validity coefficients across adjacent years were somewhat larger than the corresponding standard errors. Of greater interest is the fact that a substantial number of institutions — about one in six or seven — showed a yearly change that should nominally occur by chance only one time in 100. Results for this 1982-85 period — the most recent data available for such an analysis — were quite similar for the three predictor sets: HSR, SAT-V,M, and the three predictors combined.

Comparing 1982-85 with the period 1974-77 suggests that there has been a small increase in the degree of yearly fluctuation. The absolute correlation difference increased a bit for each predictor set, though it is not clear whether those changes are significant. The most dramatic change from the earlier to the later years was in the proportion of SAT coefficients that showed a significant change from one year to the next. In 1974-77, that proportion had been .03, barely above chance and not at all typical of results for HSR and the three-variable coefficient. For reasons not presently clear, the proportion of

150

significant SAT fluctuations climbed progressively, so that by 1982-85, it was at about the same level (.16) as the other predictor sets.

These results indicate that a number of institutions experience significant shifts in validity coefficients from year to year. Is it possible that these shifts are largely due to the fact that some colleges are on a declining or inclining trend? This is unlikely; the standard errors in Table 6-2 indicate that significant yearly shifts are on the order of .10 while the yearly change associated with long-term slopes seldom exceeds .05. As a check, however, the analysis of Table 6-2 was repeated using absolute correlation differences adjusted by the institution's characteristic yearly change as determined by its prediction slope. The results were almost identical to those shown.

Sources of Temporal Variation

The preceding analyses suggest that there are several distinct types of variation in validity coefficients over time. Imagine those coefficients in a matrix of colleges by years. Even though the matrix is quite incomplete, variance components can be estimated by fitting a series of models to the data using an appropriate least-squares criterion. (See Note 6-5.) By successively subtracting average squared residual correlations from the grand mean, the college means, the overall trend, and the college trend, one obtains the following five components of variation in the correlations:

1. College differences in average coefficient — variations in the typical level of validity coefficients from college to college.

   Three components represent *temporal* effects:

2. Overall trend — the yearly linear trend in the average correlation across all colleges.

3. College differences in trend — the extent to which coefficients are linearly going up in some colleges and down in others.

4. Yearly deviations — nonrandom deviations about the trend line for individual colleges.

   And the remainder is:

5. Error — the expected sampling fluctuation for the correlations, inversely associated with the size of the class.

Table 6-3

Sources of Variation and Temporal Effect Sizes for Validity Coefficients
Based upon Different Predictors*

Variance Component	Analysis of Validity Coefficients for:		
Due to:	HSR	SAT (V,M)	HSR,SAT
1. College differences in average coefficient	480	474	513
Temporal components			
2. Overall trend	0	16	4
3. College differences in trend	82	95	86
4. Yearly deviations	51	52	85
5. Error (sampling fluctuations)	149	169	112
Total	762	806	800
Temporal components	Effect sizes (ratio: component/error)		
2. Overall trend	.00	.09	.04
3. College differences in trend	.55	.56	.77
4. Yearly deviations	.34	.31	.76

*Variance components in the upper portion of the table are based upon average squared residual correlation coefficients. All entries are multiplied by 10^5. See Note 6-5.

Table 6-3 gives estimates of these variance components for validity coefficients based upon HSR, SAT, and the multiple correlation for both measures. Each component can be expressed as a percentage of the total. Also the size of the effects can be evaluated on the basis of the ratio of the variance component to the error. Cohen (1988, p. 410ff) calls a ratio of .35 a large effect. The uncertain nature of the sample and the missing data provide an inadequate basis for statistical inference; however, the effects are large except in the case of component 2, the overall trend in validity coefficients.

These results reflect previous findings in several respects. In general, the pattern is very similar for HSR and SAT. The relative amount of variance associated with overall validity trend (component #2) is consistent with correlational results. In this group of colleges, the

10-year change in validity coefficient was –.04 for SAT and –.01 for HSR. Table 6-3 adds the following useful new perspectives:

- The role of institutional differences in prediction trends is dramatically illustrated. These differences account for some 11-12 percent of all variation in validity coefficients — substantially larger than the variation associated with the overall trend (0-2 percent). This finding supports the view that validity trends are largely an institution-based phenomenon. Another implication is that estimates of validity trends are heavily dependent upon how representative the sample of institutions is.

- These results confirm a substantial amount of nonrandom yearly deviation in validity coefficients. The deviations may be of several varieties: curvilinear trends, cyclical effects, or yearly fluctuation associated with particular changes within the institution.

- For the two temporal components associated with institutional differences, the effect sizes are very nearly the same for SAT and HSR: .56 and .55 for college trends (component #3); .34 and .31 for college yearly deviations (component #4). For both of these types of institutional variation, effect sizes are noticeably higher for the three-variable multiple. The fact that college differences are relatively larger using the most effective combination of predictors suggests again that college differences in prediction trends have more to do with variations in the predictability of the criterion than with changes in predictors or in underlying predictor-criterion relationships.

- The total of all temporal variation is, in turn, swamped by component #1, variation in the average validity coefficient from college to college (by a factor of at least three to one). This variation in predictability is independent of range restriction, sample size, and, of course, sampling fluctuations.

WEIGHTING INSTITUTIONS IN TREND ANALYSES

Yearly changes in validity coefficients have typically been described on the basis of mean values for data available each year (Ramist, 1984). This approach to trend analysis has the effect of weighting each institution by K, the number of studies it has done, because that is how many times it is represented in determining the overall trend. The pairwise method of trend analyses used elsewhere in this volume tends to heighten that differential weighting. Since each pair of studies is weighted equally in the pairwise method, this has the effect of weighting the data of a given institution by a factor of

K(K–1)/2, the number of pairs. (See Note 6-6.) A question arises when there are institutional differences in validity trends: To what extent might estimates of overall trends be minimized or exaggerated because those institutions that have done a number of studies have changed more or less over time than those that have done only a few studies? There can be such a "repetition effect" when three conditions are met:

- There are institutional differences in number of studies K_j

- There are institutional differences in the prediction slope t_j

- There is a relationship between K and t.

Recognizing now that conditions 1 and 2 hold, the question is whether there is any relationship in these data between an institution's prediction slope and the number of studies it has undertaken. To examine that question, we used the same database as previously described, though for present purposes, it was possible to include colleges that did only two or three validity studies. This addition increased the sample to 387 colleges and 1,737 studies.

Figure 6-2

Prediction Slope (per year) for SAT Validity Coefficients—a Plot Showing Mean and Range for 387 Institutions That Conducted Different Numbers of Studies Between 1974 and 1988

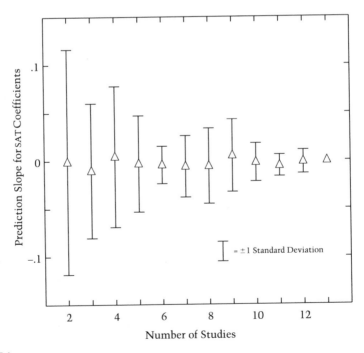

Figure 6-2 shows distributions of the SAT's slope t for those 387 colleges, sorted according to the number of studies each did. Two results are evident. One is the lack of any consequential relationship between t and K. Another is the wide variation in prediction trends among those institutions that did only a few studies. This latter result is consistent with the earlier observation that number of studies is a good predictor of stability in the institutional prediction slope. The lack of relationship between t and K in the case of the SAT is confirmed by the correlation between the two, r_{kt} = –.004. The corresponding correlation for the prediction slope of HSR was +.042.

It appears that the third condition for a repetition effect does not obtain in the case of the SAT and only very slightly, if at all, for the HSR. Pushing the issue a bit further, what are the arguments for using different weights for each institution, and how much difference does it actually make in these data? A priori, the main arguments would seem to be the following:

- *Unit weights* for institutions might be more valid because they allow better generalization to a population of institutions, but less reliable because they ignore differential stability of institutional prediction slopes;

- *K weights* would correspond to a conventional compilation of study results and would favor the more stable institutional data;

- *K(K–1)/2 weights* correspond to the pairwise analysis and place primary emphasis on stability.

Presumably unit weights would be more desirable when weighting clearly makes a difference in the outcome of the trend analysis. When weighting has little effect, the K or K(K-1)/2 weights would seem to have the advantage of producing more stable results. In order to determine the effect of these different weights, each was used in computing an average prediction slope for SAT and HSR for the 387 colleges in the period 1974-88.

Several aspects of the results shown in Table 6-4 are noteworthy. There was a small effect of weighting on the average slope for HSR, with unit weighting producing a slightly steeper negative average slope than did weighting by K, which in turn produced a slightly steeper negative value than did weighting by K(K-1)/2. This pattern is consistent with the small positive correlation (.04) observed between slope and number of studies for HSR. Given the standard errors associated with these three averages, however, it is not clear whether any substantive interpretation should be given to the differences among them. There was essentially no effect of different weighting on the SAT trend. Finally, for both SAT and HSR, the standard error of the mean slope is smallest with the K(K-1)/2 weight.

Table 6-4

The Effect on Average Prediction Slopes of
Different Weightings of the College Slope t

| | Average Slope* | |
Weight	SAT	HSR
Unit (colleges)	−.030 (.020)	−.021 (.019)
K (studies)	−.031 (.014)	−.013 (.012)
K(K−1)/2 (pairs)	−.031 (.012)	−.005 (.010)

*Standard errors in parentheses. Entries are multiplied by 10 to represent the amount of change over a decade.

An important consideration in evaluating the weighting issue is how much K varies among institutions, and this in turn depends upon how many years or points are involved in the trend analysis and how the data are aggregated. In Morgan's analysis in Chapter 10, for example, only three years are involved, so K can only be two or three. In the main analyses of Ramist and Weiss (Chapter 5) the data were grouped into periods. This practice not only stabilizes the validity estimate by averaging an institution's coefficients within periods, but also reduces markedly the possible range of K(K−1)/2.

In order to examine these effects, analyses of SAT and HSR trends using the pairwise method were carried out for all studies conducted by the 387 colleges in the period 1974 to 1988. The top portion of Figure 6-3 shows the SAT results for the conventional pairwise analysis where *pairs* are weighted equally (i.e., K(K−1)/2 weights for each college) and the same analysis when the pairs are weighted so that the data for each *college* have the same weight. Similar to the previous analysis of weighted slopes, this figure suggests no overall difference in the 12-year slopes for the two weights. There is, however, noticeable variation in individual years. In the bottom portion of Figure 6-3, the same pairwise analyses are based upon average coefficients within four periods. These results suggest that the different weights have very little effect — local or overall — on the pairwise period analysis. Results for HSR were quite similar.

Based upon these analyses, it appears that for this series of studies, it is appropriate to use the same pairwise method employed in the initial trend analyses by Morgan (1989a, and Chapter 4 of this volume). The lack of any consistent relationship between institutional

Figure 6-3

Pairwise Trend Analysis of SAT Validity Coefficients by Years
and by Periods When the Data of Each College
Were Weighted Equally or by K(K-1)/2*

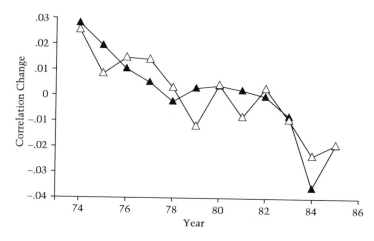

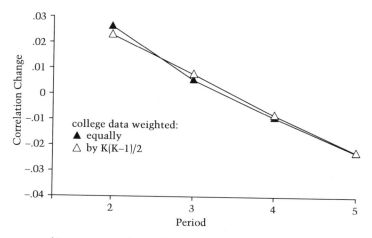

*Due to sparse data in later years, yearly points were plotted
only through 1985.

slope and number of studies and the smaller standard errors associated with the conventional pairwise method seem to make it a
reasonable choice. In these data, moreover, it seems unlikely that
different weighting will yield consequential differences in results,
though small differences are observable for HSR. On the other hand, a
better data set with representative groups of colleges doing validity
studies on a regular basis would be a much superior database for
trend analyses.

CONCLUSIONS

The principal findings of this study are as follows:

1. There were substantial institutional differences in prediction trends. In the case of the SAT, at least one validity slope went up during the 1974-1988 period for each two that went down. The percentage of total variance in SAT coefficients due to institutional differences in prediction trends (12 percent) was considerably larger than the variance associated with the overall trend (2 percent). In relation to error variance, such institutional variation in trend was comparable for HSR and SAT, but larger for the multiple correlations based on both measures.

2. The stability of institutional prediction slopes was highly predictable from institutional size, the number of validity studies conducted by each college, and particularly the range of time over which the studies were undertaken. Given the degree of institutional variation in true slope in this particular sample of colleges, the reliability of institutional slope differences could range widely (e.g., from .17 to .85), depending upon the stability.

3. The prediction slope for validity coefficients based upon HSR was strongly related to the prediction slope for coefficients based upon SAT scores. Taking account of the unreliability of the slopes and the correlated error they share, their "true" correlation was estimated to be .87.

4. Nonrandom year-to-year deviations in the validity coefficients of individual institutions were a consequential source of variation in prediction results, unrelated to long-term institutional trends. As in the case of long-term prediction slopes, this form of institutional variation was very similar (in relation to error) for validity coefficients based upon HSR and SAT, but larger in the case of multiple correlations based upon both measures. When institutions did studies in successive years, some 13-16 percent obtained results significantly different (at the nominal 1 percent level) from the previous study.

5. Institutional differences in validity level (the main effect in the analysis of variance) were quite large — three to four times greater than all temporal sources of variation combined.

6. In this data set, the direction of prediction slopes (up or down) was not significantly correlated with the number of studies an institution had conducted. Consequently, the overall results of the pairwise method of trend analysis used in other studies reported

here were not particularly sensitive to different weighting of institutional data or unduly influenced by the fact that some colleges did more studies than others.

These findings have several important implications. First, it is clear that institutional differences are a major factor in understanding and accounting for trends in validity coefficients. These institutional differences are substantial and highly similar for SAT scores and HSR. The results strongly suggest that there is an institutional basis for changes in validity coefficients, and that those changes have much more to do with variations in predictability of the criterion than with changes in the predictors or in underlying predictor-criterion relationships. Evidence from other research suggests that increases and decreases are unlikely to result from changes in the samples of entering students. It would appear, however, that institutional changes and variations in local criteria are promising places to look for correlates and mechanisms of changes in validity coefficients.

In the framework suggested in Chapter 1 of this volume, institutional differences constitute a "sample effect." A corollary of such sample effects is that one cannot hope to describe national trends — or even trends that are necessarily representative of SAT users — with a self-selected sample of validity studies. Another corollary is that some variation in the results of different analyses is likely when trend estimates are based upon different samples of colleges. That principle applies to this study as well. Although we have found substantial institutional differences, undoubtedly the pattern of results would vary somewhat with another sample of colleges.

Overall, weighting of institutional data does not seem to be a major factor in analyzing trends in these VSS data, though there may be a small effect in the case of HSR. This gives some assurance that the pairwise method is not skewing the results because some colleges did more validity studies than others. On the other hand, it is clear that there can be several sources of methodological variation in such trend analysis: pairwise vs. average slope, yearly vs. period analysis, in addition to how the college data are weighted. Differences due to the sample of institutions available for analysis may well be larger than any of these. We conclude there is no good statistical substitute for suitable validity data, consistently gathered. (See Note 6-7.)

Finally, such substantial institutional variations in predictability — both as to level and trend over time — give a new perspective on variation in validity coefficients. Validity generalization has inspired more research on such variation than any other theoretical construction (Boldt, 1986; Linn, Harnisch, & Dunbar, 1981b; Schmidt &

Hunter, 1977). That work has tended to focus on cross-sectional analysis of the factors that may obscure the essential commonality of a measure's predictive validity in most situations where it is used. On the practical side, validity studies have been primarily connected with selection and placement decisions and how those practices may need to be adjusted periodically (American College Test, 1988; College Board, 1988c), rather than with the implications that validity study results may hold for other aspects of educational programs, such as grading and instruction. An important implication of the present analysis is that such variation in validity coefficients — across colleges and over time — is a promising research topic. It does appear that these coefficients vary in consequential ways and may provide a useful means of studying college differences, educational practices, and the dynamics of institutional change.

CHAPTER 7

The Relationship of Trends in SAT Content and Statistical Characteristics to SAT Predictive Validity

GARY L. MARCO & CAROLYN R. CRONE*

Recent analyses by Morgan (1989a) and Ramist and Weiss (Chapter 5) indicated that the average multiple correlation of the SAT with college freshman grades increased in an uneven fashion by about .04 to .05 in the early 1970s and decreased gradually by about the same amount from the mid-1970s to the mid-1980s (see Table 5-5). Because changes in the test as well as other factors could have contributed to these changes in predictive validity, careful analyses were made of changes associated with the test during this time. This report provides the results of that analysis and evaluates the possible effect on predictive validity of changes in the SAT's content and format, statistical characteristics, and equating procedures. It is a shorter, more focused version of the detailed, lengthy report by Marco, Crone, Braswell, Curley, and Wright (1990), which provided extensive documentation of changes in SAT characteristics year by year.

The editions of the SAT that provided data for the study were those taken by the classes entering college from 1971 to 1985, the classes that provided data for the validity studies conducted through the College Board's Validity Study Service (VSS). More than half of the SAT scores for the high school seniors who graduated the previous spring came from the tests administered in November and December of the senior year, and 30 percent to 40 percent of the scores came from the November administration alone. The test-specific analyses for this study used item and test data from the November and December tests.

Figure 7-1 shows the average test performance of VSS samples, college-bound seniors, November and December seniors, and the

---

* Many individuals assisted with the preparation of this report. The authors thank particularly Susan Bryce, who prepared the figures; Gaye Allen and Georgiana Thurston, who typed the tables; and Jim Braswell, who provided the sample SAT items. The authors also thank reviewers Nancy Burton, Robert Linn, Sam Messick, and Warren Willingham, who suggested a number of important revisions to the review draft of the report.

161

Figure 7-1

Trends in SAT-Verbal and SAT-Mathematical Scaled-Score Means for
Various Groups of Test Takers by Year of High School Graduation

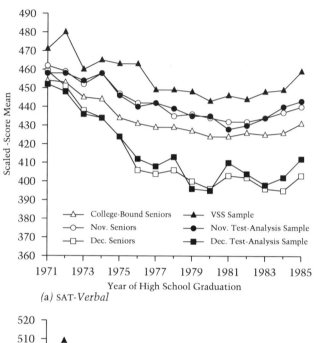

(a) SAT-*Verbal*

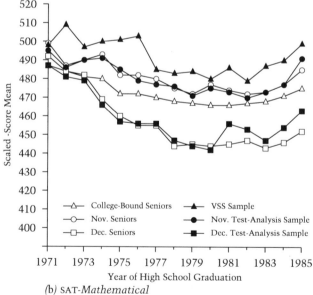

(b) SAT-*Mathematical*

test-analysis samples that provided data on the November and December SATs. The freshmen represented in validity studies scored higher on average than the seniors who took the November and December SATs, and the November senior means were higher than the December means. The test-analysis sample means, although based on data from other groups as well as seniors, were similar to the means for the November and December seniors. For all groups, the average SAT performance declined in the 1970s and moved upward slightly in the early 1980s.

This report concentrates on changes in characteristics of the test, particularly planned changes, that might have affected predictive validity. Angoff, Pomplun, McHale, and Morgan compare the predictive validity of old and new editions of the SAT administered to the same students at the same time (see Chapter 8). In addition to providing an empirical check on the results reported here, they also address the possibility that small, subtle changes in the test, spread out over a number of years, might have produced a gradual change in the statistical characteristics of the test and in predictive validity.

Here, we first address changes in test content and format and evaluate whether the changes, particularly those associated with the reformatting of the test in the fall of 1974, affected what the test was measuring. Next, we analyze changes in statistical characteristics that might have been affected by changes in test content and format and that might, in turn, have affected test validity: test difficulty, speededness of test sections, reliability, and correlational patterns. In this section, we link changes in test difficulty and speededness to changes in reliability and show the changes in validity that would be expected from classical test theory, given changes in reliability like those observed on the SAT. We then discuss trends in correlations between, for example, the SAT-Verbal (SAT-V) and the SAT-Mathematical (SAT-M), which, if substantial, could imply that what the test measured changed over time. Because the data for the study came primarily from test-analysis reports, however, only a limited amount of data was available on correlational patterns. Finally, we consider changes in equating methods and their possible effect on predictive validity. In all of these analyses, the intention is to identify trends that help account for the gradual increasing and decreasing trends in predictive validity.

TEST CONTENT AND FORMAT

Many kinds of changes in a test could affect predictive validity. Changing the number of test items without changing the types of items or their content would affect the reliability of the test and consequently validity. Changes in the types of items used on the test could also affect validity if the different types measured knowledge, skills, or abilities not measured by the original test. Moreover, changes in the content of the items (e.g., using more science-related reading items) might affect predictive validity, provided the different content related differentially to the validity criterion.

Changes in Content and Format

Primary among the changes that occurred in the SATs administered to college-bound high school seniors who graduated from 1971 to 1985 is the shortening of the SAT-V and the SAT-M from 75 to 60 minutes each in October 1974. Previously each had consisted of one 30- and one 45-minute section. Now, each was shortened to two 30-minute sections to permit the introduction of the Test of Standard Written English (TSWE) into the testing program. The revised SAT-V consisted of 85 items rather than 90; the SAT-M, like its predecessor, consisted of 60 items. To maintain high test reliability, test developers increased the proportion of items that could be answered at a faster rate by adding more Antonyms in the SAT-V and replacing Data Sufficiency items with Quantitative Comparisons in the SAT-M. (Examples of these and other item types used in the SAT during the period studied are given in Appendix A-2.)

In addition, test developers reduced the number of Reading Comprehension items in the shortened SAT from 35 to 25 by eliminating the Synthesis passage and one of the two Science passages — leaving five rather than seven reading passages. In October 1978, when three reading passages replaced two longer ones, the second Science passage was restored.

Detailed content specifications for the SAT are shown in Tables 7-1 and 7-2, along with the numbers of items actually included in the November and December tests administered in the specified period. Although the numbers of items deviated from specifications for individual tests (see also Marco et al., 1990), most of the deviations were small.

Other changes in the SAT's format and content were less likely to affect the statistical characteristics and validity of the test. These included changes in the order in which the sections of the SAT (and the TSWE from October 1974 on) were administered, changes in the order in which the verbal and mathematical items were presented, and changes in content as the result of informal and formal sensitivity reviews designed to ensure that test forms are free of material offensive or patronizing to females and minority groups. Cruise and Kimmel (1990) documented changes made to gender references used

Table 7-1

Specified* and Actual** Numbers of Items
Within Various Classifications for sat-Verbal Tests

Item Type Classification	Specified (Jan. 1961-Sept. 1974)	Nov. & Dec. Actual (1970-1973)	Specified (Oct. 1974-Sept. 1978)	Nov. & Dec. Actual (1974-1977)	Specified (Oct. 1978-Present)	Nov. & Dec. Actual (1978-1984)
Sentence						
Completions						
Content						
Aesthetics/philosophy	4	4-5	4	3-5	4	4-4
World of practical affairs	5	5-6	4	4-5	4	4-5
Science	5	5-5	4	3-4	4	3-4
Human relationships	4	3-4	3	3-3	3	3-3
(Total)	(18)	(18)	(15)	(15)	(15)	(15)
Antonyms						
Content						
Aesthetics/philosophy	4	3-5	6	5-6	6	4-7
World of practical affairs	5	4-7	6	6-7	6	5-7
Science	5	4-5	7	6-7	7	4-8
Human relationships	4	3-5	6	5-6	6	5-9
(Total)	(18)	(18)	(25)	(25)	(25)	(25)
Analogies						
Content						
Aesthetics/philosophy	5	4-6	5	5-5	5	4-6
World of practical affairs	5	4-6	5	5-6	5	5-7
Science	5	5-6	5	4-5	5	4-6
Human relationships	4	3-5	5	4-5	5	4-6
(Total)	(19)	(19)	(20)	(20)	(20)	(20)
Reading						
Comprehension						
Content						
Narrative	5	5-5	5	5-5	2-5	3-5
Biological science	5	0-10	0-5***	5-5	2-5	2-5
Physical science	5	0-5	0-5***	0-0	2-5	3-5
Argumentative	5	5-10	5	5-5	2-5	3-5
Humanities	5	5-5	5	5-5	2-5	3-5
Synthesis	5	0-5	0	0-0	0	0-0
Social studies	5	5-5	5	5-5	2-5	3-5
Functional Skill						
Main idea	7	2-8	5	3-6	5	1-6
Supporting idea	7	4-10	5	4-10	5	2-8
Inference	12	11-16	9	6-10	9	8-11
Application	3	1-4	2	1-3	2	1-3
Evaluation of logic	3	1-6	2	1-3	2	1-4
Style and tone	3	2-5	2	2-2	2	0-3
(Total)	(35)	(35)	(25)	(25)	(25)	(25)

* The specifications applied to any new test administered during the indicated period.

** Expressed as ranges

*** Only one Science passage was permitted on the test.

Table 7-2

Specified* and Actual** Numbers of Items
Within Various Classifications for sat-Mathematical Tests

Item Type Classification	Specified (Nov. 1969-Sept. 1974)	Nov. & Dec. Actual (1970-1973)	Specified (Oct. 1974-Dec. 1975)	Nov. & Dec. Actual (1974-1975)	Specified (Jan. 1976-Sept. 1981)	Nov. & Dec. Actual (1976-1980)	Specified (Oct. 1981-Present)	Nov. & Dec. Actual (1981-1984)
Regular								
Mathematics								
Arithmetic	13	13-13	12-13	12-12	12-13	12-13	12-13	12-13
Algebra	11	11-13	11	11-11	11	10-11	11	11-11
Geometry	13	12-13	11	11-12	11	11-11	11	11-11
Miscellaneous	5	4-5	5-6	5-6	5-6	5-6	5-6	5-6
(Total)	(42)	(42)	(40)	(40)	(40)	(40)	(40)	(40)
Data								
Sufficiency								
Arithmetic	4-5	4-5						
Algebra	4-5	3-5						
Geometry	6-7	5-8						
Miscellaneous	3-4	3-4						
(Total)	(18)	(18)						
Quantitative								
Comparisons								
Arithmetic			6	6-7	6	6-7	6	6-6
Algebra			6	5-6	6	5-6	6	6-6
Geometry			5-6	5-6	5-6	5-6	5-6	5-6
Miscellaneous			2-3	2-3	2-3	1-3	2-3	2-3
(Total)			(20)	(20)	(20)	(20)	(20)	(20)
All								
Setting								
Concrete	11-31	12-24	11-31	13-16	11-31	10-16	11-21	14-19
Abstract	29-49	36-48	29-49	44-47	29-49	44-50	39-49	41-46
Ability								
Solve routine problems	0-8	7-10	12-21	14-20	2-21	10-18	0-21	11-17
Demonstrate comprehension of math ideas and concepts	22-30	21-26	22-31	22-25	22-41	23-32	22-43	24-31
Apply "higher" mental processes to math	30-38	26-31	17-26	16-24	17-36	16-22	17-38	17-21
(Total)	(60)	(60)	(60)	(60)	(60)	(60)	(60)	(60)

* The specifications applied to any new test administered during the indicated period.

** Expressed as ranges

on the SAT from 1961 to 1987, including those that resulted from increased sensitivity to female concerns.

Relation to Validity

The two changes in the test most likely to affect predictive validity were decreasing the number of SAT-V items from 90 to 85 in the fall of 1974 and, at the same time, changing the numbers of items associated with the different verbal and mathematical item types. The change in test length bears directly on reliability and is addressed in the next section, which deals with changes in statistical characteristics.

The increase in the number of Antonyms used on the SAT-V and the use of Quantitative Comparison instead of Data Sufficiency items on the SAT-M could conceivably have affected the SAT's predictive validity. At issue are the relationships among the different item types and the differential validity of the various item types.

Evidence from three special studies suggests that different verbal or mathematical item types related in similar ways to freshman grade-point average (FGPA). Schrader (1973) studied the validity of the Quantitative Comparison item type before it was used operationally in 1974. A 30-minute, 55-item Quantitative Comparison test was administered to approximately 4,000 students at 12 colleges. Schrader found that, despite its shorter length, the Quantitative Comparison test had higher correlations with FGPA than the SAT-M, then composed of Regular Mathematics and Data Sufficiency items, for about half of the groups studied. He concluded that there was no marked tendency for the SAT-M to be any more valid than the Quantitative Comparison test.

In another study, Schrader (1984) provided evidence of the predictive validity of SAT-V item types. He found that, although Antonyms and Analogies had the highest validities in about twice as many of the 48 colleges included in his study as the other verbal item types, the median validities differed only slightly. Schrader concluded that the verbal item types have similar validities and that changing the mix of items in SAT-V was unlikely to affect predictive validity.

More recently, Burton, Morgan, Lewis, and Robertson (1989), in one part of their study, investigated the predictive validity of item types in the SAT and the TSWE. For the SAT-V, the most valid item type for the total group (about 49,000 students from nearly 200 colleges) was Reading Comprehension. The estimated validity of a test made up of all Reading Comprehension items was, however, the same as the operational SAT-V, composed of four item types. For the SAT-M, the Quantitative Comparison item type was more valid than Regular Mathematics items for the total group. Yet a test made up entirely of

Quantitative Comparison items was estimated to have a validity only .01 higher than the operational SAT-M, with its mixture of Regular Mathematics and Quantitative Comparison items.

The validity evidence suggests strongly that the various SAT-V or SAT-M item types correlate similarly with college grades. Therefore, the changes in the numbers of items of particular types due to the timing change in the fall of 1974 probably had little effect on the ability of the SAT to predict college grades. Moreover, if the shortening of the SAT had affected predictive validity in an important way, it presumably would have caused a substantial one-time drop in predictive validity. The average adjusted correlations from Ramist and Weiss (Chapter 5) show, however, that the decline since 1974 has been relatively gradual.

STATISTICAL CHARACTERISTICS

Presumably, if changes in the content and format of a test were important enough to influence predictive validity, they would also produce changes in the statistical characteristics of the test. For example, important changes in test length would affect reliability, because each item added or deleted affects the measurement power of the test. Important changes in content might also affect reliability in that the test items could become more or less correlated with one another. Such changes could also result in changes in the correlations of the test with other tests.

In this section, we evaluate the extent to which planned changes in format and content and in statistical characteristics actually affected test statistics and, therefore, might also have caused the validity of the test to change. Because test reliability is influenced by test length and statistical characteristics such as test difficulty and test speededness, test reliability is the single most important statistical characteristic addressed here. The item and test statistics on actual tests came from test-analysis reports for the tests administered in November and December from 1970 through 1984.

Test Difficulty

Changes in test difficulty could affect the reliability (and hence validity) of a test if they caused it to gain or lose measurement power in the score ranges of importance to the colleges conducting validity studies. To maximize the measurement power of the SAT for a given validity study sample, the test items should be concentrated at middle difficulty for the sample. Concentrating item difficulties at middle difficulty for the average sample would presumably maximize reliability for the average sample and hence the average validity. Of course, the SAT is intended to measure relatively well for a broad range of college applicants, not just the average test taker in a validity study, and thus uses a wide range of item difficulties.

Changes in specified test difficulty. Two changes occurred in the specified distribution of item difficulties for SATs administered to college-bound seniors in the 1971-85 period (see Table 7-3). With the introduction of the shortened SAT in October 1974 came a reduction in test difficulty. In the table, test difficulty is expressed in terms of

Table 7-3

Statistical Specifications for SAT-Verbal and SAT-Mathematical
Test Forms from 1966 to the Present*

Item Difficulty (Equated Delta)	SAT-Verbal			SAT-Mathematical	
	Aug. 1966-Sept. 1974**	Oct. 1974-Jan. 1982***	Jan. 1982-Present***	Aug. 1966-Sept. 1974	Oct. 1974-Present
≥ 18	0	0	0	3	3
17	2	2	0	4	4
16	4	4	2	4	4
15	8	10	6	4	4
14	10	10	14	5	4
13	10	6	10	5	4
12	10	6	8	5	4
11	10	6	7	8	8
10	10	8	7	8	8
9	8	8	10	7	8
8	7	10	8	4	5
7	6	8	6	2	1
6	3	4	4	1	2
≤ 5	2	3	3	0	1
Number of Items	90	85	85	60	60
Mean Delta	11.7	11.4	11.4	12.5	12.17-12.27
SD Delta	2.9	3.3	3.0	3.1	3.1-3.3
Mean Biserial r****	.42 (.47)	.43 (.48)	.41–.45 (.46–.50)	.47 (.53)	.47 (.53)

* The statistical specifications applied to any new test administered during the indicated periods.

** From August 1966 to July 1967 the statistical specifications for SAT-V were as follows: Mean Delta = 11.8, SD Delta = 3.0, Mean Biserial r = .42.

*** One of the two January 1982 forms was assembled to the specifications for the 1974-81 period.

**** The mean biserial r is specified in terms of pretest items, which are not included in the total-score criterion. The equivalent means for a total-score criterion that includes the item, given in parentheses, are .05 higher for the SAT-V and .06 higher for the SAT-M.

mean equated delta, the ETS measure of average item difficulty. Delta is determined by transforming the percentage of test takers who answer an item correctly into a normal curve deviate that has a mean of 13 and a standard deviation of 4. High deltas are associated with relatively difficult items and low deltas with relatively easy items. A delta of 13 corresponds to 50 percent correct. To remove the effects due to differences among groups that happen to take the SAT, ETS equates deltas observed on a particular group to a delta scale defined in terms of a common reference group.

The specified reduction in mean item difficulty is equivalent to increasing the average percentage of items answered correctly by the SAT item-analysis reference group from 63 percent to 66 percent for the SAT-V and from 55 percent to 58 percent for the SAT-M. The number of difficult items was either maintained (for the SAT-M) or increased slightly (for the SAT-V), while the number of easy items was increased somewhat in an attempt to lower difficulty and still maintain measurement power at the upper end of the score range. This change in the distribution of item difficulties resulted in an increase in the specified standard deviations of delta for both the SAT-V and the SAT-M. These changes were expected to reduce score reliability slightly for test takers scoring in the middle of the range.

In January 1982 the test-difficulty specifications for the SAT-V were again revised — this time to decrease dependence upon difficult items. The specifications decreased the number of difficult SAT-V items and increased the number of moderately difficult items. The mean item difficulty was unaffected by this change, but the standard deviation of delta decreased from 3.3 to 3.0. This change was expected to increase overall test reliability slightly while decreasing the measurement power of the test slightly for very able test takers.

Changes in actual test difficulty. A review of data from the November and December tests showed that actual mean item difficulty deviated only slightly from specified values [see panels (a) and (b) of Figure 7-2]. The SAT-V tended to be slightly harder than specified prior to 1974 and slightly easier than specified from 1974 on. The SAT-M, on the other hand, tended to be easier than specified prior to 1974, and sometimes easier and sometimes harder from 1974 on.

Panels (c) and (d) of Figure 7-2 show that, in general, the standard deviations of item difficulties for the SAT-V and SAT-M clustered around their specified values. The standard deviations of SAT-M item difficulties fluctuated more from test to test, however.

Figure 7-2

Trends in Test Difficulty and Item-Test Correlations for
November and December SATs Administered from 1970 to 1984

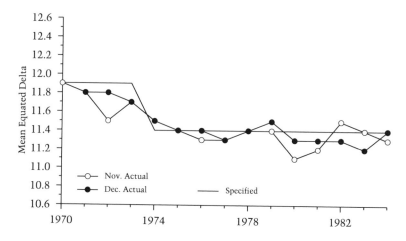

(a) *Actual and Specified Means of Equated Deltas for* SAT-V

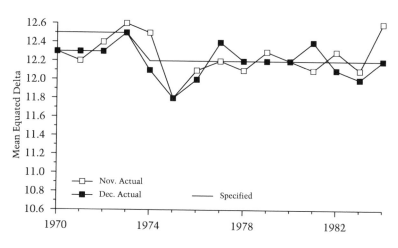

(b) *Actual and Specified Means of Equated Deltas for* SAT-M

Figure 7-2 (Continued)

Trends in Test Difficulty and Item-Test Correlations for
November and December SATs Administered from 1970 to 1984

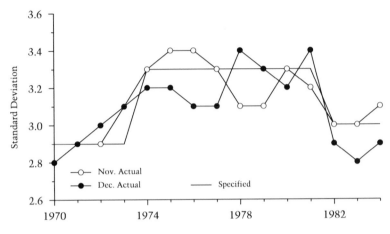

(c) *Actual and Specified Standard Deviations of Equated Deltas for* SAT-V

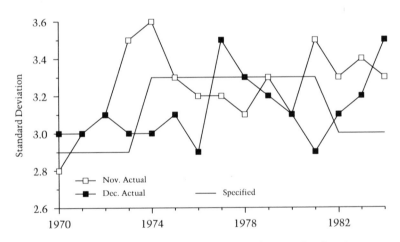

(d) *Actual and Specified Standard Deviations of Equated Deltas for* SAT-M

Figure 7-2 (Continued)
Trends in Test Difficulty and Item-Test Correlations for
November and December SATs Administered from 1970 to 1984

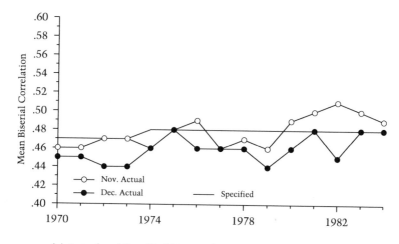

(e) Actual and Specified Means of Biserial Correlations for SAT-V

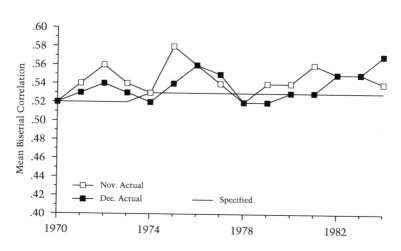

(f) Actual and Specified Means of Biserial Correlations for SAT-M

It is important to consider the relative difficulty of the test for the intended group of test takers. Analyses reported by Marco and colleagues (1990), based on the mean adjusted proportion correct (the raw score mean divided by the number of test items), showed that all of the November and December tests were relatively difficult for the test-analysis samples for all tests administered. The highest means of adjusted proportions correct (.45 for the November samples and .40 for the December samples) occurred in 1983 or 1984, indicating that the test was, if anything, more appropriate for the analysis samples in the early 1980s than in the early 1970s.

Relation to reliability and validity. Analyses based on item response theory, conducted prior to the introduction of the shortened sat in the fall of 1974, suggested that the new item-difficulty specifications would reduce measurement power slightly in the middle to upper part of the scale for the sat-V and the middle part for the sat-M. (The reduction in measurement power for the sat-V was due partly to the loss of five items.) These analyses also estimated an overall decrease in reliability of .01 for the sat-V and no overall decrease for the sat-M (Braswell & Marco, personal communication, March 1974). Because the estimated loss of measurement power was expected to occur in the neighborhood of the sat-V and sat-M means for a typical college validity sample, changes in test difficulty would presumably have lowered slightly the reliability of the test for such a sample. This reduction in reliability is too slight to have had much effect on validity, as the later discussion of reliability shows.

The other change in specifications during the period from 1970 through 1985 occurred in January 1982, when the specified distribution of item difficulties for sat-V was changed (see Table 7-3) because of the scarcity of difficult items. Analyses based on item response theory estimated a slight improvement in measurement power, relative to forms administered in 1977 and 1979, in the middle part of the score range and a slight loss elsewhere (Petersen, 1981). This change presumably would have improved very slightly the reliability of the sat for the typical college validity study sample relative to the sats given between 1974 and 1981. The effect on overall reliability would have been in the third decimal place — too small to have affected validity.

Although the November and December sats were difficult for the average test taker, they were at least as appropriate for test takers in the later years as in 1970-73. The mean adjusted proportions correct tended to increase over time, partly as a result of decreased test difficulty and partly as a result of increased score performance in the early 1980s. Thus, the SAT became slightly more appropriate in difficulty for the test-taking group. This trend would tend to improve the measurement power of the test for the middle- to low-scoring test takers and presumably for the average student in a validity study sample. If changes in test difficulty had any effect, it was to improve reliability and validity, but the changes were probably too small to notice. Certainly, no decline in reliability and validity would be expected.

Mean Item-Test Correlation

In addition to the item-difficulty distribution, SAT statistical specifications regulate the average (biserial) correlation of the items (each item scored right or wrong) with the total test score. High correlation of an item with the total score indicates that the preponderance of those who answer the item correctly also score high on the test. The average item-test correlation is related to reliability. The higher the average correlation, the higher the intercorrelations among items and the higher the test reliability.

Changes in the specified mean item-test correlation. As Table 7-3 shows, only one modification to the specified average biserial correlation was made for the SAT-V during the 1971-85 testing years. In 1974, the average was changed from .47 to .48 (expressed in terms of a total-score criterion that includes the item) because the pool of available items tended to have biserial correlations greater than .47. From January 1982 on, the SAT-V specifications permitted a deviation of .02 in the mean biserial correlation. The specified average biserial correlation for the SAT-M has remained constant at .53 from August 1966 to the present.

Changes in the actual mean item-test correlation. For the November and December SAT-V, forms generally came close to the specified value [see panels (e) and (f) of Figure 7-2]. The November mean biserial correlations were higher than those for December and varied around the specified value until 1980, after which they were higher than specified. The December SAT-V mean correlations, on the other hand, tended to be lower than specified throughout the 15-year period. The mean biserial correlations for the SAT-M fluctuated more than those for the SAT-V and tended to be higher than required.

Relation to reliability and validity. Other things being equal, the tests with mean biserial correlations higher than specified would tend to have higher reliabilities than the other tests. Thus, if anything, the November and December tests administered in the latter part of the 15-year period would be expected to have higher reliabilities. It is unlikely, however, that the slight deviations in the actual means of the item-test correlations from specifications would have altered reliability enough to affect the prediction of FGPA.

Speededness

Giving more items in the time allotted to testing, as happened with the SAT in the fall of 1974, could possibly increase test speededness. So as not to increase the speededness of the SAT in 1974, test developers included five rather than seven reading passages in the SAT-V and substituted Quantitative Comparison items for Data Sufficiency items in the SAT-M. Because of a concern about speededness, the formats of both sections were revised in 1975 in an attempt to control it. In the fall of 1978, another change occurred that could have affected speededness: The number of reading passages in the 40-item SAT-V was increased from three to four by replacing two long passages with three medium-length ones.

Speededness is affected by the ability of the test takers as well as by changes in the test. The November and December scaled-score means of the test-analysis samples decreased steadily from 1970, reaching a low during the 1979-81 period, and then rose somewhat from 1982 to 1984. Any decrease in ability would be expected to increase the speededness of the test.

The speededness of a test could affect its measurement power. For a test of developed abilities, a test that is slightly speeded for the test taker probably measures better than a test that is unspeeded. The time limits for the SAT are set to enable it to measure well in the middle to upper parts of the score range. In general, however, reduced speededness would be expected to increase the reliability of the test for the average test taker, and decrease it for high scorers.

Changes in speededness. As Figure 7-3 shows, throughout the time period, the percentage of test takers completing 75 percent of the items in a section was typically over 95 percent, indicating that the SAT-V and the SAT-M were not very speeded for the average test taker. The trends for the two SAT-V sections and the two SAT-M sections are plotted separately in the figure. The longer 50- or 45-item SAT-V section (Verbal 1) tended to become gradually more speeded after the introduction of the shortened SAT. The other SAT-V section (Verbal 2) was relatively unspeeded except in 1974. The use of four shorter reading passages instead of three in the shorter SAT-V section in 1978 seemed not to make that section more speeded. The speededness of the two SAT-M sections tended to decrease or remain stable as time went on. The longer 35-item SAT-M section (Mathematical 2) and the shorter 40-item SAT-V section (Verbal 2) became temporarily more speeded when the shortened SAT was introduced in

Figure 7-3

Trends in Speededness for November and December SATs
Administered from 1970 to 1984

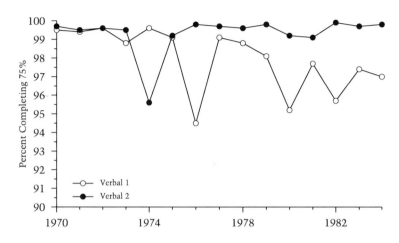

(a) *Percentages of Test Takers Completing 75% of the November*
SAT-V *Sections*

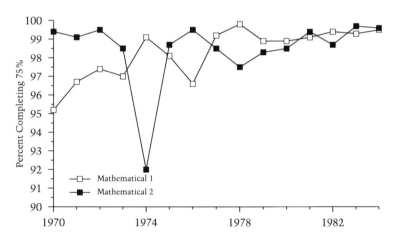

(b) *Percentages of Test Takers Completing 75% of the November*
SAT-M *Sections*

Figure 7-3 (Continued)

Trends in Speededness for November and December SATs
Administered from 1970 to 1984

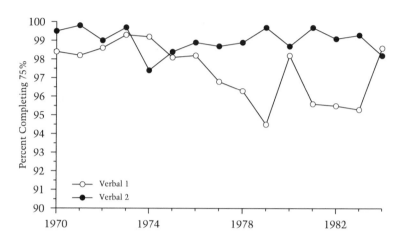

(c) *Percentages of Test Takers Completing 75% of the December
SAT-V Sections*

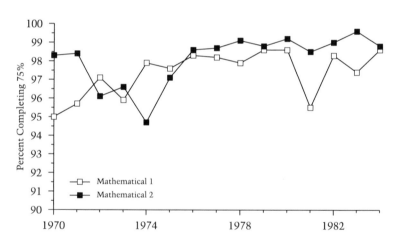

(d) *Percentages of Test Takers Completing 75% of the December
SAT-M Sections*

1974, but the change in the ordering of the items within sections in 1975 apparently reduced speededness to previous levels.

Relation to reliability and validity. Decreasing speededness would tend to improve measurement power for middle- to low-scoring test takers and possibly reduce it for high scorers. Predictive validity might improve as well for the typical college conducting validity studies. The tendency of Verbal 1 to become more speeded might have caused the SAT-V to measure average test takers less well and thus decreased the measurement power of the test. On the other hand, the decrease in speededness for the SAT-M would presumably have increased the measurement power of the test for the average test taker. Since neither test was very speeded, one would expect small, if any, effects on reliability (measurement power) and validity.

Reliability

Because test developers increased the proportion of Antonyms in the SAT-V and introduced Quantitative Comparisons in the SAT-M — items that could be answered at a faster rate — the shortened test introduced in 1974 contained the same number of SAT-M items (60) and almost the same number of SAT-V items (85 instead of 90). Application of the Spearman-Brown formula from classical test theory (see, for example, Gulliksen, 1950, p. 94) shows that a reduction from 90 to 85 items would be expected to reduce the reliability of the SAT-V, usually in the neighborhood of .91 to .92, by about .005. A test of the same length as the original test, as in the case of the SAT-M, would of course not be expected to suffer any reduction in reliability.

Changes in reliability. Figure 7-4 depicts trends in internal-consistency reliability coefficients over time. The internal-consistency reliabilities are based on the Dressel adaptation of Kuder-Richardson Formula 20, which is equivalent to coefficient alpha (see Harvey, 1989). To provide a purer measure of the reliability of the test unconfounded with differences in variation from group to group, the internal-consistency reliabilities were adjusted to reflect a constant standard deviation of 100 for the group (see Marco et al., 1990, for details). Spring-to-fall test-retest (alternative form) reliabilities are given in Table 7-4.

Figure 7-4

Trends in Reliability for November and December SATs
Administered from 1970 to 1984

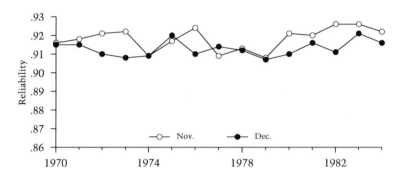

(a) *Internal-Consistency Reliabilities for* SAT-V

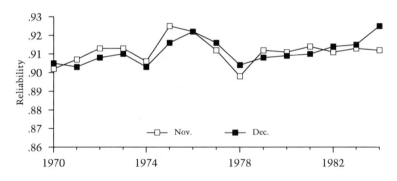

(b) *Internal-Consistency Reliabilities for* SAT-M

Figure 7-4 (Continued)
Trends in Reliability for November and December SATs
Administered from 1970 to 1984

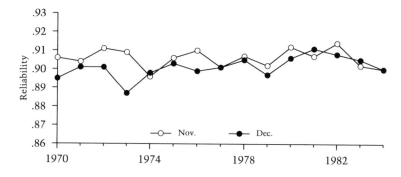

(c) *Adjusted Internal-Consistency Reliabilities (SD=100) for* SAT-V

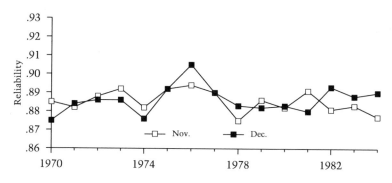

(d) *Adjusted Internal-Consistency Reliabilities (SD=100) for* SAT-M

Table 7-4

Test-Retest Correlations for the sat from 1970 to 1984*

Year	March/April-November**	May-November	June/July-November	March/April-December**	May-December	June/July-December
			sat-*Verbal*			
1970	.90	.89	.87	.90	.89	.88
1971	.89		.87	89		.88
1972	.89		.88	.89		.88
1973	.89		.88	.87		.88
1974	.88		.88	.87		.88
1975	.88		.87	.87		.87
1976	.88		.88	.87		.88
1977	.88	.88	.88	.88	.88	.88
1978	.88	.88	.87	.87	.88	.88
1979	.89	.88	.87	.87	.88	.86
1980	.89	.88	.88	.87	.87	.87
1981	.88	.88	.88	.88	.87	.88
1982	.89	.88	.88	.89	.88	.88
1983	.89	.88	.88	.89	.89	.88
1984	.89	.89	.89	.88	.89	.88
			sat-*Mathematical*			
1970	.88	.86	.86	.88	.87	.87
1971	.88		.86	.88		.87
1972	.88		.87	.89		.88
1973	.88		.87	.88		.89
1974	.87		.87	.87		.88
1975	.89		.87	.88		.88
1976	.89		.88	.90		.90
1977	.88	.89	.88	.88	.89	.88
1978	.88	.88	.88	.88	.88	.88
1979	.88	.88	.88	.88	.88	.88
1980	.88	.87	.86	.87	.87	.87
1981	.87	.88	.88	.87	.88	.88
1982	.88	.87	.88	.89	.88	.88
1983	.88	.88	.89	.88	.89	.88
1984	.88	.87	.87	.89	.88	.88

* Adaptation of Table 3.9 in Donlon (1984b)

These correlations are based on students who took the SAT in the spring of their junior year in secondary school and repeated the test in the fall of their senior year.

The ranges in numbers of repeaters for the various junior-year-to-senior-year test-taking patterns were the following:

Junior-Year Administration	Senior-Year Administration	Sample-Size Range (in 000s)
March/April	November	26-165
May	November	75-126
June/July	November	25- 66
March/April	December	11- 40
May	December	21- 66
June/July	December	9- 22

** Data are from the March administration in 1970, the April administrations from 1971 to 1976, and the March administrations from 1977 to 1984.

All internal-consistency reliabilities were very high — around .90 and .91 — for both the SAT-V and the SAT-M from 1970 to 1984, and remained relatively stable over time. No loss in reliability is evident due to shortening the time limits of the SAT in 1974. The adjusted internal-consistency reliabilities, which were lower than the unadjusted values simply because the standard deviation used for the correction was lower than the actual standard deviations of the test-analysis samples, also tended to be stable over time — except for the SAT-M during the 1974-78 period. Test-retest correlations for spring test takers who repeated the test were also high, ranging from .87 to .89. No trends were apparent.

Relation to validity. Application of the formula from classical test theory that relates changes in validity to changes in reliability (Gulliksen, 1950, p. 94) shows how changes in reliability like those observed for the SAT would be expected to affect predictive validities. These results rest on the assumption that the test remains the same in content and difficulty. Table 7-5 gives the results of applying this formula to validities ranging from .30 to .54 and to reliabilities ranging from .86 to .94, numbers that more than span the range of internal-consistency and test-retest reliabilities observed for the November and December test-analysis samples. The effects of changing reliability by –.01, –.02, and –.03 are shown in the table. Changing all of the negative signs to plus signs in the table gives the corresponding results for positive changes in reliability. The table shows that changes in reliability on the order of –.03 result at most in only a one-point shift in validity. Expressed to three decimal places, changes in validity ranged between –.002 and –.003 for changes in reliability of –.01, between –.003 and –.006 for changes in reliability of –.02, and between –.005 and –.010 for changes in reliability of –.03. The table shows that changes in reliability have a greater effect on higher initial validities (e.g., .54) than on lower initial validities (e.g., .30). Moreover, changes in lower initial reliabilities (e.g., .86) have a greater effect on validity than changes in higher initial reliabilities (e.g., .94).

Table 7-4 and Figure 7-4 clearly show that there were no systematic trends in reliability in one direction or the other. In general, the reliabilities, whether internal-consistency or test-retest reliabilities, clustered within .02 of one another; no cumulative effect was evident. The results from classical test theory in Table 7-5 indicate that changes this small in SAT reliability would result in negligible changes in validity.

Table 7-5

Changes in Validity as a Function of Changes in Reliability

Reliability	Change In Rel.	Validity							
		.30	.31	.32–.42	.43	.44	.45	.46	.47–.54
.94		.00	.00	.00	.00	.00	.00	.00	.00
.93		.00	.00	.00	.00	.00	.00	.00	.00
.92		.00	.00	.00	.00	.00	.00	.00	.00
.91		.00	.00	.00	.00	.00	.00	.00	.00
.90	−.01	.00	.00	.00	.00	.00	.00	.00	.00
.89		.00	.00	.00	.00	.00	.00	.00	.00
.88		.00	.00	.00	.00	.00	.00	.00	.00
.87		.00	.00	.00	.00	.00	.00	.00	.00
.86		.00	.00	.00	.00	.00	.00	.00	.00
.94		.00	.00	.00	.00	.00	.00	.00	−.01
.93		.00	.00	.00	.00	.00	.00	.00	−.01
.92		.00	.00	.00	.00	.00	.00	−.01	−.01
.91		.00	.00	.00	.00	.00	.00	−.01	−.01
.90	−.02	.00	.00	.00	.00	.00	−.01	−.01	−.01
.89		.00	.00	.00	.00	.00	−.01	−.01	−.01
.88		.00	.00	.00	.00	−.01	−.01	−.01	−.01
.87		.00	.00	.00	.00	−.01	−.01	−.01	−.01
.86		.00	.00	.00	−.01	−.01	−.01	−.01	−.01
.94		.00	.00	−.01	−.01	−.01	−.01	−.01	−.01
.93		.00	−.01	−.01	−.01	−.01	−.01	−.01	−.01
.92		.00	−.01	−.01	−.01	−.01	−.01	−.01	−.01
.91		.00	−.01	−.01	−.01	−.01	−.01	−.01	−.01
.90	−.03	−.01	−.01	−.01	−.01	−.01	−.01	−.01	−.01
.89		−.01	−.01	−.01	−.01	−.01	−.01	−.01	−.01
.88		−.01	−.01	−.01	−.01	−.01	−.01	−.01	−.01
.87		−.01	−.01	−.01	−.01	−.01	−.01	−.01	−.01
.86		−.01	−.01	−.01	−.01	−.01	−.01	−.01	−.01

Correlational Patterns

For the predictive validity of a test to remain stable over time, what is measured by the test and the criterion should not change. Changes in what a test measures would presumably affect predictive validity — provided that the predicted criterion did not change.

Reliability data provide evidence of consistency in measurement, but do not provide direct evidence of the extent to which the tests measured the same underlying abilities over time. The special validity studies referenced earlier (Schrader, 1973; Schrader, 1984; Burton et al., 1989) indicated that the different item types — verbal or mathematical — had similar validities, thus suggesting that the shift in the mix of items in 1974 probably did not change to any great extent what the SAT was measuring. Any large changes in what the SAT measured would be expected to show up in changes in correlations with other tests and also in correlations among subsets of test items, such as section scores or subscores.

Changes in correlational patterns. Correlational patterns among the SAT-V, the SAT-M, and the TSWE showed only slight variation from year to year (see Figure 7-5). A slight downward trend of about .02 appeared in the correlations between the SAT-V and the SAT-M, particularly for November test takers. Most of the correlations of the SAT-V with the TSWE fell between .78 and .79. Except for one outlier, those for the SAT-M with the TSWE ranged between .62 and .64. The correlations between the two SAT-V sections, and particularly between the two SAT-M sections, approached the maximum they could reach, given their imperfect reliabilities. Using the formula from classical test theory (see Gulliksen, 1950, p. 105) that corrects the correlation for attenuation due to imperfect reliability, we derived adjusted correlations that ranged from .97 to 1.00. The corrected correlations for the SAT-M tended to be slightly higher than those for the SAT-V, indicating somewhat greater homogeneity among SAT-M item types. Moreover, the correlations for the SAT-M sections tended to increase slightly over time. The correlations between the Reading and Vocabulary subscores, which were slightly less correlated than the SAT-V sections, were also relatively stable over time.

Relation to validity. Although there were a few data points that deviated from the general trends, there is no evidence to suggest any significant change in what the SAT measured over time. Any changes in the test or its other statistical characteristics had little observable effect on correlational patterns, which stayed relatively stable over time. The few trends observed in the data — for example, the gradual decrease in the correlation between the SAT-V and the SAT-M and the slight increase in the correlation between SAT-M sections — were too small to have more than a marginal effect on predictive validity.

EQUATING PROCEDURES

Equating is the process by which scores from different forms of the SAT are placed on scale. In general, equating, by making scores from different administrations more comparable, would be expected to improve validity to some extent relative to the validity of unequated scores. Because the SAT is assembled to fairly rigorous statistical specifications, however, even the unequated raw scores of its various editions are somewhat comparable. To account for increases or

Figure 7-5

Trends in Correlational Patterns for November and December SATs
and TSWE Tests Administered from 1970 to 1984

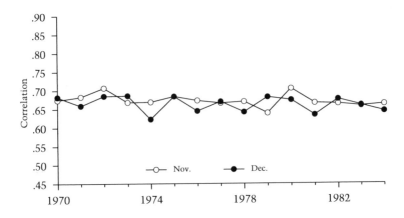

(a) *Correlations Between* SAT-V *and* SAT-M

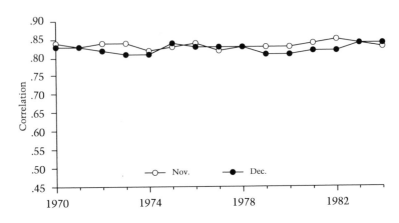

(b) *Correlations Between Sections 1 and 2 of* SAT-V

Figure 7-5 (Continued)

Trends in Correlational Patterns for November and December SATs
and TSWE Tests Administered from 1970 to 1984

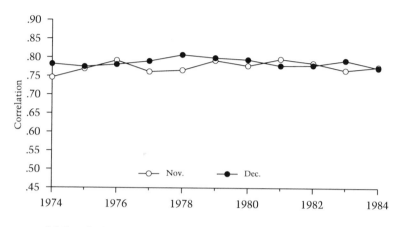

(c) *Correlations Between* SAT-V *and* TSWE

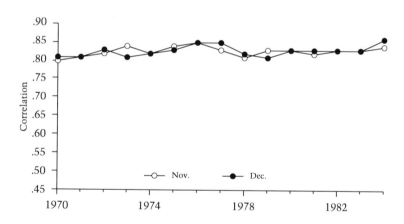

(d) *Correlations Between Sections 1 and 2 of* SAT-M

Figure 7-5 (Continued)

Trends in Correlational Patterns for November and December SATS
and TSWE Tests Administered from 1970 to 1984

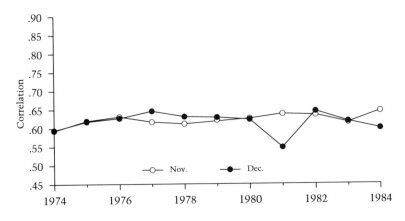

(e) *Correlations Between* SAT-M *and* TSWE

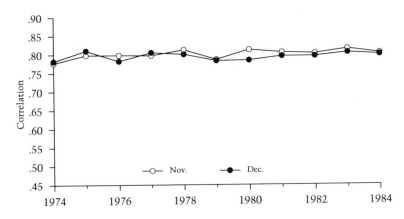

(f) *Correlations Between* SAT-V *Reading and Vocabulary Subscores*

decreases in validity, equating procedures would have had to affect scores differentially over time.

Changes in Equating Procedures

Throughout the period studied, the anchor-test equating design described in Donlon and Livingston (1984) was in use. Under this design, each edition of the SAT-V and the SAT-M was equated back to two SATs through common items, usually administered together in the variable section of the SAT test booklet. Moreover, the same linear equating methods — the Tucker and Levine methods — were used from 1970 to January 1982. Beginning in January 1982, because of the change in statistical specifications for the SAT-V, nonlinear item response theory (IRT) equating was used, sometimes in combination with linear methods, for both the SAT-V and the SAT-M. (The conversions from raw score to scaled score produced by IRT equating are nonlinear in that the graph of their relationship represents a curved line.) These various equating methods are described by Angoff (1982); Donlon and Livingston (1984); Lord (1980); Marco, Petersen, and Stewart (1983); and Petersen, Cook, and Stocking (1983).

For any given equating, two individual equating lines are averaged to produce an operational equating line. From 1970 to 1981, all of the November SAT-V and SAT-M operational equating lines came from an average of two Tucker equating lines. On the other hand, many of the December operational equating lines came from an average of Tucker and Levine lines or of two Levine lines. (Levine equating is used whenever large ability differences exist between new- and old-form equating samples.) There was no consistent trend in the use of the Levine equating method from 1970 to 1981, however. From 1982 to 1984, two IRT (nonlinear) equating lines were averaged, sometimes in combination with linear equating lines, to produce the operational score conversions.

Marco and colleagues (1990) examined several equating indices related to the November and December SAT administrations from 1970 to 1984. These included an index of the difference between the abilities of the equating samples and an index of the difference between the two equating lines, as well as a weighted composite of all the indices. Although there were some outlying values and indices fluctuated more at some times than at others, the November and December patterns were generally variable and inconsistent.

Relation to Validity

Presumably, if equating were to account for increases or decreases in validity, changes in equating procedures or results would have occurred when validity changed. Equating procedures, however, did not change much from 1970 to 1984. The same linear methods were used both before and after the introduction of the shortened SAT in the fall of 1974. The only change occurred in January 1982, when IRT equating was implemented. Moreover, indices related to the quality of equating exhibited some fluctuation but no systematic trends over time. Thus, it is not likely that changes in equating procedures affected reported scores in a way that would affect the predictive validity of the SAT. Other evidence of the effect of equating on the scaled scores that are reported and on predictive validity is discussed in this section.

Effect of equating on scaled scores. If the choice of equating procedures had little effect on reported scores, the changes in equating procedures could not have had much effect on predictive validity. Perhaps the strongest evidence of the integrity of the equating process over time comes from the scale-stability studies that have been conducted. The latest one (McHale & Ninneman, 1990) covered the period 1973 to 1984 and thus is directly relevant to the time period addressed in this study. Earlier, Modu and Stern (1975, 1977) reported that from 1963 to 1973, the scales for SAT-V and SAT-M had drifted upward by about one-and-a-half points a year. McHale and Ninneman concluded that the SAT-V scale was relatively stable from 1973 to 1984. Their study showed conflicting drifts of similar magnitude in the SAT-M scale between 1973 and 1984. At worst, the drift averaged no more than one-and-a-half scaled-score points a year. Scale shifts this small are unlikely to have any effect on validity.

Effect of nonlinear equating on scaled scores. During the 1970-74 period, before the SAT was shortened, linear methods were used to equate SAT scores. When statistical specifications for SAT-V and SAT-M were changed in 1974 and the shortened SAT was introduced, linear methods were still used — and their use continued until January 1982, when IRT methods were introduced. It is possible that the use of linear rather than nonlinear equating for the shortened SAT could have affected reported scores and predictive validity. It is likewise possible that the switch to IRT equating in 1982 could have affected reported scores in ways that influenced predictive validity.

Two analyses were conducted to determine whether the choice of equating methods affected reported scores. In the first analysis, scaled scores resulting from linear and nonlinear (equipercentile) equating were compared at midpoints of the raw-score ranges for November and December SATs administered from 1970 to 1981 (see

Marco et al., 1990, for details). The smallness of the differences suggests that reported scores would not have been much different, at least in the middle of the score range, had a nonlinear rather than a linear equating method been used, and that the continuation of linear equating with the introduction of the shortened SAT in the fall of 1974 was not inappropriate.

In the second analysis, linear and nonlinear score conversions for the full score range were compared for the November and December 1974 forms and for the January 1982 forms. Table 7-6 reports the

Table 7-6

Comparisons of Linear and Nonlinear Equating Results
for Selected SAT Administrations*

Statistic	SAT-Verbal**			SAT-Mathematical***		
	Linear	Nonlinear****	Difference (Linear Minus Nonlinear)	Linear	Nonlinear****	Difference (Linear Minus Nonlinear)
November 1974 (N = 398,604)						
Mean	446	445	.5	481	481	−.3
SD	109	109	6.6	112	112	5.1
December 1974 (N = 231,955)						
Mean	425	424	1.1	460	460	.2
SD	108	107	6.7	113	113	4.9
January 1982 (N = 74,130)						
Mean	393	394	−1.5	435	438	−3.0
SD	105	103	6.2	115	111	7.5
January 1982 (N = 44,844)						
Mean	392	394	−1.9	433	435	−2.0
SD	103	103	4.5	111	110	5.7

  * Reported scores were based on linear equating results in 1974 and on nonlinear equating results in January 1982.
  ** All SAT-V tests were assembled to new specifications except for the January 1982 SAT-V administered to 74,130 test takers.
  *** Only the 1974 SAT-M tests were assembled to new specifications.
  **** Based on equipercentile equating in November and December 1974 and item-response-theory equating in January 1982.

means and standard deviations of scores resulting from linear and nonlinear equating and the means and standard deviations of the differences between the two. Additional statistics associated with these comparisons are provided by Marco and colleagues (1990). The results show that the means and standard deviations of reported scores would not have changed much had the alternative equating method been used. The similarity of IRT and linear equating results in January 1982 indicates that the switch to IRT equating probably had little impact on reported scores.

Apparently, the choice of equating method was not a critical determinant of scores. If the scores themselves would not have changed much had an alternative equating method been used, then neither would their relationships with other variables, including freshman grades.

Effect of nonlinear equating on validity. A significant development was the decision to implement IRT equating, which produces nonlinear conversions from raw scores to scaled scores, in January 1982 when the statistical specifications for the SAT-V were changed. Little direct evidence exists regarding the effect of nonlinear equating on SAT predictive validity, as reported in studies conducted through the VSS. Data available from a sample of test takers who were included in the 1985 validity study samples, however, did permit a direct comparison of the validity of linear and nonlinear equating results (see Marco et al., 1990, for details).

A match of November 1984 testing program files with VSS files for the entering class of 1985 resulted in a sample of approximately 60,000 students from about 200 colleges who had SAT scores and FGPAS. Because IRT equating was used for both the SAT-V and the SAT-M in November 1984, scaled scores for this administration had nonlinear relationships with raw scores. The correlations of FGPAS were calculated with the scaled scores that were reported and with those that would have resulted from linear equating. These correlations differed only in the third or fourth decimal place. SAT-V linearly equated scores correlated .3662 with FGPA, while reported scores correlated .3650. The corresponding correlations for the SAT-M were .3445 and .3442. Thus, for this sample, the use of linear conversions would have had little effect on predictive validity.

The evidence presented in this section indicates that predictive validity was probably not affected by changes in the procedures used to equate scores on the SATS given to college-bound seniors from 1971 to 1985. The only change of significance was the switch to IRT equating in 1982, and special analyses showed that this change had little effect on scores. They also showed that there was little difference in the predictive validities of nonlinear and linear equating results for the November 1984 SAT.

CONCLUSIONS

The objective of this report was to evaluate the extent to which trends in SAT predictive validity for classes entering college from 1971 to 1985 might have been associated with changes in the test. The analyses of item and test statistics from November and December SAT test administrations from 1970 to 1984 provided little evidence linking changes in the test to changes in predictive validity. The major findings were the following:

- The changes in the timing, format, and content of the test in the fall of 1974 had little effect on what abilities were measured by the SAT or on predictive validity.

- Consistent with planned changes, the average item difficulty was reduced in the fall of 1974, and the test was at least as close to middle difficulty for test takers in the early 1980s as for those in the early 1970s.

- Internal-consistency and test-retest reliabilities were very stable, generally varying no more than .02 from one year to the next.

- Correlational patterns among the SAT-V, the SAT-M, and the TSWE and between parts of the SAT-V or the SAT-M provided no evidence to indicate there was a shift in what the SAT measured over time.

- Although a new equating method was introduced in January 1982, the choice of equating method was shown to have little effect on reported scores or on predictive validity.

None of the patterns of change in the various statistical or equating indices that were studied was consistent with the trends in predictive validity from 1971 to 1985. The few noticeable trends were too slight to have more than a marginal effect on predictive validity. These findings indicate that the changes in SAT predictive validity were not due to changes in test format, item types and content, statistical characteristics, or equating methods.

Comparative Study of Factors Related to the Predictive Validities of 1974-75 and 1984-85 Forms of the SAT

WILLIAM H. ANGOFF, MARK POMPLUN, FRED MCHALE, & RICK MORGAN*

PROCEDURE

This study is one of several designed to help explain the recent decline in SAT predictive validities; it is intended to determine whether the decline may be attributed to changes in the content or statistical characteristics of the SAT in recent years. It makes use of data originally developed in connection with studies of the stability of the SAT scale and provides an excellent opportunity to compare recent forms of the SAT with forms that were in use about 10 years earlier, especially with respect to factors that might have an impact on validity.

In May 1984 and again in November 1984, separate half-hour sections of SAT forms, previously administered in the academic year 1974-75, were administered in the variable (nonoperational) portion of the SAT. (See Note 8-1.) The data for those administrations have been matched with college freshman grade-point averages (FGPA) and have been combined across colleges to yield validity coefficients for the May and November 1984 sets of data. The great advantage of this data set is that it permits the direct comparison of the characteristics of the new and old forms of the test as observed in the performance of the *same* group(s) of examinees who, it is observed, took both generations of forms at the same point in time; no adjustments need be made, as are made in other studies, for the fact that different students took the new and old forms or for the fact that they took them at different times.

It is to be noted that the FGPA criterion data have simply been aggregated across the colleges without adjusting for differences in their selectivity or grading standards. Inasmuch as the data used in this study for comparing the validities of old and new test forms depend on test scores and criterion data for the very same students, it was felt that criterion adjustments for these types of differences would not necessarily serve to improve the comparisons. Indeed, if such adjustments are not entirely appropriate, they might instead

---

*The authors wish to express their appreciation to Napoleon Oleka, who conducted the data analysis for this study.

add a component of error to the statistics of interest. Accordingly, the only adjustments introduced here were those made in recognition of different *systems* of reporting the FGPAS — e.g., that grades be recorded on a 0-4 scale, with 4 representing the high-ability end of the scale.

The notation used in the tables of this report is defined as follows:

N = New forms of the SAT, introduced in the regular administrations of May and November 1984 (different forms).

O = Old forms of the SAT, originally introduced in the 1974-75 academic year, and readministered in 1984. (The sections of the old form given in 5/84 had first been given in 12/74; the sections of the old form given in 11/84 had first been given in 4/75.)

V = SAT-Verbal section.

M = SAT-Mathematical section.

1,2 = Section 1 or Section 2 of SAT-Verbal or SAT-Math. (See Note 8-2.)

FGPA = Freshman Grade-Point Average.

RESULTS

The correlations of greatest interest in these data appear in Tables 8-1, 8-2, and 8-3. Table 8-1 gives the validities and reliabilities of the entire section scores; Tables 8-2 and 8-3 give the validities of the separate item types.

We observe in both sets of data (May and November 1984) in Table 8-1 that the old Section 1 of the SAT-V shows higher correlations with FGPA than the new Section 1, but that only in the May 1984 data is the difference significant (at the one percent level). On the other hand, also in both sets of data, the new Section 2 of the SAT-V yields higher validities than the old — although the difference in validity is not significant in either set of data. On balance, it appears that the differences in favor of the old form are slightly greater than those in favor of the new form; averaging over all available observations, the validities for the new verbal forms are less than .01 lower than those for the old forms. Combining the two verbal sections and, separately, combining the two math sections (assuming correlations of .835 between the verbal sections and .815 between the math sections) yields small differences between the new and old forms, consistent with the average validities in the table. These differences all favor the old forms, but only one (math, 1984 data) approaches significance at the .01 level. On the possibility that these differences in predictive validity, however small, might be attributable to differences in reliability, Kuder-Richardson (20) reliabilities were calculated for the section scores, and are shown in Table 8-1. These reliabilities, however, throw little light on the direction of the differences in validities; overall, the reliabilities for the new forms are very little different from the reliabilities for the old.

In the case of the SAT-M, the differences in validity in three of the four instances favor the old test, but in only one of these (Section 1 in the May data) is the difference (.057) sizable and significant (at the one percent level). Again, averaging over all available observations, the validities for the new math forms are less than .02 lower than those for the old forms.

Table 8-1

Validities and Reliabilities of SAT-Verbal and SAT-Math Scores

		May 1984 Data						
Test	No. of Cases	Validities of Forms:* New	Old	Diff. in Validities: New minus Old	No. of Cases	Reliabilities of Forms:** New	Old	Diff. in Reliabilities: New minus Old
V1	1139	.326	.374	−.048***	1135	.834	.834	.000
V2	1124	.295	.275	.020	1120	.834	.791	.043
M1	1319	.284	.341	−.057***	1315	.748	.778	−.030
M2	1324	.333	.339	−.006	1320	.835	.812	.023

		November 1984 Data						
Test	No. of Cases	Validities of Forms:* New	Old	Diff. in Validities: New minus Old	No. of Cases	Reliabilities of Forms:** New	Old	Diff. in Reliabilities: New minus Old
V1	996	.347	.358	−.011	995	.815	.809	.006
V2	1014	.356	.348	.008	1010	.850	.832	.018
M1	1107	.363	.381	−.018	1105	.790	.790	.000
M2	1223	.346	.336	.010	1220	.815	.822	−.007

* Correlations with freshman grade-point average (FGPA)

** Kuder-Richardson (20) reliabilities

*** Significant at the one percent level

Note: The reliabilities and validities tabled here are based on essentially, but not quite, the same samples. The reliabilities in each instance are based on the validity samples diminished in size to the nearest multiple of 5.

It is recalled that these validities in Table 8-1 apply to half-length, not full-length, tests. On the chance that the differences in validities might be larger and more informative if corrected for length, estimates were made for the validities of the corresponding full-length tests. As expected, the new values were all larger than those reported in Table 8-1, but the differences in estimated validities for the new and old forms in every instance were the same (to the second place) for the full-length tests as for those already reported. Correction for test length did not, in fact, provide information beyond what was already known.

Table 8-2

Validities of sat-Verbal Item Types*

	May 1984 Data							
Item Type	*Section 1 Nos. of Items*	*NV1*	*OV1* (N=1139)	*Diff. New-Old*	*Section 2 Nos. of Items*	*NV2*	*OV2* (N=1124)	*Diff. New-Old*
Antonyms	15	.233	.312	−.079***	10	.185	.182	.003
Sentence Completion	10	.286	.304	−.018	5	.193	.137	.056
Analogies	10	.274	.250	.024	10	.220	.220	.000
Reading Comprehension	10	.255	.313	−.057**	15	.295	.257	.038
	November 1984 Data							
Item Type	*Section 1 Nos. of Items*	*NV1*	*OV1* (N=996)	*Diff. New-Old*	*Section 2 Nos. of Items*	*NV2*	*OV2* (N=1014)	*Diff. New-Old*
Antonyms	15	.286	.320	−.034	10	.291	.255	.036
Sentence Completion	10	.275	.244	.031	5	.230	.260	−.030
Analogies	10	.204	.232	−.028	10	.254	.238	.016
Reading Comprehension	10	.309	.305	.004	15	.326	.330	−.004

* Correlations with freshman grade-point average (fgpa)

** Significant at the five percent level

*** Significant at the one percent level

198

Tables 8-2 and 8-3 show the validities of the item types in the old and new forms; Table 8-2 reports the verbal validities, and Table 8-3, the mathematical validities. Of the 16 comparisons in Table 8-2, seven favor the old form, but only two of those are sizable and significant, one at the one percent level, the other at the five percent level. None of the eight differences that favor the new forms is statistically significant, and the comparison in one instance shows no difference at all.

Table 8-3

Validities of sat-Mathematical Item Types *

| | May 1984 Data | | | | | |
| | NM1 OM1 (N=1139) | | Difference: New minus Old | NM2 OM2 (N=1124) | | Difference: New minus Old |
Item Type						
Regular Math (25 items)	.284	.341	−.057***	—	—	—
Regular Math (15 items)	—	—	—	.297	.290	.007
Quantitative Comparison (20 items)	—	—	—	.319	.327	−.008

| | November 1984 Data | | | | | |
| | NM1 OM1 (N=1107) | | Difference: New minus Old | NM2 OM2 (N=1223) | | Difference: New minus Old |
Item Type						
Regular Math (25 items)	.363	.381	−.018	—	—	—
Regular Math (15 items)	—	—	—	.295	.332	−.037
Quantitative Comparison (20 items)	—	—	—	.329	.288	.041**

* Correlations with fgpa

** Significant at the five percent level

*** Significant at the one percent level

Note: All Regular Math items are five-choice; all Quantitative Comparison items are four-choice.

Averaging over the May and November data, separately by section, it appears that the difference in validity for Antonyms in Section 1 of the SAT-Verbal is fairly sizable (.056, on average) and in favor of the old forms. The same is true of the Reading Comprehension item type, but to a much smaller degree. Any conclusions that might be drawn from these data, however, are contravened by the data of Section 2, which are quite inconsistent with those of Section 1. There, the average difference in validity for those two item types, again averaging over the May and November data, are not only smaller, but in favor of the new forms.

Taken as a whole, the average difference in validities for the verbal item types in Section 1 is less than .02 in favor of the old forms; the average difference in validities in Section 2 is smaller, less than .015, but in the opposite direction, in favor of the new forms.

Of the six possible comparisons in Table 8-3, in which the validities of the SAT-M item types are shown, four favor the old forms, and of these, one is significant (at the one percent level).

Of the two comparisons that favor the new forms, one shows a small and nonsignificant difference; the other is significant at the five percent level.

Taken over the two sets of data, it appears that the validities of the Regular Math items in Section 1 of the old forms are greater (by .038, on the average) than those in the new forms. The new and old validities in Section 2, however, are about equal, showing an average difference of less than .001 in favor of the new forms.

It appears from Table 8-3 that the four-choice math items have maintained their predictive validity, but that the five-choice items have not. There are too few observations possible here, however, to make this generalization definitively.

The data of Tables 8-1, 8-2, and 8-3 show that the validity differences in favor of the old forms were only slightly greater than those favoring the new forms. On balance, then, the data give some, but not very convincing, support to the hypothesis that the 1984 forms showed a lower correlation with freshman grades than did the 1974 forms.

Table 8-4 provides summary statistics for the SAT-V sections, and yields observed-score and true-score correlations between corresponding new and old sections of the test. In three of the four instances (Sections 1 and 2 in the May 1984 data and Section 2 in the November 1984 data), the new form appears to be easier — i.e., it has higher means — than the old form, with differences particularly pronounced in Section 2 of both sets of data. The exception is found in Section 1 of the November 1984 data, in which the old form shows

Table 8-4

Means, Standard Deviations, and Correlations for sat-Verbal Sections

	NV1	OV1	NV2	OV2
May 1984 Data				
No. of Cases	1135		1120	
Mean	22.47	20.36	21.09	17.95
Std. Dev.	7.78	7.88	7.65	6.70
Correlation	.779		.785	
Disattenuated Correlation	.934		.966	
November 1984 Data				
No. of Cases	995		1010	
Mean	20.80	22.11	19.65	16.93
Std. Dev.	7.58	6.89	7.89	7.72
Correlation	.766		.783	
Disattenuated Correlation	.943		.931	

Note: These figures are taken from the test and item analyses of the new and old sections. The disattenuated correlations tabled here make use of the reliabilities reported in Table 8-1.

a higher mean (and is, therefore, presumably easier) than the new form. The observed (raw-score) correlations between new and old forms are all in the upper .70s. The corresponding correlations corrected for unreliability are in the low-to-middle .90s, noticeably lower than the correlations between Sections 1 and 2 as observed in regular operational test analyses. In those analyses, the disattenuated correlations are typically very close to 1.00 (i.e., .98, .99, or 1.00).

Similar observations are made in Table 8-5, which gives data corresponding to those in Table 8-4, but for sat-M. Here, too, in three of the four instances, the new math form is somewhat easier than the old. The exception is found in the November 1984 data for

Section 2, where the new form is seen to be slightly more difficult than the old. We also see in Table 8-5 that the observed correlations between the new and old forms range from the low .70s to the low .80s and that the disattenuated correlations between new and old forms are somewhat inconsistent with one another. The May 1984 data for SAT-M in Table 8-5 agree with the data in Table 8-4 for SAT-V, in which the true-score correlations are seen to fall in the middle .90s. Unlike the May 1984 data, however, the November 1984 SAT-M data show these correlations to be much closer to 1.00.

In general, like the disattenuated correlations in Table 8-4, these correlations in Table 8-5 are not as high as one would normally expect from presumably parallel forms, certainly not as high as the correlations between the two operational sections of the SAT-V or of the SAT-M, which are consistently close to 1.00. The lower correla-

Table 8-5

Means, Standard Deviations, and Correlations
for SAT-Mathematical Sections

	NM1	OM1	NM2	OM2
May 1984 Data				
No. of Cases	1315		1320	
Mean	13.81	12.64	18.38	16.41
Std. Dev.	4.55	4.93	7.29	6.84
Correlation	.730		.790	
Disattenuated Correlation	.957		.959	
November 1984 Data				
No. of Cases	1105		1220	
Mean	11.97	11.01	16.53	17.42
Std. Dev.	5.14	5.21	6.81	6.95
Correlation	.780		.829	
Disattenuated Correlation	.987		1.013	

tions observed in the present study suggest the possibility that the levels of difficulty and/or the types of test content in the new and old forms of the SAT had undergone some change after the middle 1970s.

Operating on the hypothesis that, indeed, one or more of the item types in the SAT-V and SAT-M had undergone some subtle, but significant, change between 1974 and 1984, additional tabulations were made by item type. Tables 8-6 and 8-7 give the observed and disattenuated (true-score) correlations between the new and old forms of verbal and mathematical, based on the same set of data as those in Tables 8-4 and 8-5, but separately by item type.

As seen in Tables 8-6 and 8-7, the observed-score correlations between the new (1984) and old (1974) forms of the tests are generally low, lower in the verbal tests (falling mostly in the .40s and .50s) than in the mathematical tests (.60s and .70s). The reduced size of these correlations is not overly surprising; the reliabilities of the verbal item types, based on overall numbers of items, are mostly in the .50s and .60s and the reliabilities of the math item types, also based on few items, although at higher levels, are still relatively low, mainly in the .70s.

Of greater interest than the observed-score correlations, however, are the disattenuated correlations, which should be close to 1.00 if the new and old forms of the tests are parallel in content (and roughly similar in difficulty). As it happens, the new vs. old true-score correlations for the Analogies and Reading Comprehension tests (Table 8-6) in the May 1984 data for Section 1 are only in the mid-to-high .70s; the correlations for all item types in the May 1984 data for Section 2 are considerably higher, but still only in the low-to-mid .90s. The correlations in the November 1984 data are similarly lower than one would expect. Only one (Antonyms, Section 1) of the eight correlations listed in Sections 1 and 2 is close to 1.00; the others range from .784 to .931. (The Antonyms, Section 1, data also show a high true-score correlation in the May 1984 data: .983.) To what extent these values are affected by sampling error — undoubtedly, estimates of true-score correlations from the item groupings as shown here, with as few as 5-15 items, are prone to considerable error — is not entirely clear, but the variation in these coefficients seems to be larger than one would expect, very likely too great to guide further study of these data. One possibility is that there may have been a change in the Analogies and Reading Comprehension items in Section 1. Both the May and November 1984 data for these two item types do show somewhat lower true-score correlations than do the data for the other item types.

The observed-score correlations for the SAT-M sections, shown in Table 8-7, are in the .60s and .70s, and there is some indication that

Table 8-6

Observed and Disattenuated Correlations Between New and Old
SAT-Verbal Sections by Item Type

May 1984 Data — Section 1 (N=1135)

	Nos. of Items	Observed Correlations	Reliabilities* New Form	Reliabilities* Old Form	Disattenuated Correlations
Antonyms	15	.563	.563	.582	.983
Sentence Completion	10	.559	.621	.530	.974
Analogies	10	.451	.600	.574	.769
Reading Comprehension	10	.465	.556	.643	.778

May 1984 Data — Section 2 (N=1120)

	Nos. of Items	Observed Correlations	Reliabilities* New Form	Reliabilities* Old Form	Disattenuated Correlations
Antonyms	10	.455	.520	.425	.968
Sentence Completion	5	.350	.312	.432	.951
Analogies	10	.594	.615	.633	.953
Reading Comprehension	15	.589	.705	.586	.917

November 1984 Data — Section 1 (N=995)

	Nos. of Items	Observed Correlations	Reliabilities* New Form	Reliabilities* Old Form	Disattenuated Correlations
Antonyms	15	.599	.575	.651	.979
Sentence Completion	10	.491	.564	.494	.931
Analogies	10	.420	.570	.466	.815
Reading Comprehension	10	.433	.510	.504	.854

November 1984 Data — Section 2 (N=1010)

	Nos. of Items	Observed Correlations	Reliabilities* New Form	Reliabilities* Old Form	Disattenuated Correlations
Antonyms	10	.393	.512	.490	.784
Sentence Completion	5	.389	.350	.556	.882
Analogies	10	.503	.572	.617	.847
Reading Comprehension	15	.673	.784	.680	.921

*Kuder-Richardson (20) reliabilities

Table 8-7

Observed and Disattenuated Correlations Between New and Old
sAT-Mathematical Sections by Item Type

		May 1984 Data — Section 1 (N=1315)		
		*Reliabilities**		
	Observed *Correlation*	*New* *Form*	*Old* *Form*	*Disattenuated* *Correlation*
Regular Math (25 items)	.729	.747	.778	.956

		May 1984 Data — Section 2 (N=1320)		
		*Reliabilities**		
	Observed *Correlations*	*New* *Form*	*Old* *Form*	*Disattenuated* *Correlations*
Regular Math (15 items)	.634	.703	.596	.980
Quantitative Comparison (20 items)	.695	.743	.741	.937

		November 1984 Data — Section 1 (N=1105)		
		*Reliabilities**		
	Observed *Correlation*	*New* *Form*	*Old* *Form*	*Disattenuated* *Correlation*
Regular Math (25 items)	.780	.790	.790	.987

		November 1984 Data — Section 2 (N=1220)		
		*Reliabilities**		
	Observed *Correlations*	*New* *Form*	*Old* *Form*	*Disattenuated* *Correlations*
Regular Math (15 items)	.675	.652	.693	1.005
Quantitative Comparison (20 items)	.711	.734	.717	.980

*Kuder-Richardson (20) reliabilities

the values of the correlations are related to test length; the correlations between longer sections are clearly higher than the correlations between shorter sections. The variation in reliabilities, which range from .60 to .79, also seems to be associated with test length. In any case, when corrected for attenuation, the correlations range from the middle to high .90s, but again with no discernible pattern.

In brief, this series of tabulations at the item-type level has contributed little more to our understanding of the important differences, if any, between the new and old forms. The only possibility is that, as mentioned above, the Analogies and Reading Comprehension item types may bear further editorial examination to determine whether indeed they underwent any change from the mid-1970s to the mid-1980s.

Table 8-8 presents correlations of old and new verbal and mathematical sections of the SAT with other relevant sections. The intent of these tabulations is to determine (1) whether the two current sections of verbal (or math) correlate more highly, as they should, than does an old section with a current section, and (2) whether the

Table 8-8

Correlations of Old and New Sections of the SAT with Relevant
SAT-Verbal and -Mathematical Sections

	May 1984 data				November 1984 data		
	Panel a; N = 1139				Panel e; N = 996		
	NV2	NM1	NM2		NV2	NM1	NM2
OV1	.789	.532	.562	OV1	.739	.466	.476
NV1	.824	.533	.556	NV1	.815	.515	.528
	Panel b; N = 1124				Panel f; N = 1014		
	NV1	NM1	NM2		NV1	NM1	NM2
OV2	.801	.531	.571	OV2	.778	.488	.480
NV2	.812	.515	.558	NV2	.807	.514	.506
	Panel c; N = 1319				Panel g; N = 1107		
	NV2	NM1	NM2		NV2	NM1	NM2
OM1	.506	.494	.788	OM1	.509	.540	.800
NM1	.500	.466	.754	NM1	.515	.520	.804
	Panel d; N = 1324				Panel h; N = 1223		
	NV1	NV2	NM1		NV1	NV2	NM1
OM2	.578	.550	.735	OM2	.515	.529	.788
NM2	.579	.540	.768	NM2	.504	.523	.791

current section (e.g., verbal) yields a lower correlation with the complementary current measure (e.g., math), as it should, than does an old (verbal) section.

Examination of Table 8-8 reveals that these expectations are realized in virtually every instance in the May 1984 data, but in little more than half the instances in the November 1984 data. While the correlations between current sections are nearly always higher than the correlations of current sections with old sections, current sections (e.g., verbal or math) do not correlate lower with complementary current sections (math or verbal) than with complementary old sections as often as would be ideal.

Table 8-9 gives summary statistics on the measures of item difficulty, item discrimination, numbers of items omitted, and speededness for the several forms of the SAT-V and the SAT-M. The item difficulty indices are expressed in the form conventionally used at ETS, as deltas. The item delta is calculated by transforming the p-value for the item (proportion of examinees answering the item correctly) to a normal deviate, z (mean = 0, s.d. = 1), and converting that value to a scale with mean = 13, s.d. = 4 by the linear transformation, delta = $-4z + 13$. Thus, easy items are characterized by low values of delta; hard items are characterized by high values of delta.

The item discrimination indices are simply the biserial correlations between pass-fail on the item and the total score on the section that contains the item. Both the delta and the item-test biserial correlation are the traditional measures of difficulty and discrimination used at ETS.

The number of items omitted is defined as the number of items left blank prior to the last item attempted.

Finally, the index of speededness reported here is the ratio of the variance of the number of items not reached by the students to the variance of scores.

A review of the mean deltas in Table 8-9 reveals that the new forms of the test are, in general, slightly easier than the old, although the test specifications for these forms called for no change in item difficulty. It is noted, incidentally, that these comparisons in difficulty are quite consistent with the test-score statistics shown in Tables 8-4 and 8-5. (See Note 8-3.)

The statistics on item discrimination are unremarkable; they show very little difference between the new and old forms, and whatever differences exist are entirely inconsistent, confirming the observation made earlier that there are no clear differences in reliability between the new and old forms.

Table 8-9

Summary Statistics on Item Difficulty (Delta), Item Discrimination (Biserial r), Number of Items Omitted, and Speededness

	NV1	OV1	NV2	OV2	NM1	OM1	NM2	OM2
May 1984 Data								
No. of Items	45	45	40	40	25	25	35	35
Mean Delta	11.81	12.38	11.69	12.46	11.59	12.05	11.48	11.91
S.D. of Delta	3.29	3.32	2.63	3.29	3.13	3.16	2.72	3.08
Mean r_{bis}	0.49	0.49	0.50	0.47	0.54	0.56	0.55	0.52
S.D. of r_{bis}	0.11	0.11	0.10	0.10	0.08	0.08	0.07	0.10
No. of Items Omitted								
No. of cases	1135		1120		1315		1320	
Mean	4.49	5.78	4.20	4.58	2.03	2.64	1.98	2.78
Std. Dev.	4.66	5.45	3.97	4.41	2.21	2.48	2.45	3.27
Speededness Index*	.082	.048	.044	.037	.052	.060	.029	.057

	NV1	OV1	NV2	OV2	NM1	OM1	NM2	OM2
November 1984 Data								
No. of Items	45	45	40	40	25	25	35	35
Mean Delta	12.14	12.06	11.98	12.72	12.31	12.66	12.12	11.87
S.D. of Delta	3.16	3.79	2.80	2.65	3.13	3.05	3.13	3.02
Mean r_{bis}	0.45	0.49	0.52	0.49	0.57	0.56	0.52	0.53
S.D. of r_{bis}	0.11	0.10	0.09	0.11	0.10	0.09	0.13	0.10
No. of Items Omitted								
No. of cases	995		1010		1105		1220	
Mean	4.99	4.70	4.69	4.75	2.27	2.76	2.56	2.85
Std. Dev.	4.66	4.43	4.32	4.62	2.50	2.71	3.03	3.20
Speededness Index*	.175	.039	.086	.088	.081	.055	.054	.079

* The index of speededness used here is the ratio of the variance of the number of items not reached to the variance of scores: $\sigma_{n}^2/\sigma_{x}^2$.

Note: The samples on which the reliabilities in Table 8-1 were based were also used to calculate the values in this table.

The data on items omitted show that there are generally more omits in the old verbal forms than in the new, *but* there is evidence of slightly greater speededness in the new forms than in the old (see the speededness index).

The data on the math tests show consistently fewer items omitted in the new forms but somewhat inconsistent data on speededness. Again, there is no clear pattern of differences in the comparison of new and old forms taken by the same groups of examinees.

A hypothesis had been advanced that a change in the difficulty of the tests during the years between 1974 and 1984 caused a decline in the validity of the tests at the lower ranges of ability. In order to examine this hypothesis, the distributions of scores on the two sections of the tests for both the old and new forms were divided into three segments, comprising, respectively, about 27, 46, and 27 percent of the cases. (This division of the distributions was carried out as a compromise solution. To divide the scale into three equal parts would have yielded too few cases in the end categories and too many, relatively, in the middle; on the other hand, to divide the total group into three subgroups of equal size would have resulted in three grossly unequal scale segments. The division into 27, 46, and 27 percent of the group was the outcome of a decision to avoid both of these extreme and undesirable results.) Table 8-10 presents the intercepts and slopes for predicting FGPA for each of the three segments of the distributions. Data are given for new and old forms of Sections 1 and 2 of both the verbal and mathematical tests and for both the May and November 1984 data.

The comparisons in Table 8-10 that are of particular interest are the two slope values — for the new and old forms of the test — for the lower segments of the distributions. Eight such comparisons can be made, four in the May 1984 data and four in the November 1984 data, and within those sets of data, two comparisons for the SAT-V and two for the SAT-M. In the four sets of SAT-V data (considering both the May and November 1984 data), three instances show the new form to have a steeper regression line than the old form; in the four sets of SAT-M data, three show the old form to have a steeper regression line than the new. It should be emphasized, however, that in none of these comparisons is the difference in slope at all substantial. The differences are, in fact, quite small.

In consideration of the observations made in Table 8-5, that the new forms appear to be somewhat easier than the old, attention was also directed in Table 8-10 to the slopes of the regression lines for the middle 46 percent and the upper 27 percent of the distributions. In the middle segment of the distributions, the differences in verbal appear to favor the new forms slightly; the differences in math show no pattern. In the upper segment of the distributions, the slopes for verbal show no consistent pattern of favoring one set of forms over the other; the slopes for math appear to favor the old forms slightly.

Table 8-10

Regression Lines for Predicting FGPA for Low-, Middle-, and High-Scoring Segments of the Test Score Distributions

May 1984 Data

Test Section	Low Segment Intercept	Slope	Middle Segment Intercept	Slope	High Segment Intercept	Slope
NV1	2.068	.019	1.846	.036	2.072	.026
OV1	2.000	.026	1.971	.033	2.160	.027
NV2	2.143	.019	2.009	.026	1.728	.038
OV2	2.282	.007	2.071	.029	1.963	.034
NM1	2.107	.041	1.940	.048	1.308	.083
OM1	2.018	.052	2.293	.026	1.778	.063
NM2	2.055	.036	2.150	.023	2.086	.031
OM2	2.206	.020	2.105	.029	1.804	.046

November 1984 Data

Test Section	Low Segment Intercept	Slope	Middle Segment Intercept	Slope	High Segment Intercept	Slope
NV1	1.865	.034	1.764	.040	1.902	.031
OV1	2.012	.018	1.783	.035	1.281	.053
NV2	2.012	.017	1.711	.039	1.341	.049
OV2	2.124	.004	2.258	.012	1.745	.040
NM1	1.988	.040	1.662	.071	2.073	.043
OM1	1.965	.052	1.748	.070	1.896	.056
NM2	1.976	.025	2.001	.030	1.680	.045
OM2	1.926	.036	1.903	.032	1.298	.059

In brief, there is little evidence to support the hypothesis that the new forms of the test are less clearly predictive of college success than the old forms for students at the lower end of the scale. The same is true for the middle and upper segments of the scale.

What is of some interest is that the slopes of the regression lines in Table 8-10 generally progress upward in steepness from low to high, suggesting some curvilinearity of regression over the entire range of SAT scores. This would seem to indicate that in this data set, at least, the test is a better predictor of freshman grades for higher-scoring than for lower-scoring students.

Finally, as part of this effort to determine the reason or reasons for the observed decline in the predictive validity coefficients in the colleges, the leaders in the ETS test development groups responsible for the SAT-V and SAT-M were requested to make a review of the old and new forms studied in this report. The purpose of their review was to determine whether there were any differences between the forms that might be related to the changes in validity. It should be emphasized that these reviews were entirely impressionistic, not rigorous, nor were they expected to be as intensive or informative as the reviews reported in the detailed study by Marco, Crone, Braswell, Curley, and Wright (1990).

The review of the verbal tests yielded the observation that the order of the items within the sections was changed somewhat, and that there were some detailed changes in the length of stimulus materials, especially in the Reading Comprehension item type. In addition, there were fewer especially difficult-looking, arcane words in the new forms and fewer items calling on outside knowledge. Finally, Analogy distracters that seemed to have no obvious relationship to each other were largely eliminated in the new forms.

The review of the math sections also reported that there were no discernible differences either in test content or in the ability level tested; nor were there any differences in the number of items in concrete vs. abstract settings. Recent forms, it was noted, generally have very few wordy items, fewer than in older forms. The level of geometry required to solve the questions on the newer forms is comparable to that on the older forms, and does not go beyond the specifications for the test. It was observed that a change in the placement of the Quantitative Comparison items reduced the speededness of the test. In any case, the difference was not felt to be marked, nor is it clear how this difference would have affected the predictive validity of the tests.

CONCLUSIONS

The tabulations of the validity coefficients for the scores on the sections of the SAT and for scores on the separate item types showed small and inconsistent differences in favor of the old forms of the tests. The data do not permit a clear conclusion as to whether the differences are real. In any event, the observed differences are quite small — .013, on average — in favor of the old test sections. Virtually none of the attempts to associate statistical or content changes in the test with the notion of a decline in predictive validity yielded useful results. Very few of the psychometric tabulations showed consistent differences between the two forms, and those that were found — for example, a lower-than-expected true-score correlation between the new and old forms (especially in the case of the SAT-V) and a slightly lower level of difficulty and higher level of speededness (at least in SAT-V) in the new forms — failed to identify specific characteristics in the new forms of the SAT that might have accounted for their lower validities. Impressionistic reviews of the new and old forms made by test development specialists similarly failed to identify characteristics associated with lower validities.

CHAPTER 9

Effects of Coaching on the Validity of the SAT: Results of a Simulation Study

NAZLI BAYDAR[*]

This chapter presents a simulation study that assesses the probable effects of trends in student coaching in preparation for the SAT on trends in this test's predictive validity for freshman-year performance. During the 10-year period between 1976 and 1985, the multiple correlation of SAT-Mathematical and SAT-Verbal with freshman grades declined by about .04, or 8 percent, in colleges that participated in the College Board's Validity Study Service (Morgan, 1989a). (See Note 9-1.) Using simulations, we estimate the changes in the validity of the SAT that result from hypothetical changes in the extent and effectiveness of coaching.

The SAT is designed to measure long-term developed abilities of verbal and quantitative reasoning and comprehension (Donlon, 1984a; Messick, 1980). As a predictor of freshman-year performance, the validity of the SAT hinges on two factors:

- The extent to which the SAT scores reflect verbal and quantitative reasoning abilities of students, and

- The extent to which these abilities are reflected in college performance as indicated by freshman-year grades.

Coaching will negatively affect predictive validity only if it leads to increases in test scores without corresponding improvements in the skills that are relevant to college performance. The simulations presented here examine the extent to which possible increases in the incidence and effectiveness of coaching for the SAT could have systematically degraded the SAT's predictive validity over time. Although these simulations cannot provide conclusive evidence of the existence of such coaching effects, or of the actual magnitude of the effects of coaching on the validity of the SAT, they can provide plausible bounds for the magnitude of such effects, given certain assumptions on modeling and on the incidence and effectiveness of coaching.

---

[*] The author would like to thank Paul Holland for statistical advice and Min Hwei Wang for outstanding programming assistance.

To interpret the results of the simulations correctly, it is important to distinguish three components of score gains that could result from coaching (Messick, 1982):

- Gains due to test-taking familiarization and reduced anxiety,

- Gains due to genuine improvement in reasoning and comprehension skills, and

- Gains due to learning test-specific tricks and strategies.

The first type of score gain leads to valid increases in test scores and therefore improves the validity of the test. The second type results from a genuine improvement in skills that lead to improved college performance as well as improved test scores, and hence does not affect the validity of the test. The third type of score gain (i.e., that due to learning tricks and strategies for selecting answers) leads to a spurious increase in test scores that affects test validity negatively.

Score gains over time may also occur for reasons other than coaching, such as academic growth, increased motivation, test practice, and stochastic fluctuations of the scores. Therefore, total score gains of students cannot be equated to coaching effects. Coaching effects can be measured as the average difference between the score gains of coached students and the score gains of comparable uncoached students over the same time period.

THE SIMULATIONS

Data on 1985 freshmen at two colleges are used to simulate the effects of coaching on the validity of the SAT. After the validity of the SAT for each college is estimated, a given proportion of students is picked, and score gains of given magnitude are added to the observed SAT-Verbal and SAT-Mathematical scores of each student. The validity of this new set of SAT scores is then estimated and compared to the validity of the observed scores. Each simulation provides an estimate of the change in validity of the SAT resulting from a hypothetical coaching effect of a given size for a given proportion of the freshmen.

In these simulations, an association between coaching effects and the first-year average is not modeled; hence, the design of the simulations excludes gains due to skills acquisition. The simulated coaching effects are assumed to be due to test familiarization and to trick and strategy learning (i.e., gains that do not lead to corresponding increases in freshman performance). (See Note 9-2.) However, gains associated with skills acquisition are probably included in the coaching effect estimates, reported in various studies on coaching, which are used here to determine the size of the simulated coaching effects. Hence, the results of the simulations are likely to overrepresent the impact of a given magnitude of coaching effects on the predictive validity of the SAT.

The data on SAT scores that are used in the simulations are probably already contaminated by coaching effects. Although that is a disadvantage of using real data for the simulations, using entirely simulated data would have other disadvantages. For example, observed data on student background characteristics, academic performance, and SAT scores already reflect unmeasured associations due to interactions between these variables and their common unobserved determinants (such as motivation). If simulations were based only on modeled data, introduction of such interactions and unobserved determinants would be very difficult, and hence, the relevance of the results of such simulations would be limited. The presence of actual coaching effects in the observed data may affect the observed validity coefficient. Therefore, our results emphasize the simulated *relative* changes in the validity of the SAT, obtained by comparing the observed validity coefficient to the validity coefficient obtained after coaching effects are simulated.

THE ASSUMPTIONS

Students Who Are Likely to Receive Coaching

Differences in the background characteristics of coached and uncoached students are well-documented and substantial (FTC, 1979), and it is desirable to retain these differences in the simulations. A survey of high school juniors and seniors who registered to take the SAT during 1986 and 1987 provides detailed information on the profiles of students who used various forms of SAT preparation (Powers, 1988). (See Note 9-3.) Using these data, a logistic model of the probability of being coached was developed. This model expresses the probability of being coached for each student as a function of an "average" probability of being coached and of the effects of background characteristics, including father's education, parental income, and high school grade-point average (HSGPA). This model is employed in the simulations so that a student's background characteristics contribute to the probability of that student being selected to receive simulated coaching effects (i.e., to have the observed SAT score increased by an assumed coaching effect). Different levels of distribution of propensity for being coached can be simulated by manipulating the term in the logistic model that quantifies the average probability of being coached. (See Note 9-4.)

Our estimates show that an "average" student in Powers' sample has 0.11 probability of being coached. Alderman and Powers (1980) found that about 3 percent of the students who took the SAT in December 1977 attended coaching sessions outside of school. A survey of SAT-taking juniors in 1978 (Powers & Alderman, 1979, 1983) revealed that about 5 percent had been coached. Data on 1986-87 juniors and seniors (Powers, 1988) indicate that 14 percent of the respondents were coached. These figures indicate that there has been an increase in the proportion of students who seek and receive coaching for the SAT during the past 10 years. Whitla (1988) reports that 22 percent of Harvard students had been coached, which leads one to expect that almost a quarter of the students might have received coaching in such selective institutions.

Three mean levels of probability of being coached are assumed in the simulations:

- An estimate of the level of coaching 10 years ago — 5 percent.

- The approximate current level of coaching — 15 percent.

- A high level of coaching, observed in some very selective colleges — 25 percent.

Simulated Increases in SAT Scores Due to Coaching

Although there are many studies on coaching effects, few adequately control for confounding score gains from other sources, such as learning that occurs independent of coaching, test practice, and increased motivation. The results of some nonrandomized studies are further contaminated by the fact that the profiles of coached students differ from those of uncoached students. The claims of coaching schools, on the other hand, refer to students' total score gains over time and therefore include gains from all sources.

The best information on the effects of coaching is derived from a comparison of the differences in pre- and post-test scores of coached and uncoached students who are assigned to these groups randomly (Messick & Jungeblut, 1981). Even then, it is very difficult to distinguish score increases due to trick learning from those due to learning that occurs independent of coaching, to test familiarization, to instruction in skills that are relevant to college performance, or to stochastic fluctuations of test scores.

Meta-analyses by Messick and Jungeblut (1981) and DerSimonian and Laird (1983) provide quantitative syntheses of prior studies (with a variety of program and study designs) on the magnitude of coaching effects. Hence, these two studies probably provide estimates of coaching effects that are less vulnerable to program design or methods of estimation than any particular study. Messick and Jungeblut summarize their study with a regression analysis of coaching effects on (the logarithm of) hours spent in coaching programs. The mean coaching effects are estimated at about 23 points for SAT-Math and 14 points for SAT-Verbal. DerSimonian and Laird provide estimates of coaching effects adjusted for interstudy correlations. Their estimates are 18 points for math and 19 points for verbal. Both Messick-Jungeblut and DerSimonian-Laird estimates could be somewhat high because they include data from full-time post-high school preparatory schools such as those reported by Marron (1965), which are expected to contain substantial gains due to genuine skills improvement. When the data from such long-term programs are excluded, Messick-Jungeblut estimates of coaching effects are 16 and 14 for SAT-Math and SAT-Verbal, respectively. All of these estimates are somewhat lower than those claimed by the Federal Trade Commission study (FTC, 1979), which averaged 25 and 32 points for math and verbal, respectively (Stroud, 1980). (See Note 9-5.) The Harvard study (Whitla, 1988) reported small net effects of coaching: 16 and 11 points for math and verbal, respectively. Smyth (1989) found increases (15-35 points) in math scores due to coaching but almost no increase in verbal scores.

In the simulations, it is desirable to consider a *distribution* of coaching effects because they vary from student to student. These variations could be due to:

- Differences between students in level of motivation or ability to retain coaching information,

- Differences between coaching programs, and

- Differences in the number of hours invested in the programs.

DerSimonian and Laird (1983) estimated the variance due to program differences in a group of programs that various studies reported. However, their estimates reflect a combination of variance due to program differences and variance due to hours spent in each program, because they did not control for hours. The Messick-Jungeblut meta-analysis introduces a control for hours, but it is not possible to partition the remaining variance in coaching effects into components due to differential study designs and methods of estimation, as well as program differences.

Data from 1986-87 SAT takers (Powers, 1988) show that, among the coached students, there is substantial variation in the number of hours spent in coaching. The variation in coaching effects due to the variation in hours could be estimated using the regression equations reported by Messick and Jungeblut (1981; see Note 9-6) that relate the logarithm of hours spent in coaching programs to coaching effects. This exercise leads to estimated coefficients of variation of coaching effects (standard deviation divided by mean) of .954 and .734 for SAT-Math and SAT-Verbal, respectively. Hence, in the simulations, coaching effects are assumed to be normally distributed with a given mean and a variance based on these coefficients of variation. (See Note 9-7.)

The coaching effects on SAT-Math and SAT-Verbal for a given student are probably correlated. This association might stem from two sources:

- For each student, coaching effects on both components of the SAT might reflect the same underlying factors, such as motivation and ability to retain information;

- Students are likely to receive coaching for both components from the same program, which is likely to adopt a uniform approach to mathematical and verbal coaching.

The number of hours spent on SAT-Verbal and SAT-Math coaching are almost perfectly correlated (.97), according to Powers' 1986-1987 data. In the simulations, this correlation is taken as a proxy for the correlation between math and verbal coaching effects. (See Note 9-8.)

Four sets of assumptions about the magnitude of the coaching effects underlie the simulations:

- One standard deviation unit below
  Messick-Jungeblut mean estimates:

  12 points, SAT-Math
  8 points, SAT-Verbal
  20 points, SAT total

- Messick-Jungeblut mean estimates:

  23 points, SAT-Math
  14 points, SAT-Verbal
  37 points, SAT total

- One standard deviation unit above
  Messick-Jungeblut mean estimates:

  34 points, SAT-Math
  20 points, SAT-Verbal
  54 points, SAT total

- Coaching school claims of 100-point
  total gains (including gains due
  to extraneous learning; see Note 9-9):

  62 points, SAT-Math
  38 points, SAT-Verbal
  100 points, SAT total

The first set of coaching-effect assumptions comes very close to the coaching effects reported by Whitla (1988), Smyth (1989), and Messick and Jungeblut (1981) in their meta-analysis excluding the long-term preparatory schools. These coaching effects are also almost identical to the estimates obtained when the hours of coaching reported by the members of the Powers 1986-87 sample are used to predict coaching effects using Messick-Jungeblut regression equations that relate hours to coaching effects (see Note 9-6). The third variant of coaching-effect assumptions comes very close to the FTC study estimates. The last set of coaching-effect assumptions, based on coaching school claims, should be interpreted as total score gains including the effects of the higher level of motivation of students attending coaching programs and the effects of learning that occurs independent of coaching. (See Note 9-10.)

There is no available research documenting a trend in coaching effects over the last 10 years. The College Board is now actively trying to develop tests that are robust to test-taking tricks, in response to coaching programs that are searching for more effective coaching methods. Additionally, most recent research on coaching effects (Smyth, 1988; Whitla, 1988; computations based on Powers' 1986-87 data) yields coaching-effect estimates that are in parity with earlier studies summarized in the Messick-Jungeblut (1981) and DerSimonian-Laird (1983) meta-analyses. Changes related to coaching during the last decade are more likely to be in the proportion of students coached than in the effectiveness of coaching.

RESULTS

Four colleges from the College Board's Validity Study Service 1985 database were initially chosen for simulations. The results of the simulations for two of these colleges provide bounds to the estimates of probable changes in the predictive validity of the SAT that can be attributed to the assumed changes in the prevalence of coaching. These two are referred to as Colleges A and B. College A is highly selective, with approximate mean SAT scores of 700 (S.D. = 66) for math and 670 (S.D. = 74) for verbal in 1985. College B is less selective, with average SAT scores of 440 (S.D. = 85) and 400 (S.D. = 75) for math and verbal, respectively, in 1985.

Data from 996 freshmen students of College A were available for the simulations. An average freshman has a college-graduate father and a family income slightly under $40,000 per year. The students' mean HSGPA is 3.9 and mean FGPA is 3.1. The observed multiple correlation coefficient of SAT-Math and SAT-Verbal with FGPA is .42. College B data provide information on 386 freshmen students. The average level of education of students' fathers is slightly above high school completion, and the mean parental income is slightly over $25,000 per year. The mean HSGPA of the 1985 entering freshmen is 2.9, much below that of College A freshmen. Mean FGPA is 2.4. The multiple correlation between SAT scores and FGPA is .32, substantially lower than that for College A.

Table 9-1

Multiple Correlation Coefficients of SAT-Math and SAT-Verbal Scores with FGPA When Coaching Effects Are Simulated*

	Probability of Being Coached for an Average Student**					
	College A			College B		
Coaching Effects	5%	15%	25%	5%	15%	25%
1 SD Below Messick-Jungeblut Estimates						
Mean	.4222	.4215	.4208	.3249	.3237	.3249
% Decline	0.2	0.3	0.5	–0.0	0.3	–0.0
Messick-Jungeblut Estimates						
Mean	.4208	.4184	.4162	.3245	.3218	.3223
% Decline	0.5	1.1	1.6	0.1	0.9	0.8
1 SD Above Messick-Jungeblut Estimates						
Mean	.4189	.4144	.4101	.3236	.3188	.3178
% Decline	0.9	2.0	3.0	0.3	1.8	2.2
Score Gains						
Claims of 100 Points Total						
Mean	.4133	.4016	.3909	.3196	.3061	.2993
% Decline	2.3	5.0	7.6	1.6	5.7	7.8

* Observed multiple correlation coefficient is .4228 for College A and .3247 for College B.

** Average proportions simulated are 5.5%, 16.5%, and 27.9% for College A; and 5.6%, 15.4%, and 26.0% for College B.

The multiple correlation coefficient of SAT-Math and SAT-Verbal with FGPA is computed as an indicator of the predictive validity of the SAT. The multiple correlation coefficient measures the correlation of an optimal linear combination of SAT-Math and SAT-Verbal with FGPA. Table 9-1 shows the effects of varying simulated levels of coaching prevalence and effectiveness on the predictive validity of the SAT for Colleges A and B. (See Note 9-11.)

College A

Since College A is highly selective, with students who have high socioeconomic status and high levels of academic achievement, as many as a quarter of its students' observed SAT scores may include actual coaching effects. Hence, the addition of the simulated coaching effects is expected to have a large negative impact on the estimated validity of the SAT for College A.

When the assumed effectiveness of coaching is low, the predictive validity of the SAT for College A is affected only slightly, even when the probabilities of being coached are as high as 25 percent. Assuming that the probability of being coached for an average student at College A is .25 (close to Whitla's estimate of .22 in a similar selective college) and that the coaching effects total 37 points on the average (Messick-Jungeblut mean estimates), the multiple correlation coefficient of SAT scores with FGPA decreases by 1.6 percent from the same coefficient when no coaching effects are simulated. We have very little information about the proportions coached in selective colleges 10 years ago. If we assume that the proportions coached increased by about 1 percent a year during the last 10 years, that the mean coaching effects have remained constant during this period at the level estimated by Messick and Jungeblut, and that these effects represent gains due to test familiarization and trick learning only, then we could conclude that the multiple correlation coefficient of SAT scores and FGPA for College A declined by about 0.5 percent over the last 10 years due to coaching.

If coaching school claims of 100-point gains in SAT total scores were accurate, and if all these score gains could be attributed to test familiarization and test-taking strategy or trick learning (i.e., assuming no skills training or extraneous learning effects in these estimates), then in a highly selective institution like College A, with as many as a quarter of the students receiving coaching, we may expect to find the multiple correlation of SAT with FGPA to be lower by 7.6 percent than it would have been if no simulated coaching effects were added.

Morgan (1989a) reports a 10-year decline of 8.2 percent in the multiple correlation coefficient of SAT scores with FGPA for selective colleges. If coaching effects were the only factor to account for this decline in selective colleges like College A, one would have to assume that, over the past decade, the incidence of coaching has increased at least fivefold and coaching effects have increased by 100 points, excluding increases in coaching effects due to genuine skills training. To the extent that these assumptions are unsupported by evidence, the results of the simulations indicate that coaching effects could not account for more than a minor proportion of the decline in validity of the SAT for selective colleges.

College B

In College B, changes in the multiple correlation coefficients of SAT scores with FGPA due to simulated coaching effects are smaller than those found for College A. One reason for this is that College B's students exhibit characteristics that are typically accompanied by low levels of participation in coaching programs, and therefore, the data from College B are not likely to be contaminated by actual coaching effects.

We do not have any data on the proportions of students entering less-selective colleges who receive coaching. In the absence of other data, one might assume that the proportions coached in such colleges are close to or somewhat under national proportions. If 15 percent of College B students received coaching at mean effectiveness levels that are equal to Messick-Jungeblut mean estimates, the multiple correlation coefficient of SAT scores and FGPA would be lower by 0.9 percent than if no coaching effects were simulated. The levels of coaching assumed to be present 10 years ago (5 percent) have almost no effect on the multiple correlation coefficient for College B data at the same levels of effectiveness.

The observed 10-year decline in the validity of the SAT for less-selective colleges is estimated at 13.0 percent by Morgan (1989a). The simulations indicate that such a decline could not be accounted for by trends in coaching at College B and similar institutions, even if coaching effects were assumed to have increased by 100 points and the proportions coached were assumed to have increased from zero to 25 percent.

DISCUSSION

The results of this study provide a framework for evaluating possible negative effects of coaching on the SAT's predictive validity in the contexts of different colleges. Not all types of score gains due to coaching affect the validity of the SAT negatively. In the simulations

222

presented here, coaching effects are defined as score gains due to test familiarization and trick learning. No score gains leading to genuine improvement of mathematical or verbal skills were simulated. These latter score gains are expected to lead to improved freshman-year performance and, therefore, do not affect the validity of the SAT.

In order to infer changes in the predictive validity of the SAT that can be attributed to changes in coaching effects over the last 10 years, one needs information on trends — both in the proportions of coached students entering different types of colleges and in the magnitude of coaching effects. Although measurement of the proportion of students who receive coaching is relatively straightforward, coaching effects are very difficult to measure. Often, what is reported as the coaching effect is the total score gain, including the effects of test familiarization, training, and employing test-taking strategies and tricks — and in some cases, the effects of extraneous learning and self-selection. Most of the public opinion on the effectiveness of coaching is based on advertising claims of commercial coaching schools and on news articles that are derived from these claims and report score gains that include all of these components. Research on coaching effects during the past 15 years provides no evidence that coaching effects have been increasing, although there is evidence that the proportion of students coached for the SAT has been increasing.

Morgan (1989a) and Ramist and Weiss (Chapter 5) present evidence that in the past decade, there were smaller declines in the predictive validity of the SAT in selective, small, private colleges than in less-selective, public, and large colleges. We can estimate the 10-year changes in SAT validity that are attributable to coaching using the following assumptions: that coaching effects have remained constant with a mean between 20 and 50 points total and that proportions of students coached have increased by about 1 percent a year, growing from 5 percent to 15 percent in less-selective colleges and from 15 percent to 25 percent in selective colleges. Under these assumptions, the multiple correlation coefficient of SAT scores with FGPA could be expected to decrease by less than 1 percent as a result of changes in students' coaching behavior during the last 10 years. In the Morgan (1989a) study, estimates based on data from colleges that participated in the College Board's Validity Study Service and used high school grade average or rank data from actual transcripts showed that the 10-year decline in the multiple correlation of SAT scores with FGPA was 8 percent if corrected for restriction of range, or 16 percent if uncorrected. According to the simulation results, trends in coaching might have resulted in a decline in the multiple correlation coefficient of SAT scores with FGPA of 0.5 percent in highly selective colleges

(College A) and of 0.8 percent in less-selective ones (College B) during the past decade. The simulations indicate clearly that trends in coaching could not have accounted for more than 10 percent of the last decade's decline in the validity of the SAT.

CHAPTER 10

Analyses of Predictive Validity Within Student Categorizations

RICK MORGAN

Morgan (1989a) reported that the average correlation of SAT scores with freshman grade-point average (FGPA) declined from 1976 to 1985. However, the database used by Morgan did not allow for the study of predictive validity for categories of college students (e.g., ethnic groups, intended majors, SAT score levels). Furthermore, Morgan did not have sufficient data to study whether the correlations of FGPA with other measures in the College Board's Admissions Testing Program (ATP) — i.e., the Achievement Tests and the Test of Standard Written English (TSWE) — were also declining. As a result, it was difficult to determine whether the reported changes in predictive validity were pervasive through all classifications of students and types of tests or resulted either from validity changes within specific classifications of students or from increases in the proportion of students from classifications with somewhat lower predictive validity. The limitations of Morgan (1989a) led to this study, which utilizes individual student records to examine the predictive validity of the SAT, TSWE, and three Achievement Tests. Analyses are conducted within subgroups based on gender, ethnic group, and intended college major for the enrolling classes of 1978, 1981, and 1985.

PROCEDURE

Selection of Data

Because the study focuses on within-college trends, only colleges conducting analyses in at least two of the three years under study (1978, 1981, 1985) were included. The enrolling years of 1978 and 1985 were chosen for analysis because they represent the first and last years in which SAT scores and high school grade information were matched with FGPA for substantial numbers of college students. The year 1981 was chosen for analysis because it represents an intermediate year, both for time and for predictive validity (Morgan, 1989a). The study sample included only colleges that had at least 25 complete student records of SAT scores, FGPA, and student-reported high school grade-point average (HSGPA). The data came from 198 colleges that conducted 443 different validity studies in the three years studied. Students with FGPAS and HSGPAS of zero were excluded from the analyses, because these data points may not accurately reflect student performance.

HSGPA was calculated based on responses to questions on the Student Descriptive Questionnaire (SDQ) concerning grades in six academic areas. This self-reported measure of HSGPA was used because actual high school grade information was unavailable for more than half the colleges. Thus, the use of actual high school records would have significantly reduced the number of colleges examined in the study and precluded a number of subgroup analyses. An analysis comparing the correlations of FGPA with self-reported HSGPA and actual high school record information (either HSGPA or class rank) for colleges supplying actual high school records (Morgan, 1990) showed that while actual grade information yielded correlations .05 to .06 higher, there was little difference in the trends for correlation change from 1978 to 1985.

Method of Analysis

The repeated measures estimation procedure outlined by Goldman and Widawski (1976) and utilized in Morgan (1989a) was used to produce estimates for each of the years, based on pairwise estimates of change. Formulas used for obtaining the yearly estimates and their associated standard errors can be found in Chapter 4 (see Note 4-1).

The pairwise difference estimation technique produced yearly estimates of the means for the predictor variables and FGPA to permit an examination of the trends in the means. Both raw correlations and correlations corrected for the multivariate restriction of range of SAT-V, SAT-M, and HSGPA (see Note 10-1) were estimated along with regression weights (for colleges with FGPA on a four-point scale). The correlations of FGPA with the TSWE, the English Composition Test, the Mathematics Level I Achievement Test, and the Chemistry Achievement Test were also estimated.

Grouping Variables

The second set of analyses examined the predictive validity within categories of students. This allowed for an examination of differential trends within the categories. Validity estimates using the repeated measures procedure were calculated for the following categories of student characteristics:

- Sex

- Ethnic Group
  Asian-American
  Black
  Hispanic
  White

- Intended College Major (see Note 10-2)
  Business
  Liberal Arts
  Preprofessional
  Technical

Finally, within each college, students were placed into one of three groups based on their SAT scores. For each college, separate cut-offs grouped students into top, middle, and bottom thirds according to the sum of their SAT-V and SAT-M scores. Cut-offs were based on the college's combined SAT total score distribution for each of the three years for which data were available. Regression analyses were conducted for each of the three groups within each college to examine changes in the relationship of FGPA with SAT-V and SAT-M, within SAT total score levels. Only colleges with complete data for at least 25 students within a given subgroup or Achievement Test were included in the analyses for the subgroup or test.

RESULTS

All Students

Table 10-1 provides the estimates for raw and corrected correlations of SAT scores and HSGPA with FGPA for all students. The table also shows estimates of the multiple regression weights for predicting FGPA using SAT-V and SAT-M, as well as the means of SAT-V, SAT-M, HSGPA, and FGPA. The associated standard errors for all estimates are indicated in parentheses. The numbers of colleges and freshmen associated with each estimate are also provided. The estimates for average SAT mean scores decreased between 1978 and 1981 and then rose in 1985. This parallels the national SAT score trends reported by the College Board in 1985. Mean FGPA and SAT correlations decreased across the three years. However, the decline in the correlations is less for the corrected correlations than for the uncorrected correlations. The SAT multiple regression weights are also larger for 1978 than for 1985. These patterns of decline were expected, given previous research (Morgan, 1989a).

Table 10-1

Estimated Correlations and Regression Weights for Self-Reported HSGPA and SAT Scores with FGPA for All Students

	1978	1981	1985
Raw Correlations			
HSGPA	.46(.01)	.44(.01)	.43(.01)
SAT-V	.36(.01)	.33(.01)	.32(.01)
SAT-M	.37(.01)	.33(.01)	.32(.01)
Multiple SAT	.43(.01)	.39(.01)	.38(.01)
Multiple Correlation	.55(.01)	.52(.01)	.51(.01)
Corrected Correlations			
HSGPA	.58(.01)	.58(.01)	.56(.01)
SAT-V	.51(.01)	.49(.01)	.48(.01)
SAT-M	.53(.01)	.50(.01)	.49(.01)
Multiple SAT	.57(.01)	.55(.01)	.53(.01)
Multiple Correlation	.67(.01)	.65(.01)	.63(.01)
Regression Weights			
SAT-V	.0019(.0001)	.0018(.0001)	.0016(.0001)
SAT-M	.0019(.0001)	.0016(.0001)	.0017(.0001)
Means			
SAT-V	464(4.3)	458(4.4)	463(4.6)
SAT-M	502(4.9)	499(4.9)	506(5.2)
HSGPA	3.24(.02)	3.21(.02)	3.17(.02)
FGPA	2.56(.04)	2.55(.03)	2.53(.03)
Number of Colleges	152	155	124
Number of Students	103,956	104,514	91,324

Analyses of Other Tests

Data on four other tests were examined to determine whether the trend of declining predictive validity was unique to the SAT or whether the trend was present for other ATP tests. The data in Table 10-2 are uncorrected correlations of HSGPA, SAT scores, and Achievement Tests with FGPA for the students who took each Achievement Test. Uncorrected correlations were used because different groups of students take each Achievement Test. Therefore, multivariate corrections would be correcting to different population groups for each test. Additionally, the colleges with sufficient data available are not the same for all Achievement Tests. Therefore, since the students taking each test constituted different populations and because the colleges used in the estimation procedure differ, comparisons of Achievement Test and SAT correlations across tests should be avoided.

Table 10-2

Correlation of Self-Reported HSGPA, SAT Scores, and Achievement Test Scores with FGPA

	English Composition Test			Mathematics Level I Exam		
	1978	1981	1985	1978	1981	1985
HSGPA	.43(.01)	.42(.01)	.42(.01)	.42(.01)	.41(.01)	.40(.01)
SAT-V	.33(.01)	.28(.01)	.30(.01)	.32(.01)	.28(.01)	.29(.01)
SAT-M	.33(.01)	.30(.01)	.29(.01)	.31(.01)	.29(.01)	.27(.01)
Multiple SAT	.41(.01)	.35(.01)	.36(.01)	.39(.01)	.35(.01)	.34(.01)
Achievement Test	.36(.01)	.33(.01)	.33(.01)	.32(.01)	.32(.01)	.30(.01)
Multiple Correlation	.53(.01)	.50(.01)	.51(.01)	.52(.01)	.50(.01)	.49(.01)
Number of Colleges	113	104	83	105	99	81
Number of Students	37,680	34,673	34,143	28,642	27,430	26,232

	Chemistry Test			TSWE		
	1978	1981	1985	1978	1981	1985
HSGPA	.41(.02)	.39(.01)	.39(.02)	.46(.01)	.44(.01)	.43(.01)
SAT-V	.27(.02)	.27(.02)	.26(.02)	.36(.01)	.33(.01)	.32(.01)
SAT-M	.33(.02)	.31(.02)	.30(.02)	.37(.01)	.33(.01)	.32(.01)
Multiple SAT	.38(.02)	.37(.02)	.35(.02)	.43(.01)	.39(.01)	.38(.01)
Achievement Test	.36(.02)	.36(.02)	.36(.02)	.36(.01)	.33(.01)	.32(.01)
Multiple Correlation	.52(.02)	.50(.01)	.49(.02)	.55(.01)	.51(.01)	.51(.01)
Number of Colleges	43	44	40	152	155	124
Number of Students	5,239	5,552	5,966	103,956	104,514	91,324

Within the sample of English Composition Test (ECT) examinees, the correlation with FGPA declines by .04 for SAT-M, .03 for SAT-V, and .04 for ECT. The table also indicates that the correlation of ECT with FGPA was larger than the SAT-V correlation with FGPA for each year by at least .03. One reason for higher Achievement Test correlations is that student selection to college is based more on SAT scores and HSGPA than Achievement Test scores. As a result, the correlations involving the SAT are more affected by test score range restriction than are the correlations involving Achievement Tests.

Within the sample of those taking the Mathematics Level I Test, the decline of the correlation of SAT-M with FGPA is .04, while the decline is .02 for the Achievement Test. The Level I correlation was .01 higher than the SAT-M correlation in 1978 and .03 higher in both 1981 and 1985.

No change was found in the correlation of the Chemistry Achievement Test with FGPA. However, from 1978 to 1985 the estimated univariate correlations of SAT-V and SAT-M with FGPA dropped by .01 and .03.

Because all SAT examinees take the TSWE, the data for the TSWE provide some information that is repeated from Table 10-1. Between 1978 and 1985 the correlations of both TSWE and HSGPA with FGPA declined from .36 to .32.

The data indicate that correlations of FGPA with tests other than the SAT declined from 1978 to 1985. However, the declines were generally not as large as those associated with the SAT.

Analyses by Sex

Morgan (1989a) focused analyses on estimating correlations and regression weights based on all first-year students. The present study examines several subgroups. Table 10-3 provides separate estimated correlations of SAT scores and HSGPA with FGPA, associated regression weights, means for the predictor and criterion variables for both sexes. To be used in the analyses, a college had to have data for at least 25 students of each sex.

All the correlation estimates are higher for females than males. The corrected multiple correlation of SAT scores with FGPA declined from 1978 to 1985 by .06 for males and .03 for females. There was no difference between the HSGPA corrected correlation for 1978 and 1985 for females; the correlation declined .04 for males. The corrected multiple correlation dropped from .65 to .59 for males, while only declining from .68 to .67 for females. For both sexes, SAT-M was the best single predictor of FGPA, followed by SAT-V and then TSWE. The declines in the regression coefficients of SAT-V and SAT-M scores for

Table 10-3

Estimated Correlations and Regression Weights for HSGPA and SAT Scores with FGPA for Male and Female Students

	Males			Females		
	1978	1981	1985	1978	1981	1985
Raw Correlations						
HSGPA	.43 (.01)	.41 (.01)	.40 (.01)	.45 (.01)	.45 (.01)	.44 (.01)
SAT-V	.34 (.01)	.29 (.01)	.28 (.01)	.40 (.01)	.36 (.01)	.35 (.01)
SAT-M	.38 (.01)	.32 (.01)	.31 (.01)	.42 (.01)	.38 (.01)	.37 (.01)
TSWE	.32 (.01)	.28 (.01)	.27 (.01)	.38 (.01)	.34 (.01)	.33 (.01)
Multiple SAT	.42 (.01)	.36 (.01)	.36 (.01)	.47 (.01)	.43 (.01)	.42 (.01)
Multiple Correlation	.53 (.01)	.49 (.01)	.48 (.01)	.56 (.01)	.54 (.01)	.53 (.01)
Corrected Correlations						
HSGPA	.56 (.01)	.54 (.01)	.52 (.01)	.58 (.01)	.59 (.01)	.58 (.01)
SAT-V	.48 (.01)	.45 (.01)	.44 (.01)	.53 (.01)	.51 (.01)	.51 (.01)
SAT-M	.52 (.01)	.47 (.01)	.46 (.01)	.55 (.01)	.53 (.01)	.53 (.01)
Multiple SAT	.56 (.01)	.51 (.01)	.50 (.01)	.60 (.01)	.57 (.01)	.57 (.01)
Multiple Correlation	.65 (.01)	.61 (.01)	.59 (.01)	.68 (.01)	.67 (.01)	.67 (.01)
Regression Weights						
SAT-V	.0019 (.0002)	.0016 (.0001)	.0013 (.0001)	.0022 (.0002)	.0018 (.0001)	.0016 (.0001)
SAT-M	.0024 (.0002)	.0018 (.0001)	.0017 (.0001)	.0023 (.0001)	.0021 (.0001)	.0020 (.0001)
Means						
SAT-V	464 (4.7)	460 (4.8)	466 (5.2)	467 (5.0)	459 (5.0)	463 (5.1)
SAT-M	525 (5.5)	523 (5.4)	530 (5.8)	488 (4.8)	486 (5.1)	494 (5.4)
HSGPA	3.16 (.02)	3.13 (.02)	3.10 (.03)	3.33 (.02)	3.28 (.02)	3.25 (.02)
FGPA	2.46 (.04)	2.46 (.04)	2.43 (.04)	2.63 (.04)	2.61 (.04)	2.59 (.03)
Proportion	47.7 (0.9)	46.6 (0.8)	45.6 (0.8)	52.3 (0.9)	53.4 (0.8)	54.4 (0.8)
Number of Colleges	118	120	104	118	120	104
Number of Students	47,254	46,866	42,118	47,285	49,273	45,278

males reflect the declines in the corrected correlations. The decline in the SAT-M regression coefficient for females is half the decline in the SAT-M coefficient.

The SAT means for both sexes were relatively stable for the three years, and the mean HSGPA declined by at least .06 for both groups. The percentage of females increased approximately two percent from 1978 to 1985. The SAT correlation declines shown in Table 10-1 for all students are similar to those indicated for each sex. Therefore, the decline in the correlations and regressions for all students is most likely not a function of differential validity or changes in the representation or performance of males and females for the years under study. However, it appears that the decline in the correlation of HSGPA with FGPA found in Table 10-1 results from male students.

Analyses by Ethnic Group

Tables 10-4 and 10-5 provide estimated correlations of SAT scores and HSGPA with FGPA, associated regression weights, and means for the predictor variables for Asian-American, Black, Hispanic, and White freshmen. The estimated percentages for the ethnic groups do not sum to 100, because very few colleges had the required 25 or more freshmen in each ethnic group. Since the mix of colleges is different for each ethnic group, comparisons of correlation and regression estimates should not be made across ethnic groups. Due to the small number of colleges with sufficient numbers of Hispanic students, the standard errors are large for that subgroup. As a result, fluctuations of the correlation estimates for Hispanic students should be interpreted cautiously.

Nonetheless, several points are worth consideration. All four ethnic groups had a decline of .03 to .05 for the raw multiple correlation of SAT scores with FGPA. However, the corrected multiple SAT correlation did not drop significantly for Asian-American students and actually rose for Hispanic students. For Black students, both the raw and corrected multiple SAT correlations with FGPA are larger than the correlations of HSGPA with FGPA. This suggests that SAT scores are better predictors of freshman grades than are high school grades for Black students.

SAT-M had a much higher correlation with FGPA than did SAT-V or TSWE for Asian-American students. For Hispanic students, TSWE and SAT-V had higher correlations with FGPA than did SAT-M. A similar tendency is apparent in the results for Black students. The correlations of TSWE, SAT-V, and SAT-M with FGPA are nearly the same for White students.

From 1978 to 1985, significant increases in the mean SAT scores occurred for Asian-American, Black, and Hispanic freshmen. The percentage of Asian-American freshmen increased significantly, while

232

Table 10-4

Estimated Correlations and Regression Weights for HSGPA and SAT Scores with FGPA for Asian-American and Black Students

	Asian-American Students			Black Students		
	1978	1981	1985	1978	1981	1985
Raw Correlations						
HSGPA	.36 (.04)	.36 (.03)	.37 (.03)	.31 (.02)	.27 (.02)	.27 (.03)
SAT-V	.28 (.03)	.19 (.03)	.22 (.03)	.28 (.02)	.22 (.02)	.24 (.02)
SAT-M	.36 (.03)	.33 (.03)	.33 (.02)	.28 (.02)	.23 (.02)	.22 (.02)
TSWE	.29 (.03)	.15 (.03)	.23 (.03)	.29 (.02)	.23 (.02)	.24 (.03)
Multiple SAT	.42 (.03)	.36 (.03)	.37 (.02)	.35 (.02)	.29 (.02)	.30 (.02)
Multiple Correlation	.51 (.03)	.47 (.02)	.48 (.02)	.44 (.02)	.39 (.02)	.38 (.02)
Corrected Correlations						
HSGPA	.52 (.03)	.53 (.02)	.56 (.04)	.44 (.02)	.39 (.03)	.37 (.03)
SAT-V	.43 (.03)	.39 (.03)	.43 (.02)	.43 (.03)	.35 (.03)	.35 (.03)
SAT-M	.52 (.03)	.49 (.03)	.50 (.02)	.43 (.03)	.33 (.03)	.32 (.03)
Multiple SAT	.54 (.03)	.50 (.03)	.53 (.02)	.49 (.03)	.42 (.03)	.41 (.02)
Multiple Correlation	.64 (.02)	.61 (.02)	.64 (.03)	.55 (.02)	.51 (.02)	.48 (.02)
Regression Weights						
SAT-V	.0010 (.0002)	.0004 (.0002)	.0007 (.0002)	.0016 (.0002)	.0012 (.0002)	.0014 (.0002)
SAT-M	.0023 (.0002)	.0022 (.0002)	.0021 (.0002)	.0014 (.0003)	.0009 (.0003)	.0006 (.0002)
Means						
SAT-V	446 (15.2)	442 (15.8)	468 (16.8)	390 (10.4)	397 (10.4)	408 (9.6)
SAT-M	561 (12.1)	564 (12.2)	574 (13.6)	414 (10.5)	425 (10.3)	441 (10.1)
HSGPA	3.43 (.05)	3.42 (.05)	3.45 (.05)	3.08 (.04)	3.07 (.04)	3.01 (.05)
FGPA	2.77 (.08)	2.76 (.06)	2.76 (.05)	2.12 (.07)	2.13 (.07)	2.13 (.07)
Proportion	6.7 (1.3)	8.8 (1.6)	10.5 (1.5)	16.2 (4.5)	16.6 (4.6)	16.7 (4.5)
Number of Colleges	23	28	27	48	39	34
Number of Students	2,535	3,585	4,375	5,162	4,086	5,095

Table 10-5

Estimated Correlations and Regression Weights for HSGPA and SAT Scores with FGPA for Hispanic and White Students

	Hispanic Students			White Students		
	1978	1981	1985	1978	1981	1985
Raw Correlations						
HSGPA	.33 (.04)	.39 (.03)	.34 (.03)	.46 (.01)	.45 (.01)	.43 (.01)
SAT-V	.25 (.04)	.28 (.04)	.22 (.03)	.35 (.01)	.32 (.01)	.31 (.01)
SAT-M	.20 (.03)	.24 (.04)	.21 (.04)	.35 (.01)	.31 (.01)	.30 (.01)
TSWE	.25 (.05)	.27 (.05)	.21 (.04)	.34 (.01)	.32 (.01)	.31 (.01)
Multiple SAT	.30 (.03)	.31 (.04)	.27 (.04)	.41 (.01)	.37 (.01)	.36 (.01)
Multiple Correlation	.42 (.04)	.48 (.03)	.41 (.03)	.54 (.01)	.52 (.01)	.50 (.01)
Corrected Correlations						
HSGPA	.41 (.06)	.50 (.04)	.47 (.03)	.59 (.01)	.59 (.01)	.57 (.01)
SAT-V	.33 (.05)	.35 (.05)	.36 (.05)	.50 (.01)	.49 (.01)	.48 (.01)
SAT-M	.27 (.06)	.36 (.04)	.35 (.04)	.52 (.01)	.49 (.01)	.49 (.01)
Multiple SAT	.37 (.05)	.42 (.04)	.41 (.04)	.57 (.01)	.54 (.01)	.53 (.01)
Multiple Correlation	.49 (.05)	.57 (.03)	.53 (.04)	.67 (.01)	.65 (.01)	.64 (.01)
Regression Weights						
SAT-V	.0017 (.0004)	.0010 (.0003)	.0011 (.0003)	.0019 (.0001)	.0018 (.0001)	.0017 (.0001)
SAT-M	.0004 (.0004)	.0010 (.0002)	.0010 (.0004)	.0018 (.0001)	.0015 (.0001)	.0015 (.0001)
Means						
SAT-V	421 (14.3)	417 (12.7)	423 (15.3)	474 (4.1)	467 (4.4)	472 (4.6)
SAT-M	457 (15.0)	464 (14.4)	474 (16.2)	513 (4.7)	508 (4.8)	515 (5.1)
HSGPA	3.27 (.07)	3.28 (.06)	3.22 (.08)	3.27 (.02)	3.23 (.02)	3.19 (.02)
FGPA	2.43 (.08)	2.42 (.07)	2.45 (.07)	2.60 (.04)	2.58 (.03)	2.57 (.03)
Proportion	12.2 (3.6)	12.5 (3.8)	14.7 (3.8)	88.4 (0.7)	87.6 (0.8)	86.9 (0.9)
Number of Colleges	16	23	18	147	152	121
Number of Students	1,575	1,354	2,192	89,013	89,524	74,586

there was little change in the percentage of Black students and only a marginal increase in the percentage of Hispanic students. For all practical purposes, the mean SAT total score for White students remained the same from 1978 to 1985, while a small decrease in the percentage of White students is indicated.

In summary, it appears that declines in SAT correlations with FGPA are not focused on any particular group and that the overall declines in the SAT correlations are not due in any significant degree to changes in the ethnic composition of freshman classes.

Analyses by Intended Major

Analyses were conducted within majors to determine whether the decline in overall validity may have resulted from changes in the proportion or types of students electing the four groups of majors. For example, an increase in the number of less able students taking courses in majors for which students traditionally receive higher grades would reduce the overall correlations and regression weights, but not necessarily the correlations and regression weights within the majors. Furthermore, the SAT may be a better indicator of FGPA for some majors than for others. If substantial increases occurred in the number of students majoring in areas for which SAT correlations with FGPA are relatively low, overall SAT correlations with FGPA would be likely to decline.

The analyses indicated little change from 1978 to 1985 in the SAT means for any of the four general categories of intended major. From 1978 to 1985, the percentage of business and technical majors increased by approximately four percentage points each, while there was a three percentage point drop in liberal arts majors, and an eight percentage point drop in preprofessional majors.

The patterns of decline for the multiple correlations of SAT scores and HSGPA with FGPA were similar for the four groups of intended majors. The four raw multiple SAT correlations declined by either .06 or .07, while the corrected multiple correlations declined from a low of .04 to a high of .05.

Some changes did occur in the proportion of students electing various types of majors. The declines in correlations and regression weights found in Table 10-1 were similar to those found for the four groups of intended majors. Morgan (1990) provides more details of the analyses for the intended major groups.

Analyses by SAT Levels Within College

Changes in the construction of the SAT exam (see Chapter 7), in college curricula, in college grading standards, or in the courses selected

Table 10-6.

Estimates for Regression Weights and Corrected Correlations
Within SAT Total Score Levels

	1978	1981	1985
		High Third	
Regression Weights			
SAT-V	.0019(.0001)	.0017(.0001)	.0018(.0001)
SAT-M	.0019(.0001)	.0018(.0001)	.0019(.0001)
Corrected Correlations			
HSGPA	.63(.01)	.61(.01)	.60(.01)
SAT-V	.50(.01)	.46(.01)	.47(.01)
SAT-M	.52(.01)	.49(.01)	.50(.02)
Multiple SAT	.56(.01)	.54(.01)	.54(.01)
Multiple Correlation	.70(.01)	.69(.01)	.68(.01)
Means			
SAT-V	545(4.3)	542(4.4)	541(4.5)
SAT-M	588(4.7)	586(4.5)	589(4.7)
FGPA	2.88(.04)	2.84(.04)	2.80(.04)
		Middle Third	
Regression Weights			
SAT-V	.0020(.0002)	.0020(.0002)	.0014(.0002)
SAT-M	.0021(.0002)	.0016(.0002)	.0014(.0002)
Corrected Correlations			
HSGPA	.54(.01)	.54(.01)	.49(.01)
SAT-V	.45(.02)	.42(.02)	.37(.02)
SAT-M	.47(.02)	.43(.02)	.38(.02)
Multiple SAT	.56(.02)	.50(.02)	.49(.02)
Multiple Correlation	.68(.01)	.64(.01)	.61(.02)
Means			
SAT-V	461(4.7)	459(4.8)	458(4.6)
SAT-M	502(5.4)	503(5.4)	505(5.4)
FGPA	2.54(.04)	2.55(.03)	2.51(.03)
		Low Third	
Regression Weights			
SAT-V	.0017(.0001)	.0014(.0001)	.0012(.0001)
SAT-M	.0016(.0001)	.0014(.0001)	.0012(.0001)
Corrected Correlations			
HSGPA	.50(.01)	.49(.01)	.45(.02)
SAT-V	.46(.02)	.43(.02)	.39(.02)
SAT-M	.48(.02)	.44(.02)	.41(.02)
Multiple SAT	.53(.02)	.51(.02)	.48(.02)
Multiple Correlation	.62(.01)	.60(.01)	.57(.01)
Means			
SAT-V	385(4.7)	383(4.7)	386(4.6)
SAT-M	417(5.5)	420(5.4)	420(5.5)
FGPA	2.25(.04)	2.29(.03)	2.27(.03)

by college freshmen may have caused the SAT's predictive validity to decline differentially for students with different levels of ability. In order to investigate this possibility, students were placed in three groups on the basis of their total SAT scores. In each college, students were grouped into top, middle, and bottom thirds. Within each college, SAT total scores were pooled across years to establish one set of cut-off scores for each year's data. Multiple regression using SAT scores to predict FGPA was conducted in each of the three groups for each college.

Table 10-6 presents the regression estimates and corrected correlations for each of the three SAT levels. The table shows that from 1978 to 1985, the average SAT multiple regression estimates for both SAT-V and SAT-M declined considerably for students in both the middle and lowest thirds. However, the SAT regression weights for the top third of students within colleges showed no appreciable change from 1978 to 1985. The regression weights for the three groups also indicate evidence of increased curvilinearity over time in the relationship of SAT scores with FGPA in the later years. For 1985, the regression weights are lowest in the bottom third and highest in the top third of the students. As with the regression weights, the smallest decline in all the corrected correlations occurs in the top third of students. These findings indicate that the decline in predictive validity may have been more focused on freshmen having SAT scores in the bottom two-thirds of their college classes. Table 10-6 also shows that the SAT multiple correlation is consistently higher than the correlation of HSGPA with FGPA for the lowest third of students. As a result, while the multiple SAT correlation is highest for the top third of students, SAT scores are better predictors of college performance than HSGPA for the bottom third of students.

SUMMARY AND DISCUSSION

With the important exception of freshmen who constitute the top third of their class, and the possible exception of Hispanic and Asian-American freshmen, it appears that declines of SAT correlations with FGPA were characteristic of freshmen in general. Furthermore, the overall declines in predictive validity do not seem to result directly from changes in the population of college students from 1978 to 1985. It also appears that declines in correlation were not specific to the SAT, since declines were found for other tests as well.

An important result was apparent after placing the students within each college into one of three groups based on SAT scores. Table 10-6 indicates both increasing curvilinearity in the regression plane predicting FGPA using SAT scores and a pattern of lower regression weights and corrected correlations in 1985 than in 1978 for the middle and low SAT scoring groups. Marginally lower regression weights were found for the top third of students. These findings seem to indicate that less change occurred in the predictive validity of SAT scores for these students than for the two-thirds of their college classes scoring lower on the SAT.

The evidence of declining slopes in the lowest and middle thirds of SAT scores suggests that there may be a growing tendency for colleges to reduce the likelihood of student failure. Increased remedial education and improved matching of student ability to course difficulty in initial placement are two of several measures instituted by colleges that could account for the pattern of differential decline in predictive validity, though such hypotheses were not tested in this study. Because thirds were defined within each college, there is some overlap in the groups from college to college. This fact suggests that the correlation declines may have more to do with college grades than with changes in the SAT itself. That possibility is examined in other studies (see Chapters 8 and 12).

CHAPTER 11

Predictability of College Grades: Three Tests and Three National Samples

WARREN W. WILLINGHAM, DONALD A. ROCK, & JUDITH POLLACK

Over the past two decades, the National Center for Education Statistics (NCES) has overseen the development of three databases that have proven valuable in examining questions concerning the educational experience of young adults. As it happens, these databases provide useful information pertinent to the topic of this monograph. The National Longitudinal Study (NLS) survey was based upon a nationally representative sample of secondary school seniors in 1972. The High School and Beyond (HSB) survey involved two cohorts: a nationally representative sample of secondary school seniors in 1980 and a sample of sophomores from the same schools who were followed up as seniors in 1982. Each of these three cohorts was followed into the second year of college. In addition to scores on the test battery administered to these students as part of the survey, information was retrieved on self-reported high school and college grades and their scores on two other tests: the Scholastic Aptitude Test (SAT) and the American College Test (ACT). Our purpose, then, is to examine the relationships among predictors and grade averages for these three samples of students and see if they shed light on possible changes over time in the prediction of college grades.

These data have several strengths. First, the samples are quite independent of the College Board's Validity Study Service (VSS), which generates most of the available data concerning the correlations of SAT scores and college grades. For that reason, the data provide an independent check on any trends noted in the accumulation of VSS results. Furthermore, the data are based on national samples, which is advantageous because the data are not distorted by whatever self-selective factors prompt institutions to participate in the VSS, and because such representative samples suggest that the cohorts are reasonably comparable from one year to the next.

Finally, these NLS/HSB databases include both the SAT and two other test batteries. The other measures provide useful evidence as to whether a change in the SAT's predictive validity coefficients is an isolated event or part of a more general educational phenomenon.

Along with these strengths come some weaknesses. The students in these samples fan out into many colleges, among which the grade scales are certainly not comparable. Also, test scores are normally used to help predict grades at a particular institution, not college grades generally. Finally, there are some differences in these NLS/HSB samples and measures from one cohort to another that give cause to question their strict comparability. These weaknesses are partly correctable through procedures described later, and none seems critical to our purpose.

The questions of primary interest in this analysis are the following:

- Is the downward trend in correlations between SAT scores and college grades observed by Morgan (1989a) peculiar to colleges participating in the VSS or does it also show up in these nationally representative samples?

- If there is evidence of such a general decline, is the trend associated only with SAT scores or with other predictors as well?

- Do the correlations among similar tests (e.g., verbal with verbal, mathematics with mathematics) appear to be stable over time?

Answers to these questions are not likely to yield definitive conclusions regarding underlying reasons for trends in validity coefficients. They will, however, add useful perspective to the question of overarching interest: If validity coefficients change over time, is the trend more likely due to changes in the sample on which the correlations are based, changes in the test, or changes in the grade criterion?

There have been various analyses of the NLS and HSB data directed to questions concerning educational attainment, the effects of schooling, and similar social policy issues. Ekstrom, Goertz, and Rock (1988) provide a good example and cite other examples as well. There has evidently been little published research in which the NLS and HSB data have been used to examine questions concerning test validity, although two well-known exceptions can be cited. Crouse and Trusheim (1988) have used these data on several occasions to dispute the added value of an aptitude test like the SAT in the college admissions process. In another study, Manski and Wise (1983) describe the relationship of test scores to college choice and student retention. While these authors reach starkly different conclusions regarding the usefulness of tests in college admissions, neither book contains data relevant to the topic at hand: Have there been recent changes in correlations of test scores with college grades? The following section describes the NLS/HSB data and our analyses directed to that question.

PROCEDURE

The NLS and HSB longitudinal studies have entailed continuing surveys of three representative cohorts of high school students. A variety of test information as well as personal and educational data were collected originally when these students were in secondary school. At various intervals, follow-up information has been collected concerning the students' educational and vocational experience and attainment. Detailed information concerning the samples, the test materials, and the survey procedures is found in the contractor reports (Jones, Clarke, Mooney, McWilliams, Crawford, Stephenson, & Tourangeau, 1983; Roccobono, Henderson, Burkheimer, Place, & Levinsohn, 1981; Rock, Hilton, Pollack, Ekstrom, & Goertz, 1985; Sebring, Campbell, Glusberg, Spencer, Singleton, & Turner, 1987). The background information that is most pertinent to this analysis is summarized briefly here.

Samples

The 1972 NLS survey was based upon some 16,000 seniors in more than a thousand secondary schools. The two-stage probability sample was based first on schools and then students within schools. Schools in low-income areas or with a large percentage of minority students were oversampled. The whole cohort was followed up 16 months later.

The HSB survey was initiated in 1980 with two cohorts: samples of some 28,000 seniors and 30,000 sophomores in the same 1,015 schools. The same two-stage probability sampling was employed with more complex oversampling of special groups and types of schools. Among the 1980 seniors, 12,000 were followed up some two years later.

For the sample of sophomores, secondary school data were collected for a "transcript" sample of 15,000 two years later (i.e., when they were seniors in 1982). High school transcript information as well as follow-up information is available for some 13,000 students in this "1982 senior" cohort. For each of these samples, intensive effort yielded data for over 90 percent of the students selected for follow-up.

Measures

The NLS and HSB surveys incorporated a variety of information about the student participants, but for the purposes of this study, the measures of interest are the students' grade-point averages in high school and college and those common test scores that were available for at least two of the 1972, 1980, and 1982 senior cohorts. The following measures were available for this analysis:

- Scholastic Aptitude Test
  Verbal
  Mathematics

- American College Test
  English
  Mathematics
  Social Studies
  Science

- NLS/HSB
  Vocabulary
  Reading
  Mathematics

- High school average

- College average.

The SAT and ACT scores were obtained from high school records for both the 1972 and 1982 cohorts. Admissions test scores were not originally collected as part of the survey of 1980 seniors, but SAT scores were obtained from College Board program files in conjunction with a special study by Hilton, Schrader, and Beaton (1983). The only NLS/HSB tests common to the different cohorts were the so-called skills tests: vocabulary, reading, and mathematics. While the content of these tests was generally comparable across cohorts, there were some differences in individual items and the length of two of the tests did vary somewhat. For the three years, the vocabulary test had 15, 27, and 21 items; the mathematics test had 25, 33, and 38 items. In some instances, the correlations for those two tests are shown both as they were computed and as corrected for unreliability in order to show the effect of differences in test length.

In all three samples, the high school grade-point average (HSGPA) and the college grade-point average (CGPA) were based upon information reported by the student. The reliability of these self-reported grade averages could vary, of course, depending upon how and when the information was collected. Since any such variation across samples could affect validity coefficients, the contractors' accounts of data collection procedures were carefully examined. With respect to the HSGPA, all procedures were the same for the three cohorts: the grade scale used, the wording of the question put to students, and the time of data collection. With respect to the CGPA, there were two minor differences in the NLS and HSB question, one of which was correctable in data analysis. (See Note 11-1.)

Of some possible consequence was a difference in the timing of data collection for NLS and HSB. The NLS follow-up was in the fall of the college sophomore year; the HSB follow-up was in the spring of the college sophomore year. Thus, the HSB college grade average was presumably based upon three semesters while the NLS average was based upon two. Accordingly, one might speculate that the grade criteria for the 1980 and 1982 samples are somewhat more reliable and therefore more predictable — a condition that would work against detecting any possible decline in correlations from 1972 to the subsequent years. Available data indicate, however, that there is little difference if any in the predictability of cumulative GPA in the freshman versus the sophomore year (Willingham, 1962, 1985; Wilson, 1983). Thus, for purposes of this analysis, the CGPA appears to be satisfactorily comparable for the three samples.

Analysis

The samples used in the analyses reported here were restricted to students who were located in the follow-up 16-24 months after secondary school graduation, had attended a two- or four-year college by that time, and reported a CGPA. These restrictions yielded samples of 6,900, 5,354, and 5,406 for the senior cohorts of 1972, 1980, and 1982, respectively. Test score data were available for those subsamples who took the SAT, ACT, and NLS/HSB tests as indicated in Table 11-1. Since only one in five SAT examinees took the ACT (the corresponding ratio for ACT was one in four), these two groups of students formed relatively distinct subsamples, but they are presumably representative of the national populations who take those tests. Sample weights provided by NCES were used to correct data for oversampling. Also, in order to achieve comparable data across years, the HSB tests were put on the same IRT scale as the corresponding NLS tests (see Rock et al., 1985). Two of the HSB tests show slightly larger standard deviations than their NLS counterparts — evidently a reflection of somewhat greater length and reliability. Otherwise, the data in Table 11-1 suggest a comparable range of ability in the three samples. There is no difference in average CGPA across years, though the test scores did drop somewhat from 1972 to 1980 — reflecting a national decline already well documented (College Board, 1977).

The principal analysis of interest here is the relative size of the correlation between the predictors and the CGPA for the successive cohorts. There are two reasons, however, why those correlations might not give a true picture of any trend in prediction of college

Table 11-1

Sample Sizes, Means, and Standard Deviations for Test Scores and Grade-Point Averages

Variable	NLS-1972			HSB-1980*			HSB-1982		
	N	$\bar{x}$	S.D.	N	$\bar{x}$	S.D.	N	$\bar{x}$	S.D.
SAT-Verbal	3470	467.5	106.3	2019	438.1	108.3	1928	444.1	106.5
SAT-Mathematics	3457	502.0	110.2	2019	478.8	113.6	1950	479.8	111.9
ACT-English	2308	19.0	5.0	—	—	—	1406	19.1	5.2
ACT-Social Studies	2305	20.1	6.8	—	—	—	1406	18.8	7.3
ACT-Science	2298	21.6	6.4	—	—	—	1405	22.1	6.1
ACT-Mathematics	2305	20.8	7.0	—	—	—	1405	18.6	7.7
NLS/HSB-Vocabulary	6500	8.2	3.8	4848	7.2	3.6	5401	7.6	4.0
NLS/HSB-Reading	6504	11.9	4.4	4830	10.9	4.8	5363	10.3	5.1
NLS/HSB-Mathematics	6505	16.4	6.4	4816	15.2	6.5	5342	15.1	6.6
High School Average (HSGPA)	6871	6.1	1.3	5336	6.3	1.3	5291	6.2	1.3
College Average (CGPA)	6900	5.5	1.3	5354	5.5	1.3	5406	5.5	1.3

* No ACT data available for this sample.

grades. First, the colleges represented may not be comparable, especially since the sampling of different high schools in 1972 and 1980 would create a different migratory pattern in college admissions for the NLS and HSB samples. The NLS and HSB cohorts did show numerous instances of colleges being heavily represented in one and hardly at all in the other. (See Note 11-2.)

A second problem concerns the fact that the GPA is known not to be comparable from one educational unit to another. Pooling such noncomparable grades can be expected to distort individual predictions and lower validity coefficients — as has been found in numerous other studies (see for example, Braun & Szatrowksi, 1984; Linn, 1965; Goldman & Slaughter, 1976). Looking only at data pooled across institutions, there is no way of knowing whether the effect of differences in grading standards among colleges has a comparable effect from one cohort to another.

Because of such possible distortions, we undertook additional analyses on reduced data sets that permitted pairing colleges across years and also analyzing correlations within colleges. Since these survey samples fanned out into more than 2,000 colleges, most institutions were represented by only one or two students. This was a severe problem regarding ACT and SAT scores, because those samples were smaller (see Table 11-1). Therefore, this paired analysis was carried out with the NLS/HSB test scores, for which the samples were considerably larger. There proved to be 63 colleges with seven or more students in both 1972 and 1980 (N=945 and 742, respectively). There were 69 colleges with that many students in both 1972 and 1982 (N=987 and 785, respectively). Correlations between test scores and college grades were computed for each of these four samples on the basis of data pooled across colleges and on the basis of correlations computed within individual colleges and then averaged. (See Note 11-3.)

RESULTS

Table 11-2 shows correlations between the various predictors and CGPA for the total samples for 1972, 1980, and 1982. The sample sizes correspond to data available for the different tests as indicated (with minor discrepancies) in Table 11-1. Correlations shown in parentheses are corrected for unreliability of the NLS/HSB tests in order to adjust for differences in the reliability of those tests due to different length in different years.

Table 11-2

Correlations Between Various Predictors and College Average for 1972 (NLS), 1980 (HSB), and 1982 (HSB) Total Samples*

	Correlations with College Average		
Predictors	1972 (NLS)	1980 (HSB)	1982 (HSB)
1. SAT-V	.36	.35	.33
2. SAT-M	.30	.33	.29
3. Multiple R (var. 1-2)	.37	.37	.34
4. ACT-English	.35	—	.32
5. ACT-Math	.29	—	.30
6. ACT-Social Studies	.32	—	.31
7. ACT-Science	.27	—	.24
8. Multiple R (var. 4-7)	.39	—	.35
9. NLS/HSB-Vocabulary	.29(.33)	.27(.30)	.25(.27)**
10. NLS/HSB-Reading	.27(.30)	.25(.28)	.27(.30)
11. NLS/HSB-Math	.27(.29)	.27(.29)	.26(.27)
12. Multiple R (var. 9-11)	.33(.35)	.31(.32)	.30(.30)
13. High School Average	.44	.45	.41
Multiple Rs with HSGPA:			
14. SAT & HSGPA(var. 1-2, 13)	.48	.48	.47
15. ACT & HSGPA(var. 4-7, 13)	.51	—	.46
16. NLS/HSB & HSGPA (var. 9-11, 13)	.46(.46)	.46(.47)	.42(.42)**

* Ns are approximately the same as those shown in Table 11-1. Correlations in parentheses are corrected for unreliability.
** P < .05 for 1982-1972 difference in observed r.

Across the 10-year span, the trend of the correlations is downward, though the differences are not large. The multiple correlations based on scores for the three test batteries declined between 1972 and 1982 as follows: SAT,–.03; ACT,–.04; NLS/HSB,–.03(–.05 in correlations corrected for variations in test length across years). The correlation for HSGPA also dropped .03. This pattern seems consistent with Morgan's recent analysis. He found a 10-year drop of .04 for the SAT when correlations were based upon comparable samples. As in Morgan (1989a), these data show little if any difference over 10 years in the multiple correlation of SAT and HSGPA with CGPA. Corresponding multiples did show some decline in the case of ACT (–.05) and NLS/HSB (–.04). That different result is associated with a somewhat different pattern in the correlation of these tests with high school grades. While the correlation of SAT scores with HSGPA was .06 lower in the 1982 cohort than the 1972 cohort, the corresponding declines for ACT and NLS/HSB were only .03 and .01. From this perspective, the multiple correlation of SAT and HSGPA with college grades held up somewhat better because in these samples the SAT and HSGPA were somewhat more independent predictors in 1982 than in 1972.

Table 11-2 does not show a consistent trend in the correlations for the 1980 cohort. While the 1980 HSB tests show somewhat lower correlations than the 1972 NLS tests (as would be expected from the 1972-1982 comparison), the SAT correlations show no such trend. Even though the samples may seem large, these various differences from 1972 to 1980 to 1982 — some consistent and some inconsistent with the overall pattern — are quite small and should not be overinterpreted. As previously noted, it is not clear how comparable the cohorts actually are with respect to college attended and grades assigned there. So we next analyzed data for the same colleges paired across the survey cohorts separated by eight to 10 years.

Tables 11-3 and 11-4 show the results for NLS/HSB data from such paired colleges. Table 11-3 is based upon students who went to the same colleges in 1972 and 1980; i.e., those 63 colleges that enrolled at least seven students from the survey sample in each year. Table 11-4 is similar but based upon those 69 colleges that enrolled seven or more survey students in both 1972 and 1982. Both tables show standard deviations and correlations computed two ways: from data pooled across colleges, and from data analyzed within individual colleges, then averaged.

The data in Tables 11-3 and 11-4 indicate quite similar results for the comparisons of 1972-80 and 1972-82. These reduced samples based upon paired colleges show generally similar means and standard deviations compared to the total sample figures shown in Table 11-1. The correlations between NLS/HSB tests and college grades for the paired samples are generally similar in magnitude to those of the total sample shown in Table 11-2 — with one obvious difference. The decline over time is notably larger and more consistent in these paired samples. Results for individual tests vary, but the multiple correlation of the three NLS/HSB tests with college grades was .08 lower in 1980 than in 1972. The comparison of 1972 and 1982 in Table 11-4 shows the same .08 difference. Furthermore, the correlation between HSGPA and CGPA dropped .08 in the 1972 to 1980 comparison and .06 in the 1972 to 1982 comparison.

Tables 11-3 and 11-4 also show the results when the analysis is done within individual colleges. As would be expected, the standard deviations are smaller within individual colleges than across all colleges in the pooled data. Despite the fact that the variance for the

Table 11-3

Prediction of CGPA in 1972 and 1980 from Longitudinal Tests (NLS/HSB) and HSGPA — Correlations Based upon Data Pooled Overall and Correlations Computed Separately Within Colleges and Averaged

	Standard Deviations and Correlations with College Grade Averages*											
	Pooled Overall						Average Within College					
	1972		1980		r_{diff}	SE_{diff}	1972		1980		r_{diff}	SE_{diff}
	r	s.d.	r	s.d.			r	s.d.	r	s.d.		
1. Vocabulary	.36	4.0	.24	3.8	.12	.045	.33	3.5	.23	3.1	.10	.044
2. Reading	.35	4.6	.25	4.9	.10	.044	.35	3.9	.27	4.0	.08	.042
3. Mathematics	.32	6.5	.30	6.9	.02	.043	.32	5.4	.32	5.6	.00	.041
4. Multiple R(1,2,3)	.39	—	.31	—	.08	.038	.40	—	.34	—	.06	.043
5. HSGPA	.47	1.3	.39	1.3	.08	.043	.48	1.1	.40	1.1	.08	.041
6. Multiple R(1,2,3,5)	.49	—	.41	—	.08	.037	.52	—	.45	—	.07	.042
7. CGPA	—	1.3	—	1.3	—		—	1.3	—	1.2	—	

* All 1972-1980 comparisons are based on data from 63 paired colleges with N ≥ 7 in both 1972 and 1980. Standard errors (SE) refer to differences between 1972 and 1980 correlations; total Ns in those years were 945 and 742, respectively.

Table 11-4

Prediction of CGPA in 1972 and 1982 from Longitudinal Tests (NLS/HSB) and HSGPA — Correlations Based upon Data Pooled Overall and Correlations Computed Separately Within Colleges and Averaged

*Standard Deviations and Correlations with College Grade Averages**

	Pooled Overall						Average Within College					
	1972		1982		r_{diff}	SE_{diff}	1972		1982		r_{diff}	SE_{diff}
	r	s.d.	r	s.d.			r	s.d.	r	s.d.		
1. Vocabulary	.31	3.9	.23	4.0	.08	.056	.30	3.4	.24	3.4	.06	.06
2. Reading	.30	4.5	.26	5.1	.04	.054	.30	3.9	.25	4.3	.05	.06
3. Mathematics	.28	6.4	.22	6.5	.06	.050	.28	5.4	.23	5.1	.05	.05
4. Multiple R(1,2,3)	.35	—	.27	—	.08	.040	.36	—	.29	—	.07	.05
5. HSGPA	.45	1.3	.39	1.3	.06	.055	.48	1.1	.42	1.1	.06	.06
6. Multiple R(1,2,3,5)	.46	—	.41	—	.05	.039	.50	—	.46	—	.04	.04
7. CGPA	—	1.3	—	1.3			—	1.3	—	1.2		

* All 1972-1982 comparisons are based on data from 69 paired colleges with N ≥ 7 in both 1972 and 1982. Standard errors (SE) refer to differences between 1972 and 1982 correlations; total Ns in those years were 987 and 785, respectively.

predictors is typically 25 to 30 percent smaller, the within-college multiple correlations are slightly higher than the corresponding pooled multiples. This result is consistent with the assumption that variation in grading standards across colleges restricts validity coefficients based on pooled data. There is no indication, however, that this factor operated differently over time; i.e., so as to cause the pooled correlations to decline. If that were so, the within-college correlations would have been stable through time; in fact, they showed essentially the same pattern of decline. Also, there is no indication of any consequential restriction of range that might account for lower correlations in the later years as compared to 1972.

The data in Tables 11-3 and 11-4 show a fairly consistent pattern of declining correlations from 1972 to 1980 and 1982. Comparing the differences to estimates of their standard errors (some of which may be conservative, see Note 11-4), it seems reasonably sure from the overall set of data that the correlation between these tests and CGPA declined to some degree during the 1970s. The standard errors are too large to warrant much attention to differences among the tests.

Pairing the colleges so that the cohort samples were more directly comparable yielded more consistent results than was true of Table 11-2. That is not surprising, but why should the correlations with CGPA show a larger decline in these reduced samples? In Table 11-2 the decline was .03 to .04; here the decline is .08. If the difference is real, the answer may lie in the particular colleges represented in the paired analysis. They are preponderantly large, public institutions — those most likely to meet the criterion of seven students in both cohorts. It was the "large" and "public" categories that showed larger declines in predictive validity in Morgan's (1989a) data.

One additional question of interest is how well similar tests in this data set correlate with one another in the successive samples. Do the verbal tests, for example, correlate with one another as well in 1982 as in 1972? This comparison is relevant for two reasons. First, should those correlations drop, it might indicate something unusual about the HSB samples (e.g., representativeness, accuracy of sample weights) that would suggest the drop in validity coefficients may be spurious. Second, a change in the pattern of correlations among tests measuring similar constructs could indicate that one or more of the tests is changing character or that the scores may be taking on a different meaning because of some new element, such as test security breaches or intensified test coaching.

Table 11-5 shows all correlations among the verbal tests and among the mathematics tests. Rather than declining, those correlations actually go up from 1972 to 1982. It is not clear why, though

Table 11-5

Correlations among Similar Subtests of SAT, ACT, and NLS/HSB
for 1972, 1980, and 1982

	1972		1980		1982	
	N	r	N	r	N	r
Verbal:						
SAT-V, ACT English	659	.68	—	—	361	.78
SAT-V, NLS/HSB Reading	3313	.70	1821	.70	1916	.72
SAT-V, NLS/HSB Vocabulary	3313	.78	1830	.83	1925	.79
ACT -English, NLS/HSB Reading	2108	.58	—	—	1396	.66*
ACT -English, NLS/HSB Vocabulary	2106	.60	—	—	1405	.70*
NLS/HSB Reading, Vocabulary	6498	.63	4810	.68	5361	.72*
Mathematics:						
SAT-M, ACT-Math	656	.79	—	—	368	.84
SAT-M, NLS/HSB Math	3301	.75	1816	.78	1936	.82*
ACT-Math, NLS/HSB Math	2104	.76	—	—	1392	.80

*P < .05 for 1982-1972 difference in r.

some of the increase in correlations with the NLS/HSB tests is likely due to the increased length of those tests. It does not appear that the range of talent in the three cohorts plays any significant role.

CONCLUSIONS

In this study, we have used data from the National Longitudinal Study (NLS) and the High School and Beyond (HSB) survey in order to examine correlations between three sets of test scores and college grade averages for three samples of students who graduated from secondary school in 1972, 1980, and 1982. Our principal conclusions are well-framed by the questions posed at the outset.

- Is the downward trend in correlations between SAT scores and college grades observed by Morgan (1989a) peculiar to colleges participating in the VSS or does it also show up in these nationally representative samples? A similar trend of similar magnitude was observed in these data, though not consistently in the total samples. A larger, more consistent decline was found in an analysis of the NLS/HSB scores of only those students who went to paired sets of mostly large, public institutions. Overall, these findings suggest that the decline noted in SAT correlations is not restricted to the VSS colleges but is more likely spread through at least some major sectors of higher education.

- If there is evidence of such a decline, is the trend associated only with SAT scores or with other predictors as well? These data suggest a more general phenomenon. The decline in validity coefficients was of approximately the same magnitude for the SAT, the ACT, the longitudinal survey tests, and the high school averages.

- Do the correlations among the scores on similar tests (e.g., verbal with verbal, mathematics with mathematics) appear to be stable over time? The data showed no evidence of decline in these correlations between 1972 and 1982.

These survey data are based upon carefully drawn nationally representative samples, and the followup was unusually successful. As such databases go, this one is highly regarded. Nonetheless, the results should be interpreted cautiously. As validity data, these samples are not large, and the standard errors typically do not warrant strong confidence in the results of specific analyses for specific tests. However, the findings do indicate provocative trends that deserve further attention and comparison with other relevant data.

Taken together, the findings add some generality to the changes noted in predictive validity coefficients in recent years; that is, they suggest that the phenomenon is evidently not dependent on some peculiar sample or restricted to a single test. Correspondingly, these data give less weight to test-related and sample-related hypotheses as to why the decline occurred. For example, if spurious score gains due to test-specific coaching were a significant cause of the observed decline, one would expect the SAT to show a greater decline than the other tests that are subject to less coaching effort or, in the case of the longitudinal tests, none at all as far as we know. Also, there was no sign of diminished correlations among tests measuring similar constructs. If some factor like coaching were causing scores of a particular test to correlate less well with college grades, then the test should also show declining correlations with other related measures. The same logic applies to hypotheses concerning some unrecognized deterioration in test quality due to changes in test specifications, changes in test development procedures, security breaches, and so on.

Taken alone, these findings certainly do not rule out the hypothesis that some change in the SAT or some quirk in the data samples is at the root of the trend in validity coefficients, but the results are inconsistent with that hypothesis. We have paid no attention at all here to the criterion; i.e., possible changes in its meaning or quality over time. This study underscores the need, in considering further research on this topic, to look closely at college grades — the other half of the equation that determines such validity coefficients.

CHAPTER 12

Implications of Using Freshman GPA as the Criterion for the Predictive Validity of the SAT

Leonard Ramist, Charles Lewis, & Laura McCamley[*]

Because an important function of admissions is to select the applicants most able to perform college-level work, grades constitute a logical measure of the outcome of the admissions decision: They reveal the level of academic success of the accepted applicants who enroll. The typically used measure of academic performance, freshman GPA, has many advantages: The freshman class is more representative of the applicant group than later classes, a full year of individual course grades tends to even out variations in grades from a variety of instructors and courses, and differences in the courses students take are smaller than in later years.

Nevertheless, there remain many possible flaws in the use of FGPA as a measure of academic performance. In most colleges, students have a wide choice of courses in a great variety of subject areas. Institutional response to the diversity of student needs has created options ranging from remediation to advanced placement. Course loads differ from student to student, requirements differ from course to course, and grading practices differ from instructor to instructor. All of these factors influence the reliability of grades from course to course or from term to term and the comparability of FGPA from student to student.

The predictive validity model of using the correlation between a predictor and a criterion to measure validity implicitly assumes a perfectly reliable criterion that is comparable from student to student, as well as a full range of scores on the predictor. Even though unrelated to the true validity of the predictor, any limitation in

[*] The authors wish to express gratitude to several people whose contributions made this chapter possible. Our advisory committee — Al Beaton, Rogers Elliott, Gary Marco, and Warren Willingham — put us on the right course. Jim Ferris and Judy Pollack helped us design the data input record. Celeste Gibilisco organized and supervised the massive effort of coding course categories, which was completed by Joyce Gant. Al Rogers bailed us out of programming snags. Nancy Burton, Bob Linn, Sam Messick, Howard Wainer, Gloria Weiss, and especially Larry Stricker supplied us with enormously helpful reviews. Last but not least, the colleges listed in Appendix A-3 supplied the essential raw materials — freshman course grades.

criterion reliability or comparability, or restriction of range in predictor scores, reduces the observed correlation between the predictor and the criterion. Basing the predictive validity of the SAT on its correlation with FGPA is subject to such limitations in FGPA reliability and comparability, as well as restriction of range in SAT scores.

This chapter decomposes FGPA in order to evaluate its effects on the observed correlations between the SAT and FGPA. It includes analyses of the following, annually and over longer periods:

- Student course choice,

- Student course load,

- FGPA reliability,

- Advanced and remedial course taking,

- Variety in course taking,

- Variation of student aptitude levels among courses,

- Appropriateness of average course grades,

- Student differences by sex and academic level,

- College differences by selectivity level, validity level, and level of change in validity,

- Factors that are useful in predicting both the level of and the change in correlation between the SAT and FGPA,

- Validity by course, and

- Validity by type of course.

METHODOLOGY

Participants

In order to analyze FGPA, its components — course grades associated with courses taken — had to be obtained for a representative sample of colleges. Validity studies do not typically use course grades, and therefore, data from the College Board's Validity Study Service would not have been sufficient. It was necessary to obtain the required data directly from colleges.

To minimize the amount of data transmitted, internal College Board files were utilized to the extent possible. In the process of providing summary reports of enrolled freshmen for participating colleges, the Summary Reporting Service (SRS) created annual files of test scores and other data from the Admissions Testing Program on

254

students identified as enrolled by a participating college. Among other data, these files contained SAT scores, student-reported high school GPA, and sex identification. The SRS files were used in order to maximize available data, minimize data needed from the college, and enhance comparability from college to college. (The 1985 entering class was the last one for which the SRS was available. A similar service is being introduced this year.)

To obtain course information that would provide insight into changes that were occurring, data for more than one year were needed. Data more than a few years old would have been difficult for many colleges to provide, and data from consecutive years would have provided little information about changes. Therefore, the entering classes selected for analysis were 1985, the last year of SRS data, and 1982, the earliest year feasible for colleges to supply data.

Ramist and Weiss (Chapter 5 of this volume) document that the SAT multiple correlation with FGPA, corrected for restriction of range, fell from a high of .57 in 1974 to .52 in 1985 (with further reductions after 1985). Although the period from 1982 to 1985 covers only three years of the 11-year span, 40 percent of the .05 decline (from .54 to .52) occurred during this period.

All 186 colleges that had identified their enrolled freshmen through SRS in both 1982 and 1985 were invited to participate. Of these colleges, 45 provided course identifications and grades and student identifications for their 1985 enrolled freshmen, but seven had to be excluded from most analyses because they were not able to supply usable data for the 1982 class; the other 38 supplied usable data for both classes. (See Appendix A-3.)

Table 12-1 shows that the 38 colleges represented all geographical regions; although few were in the Midwest or Southwest, the other regions were represented by approximately equal numbers. One-third were public colleges. Almost equal numbers were small (15 had fewer than 500 identified freshmen in 1985), medium-sized (11 had between 500 and 1,000), and large (12 had 1,000 or more). Almost equal numbers had 1985 SAT means of 1,100 or more (14), 1,000-1,099(11), and below 1,000 (13).

At nine of the colleges, the 1982 and 1985 multiple correlations of verbal and mathematical scores with FGPA (uncorrected for restriction of range) remained essentially unchanged (changes of less than .01 each). At another nine, these multiple correlations increased by .01 or more each. At 20 colleges, they decreased by .01 or more each. Eight colleges had changes of .10 or more each, and these were all decreases.

Table 12-1

Characteristics of Participating Colleges

Geographical Distribution	Number	SAT *Total Mean*	Number
Middle States	11	800-899	5
New England	10	900-999	8
South	7	1,000-1,099	11
West	7	1,100-1,199	8
Midwest	2	1,200-1,299	5
Southwest	1	1,300-1,399	1
	38		38

Control	Number	Change in SAT *Validity*	Number
Public	13	Increase, +.10 or more	0
Private	25	Increase, +.01 to +.10	9
	38	No change, −.01 to +.01	9
		Decrease, −.01 to −.10	12
		Decrease, −.10 or more	8
			38

Number of Identified 1985 *Enrolled Freshmen*	Number
Less than 500	15
500 up to 1,000	11
1,000 or more	12
	38

Data Preparation

In addition to supplying course identifications, course grades, and student-identifying information about their 1982 and 1985 freshmen, colleges supplied copies of their 1982 and 1985 course catalogs. These catalogs were used to classify all courses taken by freshmen.

The classification scheme of 37 categories listed in Table 12-2 was used. The scheme was established to classify courses across colleges by both subject and level. When matched against skills tested in the SAT-Verbal and SAT-Mathematical sections and in the Test of Standard Written English, subjects requiring similar skills were grouped together (for example, social sciences and humanities) and other subjects were disaggregated (nine levels of English, depending on approximately equal or unequal emphasis on reading or literature as opposed to writing or composition, and depending on advanced, regular, or remedial level). There were five levels of mathematics: postcalculus (with one year of calculus as a prerequisite), calculus,

256

Table 12-2

Course Categories

1. Postcalculus	23. History
2. Calculus	
3. Precalculus	24. Social sciences/humanities-
4. Remedial mathematics	political science, sociology,
5. Regular mathematics (other than	psychology, philosophy, religion,
1-4)	anthropology, archeology, geogra-
	phy, law, criminal justice, social
6. English-advanced	work, library science, public affairs,
7. English-regular	area studies, ethnic studies
8. English-remedial	
	25. Economics
9. Reading/literature-advanced	
10. Reading/literature-regular	26. Business/communications
11. Reading/literature-remedial	
	27. Art/music/theater-studio
12. Writing/composition-advanced	28. Art/music/theater-nonstudio
13. Writing/composition-regular	
14. Writing/composition-remedial	29. Computer
15. Biological sciences-advanced	30. Health/nursing
16. Biological sciences-intro with lab	
or for majors	31. Education
17. Biological sciences — intro with no	
lab and for nonmajors	32. Physical education
18. Physical sciences/engineering-	33. Military science
advanced	
19. Physical sciences/engineering-intro	34. Home economics
with lab or for majors	
20. Physical sciences-intro with no lab	35. Architecture/environmental design
and for nonmajors	
	36. Technical/vocational
21. Foreign languages-beyond entry	
level	37. Other
22. Foreign languages-entry level	

precalculus, regular (any course not fitting in any of the other categories), and remedial.

Records of student identifications supplied by the colleges were matched with SRS files. For the 38 colleges, 86 percent of the records were matched. In this way, student records of courses taken and grades (converted to a 0-4 scale) were augmented by SAT-Verbal and SAT-Mathematical scores, TSWE score, student-reported HSGPA, and sex.

Data Analyses

For the various courses, we attempted to characterize grading practices by calculating the grade residual: the difference between the average course grade and the average expected GPA based on HSGPA and SAT scores of students taking the course. Large positive grade residuals were taken to indicate courses for which grading tended to be lenient, and large negative residuals to indicate courses for which grading tended to be strict. ("Lenient" and "strict," as used here, are not intended to imply any judgment about the relative academic rigor of different disciplines, but merely to describe apparent differences in grading practices). Grading leniency and strictness, as well as student course taking by year, were summarized by type of course. Student choice of courses with lenient, average, or strict grading was summarized by SAT and HSGPA level for each year.

Separate validity analyses were undertaken using both FGPA and course grade as criteria in 1982 and 1985, and these results were summarized across colleges. To compensate for widely different restrictions of ranges of test scores among colleges and courses, corrections were made to the full SAT-taking group based on a model of a three-variable correction — HSGPA, SAT-Verbal score, and SAT-Mathematical score. The model assumes restriction of range either from the student (by applying, by accepting an offer of enrollment, or by choosing to take certain types of courses) or from the college (by offering admission). (See Note 12-1.)

Advanced course levels were identified in the subject areas of mathematics, English, reading/literature, writing/composition, biological sciences, physical sciences/engineering, and foreign languages. The percentage of credits in advanced courses was tabulated for each college, in both years, and was used to predict levels and changes in correlations.

Remedial course levels were identified in the subject areas of mathematics, English, reading/literature, and writing/composition. The percentage of credits in remedial courses was tabulated for each college, in both years, and was also used to predict levels and changes in correlations.

The full effect of remediation may go beyond the remedial course grades that enter into the FGPA. Some remedial courses are taken without credit and are not included as part of the FGPA criterion; the need for remediation may be reflected in smaller course loads. Also, some students take some courses on a pass-fail basis, receiving no grades to contribute to the criterion. Therefore, the average number of credits per student and the average number of courses per student with quantifiable grades were tabulated for each college for both years. Change in the average number of credits per student was used to predict changes in correlations. Because it is a more comparable measure from college to college, the average number of courses, rather than credits, per student was used to predict the levels of correlations.

The number of course grades received has a direct effect on the reliability of FGPA. For each college, FGPA reliability was established for each year by computing separate FGPAs for each of two randomly created sets of half of the course grades for each student. (See Note 12-2.) Factors associated with levels and changes in the reliability of FGPA were determined, including levels of and changes in SAT correlations with FGPA.

There may be more deleterious effects on comparability of FGPA than can be isolated in the variables related to advanced or remedial course taking or reliability of FGPA. There may simply be a change in the dispersion of course taking among courses offered. To measure the dispersion of course taking, the number of courses accounting for half of all credits was tabulated for each college for each year. Large numbers indicate great dispersion, and small numbers indicate concentration. This variable was also used to predict the levels of and changes in correlation.

If there is great variety in course taking, comparability of course grades may depend on the variation of student aptitude levels among courses. When some courses are taken primarily by students with high aptitude and others primarily by students with low aptitude, then comparability would be reduced if instructors tend to grade at similar levels in each course. To evaluate this possibility, the standard deviation of course SAT means was calculated for each college for each year. This variable was also used to predict the levels of and changes in correlation.

Even if there is great variation of student aptitude levels among courses, comparability of course grades may not be greatly compromised if the levels of the grades correspond to the levels of academic aptitude. The greatest incomparability would occur if, in addition to course variety and variability of course SAT means, course grade levels are unrelated to course SAT levels. To explore this possibility, the correlation between course grade mean and course SAT mean was tabulated for each college for each year. This variable was also used to predict the levels of and changes in correlation.

Because the FGPAs of females are predicted better by test scores and high school performance than the FGPAs of males, the percentage female at each college was tabulated and used as a variable. In addition, analyses were performed separately by sex, as well as with both sexes combined.

In addition to sex, student groupings by academic level were established at each college. An academic composite index of SAT scores and HSGPA was tabulated for each enrolled freshman. (See Note 12-3.) For each college, students were grouped into equal thirds based on the academic composite index. Separate analyses were performed for high, middle, and low student composites, first for each college and then across colleges.

Analyses of correlation levels and changes were performed for each college and for all colleges combined, by student academic composite and sex. In addition to student groupings, colleges were also grouped by selectivity level based on their 1985 SAT total mean. The 13 colleges with the highest SAT mean, the 12 in the middle, and the 13 with the lowest mean were grouped, and separate analyses were performed for each group, also by student composites and sex. In addition to selectivity level, two other kinds of college groupings were used to highlight important differences:

- High, middle, and low groupings based on the level of the corrected (for restriction of range) correlation of the SAT with FGPA; and

- High, middle, and low groupings based on the change in the level of the corrected correlation of the SAT with FGPA.

To eliminate almost all of the problems due to noncomparability of course grades, an analysis of validity for an individual course was undertaken. For each college, the individual course validities were averaged overall and by course category, weighting each course validity by the sum of the numbers of students taking the course in 1982 and 1985.

STUDENT CHARACTERISTICS

There were records of 40,622 students from the 38 colleges included in the analysis in 1985, 1,069 per college, up 9 percent from 1982. As in the overall SAT-taking population (College Board, 1982 and 1985), 52 percent were female and 48 percent male. As shown in Table 12-3, the 12 colleges of middle selectivity were larger (1,980 per college) than the colleges of high (754 per college) or low (543 per college) selectivity.

Test scores generally increased from 1982 to 1985 (by an average of 12 SAT total points), while the HSGPA mean decreased (–.04), suggesting somewhat stricter high school grading. The group of colleges with low selectivity was the only group with a decrease in the SAT mean (-2 compared with +19 and +21) and had the largest decrease in the HSGPA mean (–.08 compared with –.02 and –.03). On the average,

Table 12-3

Student Characteristics, 1982 and 1985, by Sex,
Student Composite, and College Selectivity

	All Students	Sex Males*	Females	Student Composite High	Middle	Low	College Selectivity High	Middle	Low
1985									
Number per College	1,069	540	557	369	353	346	754	1,980	543
SAT-V+M Mean	1,062	1,078	1,042	1,165	1,054	965	1,211	1,060	914
HSGPA Mean	3.35	3.27	3.40	3.75	3.39	2.91	3.61	3.40	3.04
Change, 1982 to 1985									
Number per College	+86	+39	+49	+31	+29	+16	+24	+223	+22
SAT-V+M Mean	+12	+15	+11	+6	+16	+20	+19	+21	−2
HSGPA MEAN	−.04	−.05	−.05	−.01	−.03	−.05	−.02	−.03	−.08

* Two of the colleges were all female. Data for males were averages among the 36 of 38 colleges with males.

within each college, students in the high academic composite level had the smallest increase in test scores but also the smallest decrease in HSGPA.

FRESHMAN COURSE SELECTION AND GRADING

Table 12-4 contains the percentage of students taking a course in each of the 37 course categories in 1985, the percentage change from 1982 to 1985, and 1985 student and grading characteristics. Social sciences/humanities, because it is broadly defined, was the only course category in which more than half of all students (78 percent) took a course. Half (50 percent) took a course in the calculus category and 41 percent took a regular writing course.

The course category with by far the highest 1985 SAT total mean (1,250) and also the highest HSGPA mean (3.7) was advanced mathematics. The course category with the lowest SAT mean (842) and HSGPA mean (3.0) was remedial English. Most of the courses with the highest SAT and HSGPA means were advanced, and most with the lowest means were remedial.

The 1985 average of course grades ranged from 1.9 for remedial mathematics to 3.1 for studio art/music/theater and advanced writing. All of the categories with the strictest grading (low grade-residual mean over predicted FGPA based on SAT scores and HSGPA) were science or quantitative, and none of the categories with the most lenient grading (high grade-residual mean) were science or quantitative. The strictest grading was in biology — lab/major (−.35 residual), followed by physical sciences/engineering — lab/major and calculus (both −.24). The most lenient grading was in physical education (+.78), followed by studio art/music/theater (+.56) and education (+.50).

Table 12-4

Percentage (1985) and Percentage Change (1982 to 1985)
of Students Taking a Course in Each Course Category,
with Student and Grading Characteristics

			1985 Student and Grading Characteristics			
Volume					Course	Grade
1985 % of All Students	1982 to 1985 % Change		SAT Mean	HSGPA Mean	Grade Mean	Grade Residual Mean
78%	+14%	Social sciences/humanities	1,057	3.3	2.7	+.07
50%	+6%	Calculus	1,113	3.5	2.5	–.24
41%	+5%	Regular writing	1,034	3.3	2.8	+.22
33%	+10%	Phys. sci. & engin.-nonmajor	1,114	3.4	2.5	–.09
33%	-1%	Phys. sci. & engin.-lab/major	1,095	3.5	2.5	–.24
31%	+5%	History	1,068	3.4	2.6	–.02
29%	+7%	Economics	1,087	3.4	2.5	–.17
26%	+12%	Foreign language-entry	1,077	3.4	2.8	+.20
26%	+2%	Regular English	1,039	3.3	2.8	+.21
20%	+34%	Art/music/theater-nonstudio	1,071	3.4	2.8	+.25
18%	+25%	Foreign language-beyond entry	1,093	3.4	2.9	+.28
17%	+10%	Regular reading/literature	1,116	3.4	2.9	+.14
17%	+8%	Physical education	989	3.3	3.0	+.78
17%	+6%	Business/commerce	1,013	3.3	2.7	+.14
16%	-6%	Computer	1,091	3.4	2.7	–.02
15%	+10%	Biology-lab/major	1,067	3.4	2.3	–.35
14%	+26%	Biology-nonmajor	1,058	3.4	2.5	–.07
14%	+6%	Precalculus	1,011	3.3	2.3	–.14
14%	-7%	Regular mathematics	1,022	3.3	2.5	–.05
11%	+20%	Art/music/theater-studio	1,080	3.4	3.1	+.56
9%	+5%	Other	1,073	3.4	2.9	+.39
7%	–28%	Advanced mathematics	1,250	3.7	2.9	–.06
4%	+19%	Education	984	3.3	3.0	+.50
4%	+21%	Health/nursing	948	3.2	2.9	+.40
3%	+43%	Remedial writing	889	3.2	2.5	+.23
3%	–19%	Remedial mathematics	866	3.1	1.9	–.10
2%	+33%	Home economics	886	3.1	2.5	+.36
2%	+14%	Architecture	1,076	3.3	2.7	+.25
2%	0	Military science	1,076	3.4	3.0	+.45
2%	–12%	Phys. sci. & engin.-advanced	1,202	3.6	2.6	–.06
0.9%	–23%	Remedial English	842	3.0	2.6	+.42
0.9%	–37%	Advanced English	1,172	3.6	2.8	+.26
0.8%	-7%	Advanced biology	1,192	3.5	2.6	–.04
0.5%	+23%	Advanced reading/literature	1,188	3.4	3.0	+.15
0.4%	–21%	Remedial reading/literature	936	3.0	3.0	+.28
0.4%	–21%	Technical/vocational	938	3.1	2.6	+.30
0.2%	–31%	Advanced writing	1,099	3.6	3.1	+.28

Between 1982 and 1985, the largest increases in number of students selecting categories of courses (among those offered to freshmen by at least one-third of the colleges) were in art/music/theater (nonstudio, +34 percent; studio, +20 percent), biology (nonmajors, +26 percent; lab/majors, +10 percent), foreign language (beyond entry level, +25 percent; entry level, +12 percent), and education (+19 percent). The only large decrease in a category selected by freshmen from at least one-third of the colleges was in advanced mathematics (-28 percent), which is especially surprising given the large increase in mathematics course taking in high school during this period: The percentage of SAT takers with four or more years of mathematics increased from 54 percent in 1982 to 61 percent in 1985 (College Board, 1982, 1985). There were offsetting increases in calculus (+6 percent) and precalculus (+6 percent).

Student capabilities are related to selection of courses with strict or lenient grading. For each college, students were divided into thirds in terms of their SAT scores and HSGPA, and courses were divided into thirds in terms of the mean residual of course grade and predicted FGPA based on SAT scores and HSGPA of those taking the course. Table 12-5 displays the ratio of strictly graded to leniently graded courses taken, by SAT and HSGPA level, for 1982 and 1985. Table 12-6 shows the effect of the course selection on ultimate FGPA.

Table 12-5

Ratio of Strictly-Graded to Leniently-Graded Courses Taken, by SAT and HSGPA Level, 1982 and 1985

	HSGPA							
	Lowest Third		Middle Third		Highest Third		TOTAL	
SAT	1982	1985	1982	1985	1982	1985	1982	1985
Highest third	1.00	1.07	1.09	1.12	1.12	1.16	1.07	1.12
Middle third	.93	.96	.99	1.01	1.12	1.09	1.02	1.02
Lowest third	.73	.75	.85	.88	.99	.95	.85	.86
TOTAL	.88	.92	.97	1.00	1.07	1.06	1.00	1.00

Table 12-6

Effect of Course Selection on FGPA, by SAT and HSGPA Level, 1982 and 1985

	HSGPA							
	Lowest Third		Middle Third		Highest Third		TOTAL	
SAT	1982	1985	1982	1985	1982	1985	1982	1985
Highest third	−.01	−.02	−.03	−.03	−.03	−.04	−.02	−.03
Middle third	+.01	+.01	.00	.00	−.02	−.02	.00	−.01
Lowest third	+.06	+.06	+.03	+.03	+.01	+.01	+.03	+.03
TOTAL	+.02	+.02	.00	.00	−.02	−.02	.00	.00

Students with both SAT scores and HSGPA in the lowest third took only three strictly graded for every four leniently graded courses (ratio of .75) in 1985; this selection of courses added .06 to their mean FGPA. Students in the highest third on both measures took 16 percent more strictly graded than leniently graded courses in 1985 (up from 12 percent more in 1982); this course selection subtracted .04 from mean FGPA in 1985 (.03 in 1982). It is interesting to note that, whereas the two groups of discrepant SAT and HSGPA levels had similar course selection patterns in 1982 (1.00 for high SAT/low HSGPA and .99 for low SAT/high HSGPA), by 1985 the two groups had gone in different directions, with the high SAT/low HSGPA group selecting more strictly graded courses (ratio of 1.07) and the low SAT/high HSGPA group selecting more leniently graded courses (ratio of .95).

Table 12-7 displays averages of freshman course characteristics for all colleges. These include FGPA, percentage of credits from advanced courses, percentage of credits from remedial courses, average stu-

Table 12-7

Mean Freshman Course Characteristics, 1982 and 1985,
by Sex, Student Composite, and College Selectivity

	All Students	Males	Females	High	Middle	Low	High	Middle	Low
		Sex		*Student Composite*			*College Selectivity*		
1985									
FGPA	2.64	2.54	2.70	3.00	2.61	2.32	2.88	2.69	2.37
% Advanced	5.9%	4.8%	6.4%	7.4%	5.8%	4.5%	9.3%	6.5%	2.0%
% Remedial	1.4%	1.6%	1.3%	1.0%	1.4%	1.9%	0.6%	0.3%	3.3%
Student course load	8.6	8.6	8.6	8.8	8.6	8.3	8.0	9.0	8.7
Courses accounting for 50%	16	15	17	16	15	15	18	18	12
FGPA reliability	.82	N/A	N/A	N/A	N/A	N/A	.81	.83	.83
Standard deviation of course SAT means	57	N/A	N/A	N/A	N/A	N/A	55	61	57
Correlation of course-grade and SAT means	.10	N/A	N/A	N/A	N/A	N/A	.13	.10	.09
Change, 1982 to 1985									
FGPA	−.04	−.06	−.03	−.03	−.03	−.03	+.01	+.01	−.13
% Advanced	−.3	−.4	−.2	−.5	−.3	−.1	−.7	+.5	−.5
% Remedial	−.3	−.3	−.2	−.2	−.4	−.3	−.1	0	−.7
Student course load	−.2	−.2	−.1	−.2	−.1	−.2	−.2	−.2	0
Courses accounting for 50%	+2	+2	+2	+3	+1	+1	+3	+2	+1
FGPA reliability	+.01	N/A	N/A	N/A	N/A	N/A	−.01	.00	+.03
Standard deviation of course SAT means	−2	N/A	N/A	N/A	N/A	N/A	−4	−1	−1
Correlation of course-grade and SAT means	−.01	N/A	N/A	N/A	N/A	N/A	.00	+.02	−.06

dent course load, courses accounting for 50 percent of all credits, reliability of FGPA, standard deviation of course SAT means, and correlation of course SAT means and FGPA for 1985, with changes from 1982, by sex, student composite, and college selectivity. Overall mean FGPA was 2.64 in 1985, a slight decline from 2.68 in 1982.

The mean percentages of courses that were advanced and remedial in 1985 were 5.9 percent and 1.4 percent, respectively; both declined slightly — from 6.2 percent and 1.7 percent, respectively, in 1982. The overall mean student load was 8.6 courses, a decline from 8.8 in 1982. Course variety increased, however, with an average of 16 courses accounting for 50 percent of the credits in 1985, compared to 14 in 1982. The average FGPA reliability of .82 was higher than expected. (See Note 12-2.) The average correlation between course SAT mean and course GPA of .10 was lower than expected.

Compared with males, females had a higher mean FGPA (2.70 in 1985, compared to 2.54), took advanced courses at a higher mean rate (6.4 percent compared to 4.8 percent), took remedial courses at a slightly lower mean rate (1.3 percent compared to 1.6 percent), and had greater course variety (an average of 17 courses accounting for half of all credits, compared to 15). Males and females had the same average course load (8.6).

Generally, for a higher student academic composite level, there were: a higher mean FGPA, a higher mean percentage of advanced courses, a lower mean percentage of remedial courses, and a larger mean student course load. On average, there were very small differences in course variety among the student composites.

In a similar way, for a higher college selectivity level (higher SAT means), there were: a higher mean FGPA and a higher mean percentage of advanced courses. In addition to being the only group with a decrease in SAT mean (–2) and having the largest decrease in mean HSGPA (–.08), the group of colleges with low SAT means was the only group with a decrease in mean freshman FGPA (–.13) and a decrease in the mean correlation of course SAT means and GPA (–.06).

SAT PREDICTIVE VALIDITY: USING THE TRADITIONAL FGPA CRITERION

To document the average validity of SAT scores and HSGPA in 1982 and 1985 for all 38 colleges, Table 12-8 displays mean overall correlations for the prediction of FGPA from SAT scores and HSGPA, both uncorrected and corrected for restriction of range. The average correlations for the verbal and mathematical scores were close (the verbal score had higher mean uncorrected overall correlations, but the corrected correlations were about the same). Compared with HSGPA, the mean

Table 12-8

Mean Correlations with FGPA, 1982 and 1985,
Uncorrected and Corrected for Restriction of Range

	Uncorrected			Corrected		
	1982	1985	Change	1982	1985	Change
SAT-V	.33	.29	−.042	.52	.49	−.033
SAT-M	.31	.28	−.028	.52	.50	−.023
SAT-V, M	.38	.34	−.039	.57	.54	−.030
HSGPA	.40	.39	−.009	.59	.57	−.015
SAT, HSGPA	.50	.47	−.026	.67	.64	−.026
SAT Increment	.10	.08	−.016	.08	.07	−.011

overall SAT multiple correlations (both uncorrected and corrected) were lower.

From 1982 to 1985, all average correlations for the 38 colleges declined. The decline of .03 for the mean overall SAT multiple corrected correlation (from .57 to .54) is the same amount experienced by colleges using the Validity Study Service (from .54 to .51, Chapter 5). The mean overall corrected correlation for HSGPA declined by .02 (from .59 to .57), compared with no change (at .58) for colleges using VSS. Because the average reliability of FGPA was .82, the mean overall correlations for the SAT and HSGPA would all be about .06 higher for a perfectly reliable criterion. (See Note 12-4.)

Table 12-9 displays mean corrected (overall) correlations for 1985 and changes from 1982 by sex, student composite, and college selectivity. Generally, mean correlations were higher for females than for males; higher for the high student composite than for the middle composite; higher for the middle composite than for the low composite; higher for colleges of high selectivity than for colleges of middle selectivity; and higher for those of middle selectivity than for those of low selectivity. The highest average SAT correlation (.63) and SAT increment (.10) were at the more selective colleges. The lowest average SAT correlation (.44) and SAT increment (.05) were at the less selective colleges.

For all groups, the mean corrected correlation for the SAT-Mathematical score was slightly higher than the mean corrected correlation for the SAT-Verbal score. Also, for most groups, the mean corrected correlation for HSGPA was slightly higher than the mean corrected correlation for the SAT.

Colleges of high selectivity had a higher mean SAT correlation (.63) than HSGPA correlation (.62) and a high mean SAT increment (.10). Females had equal mean SAT and HSGPA correlations (.58) and also a high mean SAT increment (.09).

Table 12-9

Mean Corrected Correlations with FGPA, 1985 and Changes from 1982, by Sex, Student Composite, and College Selectivity

	All Students	Males	Females	High	Middle	Low	High	Middle	Low
		Sex		*Student Composite*			*College Selectivity*		
1985									
SAT-V	.49	.46	.51	.53	.48	.38	.57	.50	.39
SAT-M	.50	.49	.54	.55	.48	.39	.58	.51	.41
SAT-V, M	.54	.53	.58	.60	.53	.44	.63	.56	.44
HSGPA	.57	.55	.58	.73	.58	.40	.62	.59	.50
SAT, HSGPA	.64	.62	.67	.78	.64	.50	.72	.66	.54
SAT Increment	.07	.07	.09	.05	.07	.09	.10	.07	.05
Change, 1982 to 1985									
SAT-V	−.033	−.054	−.016	−.030	+.050	−.040	−.007	−.023	−.066
SAT-M	−.023	−.027	−.010	−.026	+.057	−.013	+.008	−.019	−.059
SAT-V, M	−.030	−.044	−.013	−.030	+.039	−.031	+.002	−.022	−.070
HSGPA	−.015	−.018	−.004	+.001	+.087	−.033	−.006	−.010	−.028
SAT, HSGPA	−.026	−.040	−.010	−.015	+.045	−.036	−.003	−.018	−.055
SAT Increment	−.011	−.022	−.005	−.016	−.042	−.003	+.003	−.008	−.028

For all students, the mean correlation changes were a moderate decline for HSGPA (−.015) and a larger decline for the SAT (−.030), somewhat higher for the verbal score (−.032) than for the mathematical score (−.023). For males and for colleges with low selectivity, the mean declines were especially large for the SAT (−.044 and −.070, respectively). Colleges of high selectivity were the only group with an increasing mean SAT increment (+.003).

For students with a high academic composite, the corrected correlation for HSGPA averaged an exceptionally high .73, compared to .60 for the SAT (high in comparison to almost all groups, but small in comparison to HSGPA), and the SAT increment averaged a relatively low .05. In contrast to the high mean correlation for HSGPA for the high student composite, the mean HSGPA correlation for the low student composite was a very low .40, lower than the SAT correlation of .44, but the mean SAT increment of .09 was high.

The mean correlations with FGPA ranged from .34 for the SAT and .33 for HSGPA for the low composite group at colleges of low selectivity to .66 for the SAT and .79 for HSGPA for the high composite group at colleges of high selectivity. Regardless of the college selectivity level, the high student-composite group consistently had a mean HSGPA correlation that exceeded the mean SAT correlation by .12–.14, with low mean SAT increments of .04–.06. Also regardless of the college selectivity level, the low student-composite group consistently had

267

a mean SAT correlation that exceeded the mean HSGPA correlation by .01–.05, with high mean SAT increments of .08–.12. These data belie the common assertion that the SAT is not a good predictor for weak students; it does better than HSGPA for the low student-composite group. The highest mean SAT increment of .12 was for the low student-composite group at colleges of high selectivity.

From 1982 to 1985, average predictability of FGPA improved for the middle student-composite group, especially at colleges of both high and low selectivity, and especially for HSGPA. The largest mean decline for the SAT correlation (–.077) took place in the high student-composite group at colleges with low selectivity, for which the mean HSGPA correlation did not decline (+.023) and the mean SAT increment did (–.044).

CORRELATES OF SAT PREDICTIVE VALIDITY: USING THE FGPA CRITERION**

The SAT is designed to predict the academic performance of freshmen in college. In the predictive validity model, the correlation between the SAT and FGPA demonstrates how effective the SAT is for this purpose. But, in addition to the effectiveness of the predictor, the observed correlation can also be influenced by elements of FGPA. *Freshman GPA may not be a perfectly reliable criterion;* any unreliability reduces the observed correlation. *Grades may not be comparable* from subject to subject, course to course, and instructor to instructor; any difference from one "A" to another spuriously reduces the observed correlation and underestimates the real predictive power of the SAT.

Criterion Reliability

The reliability of FGPA was established for each college for each year by computing and correlating separate FGPAS for each of two randomly created sets of half of the course grades for each student, and then adjusting the correlation so that it applies to the full FGPA. The 1985 reliabilities ranged from .71 to .91, with an overall mean of .82.

** In this and the following section, we examine correlates of the size of validity coefficients, in effect, predicting predictive validity. In order to avoid confusing wordiness, several shorthand terms are used here without the usual qualifiers; viz., we use: "SAT validity" to describe the SAT multiple correlation coefficient of verbal and mathematical scores with FGPA; "HSGPA validity" to describe the HSGPA correlation coefficient with FGPA; and "the SAT increment" to describe the difference between the multiple correlation coefficient of HSGPA and verbal and mathematical scores with FGPA and the HSGPA correlation coefficient with FGPA.

More selective and less selective colleges had similar mean criterion reliabilities. The one-third of the colleges with the lowest SAT validities had a mean criterion reliability of about .02 below the mean for other colleges.

Among all colleges, the variables that had the greatest association with the reliability of FGPA were the average number of courses taken per student (correlation of +.64 in 1985) and the number of courses accounting for 50 percent of all credits awarded (–.52); a larger student course load and less variety of courses were associated with higher reliability. Reliability was correlated much more with SAT validity in 1982 (+.51) than in 1985 (+.12). For the correlation between reliability and HSGPA validity, the decline from 1982 (+.49) to 1985 (+.34) was smaller.

Comparability of Grades

Five variables were used to measure various aspects of grade comparability:

- The number of courses accounting for half of all credits (variety in course taking),

- The standard deviation of course SAT means (variation of student aptitude levels among courses),

- The correlation between course-grade and SAT means (appropriateness of average course grade),

- The percentage of credits from advanced courses, and

- The percentage of credits from remedial courses.

These five variables were used to predict SAT validity, together with the following three variables that were also expected to have an effect on SAT validity:

- The SAT mean (Ramist & Weiss, Chapter 5, document that more selective and less selective colleges have had different levels and patterns of SAT validity),

- The number of courses taken per student (because this variable was highly correlated with the reliability of FGPA, the latter was not included in the regressions in order to avoid multi-collinearity), and

- The percentage female (Ramist, 1984, and Morgan, 1990, document consistently higher SAT validity for females than for males).

Linear regression analyses were carried out using these eight variables to predict six criteria, each corrected for restriction of range: SAT correlations with FGPA, HSGPA correlations with FGPA, and the SAT increment over HSGPA, for 1982 and 1985. The levels of prediction were very good. For predicting SAT validity, the 1982 and 1985 multiple correlations averaged .84 (.79 after shrinkage; see Note 12-5). For predicting HSGPA validity, they were almost as high, averaging .80 (.74 after shrinkage). Similarly, for predicting the SAT increment, they were a little lower but still high, averaging .74 (.65 after shrinkage).

Each of the 1982 and 1985 regressions provides one set of estimates of the underlying relationships among the predictor and validity variables. As a summary of these results, Table 12-10 shows the average correlation, the average partial correlation (after controlling for the other variables), and the average test statistic (t with 29 degrees of freedom) for each of the eight predictors, averaged over the 1982 and 1985 regressions for all colleges.

The SAT mean was statistically significant ($p<.01$) as a predictor for SAT and HSGPA validity and had very high average partial correlations for both. Comparing colleges with high (.61–.69), medium (.51–.59), and low (.36–.50) SAT validity in 1985, colleges with high SAT validity had an SAT mean (1,159) that was almost 200 points higher than colleges with low correlations (975). Also, Table 12-9 shows that colleges of high selectivity had a mean SAT validity of .63, compared with .56 for colleges of medium selectivity and .44 for colleges of low selectivity.

Although the predictive effectiveness of the SAT mean clearly indicates that factors associated with college selectivity were also important factors associated with validity levels, it is nevertheless true that, even after removal of the SAT mean as a predictor, the remaining factors resulted in very high average correlations for predicting the validity of the SAT (.74 before and .67 after shrinkage), HSGPA (.71 and .62), and the SAT increment (.69 and .60). The three variables associated with grade comparability other than advanced and remedial course taking — course-taking variety, the standard deviation of course SAT means, and the correlation of course-grade mean and SAT mean — were identified with a "+" in Table 12-10 and provided high average multiple correlations for predicting the validity of the SAT (.69 before and .66 after shrinkage), HSGPA (.57 and .51) and the SAT increment (.63 and .59).

A variable that was fairly good for predicting HSGPA validity, but not very good for predicting SAT validity, was *course-taking variety*, measured by the number of courses accounting for 50 percent of all credits. A smaller number of courses shows less variety and would be

270

Table 12-10

Prediction of SAT Validity, HSGPA Validity, and SAT Increment Using The FGPA Criterion (Average of 1982 and 1985 Correlations and Partial Correlations, Corrected for Restriction of Range, and t Test Statistic)

	Average Correlation			Average Partial Correlation			Average Test Statistic (t)		
	SAT	HSGPA	SAT Increment	SAT	HSGPA	SAT Increment	SAT	HSGPA	SAT Increment
SAT mean	+.41	+.42	+.28	+.55	+.62	+.22	+3.7*	+4.3*	+1.4
Course-taking variety+	-.09	-.21	+.05	-.17	-.30	+.03	-1.0	-1.8	+0.2
Standard deviation of course SAT means+	-.37	-.29	-.33	-.44	-.28	-.40	-2.9*	-1.5	-2.4*
Correlation of course grade and SAT means+	+.56	+.42	+.49	+.57	+.35	+.49	+4.0*	+2.1*	+3.1*
Percentage of credits in remedial courses	-.07	-.17	+.01	+.37	+.29	+.25	+2.2*	+1.7	+1.5
Percentage of credits in advanced courses	+.26	+.17	+.27	-.19	-.29	+.01	-1.1	-1.7	+0.1
Number of courses per student	+.26	+.32	+.12	+.28	+.50	+.05	+1.6	+2.2*	+0.3
Percentage female	+.11	+.03	+.16	+.28	+.26	+.16	+1.6	+1.5	+0.9

Average multiple correlation:
(with correlation after shrinkage)**

All variables   .84(.79) .80(.74) .74(.65)
All except SAT mean   .74(.67) .71(.62) .69(.60)
+Three variables with + .69(.66) .57(.51) .63(.59)

* Significant (t≥ |2|)
** See Note 12-5.

271

expected to be favorable for validity. The average correlation, partial correlation, and test statistic for HSGPA validity were –.21, –.30, and –1.8, respectively; for SAT validity, they were –.09, –.17, and –1.0. Colleges with high SAT validity had an average of only 14 courses accounting for 50 percent of all credits, but colleges with medium validity had more courses accounting for 50 percent (18) than colleges with low validity.

For the SAT and the SAT increment level, a much better predictor was the *standard deviation of course SAT means,* measuring differences among courses of student academic ability levels. Low standard deviations show similarity in ability and are favorable for validity. In terms of its average correlation, partial correlation, and test statistic, this variable was a good predictor of both SAT validity (–.37, –.44, and –2.9, respectively) and SAT increment (–.33, –.40, and –2.4); it was a fairly good but nonsignificant predictor of HSGPA validity (–.29, –.28, and –1.5). Colleges with high SAT validity had a low average standard deviation of course SAT means (53), compared to higher average standard deviations for colleges with medium (61) and low (58) validity.

An even better predictor was the *correlation of course-grade mean and SAT mean,* showing how closely the course grading level adjusts to the aptitude level of the students in the course. More positive correlations show greater adjustment of grade level to aptitude level (as measured by the SAT) and are favorable for validity. The variable was a better predictor for SAT validity than the SAT mean: Its average correlation (+.56 compared to +.41), its partial correlation (+.57 compared to +.55), and its average test-statistic value (+4.0 compared to +3.7) were higher. Also, for the SAT increment, its average correlation (+.49), its partial correlation (+.49), and its average test-statistic value (+3.1) were all higher than those of the SAT mean. Although its average correlation was the same as that of the SAT mean for predicting HSGPA validity (+.42), its average partial correlation (+.35) and its average test-statistic value (+2.1) were lower. Colleges with low SAT validity had a very low average correlation between their course SAT and grade means (.01), compared to more moderate correlations for colleges with medium (.14) and high (.17) SAT validity.

The *percentage of credits in remedial courses* was somewhat negatively correlated with both SAT (–.07) and HSGPA (–.17) validity (remedial courses contribute to lower validity). When used with the other variables, however, it was a positive suppressor variable for both the SAT (average partial correlation of +.37 and average test statistic of +2.2) and HSGPA (+.29 and +1.7), probably as the result of its negative correlation, averaging –.42, with the SAT mean. The more selective colleges were less likely to have remedial courses. Colleges with high SAT validity had almost no remediation (0.1 percent of all credits), compared to 2.5 percent for colleges with medium validity and 1.7 percent for colleges with low validity.

The *percentage of credits in advanced courses* had a moderate and appropriately negative average partial correlation and average test statistic for SAT and HSGPA validity (as expected, advanced courses reduce validity). It was positively correlated, however, with SAT and HSGPA validity because of its positive correlation (+.70) with the SAT mean; colleges with high SAT validity had more advanced course taking (8.3 percent of all credits), compared to colleges of medium (5.3 percent) and low (4.2 percent) validity.

The *number of courses per student* was positively correlated and had moderate test-statistic levels with SAT validity (average correlation of +.26, average partial correlation of +.28, and average test-statistic value of +1.6), but had high test-statistic levels with HSGPA validity (+.32, +.50, and +2.2, respectively). A large number of courses per student was associated with high reliability of FGPA but only moderately related to SAT validity; colleges with high SAT validity had a higher average student course load (8.8) than colleges with medium validity (8.6), which in turn had a higher average student course load than colleges with low validity (8.3).

The *percentage female* was essentially uncorrelated with SAT and HSGPA validity, but was moderately related in the regressions (average partial correlations of +.26 and +.28 and average test-statistic levels of +1.5 and +1.6).

CORRELATES OF CHANGE IN SAT PREDICTIVE VALIDITY: USING THE FGPA CRITERION

Criterion Reliability

College changes in reliability ranged from a loss of −.11 to a gain of +.11. Overall, the mean reliability of FGPA was stable (at .81 in 1982 and .82 in 1985).

Reliability was an excellent predictor of SAT and HSGPA validity in 1982, but not as good in 1985, especially for the SAT. When change in reliability was correlated with change in SAT and HSGPA validity, the correlations were positive, but higher for HSGPA. The correlation with change in validity was +.05 for the SAT and +.23 for HSGPA.

Comparability of Grades

Linear regression analyses were carried out to predict change in SAT validity, HSGPA validity, and SAT increment, using both changes and levels of the same eight variables that were used to predict validity levels. To predict each of the three types of criteria, there were two regression analyses, one using 1982 levels, and the other 1985 levels, as controls.

The levels of prediction were very high, especially considering how difficult it usually is to predict change. Before correcting for shrinkage, the multiple correlations averaged .84 both for predicting change in SAT validity and for predicting SAT validity for one year. (After correcting for shrinkage, these multiple correlations averaged .70 and .79, respectively.) For predicting change in HSGPA validity, the multiple correlations averaged .76 before and .51 after shrinkage, somewhat lower than the averages for the SAT and for predicting HSGPA validity for one year. For both predicting change in the SAT increment and predicting the SAT increment for one year, the multiple correlations averaged .74 before shrinkage. (After shrinkage, these averages were .46 and .65, respectively.)

Table 12-11 displays correlations, partial correlations (after controlling for the other variables), and the average test (t) statistic for each of the eight change variables and each of the eight level variables. Data for the level variables are averages of 1982 and 1985 levels. The test statistic shown for the change variables is the average of test statistics obtained from the change variables alone, the change variables with 1982 levels, and the change variables with 1985 levels.

Additionally, Table 12-11 shows the average multiple correlations for all of the change and level variables, for the change variables alone, and for just the change variables associated with grade comparability, other than advanced and remedial course taking — change in course-taking variety, change in the standard deviation of course SAT means, and change in the correlation of course-grade mean and SAT mean. The multiple correlations for change in SAT validity were higher than for change in HSGPA validity. The three change variables associated with grade comparability had a multiple correlation for overall validity of .63 for the SAT (.59 after shrinkage), .37 for HSGPA (.25 after shrinkage), and .48 for the SAT increment (.40 after shrinkage).

Although the SAT *mean* was a strong predictor of validity within each year for both the SAT and HSGPA, it was a good predictor of validity change only for the SAT. The level of SAT mean had high simple and partial correlations for predicting change in SAT validity and the SAT increment, ranging from +.36 to +.45, significant for both SAT validity (average test statistic of +2.0) and SAT increment (+2.3). In addition to the level of SAT mean, the change in SAT mean also was related to change in SAT validity, with a simple correlation of +.45, but controlling for other variables produced a weaker partial correlation of +.25. Comparing colleges with increasing (+.01 to +.06), stable (no change to

274

Table 12-11

Prediction of Change from 1982 to 1985 in SAT Validity, HSGPA Validity, and SAT Increment, Using the FGPA Criterion (Correlations and Partial Correlations, Corrected for Restriction of Range, and t Test Statistic)

Change Variables	Average Correlation			Average Partial Correlation			Average Test Statistic (t)		
	SAT	HS-GPA	SAT Increment	SAT	HS-GPA	SAT Increment	SAT	HS-GPA	SAT Increment
SAT mean	+.45	+.23	+.33	+.25	+.15	+.12	+1.5	+0.7	+0.8
Course-taking variety+	−.22	−.07	−.19	−.47	+.24	−.46	−2.3*	+0.4	−2.1*
Standard deviation of course SAT means+	−.27	−.09	−.23	−.18	−.30	.00	−1.2	−1.2	−0.4
Correlation of course grade and SAT means+	+.49	+.34	+.35	+.38	+.46	+.15	+2.4*	+2.2*	+1.1
Percentage of credits in remedial courses	+.04	+.02	+.03	−.09	−.37	+.12	−0.5	−1.3	+0.1
Percentage of credits in advanced courses	+.08	−.06	+.11	+.02	−.46	+.29	−0.1	−2.0*	+1.0
Number of credits per student	+.09	+.01	+.07	+.17	−.21	+.20	+0.4	−0.7	+0.4
Percentage female	+.25	+.22	+.14	+.23	+.31	+.02	+1.0	+1.4	+0.1
Level Variables									
(Average of 1982 and 1985)									
SAT mean	+.36	.00	+.39	+.40	−.12	+.45	+2.0*	−0.5	+2.3*
Course-taking variety	−.05	−.22	+.17	−.34	−.33	−.12	−1.7	−1.6	−0.5
Standard deviation of course SAT means	+.27	+.33	+.11	+.35	+.30	+.14	+1.7	+1.4	+0.7
Correlation of course grade and SAT means	−.03	+.01	−.06	−.34	−.09	−.27	−1.7	−0.4	−1.3
Percentage of credits in remedial courses	−.07	−.12	+.01	−.09	−.43	+.32	+0.4	−2.2*	+1.6
Percentage of credits in advanced courses	+.20	−.15	+.29	.00	−.14	+.03	+0.3	−0.7	+0.1
Number of courses per student	−.06	−.07	−.03	+.03	−.06	+.07	+0.1	−0.3	+0.3
Percentage female	−.06	−.04	−.05	+.25	+.17	+.16	+1.2	+0.8	+0.7
Multiple Correlations									
(With Correlation After Shrinkage)									
Multiple of change variables	.73(.40).47(.07).56(.35)								
Multiple of change and level variables	.84(.70).76(.51).74(.46)								
+Multiple of three variables with +	.63(.59).37(.25).48(.40)								

*Significant (t ≥ |2|)

−.04), and decreasing (−.05 to −.22) SAT validity: Colleges with increasing SAT validity had the highest 1982 SAT means (average of 1,089) and increased the most (+21); colleges with stable SAT validity had moderate 1982 means (1,057) and increased moderately (+11); and colleges with decreasing SAT validity had the lowest 1982 SAT means (1,002) and increased the least (+5).

Course-taking variety, measured by the number of courses accounting for 50 percent of all credits, was a good predictor of the level of HSGPA validity but not SAT validity. Change in course-taking variety was very good for predicting change in SAT validity and the SAT increment, but only moderately useful as a control of level for predicting change in HSGPA validity. Change in course-taking variety had the largest partial correlations of all variables with change in validity for the SAT (–.47) and the SAT increment (–.46), both significant (average test statistics of –2.3 for the SAT and –2.1 for the SAT increment). Large increases in course-taking variety were associated with large declines in SAT validity. Colleges with declining SAT validity had an increase of four in the average number of courses accounting for 50 percent of all credits (from 14 to 18), compared with increases of only one each (from 15 to 16) for colleges with stable and increasing validity. To understand what course-taking patterns caused course-taking variety to increase, we closely examined courses taken by 1982 and 1985 freshmen in colleges with large declines in SAT validity:

- As alternatives to standard calculus courses, new courses were offered that were either for nonmajors or included a review of math fundamentals;

- Fewer students took large introductory economics courses;

- Fewer students took computer programming or computer science courses, but some instead took courses on using computers, emphasizing word processing and spreadsheet analysis;

- Instead of economics and computer science, students took a variety of other courses, including government or politics, astronomy, music, and techniques of drawing.

The *standard deviation of course SAT means* was a good predictor of SAT validity, but not of HSGPA validity, with high standard deviations associated with low SAT validity. For change in validity, the prediction was moderately good for both the SAT and HSGPA. The largest relationship with validity change involving this variable was for level of standard deviation, with high levels leading to increasing validity for both the SAT and HSGPA, demonstrated by simple and partial correlations ranging from +.27 to +.35. The change in standard deviation correlated in the expected negative direction with overall validity change: –.27 and –.18, respectively, for the SAT simple and partial correlations, and –.09 and –.30, respectively, for the HSGPA simple and partial correlations. Large decreases in the standard deviation of course SAT means were favorable for validity. Colleges with increasing SAT validity had high 1982 standard deviations that

276

averaged 66, but declined to 61 in 1985; colleges with stable validity had lower standard deviations that increased (+1, from 58 to 59), and colleges with decreasing validity had even lower standard deviations that decreased (–3, from 55 to 52).

Not only was the *correlation of course-grade mean and* SAT *mean* a good predictor of both SAT and HSGPA validity, change in the correlation of course-grade and SAT means was also a good predictor of change in both SAT and HSGPA validity; simple and partial correlations for predicting changes were +.34 to +.49, all significant (average test statistics of +2.4 for the SAT and +2.2 for HSGPA). As course-grade level became less closely related to course SAT mean level, validity declined for both the SAT and HSGPA. Colleges with decreasing SAT validity had a substantial decline of .10 (from .19 to .09) in their average correlation of course-grade and SAT means, while colleges of stable and increasing SAT validity had increases (of +.02 and +.04, respectively).

Used with the other variables, the *percentage of credits in remedial courses* was a suppressor variable for predicting the level of validity of both the SAT and HSGPA. The suppressor effect was not present for predicting change of validity. For the SAT, this variable was not useful, but it was for HSGPA. The partial correlations with change in overall HSGPA validity were –.37 (not significant) for change in remediation and –.43 (significant with an average test statistic of –2.2) for level of remediation. Colleges with increasing and with decreasing SAT validity had higher and decreasing remedial percentages, but colleges with stable validity had lower and increasing remedial percentages.

Surprisingly, the *percentage of credits in advanced courses* behaved similarly to the percentage of credits in remedial courses. Neither was useful for predicting levels of validity or for predicting change in SAT validity, but both were related to change in HSGPA validity. The partial correlation for change in advanced course taking in predicting change in overall HSGPA validity was –.46, significant with an average test statistic of –2.0.

The *number of courses per student* was moderately related to the validity levels of both the SAT and HSGPA. The relationships between change in number of credits (used instead of courses for evaluating change relationships) and change in validity were very weak.

Change in *percentage female* was moderately correlated with change in validity for both the SAT and HSGPA. Simple and partial correlations for overall validity ranged from +.22 to +.31, but were not significant.

USING COURSE GRADE AS THE CRITERION
FOR SAT PREDICTIVE VALIDITY

Freshman GPA is a composite of grades in courses taken by the student. Tables 12-4 and 12-5 demonstrate that students with high SAT scores and HSGPA tend to select different types of courses than students with low SAT scores and HSGPA. Table 12-4 also indicates that students who take certain types of courses (e.g., physical education) receive higher grades on average than expected on the basis of their SAT scores and HSGPA and that students who take other types of courses (e.g., biology — lab/majors) receive lower grades on average than expected.

Since FGPA is a composite of the grades received in courses taken by the student, it is a measure not only of student academic performance, but also of student course taking. As colleges increasingly respond to differing student needs by offering a greater variety of courses and by permitting greater choice of courses to freshmen, evaluating a student's FGPA now depends more heavily on identifying that student's courses.

It might be more useful to predict specific course grades instead of FGPA. To evaluate the possibility of course-grade criteria, all courses with at least five students registered in both 1982 and 1985 were identified — 4,680 courses, or an average of 123 per college. Separate predictions were made of the grades in each of these courses, based on SAT scores and HSGPA. Simple course-grade correlations were not permitted to go below zero, and multiple correlations were computed excluding variables with negative contributions. The course-grade correlations were corrected for restriction of range, then averaged for each college in two ways:

- By using the 1982 number of students taking a course times the number of course credits as the 1982 course weight, and the 1985 number-credit product as the 1985 course weight (not controlled for volume change); and

- By using the sum of the numbers of students taking a course in 1982 and in 1985 times the number of course credits as the course weight (controlled for volume change).

Table 12-12 displays these course-grade correlations averaged over all 38 colleges.

Although Table 12-8 shows that HSGPA had a greater corrected correlation than the SAT in predicting FGPA (.57 compared to .54 in 1985), Table 12-12 shows that the reverse was true for course grade; the 1985 SAT corrected correlation for course grade was .49, compared to

Table 12-12

Mean Correlations with Course Grade, 1982 and 1985,
Not Controlled and Controlled for Course-Volume Change,
Corrected for Restriction of Range

	Not Controlled			Controlled		
	1982	1985	Change	1982	1985	Change
SAT-V	.43	.41	−.022	.43	.41	−.021
SAT-M	.45	.43	−.015	.44	.43	−.010
SAT-V, M	.51	.49	−.022	.51	.49	−.018
HSGPA	.48	.46	−.013	.47	.46	−.009
SAT, HSGPA	.59	.57	−.020	.59	.58	−.017
SAT Increment	.13	.12	−.007	.12	.11	−.007

.46 for HSGPA. In 55 percent of the courses, SAT validity was higher than HSGPA validity (excluding courses for which both validities were negative or zero).

The mean of eight or nine course grades (mean student load was 8.6 courses) should have been much more predictable than one course grade. The Spearman-Brown formula indicates that SAT validity should have increased by .26 if course grades are comparable (see Note 12-6), from .49 in predicting one course grade to .75 in predicting FGPA. Similarly, the HSGPA validity in predicting FGPA should have increased by .25 from .46 to .71 if course grades are comparable. The noncomparability of course grades substantially offset the benefits of increased number of grades — especially for SAT validity, which increased only by .05, instead of .26, from .49 in predicting one course grade to .54 in predicting FGPA. Whereas the SAT increment to the multiple correlation (corrected for restriction of range) was .07–.08 for predicting FGPA, it was .11–.13 for predicting course grade.

Using course grade instead of FGPA as the criterion eliminated almost half of the validity declines after correction for restriction of range. Comparing Tables 12-8 and 12-2, by using course grade as the criterion and controlling for course volume change:

- The change in SAT validity from 1982 to 1985, averaging −.030 for the correlation with FGPA, was reduced to −.018;
- The change in HSGPA validity, averaging −.015 for the correlation with FGPA, was reduced to −.009; and
- The change in the SAT increment, averaging −.011 for the correlation with FGPA, was reduced to −.007.

Without controlling for course-volume change, weighting courses in each year by the volume of that year, the validity declines were .004 greater for both the SAT (−.022 not controlled instead of −.018 controlled) and HSGPA (−.013 not controlled instead of −.009 controlled). Therefore, change in course-taking volumes from courses with high to courses with low validity was a small contributor to the validity decline.

Table 12-13 displays 1982 and 1985 average corrected course-grade correlations for the SAT and HSGPA for each of the 37 course categories. For the 12 categories containing fewer than 25 courses with at least five students in each year, the 1982 and 1985 data are averaged.

Table 12-13

Average Corrected Course-Grade Correlations for the SAT and Student-Reported HSGPA, by Course Category, 1982 and 1985, for All 38 Colleges

No. of Courses	SAT-V*	SAT-M*	Course Category	SAT			HSGPA			SAT Increment		
				1982	1985	Change	1982	1985	Change	1982	1985	Change
798	.47	.43	Social sciences/humanities	.52	.50	−.02	.47	.48	+.01	.13	.12	−.01
413	.31	.36	Foreign language-entry	.42	.39	−.03	.48	.47	−.01	.09	.07	−.02
306	.41	.50	Physical science-lab/major	.54	.52	−.02	.52	.50	−.02	.12	.12	.00
299	.33	.35	Foreign language-advanced	.41	.41	.00	.46	.47	+.01	.09	.09	.00
291	.47	.40	History	.51	.53	+.02	.44	.43	−.01	.15	.16	+.01
247	.40	.53	Calculus	.55	.54	−.01	.50	.51	+.01	.13	.13	.00
201	.43	.50	Phys. sci. & eng.-nonmajor	.55	.53	−.02	.49	.45	−.04	.14	.15	+.01
189	.37	.36	Art/music/theater-nonstudio	.47	.40	−.07	.43	.42	−.01	.14	.10	−.04
176	.15	.18	Physical education	.20	.22	+.02	.25	.24	−.01	.07	.07	.00
174	.24	.26	Art/music/theater-studio	.36	.28	−.08	.25	.22	−.03	.13	.08	−.05
161	.39	.39	Business/commerce	.44	.49	+.05	.41	.47	+.06	.14	.13	−.01
145	.43	.33	Regular reading/literature	.45	.48	+.03	.43	.43	.00	.12	.13	+.01
140	.41	.38	Regular English	.47	.45	−.02	.42	.45	+.03	.13	.12	−.01
138	.50	.54	Economics	.59	.58	−.01	.52	.54	+.02	.14	.12	−.02
132	.40	.35	Regular writing	.43	.44	+.01	.37	.43	+.06	.11	.09	−.02
127	.47	.54	Biology-lab/major	.59	.57	−.02	.55	.52	−.03	.13	.13	.00
98	.54	.54	Biology-nonmajor	.61	.61	.00	.57	.57	.00	.14	.13	−.01
92	.35	.49	Regular mathematics	.51	.50	−.01	.48	.50	+.02	.12	.10	−.02
88	.32	.31	Other	.41	.38	−.03	.38	.33	−.05	.13	.12	−.01
81	.43	.54	Advanced mathematics	.53	.60	+.07	.53	.55	+.02	.13	.16	+.03
61	.26	.28	Military science	.30	.37	+.07	.30	.31	+.01	.09	.13	+.04
57	.40	.48	Computer science	.52	.50	−.02	.42	.41	−.01	.14	.13	−.01
37	.31	.48	Precalculus	.50	.48	−.02	.52	.45	−.07	.09	.11	+.02
37	.41	.39	Education	.60	.33	−.27	.54	.42	−.12	.15	.07	−.08
35	.43	.43	Health/nursing	.47	.55	+.08	.44	.44	.00	.13	.20	+.07
30	.46	.58	Phys. sci. & eng.-advanced	.57	.64	+.07	.55	.52	−.03	.16	.23	+.07
26	.40	.42	Home economics	.51	.45	−.06	.53	.38	−.15	.10	.14	+.04
25	.31	.30	Architecture	.35	.41	+.06	.25	.46	+.21	.13	.08	−.05
15	.25	.36	Remedial mathematics		.42*			.37*			.13*	
13	.36	.35	Remedial writing		.41*			.34*			.12*	
9	.22	.15	Remedial English		.25*			.31*			.07*	
9	.43	.54	Advanced biology		.60*			.39*			.24*	
9	.33	.27	Advanced reading/literature		.37*			.40*			.13*	
8	.16	.24	Technical/vocational		.27*			.35*			.06*	
6	.37	.35	Advanced English		.41*			.39*			.14*	
5	.27	.25	Remedial reading/literature		.33*			.29*			.10*	
2	.26	.38	Advanced writing		.44*			.28*			.18*	

* 1982 and 1985 correlations were averaged for the SAT-V and SAT-M correlations and for categories with fewer than 25 courses each year.

The highest average corrected course-grade correlations for the SAT-Verbal score were in biology — nonmajors (.54) and economics (.50). The highest averages for the SAT-Mathematical score were in physical sciences/engineering — advanced (.58), economics (.54), biology — lab/majors (.54), biology — nonmajors (.54), advanced mathematics (.54), and advanced biology (.54).

Table 12-14 displays the course categories with the highest and lowest SAT corrected course-grade correlations, averaging 1982 and 1985, and the average grade-residual means (from Table 12-4). The highest correlations were generally in quantitative or science course categories, which tended to be strictly graded as evidenced by their negative grade-residual means. The lowest were generally in nonacademic or remedial courses, which tended to be very leniently graded as evidenced by their large positive grade-residual means.

Table 12-14

Course Categories with High and Low Average SAT Corrected
Course-Grade Correlations, 1982 and 1985, All 38 Colleges

High Correlations	Average SAT Correlation	Grade-Residual Mean
Biology-nonmajors	.61	−.07
Physical sci. & eng.-advanced	.60	−.06
Advanced biology	.60	−.04
Economics	.58	−.17
Biology-lab/majors	.58	−.35
Advanced mathematics	.57	−.06

Low Correlations	Average SAT Correlation	Grade-Residual Mean
Physical education	.21	+.78
Remedial English	.25	+.42
Trade/vocational	.27	+.30
Art/music/theater-studio	.32	+.56
Remedial reading/literature	.33	+.28
Military science	.33	+.45

Table 12-15

Course Categories with Increases or Decreases of at Least .05
in Average SAT Correlation, All 38 Colleges

Increases		Decreases	
Health/nursing	+.08	Education	−.27
Advanced mathematics	+.07	Art/music/theater-studio	−.08
Physical sci. & eng.-advanced	+.07	Art/music/theater-nonstudio	−.07
Military science	+.07	Home economics	−.06
Architecture	+.06		

Table 12-15 displays all course-category changes of at least .05 in the average SAT corrected course-grade correlation from 1982 to 1985. Among the course categories with 25 or more courses, the only one with a change of more than .08 was education (–.27).

Table 12-4 displays the 1985 course-taking distribution and changes from 1982. Table 12-13 displays average SAT validities for each of the course categories. Table 12-16 puts these together to identify the course-category volume changes with a major impact on SAT validity using the FGPA criterion. Increases in volume for three categories with high validity had a positive impact: biology — nonmajors, biology — lab/majors, and economics. On the other hand, increases in volume for several categories with low validity had a negative impact: art/music/theater (both nonstudio and studio courses), physical education, and remedial writing. In addition, the decrease in volume of advanced mathematics courses, for which SAT validity is high, had a negative impact. As indicated by Table 12-12, negative impacts of course-volume changes slightly outweighed positive impacts, contributing .004 to the validity decline for the SAT (that amounts to less than one-fifth using course grade as the criterion and less than one-seventh using FGPA as the criterion).

To compare course-grade correlations for the SAT with those for high school performance, 27 of the 38 colleges were identified as having supplied high school record (HSR) information based on actual school

Table 12-16

Major Course-Category Volume Changes from 1982 to 1985 with a Major Impact on SAT Validity Change Using the FGPA Criterion

Positive Impact on Validity Change*	Average SAT Validity	1985 %	1982 to 1985 % Change
Biology — nonmajors	.61	14%	+26%
Economics	.58	29%	+7%
Biology — lab/majors	.58	15%	+10%
*Negative Impact on Validity Change**			
Art/music/theater-nonstudio	.43	20%	+34%
Physical education	.21	17%	+8%
Art/music/theater-studio	.32	11%	+20%
Foreign language-beyond entry	.41	18%	+25%
Advanced mathematics	.57	7%	–28%
Remedial writing	.41	3%	+43%

* Course categories are listed in order of estimated positive and negative impact based on deviation of average SAT validity from the overall mean, 1985%, and 1982 to 1985% change.

Table 12-17

Mean Corrected Correlations with FGPA and Course Grade,
1982 and 1985, for All 38 Colleges and for 27 Colleges
Reporting HSR Information

Freshman GPA 1982	1985	Course Grade 1982	1985		Freshman GPA 1982	1985	Course Grade 1982	1985
.57	.54	.51	.49	SAT-V, M	.57	.54	.50	.49
				Student-Reported HSGPA				
.59	.57	.47	.46	HSGPA	.61	.59	.50	.47
.67	.64	.59	.58	SAT, HSGPA	.69	.66	.63	.60
.08	.07	.12	.11	SAT Increment	.08	.07	.13	.13
				College-Reported HSR				
—	—	—	—	HSR	.61	.60	.49	.48
—	—	—	—	SAT, HSR	.69	.66	.61	.60
—	—	—	—	SAT Increment	.08	.06	.12	.12

All 38 Colleges (left section); *27 Colleges Reporting HSR* (right section)

grades or class rank. Table 12-17 displays corrected mean correlations with FGPA and with course grade using both student-reported HSGPA and college-reported HSR for the full group of 38 colleges and the subset of 27 colleges. (See Note 12-7.)

The subset of 27 colleges had average SAT validities that were almost identical to those of the full group. The average student-reported HSGPA validities were higher for the subset than for the full group. There was very little difference between the average student-reported HSGPA and college-reported HSR validities. They were both higher than the average SAT validity using FGPA as the criterion, but were both slightly lower than the SAT validity using course grade as the criterion. SAT validity exceeded college-reported HSR validity in 51 percent of all courses (excluding those where both validities were negative or zero). The average SAT increment for course grade over student-reported HSGPA of .13 was reduced to .12 by using college-reported HSR, still well above the .06–.08 for FGPA (using either student-reported or college-reported HSR).

Course-grade correlations for the SAT were compared with those for college-reported HSR in different types of courses. Table 12-18 displays average corrected course-grade correlations for the 26 course

Table 12-18

Average Corrected Course-Grade Correlations for the SAT and
College-Reported HSR, by Course Category, Average of 1982 and 1985,
for 27 Colleges Supplying HSR

Number			SAT	HSR	SAT Increment
Colleges	Courses				
18	87	Biology-nonmajor	.60	.56	.15
13	31	Computer science	.47	.39	.14
10	29	Health/nursing	.51	.48	.14
24	233	History	.50	.43	.14
21	115	Biology-lab/major	.57	.52	.13
25	180	Calculus	.56	.52	.13
21	159	Physical sci. & eng.-nonmajors	.55	.51	.13
19	62	Advanced mathematics	.54	.50	.13
25	246	Physical sci. & eng.-lab/majors	.55	.53	.13
7	26	Physical sci. & eng.-advanced	.49	.47	.13
16	73	Business/commerce	.47	.45	.13
26	589	Social sciences/humanities	.51	.47	.12
19	56	Economics	.55	.51	.11
19	93	Regular reading/literature	.48	.47	.11
18	75	Regular mathematics	.52	.52	.11
12	32	Education	.50	.50	.11
14	35	Other	.38	.36	.10
23	129	Art/music/theater-studio	.30	.29	.10
11	47	Military science	.29	.28	.10
17	30	Precalculus	.49	.49	.10
22	144	Art/music/theater-nonstudio	.42	.42	.10
25	351	Foreign language-entry	.44	.49	.10
16	115	Regular writing	.44	.44	.09
14	90	Regular English	.44	.49	.09
9	181	Physical education	.26	.21	.09
22	225	Foreign language-beyond entry	.38	.44	.08

categories with at least 25 courses taken by five or more students in
both years at the 27 colleges that supplied high school records. The
average SAT increment for every one of the categories ranged from .08
(for foreign language — beyond entry level) to .15 (for biology —
nonmajor). The SAT was a better or equal predictor of course grade for
all but three of the 26 course categories: foreign language — beyond
entry level, foreign language — entry level, and regular English. The
SAT was a much better predictor for computer science (average course-
grade correlation of .47 for the SAT compared to .39 for HSR) and history (.50 compared to .43).

SUMMARY AND CONCLUSIONS

Investigation

Traditionally, the predictive validity of SAT scores is expressed in terms of their correlation with the test taker's freshman grade-point average (FGPA). A number of factors affect that correlation. One of them is the restriction of range of the SAT scores of students enrolled at a particular college. (For this reason, all results in this study were corrected for restriction of range.) Two other factors related to the composition of the FGPA are:

- The reliability of FGPA, which is influenced at least partly by the numbers of courses taken and credits earned by the student; and

- The comparability of grades from student to student, which depends on how varied the courses taken by freshmen are, how student academic levels differ from course to course, and how closely grading levels match academic levels.

In this study, we have examined the implications of using FGPA as the criterion for predictive validity. In order to do so, we obtained course titles and grades for freshmen enrolled at 38 diverse colleges in 1982 and 1985. We classified the courses into 37 categories defined by subject and level. Then we conducted numerous analyses in order to:

- Examine FGPA as the criterion for SAT validity studies, calculating its correlations with SAT scores and high school grades;

- Determine the impact of various factors on the predictability of the FGPA; and

- Explore the alternative of using course grade as the criterion, averaging correlations overall and within course categories, and weighting them to control for shifts in enrollment volume from 1982 to 1985.

Among our analyses were separate ones for students grouped by sex and ability level as measured by a composite of SAT scores and HSGPA, and for colleges grouped by selectivity level based on SAT means. We also analyzed the correlation of the SAT with FGPA by level and by change from 1982 to 1985.

Findings

FGPA as the criterion. Using the traditional criterion, certain overall trends emerged from our analyses. Conceptually, some of these trends are associated with increases in SAT validity coefficients and others are associated with decreases. Trends conceptually associated with increases in SAT validity coefficients were decreases in the variability of course SAT means, decreases in remedial course taking, and decreases in advanced course taking, as well as increases in the reliability of FGPA. Trends conceptually associated with declines in SAT validity coefficients were increases in course variety, decreases in student course load, and decreases in the correlation between course SAT means and grade averages.

Regardless of the selectivity of the college, students in the top third of the academic composites (based on HSGPA and SAT scores) had high average corrected predictor correlations with FGPA, both for the HSGPA (average of .73 for all 38 colleges in 1985) and for the SAT (.60). For students in the lowest third of the academic composites, the correlations were considerably lower (averages of .40 for the HSGPA and .44 for the SAT). On the other hand, the SAT increment was greater for the bottom third. Therefore — and this may come as a surprise to some — in terms of its incremental prediction over HSGPA, the SAT was a more useful predictor for students with academic composites in the bottom third of their freshman class than for students in either the top or middle third.

On average, the SAT's predictive validity declined .030 at the 38 colleges from 1982 to 1985. Changes in course-enrollment volumes had both positive and negative impacts on validity coefficients, but the negatives slightly outweighed the positives, contributing .004 to the average decline in correlations. Changes in SAT and HSGPA validity coefficients were highly related to changes in grade comparability.

Three new variables and the methods of measuring them were proposed to describe grade comparability. They were:

- *Variety in course taking* as measured by the number of courses accounting for half of all credits taken by freshmen;

- *Variation of student academic levels among courses* as measured by the standard deviation of course SAT means; and

- *Appropriateness of average course grade* as measured by the correlation between SAT and course-grade means.

The average multiple correlations of these three variables for predicting the levels of SAT and HSGPA validity in 1982 and 1985 were very high (.44–.78 after shrinkage). In addition, the average multiple correlation of change in these three variables for predicting change was very high for SAT validity coefficients (.59) and moderately high for HSGPA validity coefficients (.25). Freshman grades were not as comparable across students as they once were, and that had negative effects on the predictive validity coefficients of both the SAT and the HSGPA. Other factors examined as predictors of SAT and HSGPA validity coefficients included: the college's level of selectivity, percentages of credits in remedial courses and in advanced courses, average student course load, and percentage of female students.

At colleges that showed very large declines in SAT correlations from 1982 to 1985, these patterns emerged:

- Fewer students took introductory economics and computer science courses, both of which have high correlations with SAT scores;

- As alternatives to standard calculus courses, new mathematics courses were offered, either including reviews of math fundamentals or designed for nonmajors; and

- More students took courses in which grades have low correlations with SAT scores (e.g., foreign language, art, music, theater, or education courses).

Course grade as the criterion. The SAT's correlation with a single course grade, averaged over 4,680 courses, was a surprisingly high .49 — only .05 lower than its average correlation of .54 with the average of the eight or nine course grades that make up the FGPA. If course grades had been comparable, the SAT validity for predicting FGPA would have reached .75, up .26 from the single course-grade validity. The benefits of the increased number of courses contributing to the FGPA were heavily offset by the noncomparability of course grades.

Using course grade instead of FGPA as the criterion reduced the declines in validity coefficients from 1982 to 1985 by almost half for both the SAT and HSGPA. Comparing the SAT and HSGPA for predicting course grade, we found that the average SAT correlation was slightly higher than the average HSGPA correlation, equaling or exceeding it in all but three of the 26 course categories. Additionally, the SAT increment for predicting course grade was higher for every category of courses (.08–.15) than the SAT increment for predicting the FGPA (.06–.07).

Typically, quantitative or science courses had the highest SAT validity coefficients and nonquantitative and traditionally nonacademic courses had the lowest. As indicated by the grade residuals (the differences between average course grade and predicted FGPA), the quantitative and science courses were strictly graded and the nonquantitative, nonacademic courses were leniently graded. Students with low SAT scores tended to select courses that were graded more leniently, which raised their FGPAS, and students with high SAT scores increasingly tended to take courses that were graded more strictly, which lowered their FGPAS.

Because comparisons of FGPA from student to student are becoming more and more problematic, it may be necessary, in future validity studies, to forsake measuring predictive validity only in terms of the FGPA criterion. If grades were predicted in each course separately, then an average of the appropriate course-grade predictions for each student would represent a more realistic prediction of first-year performance in the courses individual freshmen actually take, and would be a more accurate basis for estimating the correlation between predictions and FGPA. This procedure is akin to the common practice of predicting grades separately within individual colleges of a university where criterion differences are well recognized.

CHAPTER 13

A Preliminary Evaluation of the Stability of Freshman GPA, 1978-1985

MARK POMPLUN, NANCY BURTON, & CHARLES LEWIS

This study is one of several seeking information about a decline in the predictive validity of SAT scores and high school grades for a self-selected group of colleges. These were colleges that submitted data to the College Board Validity Study Service for freshman classes entering between 1976 and 1985. (For a further description of these trends, see Ramist, 1984, and Morgan, 1989a.) Most of these studies ask whether changes in the predictors or the populations involved might be related to the observed validity trends; this study addresses the question of whether the criterion, freshman grade-point average (FGPA), may have changed.

In this study, we will look for possible changes over time in the mix of skills, abilities, and subject-area knowledge that students are required to use in earning their freshman-year grades. The indicators of these academic skills are those available in the Educational Testing Service files: the verbal and mathematical reasoning abilities measured by the Scholastic Aptitude Test (SAT); the skills involved in responding to the Test of Standard Written English (TSWE) or the English Composition Achievement Test (ECT); the mathematical and foreign language reading skills measured by other Achievement Tests; the subject-area knowledge covered in the history and science Achievement Tests.

These indicators are necessarily somewhat narrow. Largely they are one-hour multiple-choice tests based on content specifications established by national consensus. (See Note 13-1.) Typically earned during the junior or senior year of high school, the test scores are also somewhat outdated as indicators of the skills utilized in earning the FGPA. The academic skills that they estimate probably improve throughout the freshman year, and at different rates for different students. Nevertheless, these test scores are valuable resources, in that they cover a wide spectrum of ability, knowledge, and skill; they are comparable across all students and colleges; and, most important, they have remained almost completely constant, on average, over the period covered by this study.

While the analysis appears similar in design to a conventional predictive validity study, with FGPA being regressed on a set of measures intended to predict success in college, the regression analysis is in fact being used to make inferences about whether the academic skills required in freshman classes have changed. The measures that would usually be thought of as "predictor variables" are being used as indicators of the concurrent academic components that make up the multidimensional composite FGPA. Possible changes in the components of FGPA over time are evaluated by controlling as many external sources of change as possible.

- Academic indicators were kept constant over time by using Admissions Testing Program tests that are developed to rigidly controlled content and statistical specifications and equated to a common scale. The only indicator measure that could not be so controlled was the high school grade-point average (HSGPA). However, instead of using actual HSGPA, which was not available for all students, we used an average of self-reported grades in six academic subjects, which controlled for variations in curriculum among students and over time.

- To tighten the control of chance variations in the academic indicators, a true-score regression technique was used to estimate indicator factor scores. These scores should be less likely than observed scores to vary due to chance differences in measurement quality for the samples being analyzed.

- To control for college-to-college variations in student ability, typical freshman curriculum, and grading standards, only colleges with data available for all the entering classes being studied were included in the sample.

With these external sources of variation held constant, regression equations fitting the data for two entering freshman classes — from the fall of 1978 and the fall of 1985 — can be compared to determine whether the academic ability, skill, and knowledge components underlying FGPA appear to have changed over time. Several hypotheses concerning specific changes that may have occurred can be evaluated based on our prediction of how each would affect the relationship between academic factors and FGPA.

For example, the kinds of courses freshmen take may have changed. There has been a growth in the popularity of courses in technical areas, such as engineering and computer science, that might have led to a decline in the importance of the skills and abilities measured by the SAT-Verbal, the TSWE, and the English, history, and foreign language Achievement Tests.

There was also a trend through the '70s and early '80s for some colleges to drop or modify their core requirements; it may be that

FGPA became less comparable from student to student and, therefore, less predictable. In that case, one would expect a decline in the contribution of all academic indicators.

Some colleges may have replaced academic core courses with more practical courses — in business or vocational areas, for example — that do not make heavy demands on analytical reasoning skills. In that case, one would predict a decline in the contribution of the SAT's more academic and analytical measures, but not necessarily in specific skill or knowledge measures, such as the various Achievement Tests.

The results of this study must be considered preliminary, both because the indicators were not collected concurrent with FGPA and because they do not cover all the abilities (particularly the noncognitive abilities) used in the freshman year. On the other hand, most important changes in the construct measured by FGPA should be at least somewhat reflected in these analyses. Even a change in a dimension not well-measured by the available indicators would be likely to perturb one or more of the regression relationships under investigation. Any area of change detected in the current study will require further investigation in a group of colleges willing to collect concurrent measures of skills, knowledge, and ability, as well as some important noncognitive components.

The current study, while it is not a predictive validity study, is important to the validation of the College Board's admissions tests. It is necessary to determine periodically whether the construct of success in college is changing. If it is, admissions tests also will need to change to meet the changing goals of the College Board's membership.

PROCEDURE

Sample

The data for this study were chosen from November 1977 and 1984 administrations of the SAT and the TSWE, which included nearly half the cohort of graduating seniors who took the SAT. The samples were 1978 and 1985 high school graduates who had SAT and TSWE item-response data from those administrations. These files were matched with College Board Validity Study Service (VSS) records to obtain freshman grades for the subset who attended participating colleges.

In all, 52,948 records were selected from the 1985 group and 6,814 from the 1978 sample. (The sample is smaller for 1978 because only a spaced sample of one-seventh of the data was retained in ETS program archives.) The students were divided into two subsamples:

One consisted of students from colleges that did validity studies for both the 1978 and 1985 entering freshmen, and the other contained the students from nonmatched colleges. The matched sample, which included 86 colleges with 2,984 students in 1978 and 32,338 students in 1985, was used to analyze the stability of FGPA over time. The nonmatched sample was used for exploratory model fitting.

Measures and Models

Although measures of various abilities (SAT-Verbal and SAT-Mathematical); skills (such as writing and foreign language fluency); subject-area knowledge (such as knowledge of science or history); and grades were available, these are observed measures with measurement error. In this study, models were developed using subscores from the SAT and TSWE to estimate factors free from measurement error that were then correlated with observed FGPA.

These models were analyzed through LISREL VI (Jöreskog & Sorbom, 1986), which allows the user to combine the factor analytic and regression models into one. The factor analytic part of the resulting model specifies how observed variables are related to the latent factors; the regression part specifies the relationship between the latent factors and the criterion latent factor. In this study, the model's factor analytic part defines various latent academic factors, such as verbal and mathematical reasoning and writing skill, through SAT and TSWE subscores; the regression part specifies the relationship between the latent academic factors and the observed criterion, FGPA.

The SAT-TSWE models were based on data that were available for the entire sample — high school grades and measures that could be constructed from SAT and TSWE items. SAT results were divided into subscores based on item format (analogies, quantitative comparisons, etc.), content (science vocabulary, algebra, geometry, etc.), or cognitive level (application, insight, etc.) as defined by Rock, Johnson, and Pollack (personal communication, 1989). TSWE items were divided into item format subscores only, because each of the numerous content classes contained too few items to form subscores that could be compared over time. Because HSGPA and FGPA are observed variables, they are used intact as factors in the models.

In the item-type model displayed in Figure 13-1, ad hoc SAT-V subscores created from the analogies, antonyms, reading comprehension, and sentence completion item formats are the observed measures (observed measures are represented by squares in Figure 13-1) defining a verbal reasoning factor (factors are represented by circles in Figure 13-1). Ad hoc SAT-M subscores created from quantitative comparison and regular multiple-choice item formats define the mathematical reasoning factor. TSWE subscores based on the sentence correction and usage formats define the writing skill factor. Student-reported HSGPA was the only available measure of high school achievement. As shown by the direction of the causal paths (arrows)

Figure 13-1

An Example of the SAT-TSWE Models: The Item-Type Model

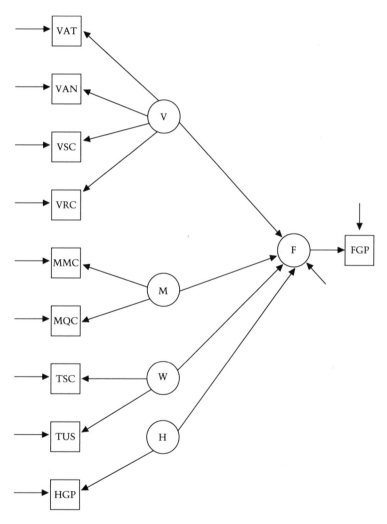

NOTE: VAT = SAT-V Antonyms, VAN = SAT-V Analogies, VSC = SAT-V Sentence Completion, VRC = SAT-V Reading Comprehension, MMC = SAT-M Multiple Choice, MQC = SAT-M Quantitative Comparison, TSC = TSWE Sentence Correction, TUS = TSWE Usage, H and HGP = High School Grade-Point Average, V = Verbal, M = Mathematical, W = Writing, F and FGP = Freshman Grade-Point Average.

in Figure 13-1, freshman success as measured by FGPA was regressed on the verbal, mathematical, writing, and HSGPA factors. (Other arrows to the observed and FGPA variables represent residual variances.)

In the item-content model, verbal and mathematical reasoning are defined by ad hoc subscores based on item-content specifications for the test. SAT-V practical affairs, human relations, science, and aesthetic/philosophical "subscores" define the verbal reasoning factor. (Because the content categories of reading comprehension items are more finely differentiated than the item-content categories for vocabulary and sentence items, and the test-development specialists advised us not to try to collapse the two categorization systems, the reading items were not included in the item-content analysis.) SAT-M geometry, algebra, arithmetic, and miscellaneous math "subscores" define the mathematical reasoning factor. The TSWE and HSGPA measures are the same as in the previous model.

In the item cognitive-level model, ad hoc cognitive-level subscores were defined only for the SAT reading comprehension items (D. Rock, personal communication, October 20, 1989). It was possible to use all the mathematical items in defining the math cognitive levels (Rock, Johnson, & Pollack, personal communication, 1989). These subscores, unlike the item-type and item-content subscores, were not based on the specifications used to develop the test. Three SAT-V cognitive-level subscores (reproduction, evaluation, and inference) define the verbal factor, and three SAT-M cognitive-level subscores (application, insight, and production) define the mathematical factor. The TSWE and HSGPA measures are unchanged from the other two models.

The second group of models was a series that included Achievement Test scores along with SAT and HSGPA measures. Because only about one SAT examinee in every five takes any Achievement Test, the samples available for these analyses were much smaller. Ideally, measures of all the different Achievement Tests would be included in the same regression model in order to capture any change over time in the pattern of relationships, but the combination of small 1978 samples and missing correlations among Achievement Tests (most students who take these tests take only two or three of the 15) made several compromises necessary in the analysis of models that include Achievement Test measures.

In order to enlarge samples used in the analyses, a score on any of the science tests (Biology, Chemistry, and Physics) was treated as a science score. Scores on all foreign language tests (Spanish, French, Latin, German, Hebrew, and Russian) were also treated as interchangeable, as were scores on Mathematics Levels I and II (as mathematics scores) and American and European History (as history scores).

There was a separate model for each of the achievement areas. Each model included one Achievement Test area and also included the SAT item-type subscores as measures of the latent verbal and mathematical reasoning factors and HSGPA as predictors of FGPA. In each achievement model, FGPA was regressed on the verbal, mathematical, HSGPA, and achievement area factors. One achievement model included two achievement areas: both the foreign language area and the English Composition Test. Two achievement models, science and mathematics, did not include the SAT mathematical reasoning factor because of collinearity between the observed scores.

Analysis

In this analysis, the chosen variables were standardized within colleges before all students were pooled into a single analysis sample. The regression equation derived from the models can be considered a weighted average of within-college equations.

LISREL was used to assess the fit of the same overall model to the freshmen entering college in 1978 as compared to those entering in 1985. In addition to looking at the overall fit, we examined specific parameters relating the observed indicators to the academic factors (the "factor analytic" part of the model) and the parameters relating the academic factors to observed FGPA (the "regression" part of the model).

Change over time was investigated by comparing the results for two different levels of constraint on each model. The less restricted condition studied is called the "similar" condition. In this condition, the pattern of relationships between the observed variables and the factors, and the factors and FGPA, were set to be similar but not identical in the two years. That is, the size of the factor loadings (see Note 13-2) and regression weights for the variables assumed to be related was allowed to vary, but for the variables assumed to be unrelated, parameters were set to zero in both samples.

In the second condition, called "invariant," the factor loadings and regression weights were required to be equal in 1978 and 1985. The fit of the models in each of these conditions was assessed through two fit indices.

Although several measures of overall fit are available, this study used the goodness-of-fit index (Jöreskog & Sorbom, 1986) provided by LISREL and an adaptation of the Tucker-Lewis index (Tucker & Lewis, 1973) to assess the fit of the models. Fit for each year separately was assessed by the LISREL goodness-of-fit index, and fit for both years together by the Tucker-Lewis index. The goodness-of-fit index measures how well the model reproduces the matrix of observed variances and covariances. The index ranges between 0 and 1; for this study, values below .90 are required for the fit of the model to be rejected.

The adapted version of the Tucker-Lewis measure created for this study is an index that represents the percent of residual variance from the fit of the more restrictive ("invariant") model that is explained by the less restrictive ("similar") model. Because it is based on residual variance rather than total variance, it can be viewed as analogous to a partial correlation. This index has an expected value of zero but is permitted to have small negative values. Whenever the index is near zero or negative, we conclude that the same model and parameters fit the data for both years. (For more information about the procedures and results of this study, see Pomplun, Burton, & Lewis, in preparation.)

RESULTS

Table 13-1 displays the fit indices for the SAT-TSWE and achievement models for the two years. In interpreting these results, it is important to recall that the samples for 1985 are more than 10 times larger than those for 1978. Because LISREL combines data from both years in this type of analysis, data from 1985 dominate the combined data set. So when parameters are constrained to be equal in the two years (the "invariant" condition), these values are very close to the 1985 values. It may be helpful to think of the goodness-of-fit index as measuring the extent to which the 1978 freshmen can be treated as a sample of the "population" defined by the larger group of 1985 freshmen. If the two years require different models, the goodness-of-fit index will drop when the parameter estimates are constrained to be equal or invariant for the two years, and nearly all of the drop will be associated with the 1978 sample.

Table 13-1 displays goodness-of-fit and Tucker-Lewis indices for each model for both conditions and years. The goodness-of-fit indices are all high, indicating that the models reproduce almost all of the observed variances and covariances.

Table 13-1 also displays the Tucker-Lewis index that compares the similar and invariant conditions. Whenever the index is near zero or negative, one can conclude that the same model and parameters fit the 1978 and 1985 data. The Tucker-Lewis partial indices are all low, indicating that relaxing the model assumptions in the similar condition adds no improvement in fit over the invariant condition. Both fit indices agree that the models and their parameters appear nearly identical for the two years.

Table 13-1

Fit Indices for SAT-TSWE and Achievement Models

	Goodness of Fit				
	Restrictiveness of Model Assumptions				
	Similar		Invariant		Tucker-Lewis Partial Index
	1978	1985	1978	1985	
SAT-TSWE *Models*					
Item Type	.994	.991	.993	.991	−.17
Item Content	.991	.997	.989	.997	−.10
Item Cognitive	.995	.995	.988	.995	−.02
Achievement Models					
English Composition Test (ECT)	.993	.988	.991	.988	−.19
Foreign Language Area (FL)	.986	.987	.984	.987	−.22
History Area	.987	.982	.979	.982	−.17
Mathematics Area	.996	.989	.994	.989	−.27
Science Area	.992	.992	.988	.992	−.26
ECT and FL	.987	.988	.983	.988	−.21

Because the primary concern of this study was change in the criterion, the parameters for the relationship between the academic skill factors and FGPA are shown in Table 13-2. Table 13-2 displays the regression weights and standard errors for the SAT-TSWE and achievement models. There is some indication that history knowledge became a less important component of FGPA between 1978 and 1985. The regression weight for history was 2.6 standard errors smaller in 1985 based on the larger of the two standard error estimates ((.265 - .101)/.064). This result must be interpreted with caution, however, because the fit statistics for the overall model in Table 13-1 indicate a lack of significance.

Table 13-2

Regression Weights and Standard Errors, SAT-TSWE and Achievement Models

SAT-TSWE Models	Year	Writing	Verbal	Mathematical	HSGPA
Item Type	1978	.120 (.049)	.115 (.056)	.166 (.029)	.316 (.017)
	1985	.102 (.015)	.154 (.015)	.154 (.009)	.308 (.005)
Item Content	1978	.137 (.047)	.092 (.054)	.169 (.030)	.318 (.017)
	1985	.133 (.014)	.109 (.014)	.162 (.009)	.308 (.005)
Item Cognitive Level	1978	.137 (.047)	.130 (.061)	.170 (.031)	.315 (.017)
	1985	.124 (.013)	.171 (.015)	.177 (.012)	.308 (.005)

Achievement Models	Year	Achievement Test	Verbal	Mathematical	HSGPA
English Composition Test (ECT)	1978	.168 (.039)	.039 (.064)	.190 (.047)	.280 (.027)
	1985	.114 (.012)	.138 (.018)	.163 (.014)	.288 (.008)
Foreign Language Area (FL)	1978	.075 (.057)	.197 (.108)	.156 (.107)	.265 (.055)
	1985	.111 (.015)	.239 (.026)	.175 (.026)	.287 (.015)
History Area	1978	.265 (.064)	.089 (.109)	.027 (.088)	.236 (.054)
	1985	.101 (.026)	.171 (.041)	.130 (.031)	.297 (.018)
Mathematics Area*	1978	.201 (.028)	.225 (.040)	*	.272 (.027)
	1985	.150 (.009)	.246 (.013)		.287 (.008)
Science Area*	1978	.278 (.048)	.107 (.072)	*	.270 (.042)
	1985	.188 (.015)	.181 (.022)		.311 (.012)
ECT and FL	1978	.078 (.058)	.216 (.135)	.158 (.108)	.267 (.055)
	1985	.105 (.015)	.185 (.033)	.160 (.026)	.284 (.015)
	1978	−.023 (.081)			
	1985	.072 (.021)			

*SAT-M was dropped from these achievement models because of collinearity.

Although other regression weights in Table 13-2 fluctuated somewhat, the fluctuations do not appear significant when standard errors are considered. Thus, the results for the regression weights are consistent with the results from the fit indices. It appears that the same model fits the data for both years.

CONCLUSIONS

The purpose of this study was to investigate possible changes in FGPA as a factor in the decline of SAT validity. The changes investigated were primarily in the skills, subject knowledge, and cognitive levels measured by the SAT, TSWE, and Achievement Tests. The primary finding was the stability of these academic indicators with respect to FGPA. This study found no evidence that a change in the meaning of FGPA has contributed to the decline in predictive validity described by Morgan and others. Although there are limitations in the indicator variables used to define the dimensions of FGPA, these results clearly suggest that the meaning of FGPA remained stable despite hypothesized changes between 1978 and 1985 in the kinds of students admitted to college and in the types of courses typically taken by freshmen. The fact that results stayed stable over a number of different indicators, and over a number of ways of combining the indicators, suggests that the construct of FGPA has not changed in the colleges included in this study.

Appendix A

Appendix A-1

Correlations Between SAT Scores and Other Verbal and Mathematical Tests, By Year*

								YEARS								
	70	71	72	73	74	75	76	77	78	79	80	81	82	83	84	85
SAT-V correlation with:																
ATP																
1. English Composition									.77			.78				
2. Test of Stand. Written Eng.					.75	.77	.79	.76	.77	.79	.78	.80	.79	.77	.78	.77
NJ																
3. Reading Comprehension									.74					.71	.75	.73
4. Sentence Structure									.66					.63	.68	.66
5. Essay									.50					.53	.48	.46
WPC																
6. English Usage	.73					.71									.67	
7. Spelling	.53					.53									.51	
8. Reading Comprehension	.76					.72									.73	
9. Vocabulary	.84					.84									.83	
NLS																
10. Reading			.70								.70		.72			
11. Vocabulary			(.89)								(.91)		(.86)			
ACT																
12. English			.68										.78			
SAT-M correlation with:																
ATP																
13. Mathematics Achievement									.82	.82		.80				.82
NJ																
14. Computation									.71					.72	.76	.71
15. Elementary Algebra									.76					.72	.76	.72
WPC																
16. Quantitative Skills	.82					.84									.75	
17. Applied Mathematics	.73					.75										
18. Mathematics Achievement	(.87)					(.89)									(.88)	
NLS																
19. Mathematics			(.81)								(.85)			(.86)		
ACT																
20. Mathematics			.79										.84			

* See Note 2-13 and text, p. 2-42. Correlations in parentheses are corrected for unreliability to adjust for differences in test length across years. Testing programs are: ATP (Admissions Testing Program), NJ (New Jersey College Basic Skills Placement Test), WPC (Washington Pre-College Test), NLS (National Longitudinal Study/High School and Beyond), ACT (American College Test).

Appendix A-2

SAT DIRECTIONS AND SAMPLE QUESTIONS

SAT-VERBAL

Antonyms, Analogies, Sentence Completions, Reading Comprehension

SECTION **1**	Time—30 minutes 40 Questions	For each question in this section, choose the best answer and fill in the corresponding oval on the answer sheet.

Antonyms

Each question below consists of a word in capital letters, followed by five lettered words or phrases. Choose the word or phrase that is most nearly opposite in meaning to the word in capital letters. Since some of the questions require you to distinguish fine shades of meaning, consider all the choices before deciding which is best.

Example:

GOOD: (A) sour (B) bad (C) red (D) hot (E) ugly

Ⓐ ● Ⓒ Ⓓ Ⓔ

Analogies

Each question below consists of a related pair of words or phrases, followed by five lettered pairs of words or phrases. Select the lettered pair that best expresses a relationship similar to that expressed in the original pair.

Example:

YAWN : BOREDOM :: (A) dream : sleep (B) anger : madness (C) smile : amusement (D) face : expression (E) impatience : rebellion

Ⓐ Ⓑ ● Ⓓ Ⓔ

Sample Questions

1. SURPLUS : (A) shortage (B) criticism (C) heated argument (D) sudden victory (E) thorough review

2. TEMPESTUOUS : (A) responsible (B) predictable (C) tranquil (D) prodigious (E) tentative

   Correct Answers: 1. A
   2. C

Sample Questions

3. APPAREL : SHIRT :: (A) sheep : wool (B) foot : shoe (C) light : camera (D) belt : buckle (E) jewelry : ring

4. BUNGLER : SKILL :: (A) fool : amusement (B) critic : error (C) daredevil : caution (D) braggart : confidence (E) genius : intelligence

   Correct Answers: 3. E
   4. C

Each sentence below has one or two blanks, each blank indicating that something has been omitted. Beneath the sentence are five lettered words or sets of words. Choose the word or set of words that, when inserted in the sentence, <u>best</u> fits the meaning of the sentence as a whole.

Example:

Although its publicity has been ----, the film itself is intelligent, well-acted, handsomely produced, and altogether ----.

(A) tasteless. .respectable (B) extensive. .moderate (C) sophisticated. .amateur (D) risqué. .crude (E) perfect. .spectacular

●ⒷⒸⒹⒺ

5. Either the sunsets at Nome are ----, or the one I saw was a poor example.

(A) gorgeous   (B) overrated   (C) unobserved (D) exemplary   (E) unappreciated

6. Specialization has been emphasized to such a degree that some students ---- nothing that is ---- to their primary area of interest.

(A) ignore. .contradictory
(B) incorporate. .necessary
(C) recognize. .fundamental
(D) accept. .relevant
(E) value. .extraneous

Correct Answers: 5. B
                          6. E

Each passage below is followed by questions based on its content. Answer the questions following each passage on the basis of what is <u>stated</u> or <u>implied</u> in that passage.

From the beginning, this trip to the high plateaus in Utah has had the feel of a last visit. We are getting beyond the age when we can unroll our sleeping bags under any pine or in any wash, and the gasoline situation throws the future of automobile touring into doubt. I would hate to have missed the extravagant personal liberty that wheels and cheap gasoline gave us, but I will not mourn its passing. It was part of our time of wastefulness and excess. Increasingly, we will have to earn our admission to this spectacular country. We will have to come by bus, as foreign tourists do, and at the end of the bus line use our legs. And if that reduces the number of people who benefit every year, the benefit will be qualitatively greater, for what most recommends the plateaus and their intervening deserts is not people, but space, emptiness, silence, awe.

I could make a suggestion to the road builders, too. The experience of driving the Aquarius Plateau on pavement is nothing like so satisfying as the old experience of driving it on rocky, rutted, chuckholed, ten-mile-an-hour dirt. The road will be a lesser thing when it is paved all the way, and so will the road over the Fish Lake Hightop, and the one over the Wasatch Plateau, and the steep road over the Tushar, the highest of the plateaus, which we will travel tomorrow. To substitute comfort and ease for real experience is too American a habit to last. It is when we feel the earth rough to all our length, as in Robert Frost's poem, that we know it as its creatures ought to know it.

7. According to the author, what will happen if fewer people visit the high country each year?

(A) The characteristic mood of the plateaus will be tragically altered.
(B) The doctrine of personal liberty will be seriously undermined.
(C) The pleasure of those who do go will be heightened.
(D) The people who visit the plateaus will have to spend more for the trip.
(E) The paving of the roads will be slowed down considerably.

8. The author most probably paraphrases part of a Robert Frost poem in order to

(A) lament past mistakes
(B) warn future generations
(C) reinforce his own sentiments
(D) show how poetry enhances civilization
(E) emphasize the complexity of the theme

9. It can be inferred from the passage that the author regards the paving of the plateau roads as

(A) a project that will never be completed
(B) a conscious attempt to destroy scenic beauty
(C) an illegal action
(D) an inexplicable decision
(E) an unfortunate change

Correct Answers: 7. C
                          8. C
                          9. E

Regular Mathematics, Data Sufficiency, Quantitative Comparisons

SECTION **2**	Time—30 minutes 25 Questions	In this section solve each problem, using any available space on the page for scratchwork. Then decide which is the best of the choices given and fill in the corresponding oval on the answer sheet.

The following information is for your reference in solving some of the problems.

Circle of radius r: Area = πr^2; Circumference = $2\pi r$
   The number of degrees of arc in a circle is 360.
The measure in degrees of a straight angle is 180.

Definition of symbols:
= is equal to	≦ is less than or equal to
≠ is unequal to	≧ is greater than or equal to
< is less than	‖ is parallel to
> is greater than	⊥ is perpendicular to

Triangle: The sum of the measures in
   degrees of the angles of a
   triangle is 180.

If $\angle CDA$ is a right angle, then

(1) area of $\triangle ABC = \dfrac{AB \times CD}{2}$

(2) $AC^2 = AD^2 + DC^2$

Note: Figures that accompany problems in this test are intended to provide information useful in solving the problems. They are drawn as accurately as possible EXCEPT when it is stated in a specific problem that its figure is not drawn to scale. All figures lie in a plane unless otherwise indicated. All numbers used are real numbers.

Regular Mathematics

Sample Questions

1. If $2y = 3$, then $3(2y)^2 =$

  (A) $\dfrac{27}{4}$

  (B) 18

  (C) $\dfrac{81}{4}$

  (D) 27

  (E) 81

2. Of seven consecutive integers in increasing order, if the sum of the first three integers is 33, what is the sum of the last three integers?

  (A) 36
  (B) 39
  (C) 42
  (D) 45
  (E) 48

Correct Answers: 1. D
                  2. D

Data Sufficiency

Example:

In $\triangle PQR$, what is the value of x?

(1) $PQ = PR$

(2) $y = 40$

Explanation: According to statement (1), $PQ = PR$; therefore, $\triangle PQR$ is isosceles and $y = z$. Since $x + y + z = 180$, $x + 2y = 180$. Since statement (1) does not give a value for y, you cannot answer the question using statement (1) by itself. According to statement (2), $y = 40$; therefore, $x + z = 140$. Since statement (2) does not give a value for z, you cannot answer the question using statement (2) by itself. Using both statements together, you can find y and z; therefore, you can find x, and the answer to the problem is C.

Sample Questions

3. Is $a + b = a$?

   (1) $b = 0$

   (2) $a = 10$

4. Is rectangle R a square?

   (1) The area of R is 16.

   (2) The length of a side of R is 4.

Correct Answers: 3. A
                   4. C

Quantitative Comparisons

Questions 5-6 each consist of two quantities, one in Column A and one in Column B. You are to compare the two quantities and on the answer sheet fill in oval

A if the quantity in Column A is greater;
B if the quantity in Column B is greater;
C if the two quantities are equal;
D if the relationship cannot be determined from the information given.

AN E RESPONSE WILL NOT BE SCORED.

	EXAMPLES		
	Column A	Column B	Answers
E1.	2×6	$2 + 6$	● Ⓑ Ⓒ Ⓓ Ⓔ
E2.	$180 - x$	y	Ⓐ Ⓑ ● Ⓓ Ⓔ
E3.	$p - q$	$q - p$	Ⓐ Ⓑ Ⓒ ● Ⓔ

Notes:

1. In certain questions, information concerning one or both of the quantities to be compared is centered above the two columns.
2. In a given question, a symbol that appears in both columns represents the same thing in Column A as it does in Column B.
3. Letters such as x, n, and k stand for real numbers.

Sample Questions

Column A	Column B
5. The least positive integer divisible by 2, 3, and 4	24

Parallel lines ℓ_1 and ℓ_2 are 2 inches apart. P is a point on ℓ_1 and Q is a point on ℓ_2.

6. Length of PQ	3 inches

Correct Answers: 5. B
6. D

Appendix A-3
Participating Colleges

The following colleges participated in the study reported in Chapter 12 by supplying freshman course grades:

Arizona State University
Auburn University
Augusta College*
Boston College
Bryant College
Bucknell University
California State University, Sacramento
Carleton College
Colby College
Colgate University
Columbia University*
Dartmouth College*
Dickinson College
Duke University
Franklin & Marshall College*
George Washington University
Harvard University
Kutztown University*
La Salle University
Lehigh University
Marquette University
Mary Washington College
Marywood College
Mount Holyoke College

New Hampshire College
Ohio State University*
St. Michael's College
Slippery Rock University
Suffolk University
Susquehanna University
Swarthmore College
University of California, Berkeley
UCLA
University of Central Florida
University of Maryland, Baltimore County*
University of Maryland, College Park
University of North Carolina, Chapel Hill
University of Southern California
University of Texas, Austin
University of Washington
Vanderbilt University
Wellesley College
Wesleyan University
Western Carolina University
Whitman College

*Supplied data for 1985 only.

Appendix B

Appendix B: Notes

Chapter 1

1-1. There are several ways of evaluating the size of a correlation coefficient. Some statisticians favor r^2 because it expresses the percentage of variation in one measure (e.g., predicted FGPA) that is accounted for by another measure (e.g., SAT scores). Measurement specialists use r as an indication of what proportion of the maximum possible selection utility a measure actually provides in practice (Cronbach, 1971; Linn, 1982b). Similarly, Brogden (1946) showed that the correlation coefficient indicates the proportional improvement in criterion performance that is attainable from selecting with a predictor instead of the criterion itself. For example, if one selected at the end of the year those 100 freshmen with the highest grades, and found that their average FGPA was one letter grade above the class average, then with a predictor that correlated .50 with FGPA one could select before matriculation 100 students who would have an average FGPA one-half letter grade above the class average. The usefulness of an admissions test will tend to appear more favorable with r or r^2 depending upon what type of comparison one is making (e.g., absolute level of test validity versus proportional improvement over high school record). The r statistic is used here since that is the one normally employed in research on test validity.

1-2. In Table 1-1 the statistics for 1985 come from Morgan (1989a). All other data come from Ramist (1984), except the SAT increments, which are simply column 4 minus column 3. The yearly averages for 1970, 1975, 1980, and 1985 include repeated studies from the same colleges. All other data are based upon one study (always the most recent) from each of the 685 institutions that conducted studies through the College Board's Validity Study Service during the years 1964-1981. When the 685 colleges are sorted into ranges according to average SAT score of the freshman class, the average correlation of predictors with freshman grades goes up with average SAT score and then down. The three score ranges shown in Table 1-1 are the two extremes and the score range in the middle, where the correlations peak.

Chapter 2

2-1.   The period labeled "Pre-1973" in the Ramist-Weiss analysis in Chapter 5 extended from 1964 to 1972, but the studies were somewhat more heavily represented in the later years. In 1985-88, the majority of the studies were in 1985. In order to represent these data more accurately on the time line, the center of those periods was set at approximately the average year of studies in the period. Accordingly, Pre-73 is depicted as six years prior to 1974-77 instead of 6.5, and 1985-88 is depicted as three years beyond 1981-84 instead of four.

2-2.   Missing data pose problems for both of these methods. With incomplete data, the pairwise method places undue emphasis on any particular year that may be out of line because the sample of studies for that year is small. It also places heavy emphasis on colleges that do multiple studies, and that can affect estimates if those colleges have atypical trends. Trend estimates based upon average slopes can be affected by the instability of college slopes based upon only two or three studies or a short time span. These complications are discussed in Chapter 6. Both types of estimates can be affected by the fact that different colleges represented in different parts of the time span may have characteristically different trends.

2-3.   In Figure 2-2, the slopes for HSR and SAT in 1974-88 are the same as reported by Willingham and Lewis in Chapter 6. The additional slopes in that figure were not part of the analysis reported in Chapter 6, but they are estimated by the same method, using the same parent database from Ramist-Weiss (Chapter 5).

2-4   During the period when validity studies were done for classes entering in fall 1986 and 1987, computer systems used by VSS were being redesigned. As a result, validity studies through VSS were cumbersome for the colleges, and few studies were done during that period. VSS was restored to full efficiency for the entering class of 1988, but most colleges were not able to provide data early enough for analysis and inclusion in this report.

2-5.   Thirty years ago Fishman and Pasanella (1960) reviewed 580 studies on college-grade prediction and concluded (a) that prediction of intellective criteria like grades is not likely to be improved much beyond the moderate accuracy afforded by HSR and SAT, and (b) that the future of prediction research lies in predicting nonintellective criteria with nonintellective predictors. Not much has changed. Breland (1981) confirmed that no new predictors were developed in the ensuing two decades that could boost validity coefficients and were also practical for use in admissions. Some measures, like personality tests, might improve grade prediction somewhat through assessment of "motivation," but such measures can usually be faked and also raise ethical problems. Other measures, like actual writing samples, might add a truly different and relevant competence to the traditional predictors, but cost and other practical problems have discouraged the use of such samples of student performance. In a recent extensive study involving some 100 predictors (Willingham, 1985), it was once again demonstrated that, if predicting FGPA is the goal, other predictors do not add much to HSR and an admissions test. That study did clearly demonstrate two points. First, for college faculty, success in college goes beyond FGPA. Second, other measures (notably "productive follow-through" or demonstrated accomplishments in and outside the classroom) are necessary in order to identify college applicants who are likely later to be regarded as most successful by faculty. While researchers have been consistently disappointed in their search for an improved predictor of FGPA, recent studies and findings reported here suggest that working toward a more predictable FGPA is a more attainable goal.

2-6. Among the 387 college prediction slopes computed by Willingham and Lewis (Chapter 6) for the period 1974-88, 35 percent were positive. Among the 399 colleges in the pairwise period analyses reported by Ramist and Weiss (Chapter 5), 38 percent had a higher average correlation in the 1985-88 period than in the 1973-76 period.

2-7. Willingham and Lewis (Chapter 6) examined prediction slopes for 192 colleges that did enough studies (4 or more) to afford a reasonably stable estimate of trend. Twenty-nine of those institutions met a liberal definition of a significant change in SAT validity coefficients during the period 1974-88: a slope coefficient significant at the .10 level, and a slope difference (correlation change) of at least .05 over the period for which the college did studies. Of the 29 colleges that experienced a significant change, 22 were decreases and 7 were increases. Among the 22 colleges that had a decrease, 13 were below average on SAT mean and 9 were above average (14 percent and 9 percent, respectively, of the total number of such colleges in the group).

2-8.   There have been substantial increases in both foreign and older students in higher education in recent years. At the undergraduate level, foreign students approximately doubled from 1975 to 1985 (Zikopoulos, 1987), but still appear to constitute less than 2 percent of enrollment. In the same period, total enrollment throughout higher education of students age 30 or older increased from 21 percent to 26 percent, (Snyder, 1987), though most of that increase represents part-time students. While some institutions may now enroll significant numbers of foreign or older students, their direct effect on correlations reported here is minimal because very few such students were in the database. No college had as many as 25 foreign students in a study, probably because of noncomparable HSRS. Some 90 percent of these studies were based only on high school graduates of the previous year, so would include almost no older students.

2-9.   Hypothetically, if the "additional" women enrolled in these colleges in 1985 made higher grades than men relative to test scores, as was the case in 1978, this gender-related performance discrepancy could cause some reduction in the 1985 pooled coefficient. The observed pattern of male and female means does not fit that hypothesis. Either the additional women did not achieve the same pattern of high grades relative to test scores as in 1978 or that pattern shifted somewhat over all men and women from 1978 to 1985. In any event, there is no indication of net change in validity coefficients due to this factor.

2-10.   These correlations are uncorrected. Corrected coefficients are, in this case, not critical because the comparison of interest is between the SAT and the achievement test rather than year to year. Corrected coefficients might be misleading because the populations taking the various achievement tests are not comparable to the SAT examinee group and the proper basis for a comparable correction is not apparent. (See Table 10-2 and accompanying text.)

2-11. Willingham-Lewis used the same database as Ramist-Weiss, but W-L worked from the peak year 1974 forward while R-W used 1973 in the 1973-76 period. That accounts for the difference in the N's and the slightly greater slope in the pairwise analyses shown in Figure 6-3 compared to the one reported in Table 5-6. A few colleges had matchable studies based on more than one type of high school record. For those colleges, W-L used average slopes based on the separate types of record.

2-12. As reported in *Research Services Summary Tables*, ACT (undated). Based on institutions in The Standard Research Service for 1985-86, 1986-87, and 1987-88.

2-13. The trends shown in Figure 2-8 represent results of a pairwise analysis of the correlations in Appendix A-1. The analysis was based upon average correlations for three periods: 1970-74, 1975-80, and 1981-85. The sources of the data in Appendix A-1 were as follows:

ATP English Composition and ATP Mathematics Achievement — special analyses conducted by Morgan using the database from Chapter 10 of this volume;

Test of Standard Written English — Marco et al. (1990);

New Jersey Basic Skills Placement Test — Hecht (1978) and Mazzeo, Livingston, and Feryok (1986);

Washington Pre-College Testing Program — Greenmun, R. (1971, 1976, 1986);

National Longitudinal Study/High School & Beyond — Chapter 11 of this volume (Willingham, Rock, & Pollack);

American College Test — Chapter 11 of this volume (Willingham, Rock, & Pollack)

Chapter 4

4-1. Yearly estimates: Suppose there is some measure of interest (such as a correlation coefficient) that is available for some colleges in some years. Denote it by y_{ij} for college i and year j. For each pair of years, all colleges that have the measure available for both years are used to compute the difference between the two values. Thus, for years j and k, if college i has the measure for both years, the difference is computed by:

$$d_{ijk} = y_{ij} - y_{ik} .$$

Next, such differences for these two years are averaged. If there are n_{jk} colleges with the statistic for the two years, the average is given by

$$d_{jk} = \sum_{i=1}^{n_{jk}} d_{ijk} / n_{jk} .$$

Note that

$$d_{kj} = - d_{jk}$$

and let

$$d_{jj} = 0 .$$

Then for year j, the average deviation effect (a_j) is estimated as follows:

$$a_j = \sum_{k=1}^{n} d_{jk} / n$$

where n is the number of years to be estimated.

For the actual tables and figures, these deviation effects were added to an overall mean, determined as follows: The mean value of the measure for year j was averaged over all colleges having a value of the statistic for that year. The result was y_j. The unweighted mean of these values was the overall level, namely

$$y = \sum_{j=1}^{n} y_j / n .$$

Thus, the values $t_j = y + a_j$ describe average yearly estimates for the measure y_{ij}.

Standard errors of yearly estimates: Due to the complexity of the dependencies in the terms used to compute yearly estimates, there does not appear to be any straightforward way to obtain standard errors for the estimates. Consequently, it was decided to use jackknifing to provide approximate standard errors.

The jackknifing proceeded by first computing the vector of estimates based on all colleges, say t_{all}. Next, one college was left out at a time. For each college, this meant leaving out at least two records, since each college included in this analysis must have data for at least two years. For each reduced set of colleges, the corresponding vector of estimates, say $t_{(i)}$ when college i is left out, was obtained. Finally, this set of estimate vectors produced a jackknifed estimate vector t. and an estimated variance-covariance matrix S. for this estimate. From S., standard errors for each element in t. were computed.

More specifically, the jackknifed estimate for year j may be written as

$$t_{j\cdot} = (n)t_{j,all} - (n-1)t_{j(.)}, \text{ where}$$

$$t_{j(.)} = \sum_{i=1}^{n} t_{j(i)} / n \text{ and there are a total of n colleges .}$$

For the estimation method used here, it turns out that $t_{j*} = t_{j,all}$. The elements of S* are given by

$$s_{jk*} = [(n-1)/n] \sum_{i=1}^{n} [t_{j(i)} - t_{j(.)}] [t_{k(i)} - t_{k(.)}].$$

The jackknifed estimate of the standard error for t_{j*} is

$$s_{j*} = (s_{jj*})^{1/2}$$

4-2.   The multivariate restriction of range formula was supplied by Charles Lewis (personal communication, April 1989). It is equivalent to the formula for selection found in *Theory of Mental Tests* by H. Gulliksen (1950, pp. 165-166). Reference correlations and standard deviations were based on the data from the vss database for the enrolling class of 1985. As a result, the corrected correlations refer to the population of enrolling students, rather than the population administered the SAT. The reference group had average scores for both SAT-V and SAT-M approximately 40 points higher than the population of students administered the SAT in 1985. The reference group was also less variable, with the SAT-V and SAT-M standard deviations approximately 10 points less than those for the population administered the test.

Chapter 5

5-1. vss automatically converts rank to a normally distributed 20-to-80 scale, with a mean of 50 and a standard deviation of 10 for all ranks (see *Guide to the College Board Validity Study Service*, College Board, 1988c, p. 58).

5-2. The Pearson-Lawley multivariate correction for restriction of range was used (Gulliksen, 1950, pp. 165-166). The estimates of standard deviations for test takers were 109 for the sat-Verbal score, 120 for the sat-Mathematical score, .61 for hsgpa (only studies using gpa on a 0-4 scale were corrected), and 8.2 for high school rank (on a 20-80 scale). The estimates of correlations among the predictors for test takers were .67 for sat-Verbal and sat-Mathematical scores, .45 for the sat-Verbal score and hsr, and .50 for the sat-Mathematical score and hsr. Estimates were based on sat scores and on hsr from the sdq for all sat takers in a representative sample of years during the 1972-1988 period.

The comparison between college-reported (.52) and the sdq-based (.51) average standard deviations for hsgpa of enrolled freshmen was used to estimate the college-reported standard deviation for hsgpa of all sat takers (.61) from the sdq-based average standard deviation for hsgpa of all sat takers (.60). Comparison between the college-reported (7.5) and sdq-based (5.5) average standard deviations for high school rank of enrolled freshmen and also between the college-reported (10.0) and sdq-based (8.9) average standard deviations for high school rank of all high school seniors were used to estimate the college-reported average standard deviation for high school rank of all sat takers (8.2) from the sdq-based average standard deviation for high school rank of all sat takers (6.4). The estimates of standard deviations for hsr were:

Estimates of Standard Deviations

HSGPA			High School Rank	
College-Reported	sdq		*College-Reported*	sdq
.86	.85	All high school seniors	10.0	8.9
.61	.60	All sat takers	8.2	6.4
.52	.51	Enrolled freshmen at a college	7.5	5.5

5-3.　SAT means and standard deviations were treated as continuous variables. All other variables except control were treated as categorical variables. Control necessitated an artificial scale, with "four-year public" = 0, "four-year private" = 1, and "other" not included. Scales for the categories of other variables were:

- Freshman-class size: 250, 1,000, 2,000
- Percent part-time students: 17, 50, 83
- Number of remedial services: 1, 4, 7
- Percent of degrees occupational: 5, 30, 75

5-4.　To determine whether this correlation is due to the regression effect of including 1973-1976 data in the pre-1973 to 1973-1976 change and in the 1973-1976 to 1985-1988 slope, the analysis was repeated to correlate the pre-1973 to 1973-1976 change with the 1977-1980 (instead of 1973-1976) to 1985-1988 slope. For the 100 colleges with sufficient data to calculate both a pre-1973 to 1973-1976 change and a 1977-1980 to 1985-1988 slope, the correlation between the two variables was −.24, reduced from −.43 for the correlation between the pre-1973 to 1973-1976 change and the 1973-1976 to 1985-1988 slope. The reduction may be due to the shorter period for the slope or to the elimination of the direct regression effect of including 1973-1976 data in both variables. Nevertheless, the relationship for the shorter period is still significant without the direct regression effect.

Chapter 6

6-1.　Based on equation 4 in the text, the theoretical regression weight for the logarithm of the variance of years in predicting the logarithm of the standard error for the slope is −0.50, while the corresponding empirical weights in Table 6-1 are −0.62, −0.59, and −0.61, respectively, for the three types of slopes. Thus, there is agreement between theory and data. Moreover, the direction of the discrepancy suggests that, if anything, slopes become stable *more* rapidly with increasing variance of years than theory would predict.

6-2.　Using the first two sets of regression weights in Table 6-1, supplemented by the corresponding intercepts (−2.68 and −1.57), predicted values for the standard errors were computed for each of the two types of slopes. For SAT prediction slopes, these predicted standard errors are 0.023 for small colleges with four studies and 0.004 for large colleges with 10 studies. For HSR slopes, they are 0.020 and 0.005, respectively. Next, true slope variances were estimated by subtracting the appropriate average error variance (given in equation 3) from the total variance for SAT and HSR slopes. Expressed as standard deviations, these are 0.010 for SAT and 0.008 for HSR. Finally, the four reliabilities given in the text were obtained as ratios of true variance to true-plus-error variance. Thus, for SAT slopes and small colleges,

$$\text{Reliability} = (0.010)^2/[(0.010)^2 + (0.023)^2].$$

6-3. Let r_{Hj} and r_{Sj} denote the validities of HSR and SAT, respectively, for a single college in a year y_j when that college had a validity study. Then the prediction slope t_H for validities r_{Hj} is given by

$$t_H = \frac{\sum (r_{Hj} - \bar{r}_H)(y_j - \bar{y})}{\sum (y_j - \bar{y})^2}$$

with a similar expression for the prediction slope t_S.

In the same way that residuals are used to estimate the sampling variance of a given slope, they may be used to estimate the sampling covariance between two such slopes. Thus, the estimated sampling covariance between t_H and t_S for this college is given by

$$\hat{\sigma}(t_H, t_S) = \frac{\sum (r_{Hj} - \bar{r}_H)(r_{Sj} - \bar{r}_S) - t_H t_S \sum (y_j - \bar{y})^2}{(k - 2)\sum (y_j - \bar{y})^2}$$

where k is the number of years the college had studies. Taking an unweighted mean of these estimates over all colleges in our sample provides an estimate of the average error covariance between t_H and t_S, which turns out to be .000076. This estimate may be subtracted from the observed covariance between t_H and t_S to obtain an estimated covariance between the true prediction slopes: .000147 – .000076 = .000071. This is actually the same way that the estimated true variances (used to compute the reliability of the slopes) were obtained: .000236 –.000172 = .000064 and .000302 – .000197 = .000105 for HSR and SAT, respectively. Once we have the estimated true covariance and variances, the estimated true correlation may be found:

$$\frac{.000071}{\sqrt{(.000064)\,(.000105)}} = .87$$

6-4. The sampling variance for a simple (or multiple) correlation r may be estimated by $(1-r^2)^2/n$, where n is the number of observations in the sample from which r is computed. Thus, the sampling variance for the difference between two correlations based on independent samples may be estimated by summing two such expressions. The square roots of such sums are the standard errors referred to in the text. Since the correlations used in this analysis are corrected for restriction of range and based on nonnormal samples, these standard errors are probably too small. The statistical tests referred to are not based on these standard errors, but rather on the Fisher z transformation. Thus, the absolute value of the difference $\tanh^{-1}(r_1)$ – $\tanh^{-1}(r_2)$ is compared to the square root of its sampling variance: $(n_1-3)^{-1} + (n_2-3)^{-1}$. Again, we would expect this to be too small, so the computed test statistics are probably somewhat larger than they should be.

6-5. The approach used to produce the variance components in Table 5-3 is formally similar to a two-way analysis of variance, including a linear trend analysis of one of the factors (years). The primary difference is that this analysis is descriptive rather than inferential. Thus, no hypothesis tests are carried out, and no attempt is made to estimate population quantities. Instead, models are fit to the data, and the quality of the fits is summarized with mean squared residuals. To be more explicit about this process, some notation will be required. We use r_{ij} to denote a corrected validity coefficient for college i (i=1, ... 192) in year y_j (j=1, ... 15), and δ_{ij} ($\delta_{ij} = 0$ or 1) to indicate whether or not the college had a study in that year. Now r_{ij} only exists if $\delta_{ij} =1$, but we will ignore this in the development that follows, since we only work with quantities of the form $\delta_{ij}\, r_{ij}$. Let k_i denote the number of studies for college i. Finally, we will use ρ_{ijk} to represent the fitted value for r_{ij} based on model k, where individual models will be defined below. Model k is fit to the r_{ij} to minimize the following criterion:

$$V_k = \sum_{i=1}^{192} \left[\frac{\sum_{j=1}^{15} d_{ij}(r_{ij} - r_{ijk})^2}{k_i} \right] / 192$$

In V_k, a mean squared residual is computed for each college, and then an unweighted average is taken over colleges.

The following models were fit to the data:

$$\rho_{ij1} = \mu$$

$$\rho_{ij2} = \mu_i$$

$$\rho_{ij3} = \alpha_i + \beta y_j$$

$$\rho_{ij4} = \alpha_i + \beta_i y_j$$

Differences between successive mean squared residuals for these models may be interpreted as components of the variance of r_{ij} associated with different elements of the models. The first model serves as a baseline from which to compare the others. In this sense, V_1 may be thought of as the total variance of r_{ij}. The difference $V_1 - V_2$ is the variance associated with college differences in validity and may be thought of as representing the main effect for colleges.

The next successive difference, $V_2 - V_3$, is the variance associated with a linear trend in validity, after accounting for overall college differences in average validity. It represents a portion of the main effect for years. Note that the third model is formally identical to the model used in the analysis of covariance, with years (y_j) in the role of covariate. The main distinction is that for analysis of covariance, the interest is in the effect of college differences adjusted for years.

The difference $V_3 - V_4$ is the variance of r_{ij} associated with differences in linear validity trends among colleges, adjusting for the first two effects. It may be thought of as representing a portion of the colleges x years interaction.

The mean squared residual for the college-specific linear trends model, V_4, may be further partitioned if we are willing to estimate a component of variance due to sampling fluctuations associated with an individual study. In an analysis of variance, this component would correspond to a within cells or error term in the model. Using the estimate of sampling variance for r_{ij} given in Note 6-3, we obtain

$$V_5 = \sum_{i=1}^{192} \left[\frac{\sum_{j=1}^{15} \delta_{ij} (1 - r_{ij}^2)^2 / n_{ij}}{k_i} \right] / 192$$

It should be emphasized that V_5 differs from the previous mean squared residuals in the sense that it is an estimate of a population quantity, rather than a descriptive summary of the result of fitting a model to the data. Nonetheless, it does correspond to a standard "minimal" error term and, as such, is a useful reference for assessing the size of the other variance components. Moreover, it allows us to estimate one additional component, namely $V_4 - V_5$.

This may be thought of as variance associated with systematic deviations of the r_{ij} from the fitted linear trends, beyond what would be expected as a result of sampling fluctuations.

Finally, it should be noted that, since the individual sampling variance estimates used to obtain V_5 are probably too small (see Note 6-4), V_5 itself is probably an underestimate of the error variance component. For the same reason, the estimate of the component associated with systematic deviations from linearity ($V_4 - V_5$) is probably somewhat too large. Nonetheless, the estimates should give some idea of the role played by these two sources of variation in the r_{ij}.

6-6. The actual situation is very similar to this, but somewhat more complicated. In the pairwise method of analysis, a years x years table is set up. All pairwise differences corresponding to a particular pair of years are averaged and the result is placed in the corresponding cell of the table. The diagonal cells all contain zero. Year effects are computed by a simple averaging of all cells in a given row of the table. Thus pairs are weighted equally within cells but may be unequally weighted between cells. For our data, pairwise weighting and cellwise weighting produced essentially identical results, so all comparisons here are made using only pairwise weighting.

6-7. See Wainer (1989) and accompanying articles for an illuminating technical discussion of the pervasive problem of missing or self-selected data in social research.

Chapter 8

8-1. In the usual SAT administration, which calls for three hours of testing time, two separately timed half-hour sections are devoted to the verbal test, two to the mathematical test, one to the Test of Standard Written English (not under consideration here), and one half-hour to special nonoperational purposes such as pretesting and equating. As many as 40 different tests may be administered during this nonoperational time slot, with the tests spiraled among the students tested at any given administration of the SAT.

8-2. Sections 1 and 2 of SAT-V both contain the same four item types: Antonyms (25 items in all), Sentence Completion (15 items), Analogies (20 items), and Reading Comprehension (25 items). Section 1, however, consists of 45 items in all; Section 2, 40 items. Section 1 of SAT-M contains 25 Regular Math (problem-solving, 5-choice) items. Section 2 contains 15 Regular Math items and 20 4-choice Quantitative-Comparison items. All sections of the SAT are given in 30-minute periods timed separately.

8-3. It is noted that the delta values in Table 8-6 are raw (observed), not equated, deltas. For the purposes of this study, in which the comparisons of interest are made only between the new and old forms, delta equating is unnecessary.

Chapter 9

9-1. This is the decline estimated for colleges that provided data on actual (rather than student-reported) HSGPA or high school class rank. The 8 percent decline is estimated for the multiple correlation coefficient that was corrected for restriction of range. The decline in the uncorrected multiple correlation coefficient of SAT scores and FGPA is 16 percent. Comparable figures were estimated by Ramist and Weiss (Chapter 5, this volume) on a larger sample of colleges that participated in the

College Board Validity Study Service. Ramist and Weiss estimated a 7 percent decline in the corrected multiple correlation coefficient and an 18 percent decline in the uncorrected multiple correlation coefficient.

9-2.   The gains due to test familiarization could be achieved in a variety of ways other than coaching. Many high schools provide SAT familiarization courses (Powers, 1988). Additionally, textbooks and a variety of printed, computer-based, and audiovisual documents published by the College Board provide effective test familiarization (College Board, 1989).

9-3.   Questionnaires were sent to 2,378 students. The response rate was 54 percent, with an overrepresentation of females, Asian Americans, students aspiring to advanced degrees, and students who ranked in the top 10 percent of their high school classes. Further details on the data can be found in Powers (1988). Being "coached" was defined, on the basis of self-reports, as having attended an SAT preparation program either outside of high school or at high school, but conducted by an outside organization. From 1,287 students who responded to the survey, the coaching status of 1,243 students could be determined.

9-4.   In the simulations, the background variables of the students were standardized to have means of zero so that the probability that an average student is coached remains approximately equal across colleges for a given variant of simulations.

9-5.   Note that except for the FTC and DerSimonian-Laird studies, all coaching-effect studies estimate larger coaching effects for SAT-Math than SAT-Verbal. A reanalysis of the FTC data accounting for differential growth rates of coached and uncoached students estimated an SAT-Verbal coaching effect of 17 points (Rock, 1980), which is smaller than the SAT-Math effect.

9-6.   Regression equations of coaching effects are:

SAT-Math $= -14.072 + 26.646 \log_{10}$ (hours spent for SAT-M coaching);

SAT-Verbal $= -6.587 + 15.155 \log_{10}$ (hours spent for SAT-V coaching).

9-7.   The variance for each mean level of simulated coaching effects is computed using the same coefficient of variation, ensuring that the dispersion of the normal distribution of coaching effects remains the same between different variants of the simulations. The resulting normal distribution may contain negative coaching effects. Although some studies document large negative coaching effects, it was decided to impose a restriction on the magnitude of the possible negative effects. In the Messick-Jungeblut (1981) meta-analysis, it was estimated that a minimum of one hour of coaching will result in losses of 14.1 points on SAT-Math and 6.6 points on SAT-Verbal. In the simulations, all negative effects are truncated at these values. Alongside the assumptions on the nature of the coaching effects, in the simulations, this restriction will contribute to the overrepresentation of the impact of coaching on the validity of SAT.

9-8.   From the Messick-Jungeblut study, it is known that the number of hours spent in coaching are highly correlated with coaching effects. Analytical derivations and simulations (Baydar, 1990) show that the magnitude of the correlation of math and verbal coaching effects is of little consequence to the predictive validity of the SAT.

9-9.   Claims by Princeton Review (*Houston Post*, 1985; *The Record*, Bergen Co., NJ, 1985). The 100 points were partitioned into mathematical and verbal coaching effects using the ratio implied by the Messick-Jungeblut estimates.

9-10.   If 100-point gains were coaching effects, one would expect, on the basis of the Messick-Jungeblut regression equations, that the students received 791 hours of coaching for SAT-Math and 875 hours of coaching for SAT-Verbal. It is clear that even if such gains were possible, they could not be attributed to test familiarization or trick learning only.

9-11.   Simulations for each combination of assumptions have been repeated five times in order to account for possible random fluctuations. The entries on Table 9-1 are the means of five repetitions. When the sample size is large, the effect of random fluctuations is negligible and the standard deviation of the estimates between repetitions is fairly low (see Baydar, 1990).

Chapter 10

10-1. The multivariate restriction of range formula was employed (see Note 4-2). Reference correlations and standard deviations were based on data from Morgan (1989b), which provided the most recent data for college-bound seniors (SAT examinees). The estimated population standard deviations were 109 for the SAT-V, 120 for the SAT-M, and .61 for HSGPA. The estimated population correlations were .67 for SAT-V with SAT-M, .45 for SAT-V with HSGPA, and .50 for SAT-M with HSGPA. The estimated population parameters in Morgan (1989a) were based on enrolled freshmen. Consequently, the population standard deviations in Morgan (1989a) are smaller.

10-2. The categorization of intended major was based on the first choice of major by each examinee on the SDQ. Fields of study were classified as follows: Business majors included all fields classified on the SDQ as business; liberal arts majors included English, ethnic studies, foreign languages, history, political science, geography, music, philosophy, psychology, sociology, and theater arts; preprofessional majors included agriculture, architecture, art, communications, education, home economics, library science, military science, and nursing; technical majors included computer science, engineering, mathematics, physical science, and premed.

Chapter 11

11-1. The wording of the college grade scale was consistent in the NLS and the HSB questionnaires, but the HSB question included a grade range while the NLS question did not. For example, the two-question formats appear as follows:

NLS: 1. Mostly A
     2. About half A and half B. . .

HSB: 1. Mostly A (3.75-4.00 GPA)
     2. About half A and half B (3.25-3.74 GPA). . .

Also the NLS scale differentiated "Mostly D" and "Mostly below D" while the HSB scale collapsed the two. In this analysis, "D" and "below D" were also collapsed in the NLS data in order to make the two scales comparable.

11-2. In order to examine the degree of overlap among the cohorts, colleges were coded zero or one in each year, depending upon whether they enrolled seven or more NLS/HSB students (the criterion used in selecting colleges for the "paired" analysis reported in Tables 11-3 and 11-4). As would be expected, the colleges so selected overlapped far more in the two HSB cohorts (Phi=.56) than between the NLS and each of the HSB cohorts (Phi=.27 and .28). This is due to the fact that the two HSB cohorts were based on students from the same high schools.

11-3. The within-college correlations were computed from averaged within-college covariance matrices, weighted by college N. Findings based on weighted and unweighted data were similar for both the overall and the within-college analyses, though the unweighted data gave more stable results and are reported here.

11-4. Tables 11-3 and 11-4 show jackknifed standard errors, treating colleges as the sampling unit, which seems appropriate for the within-college analysis. Conventional standard errors, using students as the sampling unit, may be more appropriate for the overall analysis. The latter gave comparable results to the jackknifed estimates for the 1972-80 comparisons, but smaller standard errors than are shown in Table 11-4 for the 1972-82 comparisons. The jackknifed estimates are based on successive replications of the correlational analysis, each time leaving one and then another college out of the analysis. For an overview of jackknifing, see Mosteller and Tukey (1977, pp. 133-136).

Chapter 12

12-1 The Pearson-Lawley multivariate correction for restriction of range was used (Gulliksen, 1950, pp. 165-166). The estimates of standard deviations for test takers were 109 for the SAT-Verbal score, 120 for the SAT-Mathematical score, and .61 for HSGPA. The estimates of correlations among the predictors for test takers were .67 for SAT-Verbal and SAT-Mathematical scores, .45 for the SAT-Verbal score and HSGPA, and .50 for the SAT-Mathematical score and HSGPA. Estimates were based on SAT scores and on HSGPA from the SDQ for all SAT takers during the 1982-1985 period.

12-2 The Spearman-Brown split-halves method was used. For each student, courses were alternatively assigned to one of two sets, with odd courses alternatively assigned to one set for one student and to the other set for the next student. The GPAs for the two sets were correlated (r). The reliability of FGPA was estimated to be $2r/(1 + r)$.

12-3   The weights used were averages of weights from all prediction equations produced through validity studies using SAT scores and HSGPA on entering classes 1981 to 1985: .00118 for the verbal score, .00100 for the mathematical score, and .55498 for HSGPA.

12-4   The validity with a perfectly reliable criterion is:

$$\text{observed validity} \ / \ \sqrt{\text{criterion reliability}}.$$

12-5   When the number of cases (N) is small and the number of predictors (p) is relatively large, the sample multiple correlation coefficient is positively biased as an estimator of the corresponding population quantity. Lord and Novick (1968, pp. 286-287) provided an updated version of the approximate correction for this bias proposed by R.J. Wherry:

$$\hat{R} \ = \ \sqrt{\frac{(N-1)R^2 - p}{N-p-1}}$$

Although our 38 colleges are not a random sample of the population of colleges of interest, it may still be useful to be aware of the magnitude of the correction in this case (N=38, p=8).

12-6   The Spearman-Brown formula for the reliability of a test of length N (Guilford & Fruchter, 1978, p. 426) is:

$$R_{NN} \ = \ \frac{NR_{11}}{1 + (N-1) \ R_{11}}$$

where R_{11} is the reliability of a test of unit length. Solving for R_{11}:

$$R_{11} \ = \ \frac{R_{NN}}{N - (N-1) \ R_{NN}}$$

The assumption that course grades are comparable and parallel measurements, with FGPA reliability (R_{NN}) averaging .82 and an average of N=8.6 course grades per student, implies that the reliability of one course grade (R_{11}) was .346. The validity of one course grade that is perfectly reliable would then be (see Note 12-4) .833:

$$\frac{\text{Validity with perfectly}}{\text{reliable criterion}} = \frac{\text{Observed validity}}{\sqrt{\text{Criterion reliability}}} = \frac{.49}{\sqrt{.346}} = .833$$

Solving for the observed validity:

$$\frac{\text{Observed}}{\text{validity}} = \left(\sqrt{\frac{\text{validity with perfectly}}{\text{reliable criterion}}} \right) \left(\frac{\text{criterion}}{\text{reliability}} \right)$$

Given comparable and parallel measurements, the validity of .833 with a perfectly reliable criterion and an FGPA reliability of .82 imply an observed validity for predicting FGPA of .75: $(.833)(\sqrt{.82}) = .75$. The observed correlation (corrected for restriction of range) between SAT scores and FGPA of only .54 clearly repudiates the assumption that course grades are comparable and parallel measurements. Similarly, the implied validity of HSR for predicting an FGPA based on comparable course grades would be .71 instead of the observed .57.

12-7 The correction for restriction of range for college-reported HSGPA was the same as for student-reported HSGPA, both in terms of the Pearson-Lawley multivariate formula and in terms of the parameters (see Note 12-1). For college-reported high school rank on a 20 to 80 normalized scale with a mean of 50 and standard deviation of 10 for all high school graduates, the only differing parameter was 8.2 for the estimated standard deviation for all SAT takers. This estimate was based on high school rank from the SDQ for all SAT takers in a representative sample of years during the 1982-1985 period.

Chapter 13

13-1. Once a year, the English Composition Test includes a 20-minute impromptu essay; about 40 percent of the students submitting ECT scores take this version of the test.

13-2. Here the weights of the latent variables for reproducing the observed variables are labeled "factor loadings" to distinguish them easily from the weights of the latent variables for reproducing FGPA, called "regression weights."

References

Aiken, L. R. (1963). The grading behavior of a college faculty. *Educational and Psychological Measurement, 23,* 319-322.

Alderman, D. L., & Powers, D. E. (1980). The effects of special preparation on SAT-Verbal scores. *American Educational Research Journal, 17*(2), 239-251.

American College Testing Program. (1988). ACT *Assessment Program technical manual.* Iowa City: Author.

American Educational Research Association, American Psychological Association, and National Council on Measurement in Education. (1985). *Standards for educational and psychological testing.* Washington, DC: American Psychological Association.

Angoff, W. H. (Ed.). (1971). *The College Board Admissions Testing Program: A technical report on research and development activities relating to the Scholastic Aptitude Test and Achievement Tests.* New York: College Entrance Examination Board.

Angoff, W. H. (1982). Summary and derivation of equating methods used at ETS. In P. W. Holland & D. B. Rubin (Eds.), *Test equating* (pp. 55-69). New York: Academic Press.

Baratz-Snowden, J. (1987). Good news, bad news. *Change, 19*(3), 50-54.

Baydar, N. (1990). *Effects of SAT coaching on the validity of the SAT: A simulation study.* (ETS Research Report 90-4). Princeton, NJ: Educational Testing Service.

Bejar, I., & Blew, E. O. (1981). *Grade inflation and the validity of the Scholastic Aptitude Test.* (College Board Report No. 81-3). New York: College Entrance Examination Board.

Boldt, R. F. (1986). *Generalization of SAT validity across colleges.* (College Board Report No. 86-3 and ETS Research Report 86-24). New York: College Entrance Examination Board.

Braun, H. I., & Szatrowski, T. H. (1984). Validity studies based on a universal criterion scale. *Journal of Educational Statistics, 9*(4), 331-344.

Breland, H. M. (1981). *Assessing student characteristics in admissions to higher education.* (Research Monograph No. 9). New York: College Entrance Examination Board.

Breland, H. M., Wilder, G., & Robertson, N. J. (1986). *Demographics, standards, and equity: Challenges in college admissions — Report of a survey of undergraduate admissions policies, practices, and procedures.* American Association of Collegiate Registrars and Admissions Officers, American College Testing Program, College Entrance Examination Board, Educational Testing Service, and National Association of College Admission Counselors.

Brogden, H. E. (1946). On the interpretation of the correlation coefficient as a measure of predictive efficiency. *Journal of Educational Psychology, 37*(2), 65-76.

Burton, N. W., Morgan, R., Lewis, C., & Robertson, N. J. (1989, March). *The predictive validity of sat and tswe item types for ethnic and gender groups.* Paper presented at the annual meeting of the American Educational Research Association, San Francisco.

Butler, R. P., & McCauley, C. (1987). Extraordinary stability and ordinary predictability of academic success at the United States Military Academy. *Journal of Educational Psychology, 79*(1), 83-86.

Clark, M. J., & Grandy, J. (1984). *Sex differences in the academic performance of Scholastic Aptitude Test takers.* (College Board Report No. 84-8 and ETS Research Report 84-43). New York: College Entrance Examination Board.

Cohen, J. (1988). *Statistical power analysis for the behavioral sciences* (2nd ed.). Hillsdale, NJ: Lawrence Erlbaum.

College Board. (1977). *On further examination: Report of the Advisory Panel on the Scholastic Aptitude Test Score Decline.* New York: College Entrance Examination Board.

College Board. (1982). *National college-bound seniors, 1982.* New York: College Entrance Examination Board.

College Board. (1984). *College-bound seniors: Eleven years of national data from the College Board's Admissions Testing Program, 1973-1983.* New York: College Entrance Examination Board.

College Board. (1985). *National college-bound seniors, 1985.* New York: College Entrance Examination Board.

College Board. (1986a). *Annual survey of colleges, 1986-87: Summary statistics.* New York: College Entrance Examination Board.

College Board. (1986b). *Measures in the college admissions process: A College Board colloquium.* New York: College Entrance Examination Board.

College Board (1987). *Annual survey of colleges.* New York: College Entrance Examination Board.

College Board (1988a). *The College Board technical manual for the Advanced Placement Program.* New York: College Entrance Examination Board.

College Board. (1988b). *College-bound seniors, national report: 1988 profile of sat and Achievement Test takers.* New York: College Entrance Examination Board.

College Board. (1988c). *Guide to the College Board Validity Study Service.* New York: College Entrance Examination Board.

College Board. (1989). *1989-90 featured publications and software from the College Board.* New York: College Entrance Examination Board.

Cronbach, L. J. (1971). Test validation. In R. L. Thorndike, *Educational Measurement* (2nd ed.), pp. 443-507. Washington, DC: American Council on Education.

Crouse, J., & Trusheim, D. (1988). *The case against the SAT.* Chicago: The University of Chicago Press.

Cruise, P. L., & Kimmel, E. W. (1990). *Changes in the SAT-Verbal: A study of trends in content and gender references, 1961-1987.* (College Board Report No. 90-1 and ETS Research Report 89-17). New York: College Entrance Examination Board.

Cureton, L. W. (1971). The history of grading practices. *Measurement in Education, 2*(Whole No. 4).

Dawes, R. M. (1975). Graduate admissions variables and future success. *Science, 187,* 721-723.

DerSimonian, R., & Laird, N. M. (1983). Evaluating the effect of coaching on SAT scores: A meta-analysis. *Harvard Educational Review, 53*(1), 1-15.

Donlon, T. F. (Ed.). (1984a). *The College Board technical handbook for the Scholastic Aptitude Test and Achievement Tests.* New York: College Entrance Examination Board.

Donlon, T. F. (1984b). The Scholastic Aptitude Test. In T. F. Donlon (Ed.), *The College Board technical handbook for the Scholastic Aptitude Test and Achievement Tests* (pp. 37-67). New York: College Entrance Examination Board.

Donlon, T. F., & Livingston, S. A. (1984). Psychometric methods used in the Admissions Testing Program. In T. F. Donlon (Ed.), *The College Board technical handbook for the Scholastic Aptitude Test and Achievement Tests* (pp. 13-36). New York: College Entrance Examination Board.

Dorans, N., & Lawrence, I. (1987). *Internal construct validity of the SAT* (ETS Research Report 87-35). Princeton, NJ: Educational Testing Service.

Duran, R. P. (1983). *Hispanics' education and background: Predictors of college achievement.* New York: College Entrance Examination Board.

Dyer, H.S., & King, R. G. (1955). *College Board scores: Their use and interpretation* (No. 2). New York: College Entrance Examination Board.

Educational Testing Service. (1980). *Test use and validity.* Princeton, NJ: Educational Testing Service.

Ekstrom, R. (in preparation). *Gender differences in high school grades: Developing a theoretical model.* Princeton, NJ: Educational Testing Service.

Ekstrom, R. B., Goertz, M. E., & Rock, D. A. (1988). *Education and American youth.* Philadelphia: The Falmer Press.

Elliott, R., & Strenta, A. C. (1988). Effects of improving the reliability of the GPA on prediction generally and on comparative predictions for gender and race particularly. *Journal of Educational Measurement, 25*(4), 333-347.

Elliott, R., & Strenta, A. C. (1990, January). *Is the SAT redundant with high school record in college selection?* (Research and Development Update). New York: College Entrance Examination Board.

Federal Trade Commission, Bureau of Consumer Protection. (1979). *Effects of coaching on standardized admission examinations: Revised statistical analysis of data gathered by Boston Regional Office of the Federal Trade Commission.* Washington, DC: Federal Trade Commission.

Fincher, C. (1990). *Trends in the predictive validity of the Scholastic Aptitude Test.* (ETS Research Report 90-13.) Princeton, NJ: Educational Testing Service, Princeton, NJ.

Fishman, J. A. (1958). Unsolved criterion problems in the selection of college students. *Harvard Educational Review, 28*(4), 340-349.

Fishman, J. A., & Pasanella, A. K. (1960). College admission-selection studies. *Review of Educational Research, 30*(4), 298-310.

Ford, S. F., & Campos, S. (1977). Summary of validity data from the Admissions Testing Program Validity Study Service. In College Board, *Appendixes to "On further examination: Report of the Advisory Panel on the SAT Score Decline."* New York: College Entrance Examination Board.

Fraker, G. A. (Winter 1986-87). The "Princeton Review" reviewed. *The Newsletter.* Deerfield, MA: Deerfield Academy.

Freeberg, N. E. (1988). *Analysis of the revised Student Descriptive Questionnaire, Phase I — Accuracy of student-reported information.* (College Board Report No. 88-5 and ETS Research Report 88-11). New York: College Entrance Examination Board.

Freeberg, N. E., Rock, D. A., & Pollack, J. (1989). *Analysis of the revised Student Descriptive Questionnaire, Phase II — Predictive validity of academic self-report.* (College Board Report No. 89-8 and ETS Research Report 89-49). New York: College Entrance Examination Board.

French, J. W. (1961). *A machine search for moderator variables in massive data.* (ONR Technical Report). Princeton, NJ: Educational Testing Service.

Ghiselli, E. E. (1963). Moderating effects and differential reliability and validity. *Journal of Applied Psychology, 47,* 81-86.

Goldman, R. D., & Hewitt, B. N. (1975). Adaptation-level as an explanation for differential standards in college grading. *Journal of Educational Measurement, 12*(3), 149-161.

Goldman, R. D., & Slaughter, R. E. (1976). Why college grade point average is difficult to predict. *Journal of Educational Psychology, 66*(1), 9-14.

Manning, W. H. (1977). The pursuit of fairness in admissions to higher education. In *Selective admissions in higher education: Comment and recommendations and two reports* (a report of the Carnegie Council on Policy Studies in Higher Education, pp. 20-64). San Francisco: Jossey-Bass.

Manski, C. F., & Wise, D. A. (1983). *College choice in America.* Cambridge, MA: Harvard University Press.

Marco, G. L., Crone, C. R., Braswell, J. S., Curley, W. E., & Wright, N. K. (1990). *Trends in sat content and statistical characteristics and their relationship to sat predictive validity.* (ets Research Report 90-12). Princeton, NJ: Educational Testing Service.

Marco, G. L., Petersen, N. S., & Stewart, E. E. (1983). *A large-scale evaluation of linear and curvilinear score equating methods, Vol. I* (ets Research Memorandum 83-2). Princeton, NJ: Educational Testing Service.

Marron, J. E. (1965). *Preparatory school test preparation: Special test preparation, its effect on College Board scores and the relationship of affected scores to subsequent college performance.* West Point, NY: Research Division Office of the Director of Admissions and Registrar, U. S. Military Academy.

Mazzeo, J., Livingston, S. A., & Feryok, N. J. (1986). *The relationships between njcbspt scores and scores on sat-V, sat-M, and tswe.* Unpublished manuscript, Educational Testing Service, Princeton, NJ.

McCornack, R. L., & McLeod, M. M. (1988). Gender bias in the prediction of college course performance. *Journal of Educational Measurement, 25*(4), 321-331.

McHale, F. J., & Ninneman, A. M. (1990). *The stability of the score scale for the Scholastic Aptitude Test from 1973 to 1984.* (ets Research Report 90-6). Princeton, NJ: Educational Testing Service.

Messick, S. (1980). *The effectiveness of coaching for the sat: Review and reanalysis of research from the fifties to the ftc.* Princeton, NJ: Educational Testing Service.

Messick, S. (1982). Issues of effectiveness and equity in the coaching controversy: Implications for educational and testing practice. *Educational Psychologist, 17*(2), 67-91..

Messick, S. (1988). Validity. In R. L. Linn, (Ed.), *Educational Measurement* (3rd ed., pp. 13-104). New York: American Council on Education and Macmillan Publishing Company.

Messick, S., & Jungeblut, A. (1981). Time and method in coaching for the sat. *Psychological Bulletin, 89*(2), 191-216.

Modu, C. C., & Stern, J. (1975). *The stability of the sat score scale* (College Entrance Examination Board Research and Development Report 74-75 No. 3 and ets Research Bulletin 75-9). Princeton, NJ: Educational Testing Service.

Modu, C. C., & Stern, J. (1977). The stability of the sat-Verbal score scale. In College Board, *Appendixes to "On further examination: Report of the Advisory Panel on the Scholastic Aptitude Test Score Decline.* New York: College Entrance Examination Board.

Morgan, R. (1989a). *Analyses of the predictive validity of the sat and high school grades from 1976 to 1985* (College Board Report No. 89-7 and ets Research Report 89-37). New York: College Entrance Examination Board.

Morgan, R. (1989b). *An examination of the relationships of academic coursework with admissions test performance* (College Board Report No. 89-6 and ets Research Report 89-38). New York: College Entrance Examination Board.

Morgan, R. (1990). *Predictive validity within categorizations of college students: 1978, 1981, and 1985* (ets Research Report 90-14). Princeton, NJ: Educational Testing Service.

Mosteller, F., & Tukey, J. W. (1977). *Data analysis and regression: A second course in statistics.* Reading, MA: Addison-Wesley Publishing Company.

Munday, L. A. (1970). Factors influencing the predictability of college grades. *American Educational Research Journal, 7*(1), 99-107.

National Commission on Excellence in Education. (1983). *A nation at risk: The imperative for educational reform.* Washington, DC: U. S. Department of Education, U. S. Government Printing Office.

Nichols, R. C., & Holland, J. L. (1963). Prediction of the first year college performance of high aptitude students. *Psychological Monographs: General and Applied, 77*(7, Whole No. 570), 1-29.

Owen, D. (1985). *None of the above: Behind the myth of scholastic aptitude.* Boston, MA: Houghton Mifflin Company

Pennock-Roman, M. (1990). *Test validity and language background: A study of Hispanic-American students at six universities.* New York: College Entrance Examination Board.

Petersen, N. S. (1981, April). *Interim delta specifications for sat-Verbal.* Unpublished memorandum, Educational Testing Service, Princeton, NJ.

Petersen, N. S., Cook, L. L., & Stocking, M. L. (1983). IRT versus conventional equating methods: A comparative study of scale stability. *Journal of Educational Statistics, 8*(2), 137-156.

Pomplun, M., Burton, N., & Lewis, C. (in preparation). *An exploration of the stability of freshman gpa, 1978-1985.* Educational Testing Service, Princeton, NJ.

Powers, D. E. (1986). Relations of test item characteristics to test preparation/test practice effects: A quantitative summary. *Psychological Bulletin, 100*(1), 67-77.

Powers, D. E. (1988). *Preparing for the SAT: A survey of programs and resources* (College Board Report No. 88-7 and ETS Research Report 88-40). New York: College Entrance Examination Board.

Powers, D. E., & Alderman, D. L. (1979). *The use, acceptance, and impact of "Taking the SAT" — A test familiarization booklet* (College Board Research and Development Report 78-79 No. 6 and ETS Research Report 79-3). Princeton, NJ: Educational Testing Service.

Powers, D. E., & Alderman, D. L. (1983). Effects of test familiarization on SAT performance. *Journal of Educational Measurement, 20*(1), 71-79.

Ramist, L. (1984). Predictive validity of the ATP tests. In T. F. Donlon (Ed.), *The College Board technical handbook for the Scholastic Aptitude Test and Achievement Tests* (pp. 141-170). New York: College Entrance Examination Board.

Richards, J. M., Jr., Holland, J. L., & Lutz, S. W. (1967). Prediction of student accomplishment in college. *Journal of Educational Psychology, 58*(6), 343-355.

Roccobono, J., Henderson, L., Burkheimer, G., Place, C., & Levinsohn, J. (1981). *National longitudinal study: Base year (1972) through fourth follow-up (1979) data user's manual, volume 1* (Contract No. OEC-0-73-6666). Washington, DC: National Center for Education Statistics.

Rock, D. A. (1980). Disentangling coaching effects and differential growth in the FTC commercial coaching study. In S. Messick, (Ed.), *The effectiveness of coaching for the SAT: Review and reanalysis of research from the fifties to the FTC* (pp. 123-135). Princeton, NJ: Educational Testing Service.

Rock, D., Hilton, T., Pollack, J., Ekstrom, R., & Goertz, M. (1985). *Contractor report, psychometric analysis of the NLS and the high school and beyond test batteries — a study of excellence in high school education — educational policies, school quality, and student outcomes* (Contract No. OE-300-83-0247). Washington, DC: National Center for Education Statistics.

Rowe, J. (December 27, 1985). The SAT cult: Getting help to score highest points is name of the game. *The Houston Post.*

Sawyer, R., Laing, J., & Houston, M. (1988). *Accuracy of self-reported high school courses and grades of college-bound students* (ACT Research Report Series 88-1). Iowa City: American College Testing Program.

Schmidt, F. L., & Hunter, J. E. (1977). Development of a general solution to the problem of validity generalization. *Journal of Applied Psychology, 62*(5), 529-540.

Schmitt, A. P., & Dorans, N. J. (1990). Differential item functioning for minority examinees on the SAT. *Journal of Educational Measurement, 27*(1), 67-81.

Schrader, W. B. (1971). The predictive validity of College Board admissions tests. In W. H. Angoff (Ed.), *The College Board Admissions Testing Program: A technical report on research and development activities relating to the Scholastic Aptitude Test* (pp. 117-145). New York: College Entrance Examination Board.

Schrader, W. B. (1973). *Validity of the quantitative comparison test* (ETS Statistical Report 73-60). Princeton, NJ: Educational Testing Service.

Schrader, W. B. (1984). *Three studies of SAT-Verbal item types* (College Board Report No. 84-7 and ETS Research Report 84-33). New York: College Entrance Examination Board.

Sebring, P., Campbell, B., Glusberg, M., Spencer, B., Singleton, M., & Turner, M. (1987). *Contractor report, high school and beyond 1980 sophomore cohort third follow-up (1986), volumes I and II, data file user's manual* (Contract No. OE-300-84-0169). Washington, DC: National Center for Education Statistics.

Smyth, F. L. (1989). Commercial coaching and SAT scores. *Journal of College Admissions, 123*(Spring), 2-7.

Snedecor, P. J. (1989). Coaching: Does it pay — revisited. *Journal of College Admissions, 125*(Fall), 15-18.

Snyder, T. D. (1987). *Digest of education statistics, 1987.* Washington, DC: National Center for Education Statistics.

Starch, D., & Elliott, E. C. (1913). Reliability of grading work in mathematics. *School Review, 21,* 254-295.

Strenta, A. C., & Elliott, R. (1987). Differential grading standards revisited. *Journal of Educational Measurement, 24*(4), 281-291.

Stricker, L. J. (1966). Compulsivity as a moderator variable: A replication and extension. *Journal of Applied Psychology, 50*(4), 331-335.

Stricker, L. J. (1982). *Test disclosure and retest performance on the Scholastic Aptitude Test* (College Board Report No. 82-7 and ETS Research Report 82-48). New York: College Entrance Examination Board.

Stricker, L. J. (1990). *SAT scores and academic performance in high school.* (ETS Research Report 90-1). Princeton, NJ: Educational Testing Service.

Stroud, T. W. F. (1980). Reanalysis of the Federal Trade Commission study of commercial coaching for the SAT. In S. Messick, (Ed.), *The effectiveness of coaching for the SAT: Review and reanalysis of research from the fifties to the FTC* (pp. 97-110). Princeton, NJ: Educational Testing Service.

Sue, S., & Abe, J. (1988). *Predictors of academic achievement among Asian American and White students.* (College Board Report No. 88-11). New York: College Entrance Examination Board.

Thorndike, R. L. (Ed.). (1949). *Personnel selection: Test measurement techniques.* New York: John Wiley & Sons.

Thorndike, R. L. (1969). Marks and marking systems. In R. L. Ebel (Ed.), *Encyclopedia of educational research* (4th ed.) (pp. 759-766). New York: Macmillan.

Tomlinson, L. M. (1989). *Postsecondary developmental programs: A traditional agenda with new imperatives* (AAHE-ERIC Higher Education Report 3). Washington, DC: The George Washington University.

Tucker, L. R., & Lewis, C. (1973). A reliability coefficient for maximum likelihood factor analysis. *Psychometrika, 38,* 1-10.

Verdon, J. (1985, August 15). SAT service, instructor argue copyright case. *The Record,* Bergen County, NJ, p. A-28.

Wainer, H. (1989). Eelworms, bullet holes, and Geraldine Ferraro: Some problems with statistical adjustment and some solutions. *Journal of Educational Statistics, 14*(2), 121-140.

Washington, W. E., et al. (Petitioners) vs. Davis, A. E., et al. (Respondents). *Motion for leave to file brief as amicus curiae and brief amicus curiae for Educational Testing Service* (on writ of certiorari to the United States Court of Appeals for the District of Columbia Circuit). Supreme Court of the United States, October term, 1975.

Webb, S. C. (1959). Measured changes in college grading standards. *College Board Review,* (39), 27-30.

Werts, C., Linn, R. L., & Jöreskog, K. G. (1978). Reliability of college grades from longitudinal data. *Educational and Psychological Measurement, 38,* 89-95.

Whitla, D. K. (1988). Coaching: Does it pay? Not for Harvard students. *College Board Review, Summer*(148), 32-35.

Wilder, G. Z., & Powell, K. (1989). *Sex differences in test performance: A survey of the literature.* (College Board Report No. 89-3 and ETS Research Report 89-4). New York: College Entrance Examination Board.

Willingham, W. W. (1962). *Longitudinal analysis of academic performance* (Evaluation Studies, Research Memorandum 62-5). Atlanta: Georgia Institute of Technology, Office of the Dean of Faculties.

Willingham, W. W. (1963). *The effect of grading variations on the efficiency of predicting freshman grades.* (Evaluation Studies, Research Memorandum 63-1). Atlanta: Georgia Institute of Technology, Office of the Dean of Faculties.

Willingham, W. W. (1985). *Success in college: The role of personal qualities and academic ability.* New York: College Entrance Examination Board.

Willingham, W. W., & Breland, H. M. (1977). The status of selective admissions. In *Selective admissions in higher education: Comment and recommendations and two reports* (a report of the Carnegie Council on Policy Studies in Higher Education, pp. 65-252). San Francisco: Jossey-Bass.

Willingham, W. W., & Breland, H. M. (1982). *Personal qualities and college admissions.* New York: College Entrance Examination Board.

Willingham, W. W., & Johnson, L. M. (1989). *Program Research Review, 1989.* Princeton, NJ: Educational Testing Service, Princeton, NJ.

Willingham, W. W., Ragosta, M., Bennett, R. E., Braun, H., Rock, D. A., & Powers, D. A. (1988). *Testing handicapped people.* Needham Heights, MA: Allyn and Bacon.

Wilson, K. M. (1983). *A review of research on the prediction of academic performance after the freshman year* (College Board Report No. 83-2 and ETS Research Report 83-11). New York: College Entrance Examination Board.

Young, J. W. (1990a). Adjusting the cumulative GPA using item response theory. *Journal of Educational Measurement, 27*(2), 175-186.

Young, J. W. (1990b, April). *Gender bias in predicting college academic performance: A new approach using item response theory.* Paper presented at the annual meeting of the American Educational Research Association, Boston, MA.

Zikopoulos, M. (Ed.). (1987). *Open doors: 1987/88 — Report on international educational exchange.* New York, NY: Institute of International Education.

Zuman, J. P. (1988). The effectiveness of special preparation for the SAT: An evaluation of a commercial coaching school. *Dissertation Abstracts International, 48,* 1749A-1750A. (University Microfilms No. DA8722714).